Public Health
and the U.S. Military

Routledge Advances in American History

Public Health and the U.S. Military

A History of the Army Medical Department, 1818–1917

Bobby A. Wintermute

Routledge
Taylor & Francis Group
New York   London

First published 2011
by Routledge
711 Third Avenue, New York, NY 10017

Simultaneously published in the UK
by Routledge
2 Park Square, Milton Park, Abingdon, Oxfordshire OX14 4RN

First issued in paperback 2014

Routledge is an imprint of the Taylor and Francis Group, an informa business

© 2011 Taylor & Francis

The right of Bobby A. Wintermute to be identified as author of this work has been asserted by him/her in accordance with sections 77 and 78 of the Copyright, Designs and Patents Act 1988.

Typeset in Sabon by IBT Global.

Library of Congress Cataloging in Publication Data
Wintermute, Bobby A.
   Public health and the US military : a history of the Army Medical Department, 1818–1917 / Bobby A. Wintermute.
      p. cm. — (Routledge advances in American history ; no. 3)
   Includes bibliographical references and index.
   ISBN 978-0-415-88170-8 (hbk) — ISBN 978-0-203-84059-7 (ebk) 1. United States. Army Medical Dept—History. 2. Medicine, Military—United States—History. 3. United States. Army—Sanitary affairs. 4. Military hygiene—History. 5. Public health—History. I. Title.
   UH223.W56 2011
   355.3'45097309034—dc22
                                    2010017409

ISBN 978-0-415-88170-8 (hbk)
ISBN 978-1-138-86756-7 (pbk)
ISBN 978-0-203-84059-7 (ebk)

Contents

Illustrations

Introduction

Waging Health—The U.S. Army Medical Officer's Quest for Identity and Legitimacy

Even before the cease-fire was established at Santiago halting the Spanish-American War, senior American officers recognized the near-catastrophic state of health in Cuba. Years of civil war, Spanish resettlement policies, and neglect by the Spanish colonial government resulted in the collapse of nearly all public health systems on the island. The situation was even worse in the rural backcountry, where sanitation and hygiene among the island's *mestizos* was virtually non-existent. Added to this was the very real danger of endemic tropical disease, including yellow fever and malaria, as well as more familiar diseases such as dysentery and smallpox. The first task of the American forces in Cuba would be how best to improve these conditions. As Major General Leonard Wood recalled, the health risks were great indeed:

> Yellow fever, pernicious malaria and intestinal fevers were all prevalent to an alarming extent. The city and surrounding country was full of sick Spanish soldiers, starving Cubans and the sick of our own army. The sanitary conditions were indescribably bad. There was little or no water available and the conditions were such as can be imagined to exist in a tropical city following a siege and capture in the most unhealthy season of the year. . . . The death rate among our own troops was heavy and the percentage of sick appalling.[1]

Cuban laborers were immediately set to cleaning the area around Santiago. In the city proper, water and sewage pipes were laid beneath a new asphalt road system. The port's waterfront was dredged and a new sea wall built along its length. In the city and throughout the province, workers drained and filled in swamps and old canals. Likewise, the region's privy vaults and sinks, "enormous affairs, and as a rule cleaned only once in a generation," were drained, and if necessary, replaced.[2] This work, the renovation of hospitals and government buildings, and a general cleanup transformed the city, so that "the general appearance of Santiago has in the last year completely changed, and while still an old, tumble-down Spanish town, it presents some marks of modern civilization."[3] A rural sanitary guard was created to ensure compliance with a sweeping new regimen of public health directives issued for the province. Furthermore, when smallpox was uncovered in the towns evacuated by the Spanish Army in the province, some 30,000 civilians were promptly vaccinated, a remedial intervention that sped the disease's eradication in Cuba.[4]

After the peace settlement came into effect on December 10, 1898, relief poured into Cuba and other soon-to-be-former Spanish colonial possessions from American charitable organizations. In Havana alone, over 2,251,000 rations, as well as "great quantities of clothing, medicine and other supplies," were delivered to provide for the needs of the city's poor indigenous and refugee populations.[5] Army occupation authorities quickly realized that charitable contributions alone would not be enough. Wood's headquarters ordered department commanders to inspect all Cuban hospitals, jails, asylums, workhouses, and other such public facilities. Subsequent tours revealed the entire island's public health and relief infrastructure was in disarray. During the war, Cuba's hospitals were occupied by the Spanish Army, which exhausted their own resources while simultaneously disrupting the tenuous system of public and private financing that kept the facilities operational. Compounding the problem was a culture of graft that had eroded the hospitals' operating funds. The effects of the long Cuban insurrection were seen in other areas as well. Workhouses for the poor had fallen into disrepair, machinery not destroyed by the rebels rusting on the shop floor. During their withdrawal from the island, the Spaniards looted the hospitals they had occupied.[6]

Reconstructing Cuba's tattered public health infrastructure was the occupation administration's primary concern. Replenishing medical supplies looted by the Spanish was the simplest problem. Existing buildings needed repair, while new hospitals, orphanages, and work houses were also needed. Throughout the island water and sewage systems were non-existent. Many families drew drinking and cooking water from wells and cisterns contaminated by nearby open sewers and cesspools, while garbage disposal was unheard of. These real problems were exacerbated by the occupier's low esteem for the Cubans' ability to manage their affairs. The Army's immediate solution was to place the island's hospitals, orphanages, prisons, and other public charities directly under the control of the Medical Department. In Havana, a municipal Sanitary Department was organized as soon as American troops entered the city. Modeled along the same lines as the New York Sanitary Department, this new organization immediately set out to clean up the city. Over an eighteen-month period, starting on January 1, 1899, nearly five million dollars were spent on public works projects in Havana alone.[7] Street cleaners were sent out to sweep the garbage and filth clogging the city's open sewers. New macadamized roads were laid out, with underground sewer lines to pipe personal waste out of the city. Public and private buildings alike were scrubbed, painted, and cleaned, and orders were issued to regulate the ongoing cleanliness of courtyards, patios, porches, and sidewalks throughout the urban core. New enforcement power was given to a revitalized Health Department, overseen by Army medical officers and carried out by professional Cuban experts and physicians. Mandatory guidelines for the isolation, quarantine, and treatment for yellow fever patients were carried out throughout the city. "By the middle of the year 1900 all the city governments were perfectly organized, and were accomplishing all that it was possible for them to accomplish," William Crawford Gorgas later recollected, adding, "I believe that Havana was cleaner than any other city had ever been up to that time."[8]

Yet people still died. Despite all the work cleaning Havana, new yellow fever cases appeared almost daily. Indeed, in 1900, the rate of infection steadily rose to a level not known in several years, with 310 fatal cases reported.[9] A new sense of panic began, as it became clear the sanitary project had no discernable effect upon the disease. Most distressing was the distribution of yellow fever in Havana, in upper class districts and the homes and hotels frequented by Americans and the resident elites suffering the greatest during the new outbreak. Military administrators attached to Major General Wood's staff, unable to leave Havana, took to burning sulphur candles at their desks to keep the miasmas at bay. All was to no avail. Left and right, members of Wood's staff fell ill. A grim toast—"Here's to the last man gone. Here's to the next man to go."—began to be raised among the dwindling survivors. Throughout the city, daily business and social life came to a halt, as people locked themselves away in their houses or fled the city to escape the outbreak.[10]

Amidst the fever outbreak, three medical officers under the direction of the Army Medical School's expert microbiologist, Major Walter Reed, arrived in Havana to investigate the epidemic. With little direct support for their lines of research into a possible vector for the disease, the Reed commission appealed to the island's military governor for funds. Major General Wood, a former physician and Army contract surgeon before his military career, immediately recognized the significance of the Reed project. He forwarded $10,000 to Reed, with the promise of another $10,000 should more money be needed.[11]

So begins one of the most iconic accounts of American scientific medicine, the successful discovery of the mosquito vector as the sole agent of yellow fever transmission. Reed's story has become an object lesson in the alleged success of the scientific medical research model, recounted to the point where he has become part scientific detective, unraveling the mystery of an undecipherable disease, and part secular saint, an iconic exemplar of American microbiology.[12] Major Reed's accomplishments, his insights, and his unexpected death from complications arising from appendicitis have combined to elevate his reputation in American medicine despite later questions about his casual use of live test subjects, his failure to properly acknowledge the support and work of earlier experts in the field, and his increasingly troubled relationship with his superiors in the Medical

Department. Nevertheless, Walter Reed is an important link in the history of his institution, the science and practice of medicine, and American imperial policy. Throughout the nineteenth century, the Army medical officer underwent an arduous process of professional identity formation, shaping his core identity as a resident of two distinct professional spheres—the military officer and the physician. The successful integration of these dual identities occurred at the same time germ theory was increasingly accepted as the cause of disease in American science.

As a practicing microbiologist, Reed was one of a new sort of military physician who was remaking the image of the medical officer as the primary agent of national defense against a familiar scourge: infectious disease. Educated at the University of Virginia School of Medicine and at New York's Bellevue Hospital Medical College before entering the Army Medical Department, Reed was part of a very small and privileged elite. Once decried as whiskey-tippling "sawbones," U.S. Army medical officers under the tutelage and guidance of Surgeon General George Miller Sternberg were reinvented as the nation's premier body of medical researchers in the 1890s. This was taking place against the backdrop of the rise of two new professional specializations in American medicine. Sanitarians and microbiologists/researchers provided the Medical Department its greatest successes between 1890 and 1920, helping to position the branch as a model of progressive action not only for the general public but the Army as well. After 1898, the partnership between sanitarians and researchers grew stronger, while also asserting greater authority over medical affairs within the Army. By 1916, a clear hierarchy of authority based upon professional knowledge had arisen in the Medical Department, with sanitarians claiming the highest point of relevance, followed by researchers, with the more traditional general practitioner/surgeon at the bottom.

After 1898, medical officers like Walter Reed were dispatched across the globe to study, classify, and, if possible, treat a wide range of infectious diseases that, if transferred to the United States, could cause untold damage and harm. In the process, Army medical officers undertook—at times with great reservation—the role of health proconsul in the American imperial periphery and beyond. As the Caribbean became an American lake after 1898, Army physicians were increasingly invested with the authority to transform entire indigenous societies and disrupt the environment itself, all in the name of identifying and remediating disease. Not surprisingly, these same physician-scientists, inculcated with American concepts of racial hierarchy and white superiority, came to view their imperial wards through an increasingly complex and limiting lens of race and environment. Even as they were making real scientific contributions, Army medical officers were systematizing a racialist perspective that would in turn shape American assumptions about whiteness for the next generation and beyond.

This is not the first study of the U.S. Army Medical Department. Unlike its predecessors, however, it is perhaps the first to consider the department's

institutional quest for identity and legitimacy, both within the Army itself
and American society at large. Many previous studies begin with combat
medicine, either focusing on it exclusively or privileging it as the chief role
of the Army Medical Department.[13] Other monographs that do consider
American military medicine in its public health role are generally limited
to single case studies, with the emphasis on particular diseases or conflicts,
nursing and other specific forms of medical care, or biographical studies of
individual figures.[14] In this study, I have decided to eschew combat medicine and surgery in favor of focusing on the institutional culture of an organization that was an active force in establishing the contours of American
medicine. Further, I also introduce the premise that public health, not combat medicine, was the primary mission of the Army Medical Department.
To help satisfy this, I position the first century of the Medical Department as a transformational experience similar to that undergone by the
U.S. Army, which ultimately established the service as a highly rationalized
and bureaucratized professional organization. Though much has been said
about the Army's rebirth as a progressive institution, the changes in the
Medical Department have received very little attention.[15] Before 1890, the
Army Medical Department occupied two places within the army: first, it
was the branch responsible for ensuring the health of the soldiery in peace
and war, thus vouchsafing the army's continued effectiveness; second, it
constituted a group of alien professionals who, though necessary, were outside the normal command hierarchy trained at West Point. Considered to
be outsiders, medical officers were tolerated throughout much of the nineteenth century as a necessary, if confusing, adjunct to the Army's line and
staff branches. The result of this accommodation was a thorny and strained
relationship between regular line and staff officers and the physicians who
served in the department. The army's own tenuous claim to validity and
status in civil society gave officers pause when it came to accepting outsiders into their community, as evidenced in the treatment accorded medical
officers seeking the same prerogatives and privileges of rank held by the line
and staff.

For their part, medical officers were also in a bind. The term itself indicates that army physicians occupied two distinct professional spheres. As
Army officers they were willing members of the military profession, and
wished to make their own contributions in their own way to better the
institution. As trained physicians, they remained conscious of their place in
the medical profession, which was striving to stake out its own claim as the
privileged voice in managing the health of the individual and the society.
Indeed, as medical historian Paul Starr has noted in *The Social Transformation of American Medicine*, the physician's quest for legitimate authority was paralleled by the experience of the military officer. Over the same
century-long period, extending from roughly the 1820s through the 1920s,
both professional groups waged a bitter struggle against competing forces
in American society to achieve legitimate authority over highly specialized

bodies of knowledge. In both cases, society ultimately acceded authority—"professional sovereignty" according to Starr—over their respective fields to the two professions only after lengthy and bitter struggles to attain recognition.[16]

The struggles of the two professions—physicians and military officers—were exceeded only by the challenge posed to medical officers in their own quest for *dual* legitimacy within two distinct professional spheres. From the establishment of the Army Medical Department in 1818, medical officers faced numerous challenges to their authority from suspicious line and staff peers. While these officers did not attempt to directly interfere or challenge the clinical authority of uniformed physicians, they frequently obstructed the medical officers' efforts to impose health and wellness directives. The explanation offered by line officers for such actions was simple: command was the sole prerogative of the military officer. Physicians in the employ of the Army were essentially contractors, and should not exceed their place in the institution's culture by presuming officership. The first challenge for medical officers, therefore, was to convince their military peers of the legitimacy of their claims to rank and status.

By 1890, much of the work toward the first goal, acceptance within the military as an agent of binary professional responsibility, had been achieved. To reinforce their newfound status, and to establish their credentials as practitioners of *modern* scientific medicine, medical officers pursued two different courses in the Progressive Era. Capitalizing upon the public relations disaster that ensued after the humiliating experience of widespread typhoid fever in the volunteer camps in the Spanish-American War, the Army Medical Department was positioned as a primary advocate of public health. At the same time, the Army Medical Department became the nation's chief agent of institutionalized medical science in the first decades of the twentieth century. In both cases, the sudden acquisition of empire after 1898 proved fortuitous for the Medical Department. While the line and staff debated the merits of taking on the role of imperial administrator in the Philippines, Puerto Rico, Guam, Panama, and briefly, Cuba, the Medical Department jumped at the opportunity. Outside of the United States, army medical officers enjoyed unfettered access to tropical locales and control populations upon whom their vision of public health and medical science could be exercised.

Within the last fifteen years, the history of military medicine has undergone a sort of revival, as medical historians, anthropologists, and literary critics introduced a new line of inquiry, emphasizing the body as a contested terrain of meaning and control, with medical officers often acting as surrogates for the state on unwilling subject civilians and soldiers alike. Much of this work has occurred in Britain, where scholars associated with the Wellcome Institute and independent researchers have published salient works on the social and cultural nexus of war and medicine. For the most part, however, while focusing on military medicine, much of this work is also transfixed on now classical questions of modernity and the body. Much recent British research attempts to conceptualize medicine as a response to war, rather than as a component of military culture itself.[17] Collections like Roger Cooter, Mark Harrison, and Steve Sturdy's 1998 volume *War, Medicine and Modernity* consider military medicine as a part of the militarized bureaucratic regime associated with the wars of the twentieth century, its practitioners awkward uniformed civilian interlopers who are no less cogs in the machine than the soldiers they treat and return to war. Fixated on Weberian critiques of modernity and rationality, they consider the relationship between medicine, the military, and society as a temporary expediency, in which medical practitioners are subjected to the same coercive statist forces in the name of war that consume individual societies themselves.[18] Associated with this are more overt considerations of the body as a post-modern landscape, contested terrain in which conventions of masculinity—fitness, sexuality, identity—collided with the state's impulse toward abject control of individual soldiers and the personal annihilative force of modern industrial warfare. As Joanna Bourke notes in her study of men's bodies in the First World War,

> They expressed their freedom through their bodies, but were besieged on all sides by military, medical and educational disciplines which were governed by different aesthetics, economic objectives, and moral economies. The corporeal male would eventually become a corpse on some battlefield or mortuary slab, inviting reconstruction through the memories of loved ones. All men's bodies were endowed with signs and declarations of age, generation, class and ethnicity. It was within this socially constructed "frame" that bodies lived, were imagined, and died.[19]

The complete and total control of men's bodies is the object of Bourke's premier foray into war and medicine, a theme she returns to in a 2008 essay for the Wellcome Collection and the Deutsches Hygiene-Museum's joint exhibit guide *War and Medicine*. In a summary of primarily British military medicine in the First and Second World Wars, she presents the medical establishment as an essential partner with the military in "defining and expanding military power so that the armed forces could control and direct the emotional as well as the material lives of its recruits with greater effectiveness."[20] Again, the state uses the healing profession to control the minds and bodies of individuals in order to wage war. For Bourke and many other historians and scholars, this perverse corruption of the healer's mission is the implicit truth to be brought into the daylight of public understanding.

Certainly these critiques offer crucial insights into the unspoken discourses of power that reside beneath the surface in military institutions. They may also be used to understand how military medicine operated in peacetime; specifically, how uniformed physicians were elevated as models of public health management and medical science in civilian culture. Consider the influence of empire.[21] An important direction in imperial studies has been the consideration of colonial and tropical medicine as a tool used to assert coercive power by colonial administrators. Accordingly, Western physicians and health administrators played major roles in depriving indigenous peoples of agency, through subordinating local values, bodies of knowledge, and historically valid cultural perceptions of what constituted health, wellness, and treatment to an allegedly superior system of knowledge. Much of this story of the "colonization of the body" by Western medicine has been told from the perspective of the British Empire, particularly in Britain and Africa. Only recently has the focus shifted to the American colonial experience, with the Philippine Islands often the focus of special attention.[22] So much of the U.S. Army Medical Department's work in the Progressive Era was undertaken outside of the United States—the Philippines, Puerto Rico, Cuba, Panama, Hawaii, Mexico, and China—that the colonial possessions have been described as "America's tropical laboratory."[23] This study reveals that America's imperial experience provided more than a secure environment for studying epidemiology and bacteriology, but that it also offered an opportunity to develop a comprehensive doctrine of public health and sanitary reform that was put to use at home as well as abroad.

At the same time, army medical officers were at the forefront of introducing to the American public what Nancy Tomes describes as a "gospel of germs."[24] Army physicians from Surgeon General Sternberg to the newest graduate of the Army Medical School constructed a new identity as the nation's first line of defense against microbial agents foreign and domestic. Indeed America's imperial moment at the turn of the twentieth century offered a solution to a problem that had vexed the Army Medical Department since its formation in 1818. As the chief representatives of the American regular therapeutic approach to medicine—that group castigated in the antebellum years as "allopaths"—Army physicians were held in high regard by their civilian fellows. Hence, medical officers sought legitimacy across two spheres. Whereas their status in the first sphere—as physicians imbued with legitimate authority—was more or less taken for granted, their status and legitimacy as military experts was denied and resisted throughout the nineteenth century. In response, medical officers campaigned within the Army for recognition, employing numerous claims and criticisms to win over support. In due course, the Army medical practitioner settled on public health, sanitation, and medical research as linked vehicles to establish their credibility as military experts—*real* officers imbued with special authority over the body in uniform—worthy of recognition. Viewed in this light, medical officers *before* the societal transformative experience of the First World War were not civilians in uniformed mufti, acting under the restraints of militarized modernity. They were fully vested participants of a military organization, chafing under the *denial* of full recognition and legitimacy by the rest of the institution, eager to lend the benefit of their expertise in the name of honor, status, and service.

The conventional narrative of Walter Reed's yellow fever work takes on a different light when considered as part of the larger experience of the Army Medical Department as a cultural force for American medicine. For nearly a century, the successful discovery of the mosquito vector was hailed as the chief accomplishment of Army bacteriology. Reed's discovery was in turn bolstered by the high drama of the death of several volunteer test subjects and Reed's own passing in 1902. It would be unfair to deny Reed and his immediate colleagues and test subjects the credit for their achievement. Realizing the connection between the *Stegomyia culex* mosquito and yellow fever was one of the greatest discoveries of the twentieth century, offering new possibilities for social and commercial development throughout those tropical zones afflicted. Still, it is important not to lose sight of the work remaining after Reed's discovery. The actual bacteriologic agent responsible for the disease remained unseen, leaving the great goal of a vaccine unrealized. In this sense, the Reed Commission failed to fulfill the chief object of Army microbiology; it also set the stage for the rise of the sanitarian as the chief spokesman group within the Medical Department and in the eyes of the Western public. The successful promotion of an environmentally focused vector eradication program by Army sanitarian Colonel William Crawford Gorgas quickly caught the imagination of both the public and official Washington. The ease with which vector eradication was pursued by Gorgas' cadre of white American and native sanitarians solidified the sanitary-minded practitioner's hold on the Medical Department during the first decade of the twentieth century. Coming on the heels of the strong defense of their actions amidst the fever camps fiasco of 1898, Gorgas' vector eradication scheme established the Army Medical Department in the public's eye at the top rank of the nation's progressive-minded institutions. The department's sanitarians, led by Gorgas and others, turned their successes in the American imperial periphery to their advantage. With Gorgas' appointment as Surgeon General in January 1914, the process begun during the prior decade of establishing the Medical Department's primary mission as a public health mission was solidified. A triumph for practical applied sanitary medicine, the now validated hierarchy of sanitarians first, supported by microbiologists, with general practitioners and surgeons relegated to a tertiary support status would survive until 1917.

Aside from a discussion on sanitary tactics in Chapter 5, this work generally avoids the subject of combat medicine and surgery. While important aspects of military medicine, they did not form the core of the medical officer's experience and training in the nineteenth and early twentieth centuries. Similarly, while this monograph begins with the Army Medical Department's formation in 1818, the greater weight of study is located in the Progressive Era, particularly between 1890 and 1917. The occasion of America's entry into the First World War seems to offer a natural break in the overall study of the Army Medical Department; I hope to return to the subject to resume the study of how the professional triad structure fared during the war, and how Army public health practices and ideology were themselves transformed into a global public health system after 1918.[25] Likewise, I have emphasized the Army's activities in the Caribbean over the Philippines; Warwick Anderson's *Colonial Pathologies: American Tropical Medicine, Race, and Hygiene in the Philippines* offers an excellent account of American activities there.[26] Rather than duplicate his efforts, I chose to complement his monograph by studying American activities in its other imperial periphery.

Chapter 1 places the origins of the Army Medical Department and its quest for legitimacy within proper historical context, offering an analytical narrative of the two struggles for legitimate authority that the medical and military professions faced in the nineteenth century. Focused primarily on identity formation, it also examines the growing dialogue between military and medical professionals following the Civil War. The quest for the legitimacy conferred by rank and status is balanced by the growing self-realization of the medical officer's identity as being rooted in scientific medicine. The transformation of the medical officer from a necessary adjunct who accompanied troops west into a legitimate member of the officer community endowed with a highly specialized knowledge set is at the core of the chapter.

Chapter 2 considers the development of professional institutions within the Army Medical Department and their influence upon the growing debate over specialization among its commissioned members. Taking place in the 1890s, the creation of professional institutions—a professional association, the group's journal, and the foundation of the Army Medical School—all show how the Medical Department was being recast both as a legitimate branch within the Army and as the gatekeeper of access to a new medical specialty. Yet, even as military medicine was accepted as a legitimate specialized practice, medical officers remained skeptical of the need to permit further sub-specialization, seeing such diversity as a means to dilute their newly achieved authority and professional status.

The Spanish-American War is the focus of Chapter 3. In 1898, the Army Medical Department had been under the control of a well-respected bacteriologist for five years. Yet, despite the leadership of Surgeon General George Miller Sternberg, the institution was embarrassed by a series of deadly typhoid fever outbreaks in the Army's volunteer encampments. This chapter will examine the epidemic, and the Medical Department's response, in some detail. It will also consider the influence of Surgeon General Sternberg's pre-war reforms and the public outcry against him that followed, as well as the findings of the Dodge Commission Report that exonerated Sternberg and his department.

Chapter 4 moves away from the problems associated with developing an identity within the Army to consider how the Medical Department became the nation's chief agent of scientific public health in the new tropical periphery. At the same time they served as imperial health proconsuls, Army physicians also seized the opportunity to use the colonial environment as a laboratory for medical research and public health reform. At every possible occasion, Western physicians and scientists tried to expand upon the growing nosology of tropical diseases, while incorporating new scientific methods, including bacteriology, parasitology, and physiology, to treat, cure, and prevent these diseases. American physicians, acting out under the guise of legitimacy conveyed by the Army Medical Department, transformed Cuba, Puerto Rico, and Panama into Edenic gardens safe for whiteness.

Chapter 5 returns to the issue of institutional and intellectual reform within the Army Medical Department. Thanks largely to the success of the sanitary models promoted by Colonel William Crawford Gorgas in Cuba and Panama, a triad of legitimacy took shape within the department conferring privileged status upon sanitarians over the institution's medical researchers and general practitioners. In the decade before America's entry into the First World War, this group of sanitary-minded medical officers exerted great influence over the department's planning. Their efforts culminated in the development of *sanitary tactics* as a concept emphasizing the practice of a militarized public health as the foremost responsibility of the medical officer in wartime.

Chapter 6 examines the Medical Department's public health campaign against vice, primarily in the form of alcohol consumption and venereal disease. Over a twenty-five year period, from 1889 through 1914, medical officers experienced a general transformation in their position on the acceptability of light alcohol consumption in controlled environments as a means to control venereal disease. Initially supportive of the post canteen's sale of beer, wine, and hard cider, the Army's medical establishment gradually revised its position to oppose alcohol use in any form, on the premise it was a "gateway" to inevitable moral collapse and eugenic decline. As venereal infection rates skyrocketed following the acquisition of new imperial obligations after 1898, medical officers embraced prophylaxis in various forms, from urethral flushes to Salvarsan, all as part of a larger effort to control sexually transmitted diseases through coercion, education, and treatment.

As I have noted earlier, this monograph is but a single part of a larger effort, representing the bulk of my doctoral dissertation. The missing component of that work, dealing with the Army Medical Department's public health activities at home and abroad during the First World War, the ultimate failure of the sanitarian- and microbiologist-dominated regime in the Surgeon General's Office in the face of the war's tremendous toll and the unstoppable influenza epidemic, and the migration of the Medical Department's discredited sanitarians to the Rockefeller Foundation's International Health Board in the 1920s, will be addressed in a second book. Taken together, the two works will offer a new interpretation of the interrelations of state-run public health and corporate-based philanthropic public action in the twentieth century, while also providing a new perspective in the interconnectivity of military and civilian medical science and public health.

ACKNOWLEDGMENT

This project, which has consumed so much of my energy and thoughts since I first envisioned it in a graduate seminar paper in 1997, would never have reached fruition were it not for the support and assistance of a legion of friends, colleagues, supporters, and family. So many people have influenced me in the writing of this book, it would be nigh impossible to thank them individually by name in a chapter, let alone the few words I have here. But there are a special few who I could not but thank. I apologize to those who may be left out; be assured I cherish your support as well.

First, I wish to thank my family. Their patience, support, and good cheer kept me going through a difficult period and over the long haul. I would also like to thank my dissertation advisors—Richard H. Immerman, Morris J. Vogel, Jay Lockenour, and David Farber of Temple University, and Conrad B. Crane of the U.S. Army Heritage and Education Center. Their advice and support, even if it didn't always appear in the dissertation, made it through into the book. It's a much leaner and precise book thanks to your advice and support. Thanks to the U.S. Army Center of Military History and the Army Heritage Center Foundation for their generous assistance. Their support enabled me to spend the better part of two years at the U.S. Army Heritage and Education Center in Carlisle, Pennsylvania, where I met and was helped by some of the most gracious archivists and librarians in the profession. Thanks especially to Richard Sommers, David Keough, Louise Arnold-Friend, Kathy Olsen, and Rich Baker—your help was beyond measure. The College of Physicians of Philadelphia's Wood Library hosted me over a summer and opened their doors to me in countless return visits. Much of the old staff there is gone, but I would be remiss if I didn't thank Richard Fraser and Edward Norton for their assistance. Access to their outstanding collection was essential for this book.

A special thank you is in order to the Rockefeller Archive Center in Pocantico Hills, New York. Darwin Stapleton and Thomas Rosenbaum were magnificent hosts, offering not only unique paths of research that will appear in greater detail in the follow-up volume to this book. They extended great advice and emotional support at a crucial time. Special thanks also go out to my dear friends at the Army Heritage Center Foundation—Lorraine Luciano and Casandra Jewell. You helped me through a very difficult period, and your friendship has meant so much to me. Thanks for being there then and now.

So many other friends and colleagues were of tremendous help as well: Ginger Davis and David Ulbrich of Temple University gave sound advice and remain very dear friends; Paley Library's John Oram offered excellent support and advice—not to mention a good pint or two—along the way; the Lawless family provided relaxation, reality checks, and friendship at tough times; Fiona Rimmel and her children took me in and helped keep me sane; Regina Gramer has been a boon colleague and good friend; Michael Stalker is a tremendous inspiration, as was Alex and Jen Douville. Dave Kearns provided help at an important time, for which I am grateful. My colleagues at Queens College—especially Joel Allen, Katherine Antonova, Kristin Celello, Peter Conolly-Smith, Sarah Covington, Kristina Richardson, Julia Sneeringer, and Peter Vellon—have been a tremendous support. And most important of all, there is Phil Gibbon. Since our days together at Temple, Phil has been there as a scholar, a work partner, and, most of all, a friend. Long live Phob.

Some acknowledgments are tougher than others. Along the way to completion, I lost three very important people. Mary Procida was to be my guide through the historiography and interpretation of imperial history when she became ill. I still cannot think of what this dissertation has become without pausing to think of what it could have been. Thank you, Mary, for all of your help.

I came to Temple University in 1997 knowing only one thing: I wanted to work under Russell F. Weigley. Years before, I made the acquaintance of his scholarship through *Age of Battles*, and I was determined to study under him if the fates took me to Temple. I count myself fortunate to have worked with him as one of the last students he took on. His scholarship and incisive intellect were tremendous assets, to be sure; but what touched me the most during my short academic relationship with Dr. Weigley was the tremendous humanity, dignity, and grace he possessed. He will always be a model of professional excellence for me, a model I can only hope to do proud.

It's hard to believe it has been six years since my wife passed away. Priscilla was more than my spouse. She was my best friend, my touchstone, my co-worker, the anchor which I so often took for granted. I came so close to throwing this all away when she became ill, and for some time after her death, I was lost in the woods. Yet somehow I came through and managed to finish the dissertation, thanks in part to the drive to fulfill your best wishes and hopes for us together.

The last person to thank is the one who has become my closest and dearest support. I met Cleo almost three years ago, when I was in a very uncertain place. Since then she has been the brightest light and the strongest support for me, even when I'm at my worst. No one could ask for a better companion and life partner, and for that, I am and will remain grateful. So it is that I dedicate this book jointly to both Priscilla and Cleo.

1 Practice, Status, Public Health, and the Army Medical Officer, 1818–1890

"A few medical officers had long seen the need for an improved military status for themselves and their fellow, and by their insistence upon military forms, titles, salutes, drills, and other outward symbols they incurred no little ridicule," wrote Colonel Percy Moreau Ashburn, U.S. Army Medical Corps, about his onetime mentor and friend, Major John Van Rensselaer Hoff.[1] Described as an eccentric "tin-soldier" by critics and friends alike, Hoff embodied the medical officer in his struggle for legitimacy and status. He and others like him cared little for the comments of others as they sought recognition within the Army community. Yet, as Ashburn noted: "To those who did know them, whether in the field or in garrison, their abilities, courtesy, learning, high character, efficiency, and dignity were such as to stifle ridicule. Without shadow of turning they held their way."[2]

Commissioned as an assistant surgeon in 1874, Hoff witnessed the Army's waning days on the frontier firsthand. He spent part of his early career on the shrinking American frontier, at such famous places as Fort Leavenworth, Fort Reno, and Fort Riley. Hoff was present at the Sioux's last gasp at Wounded Knee, where he was mentioned in orders and recommended for the Medal of Honor "for conspicuous bravery and coolness under fire in caring for the wounded in action."[3] Such displays of bravery were fortuitous, coming after he made his name within the Army as a harsh disciplinarian and Prussian-style martinet. In 1887 at Fort Reno, Hoff created the first formal manual of drill for Hospital Corps and Company bearers. The sight of his putting the enlisted orderlies through their paces brought laughter and ridicule. But their conduct at Wounded Knee, where his orderlies and bearers performed admirably, proved the merit in Hoff's method. As future Surgeon General Merritte W. Ireland later noted:

His name was at this time universally associated with the militarization of the medical service—an advance which was much needed as the lessons of the Civil War had by this time been almost completely forgotten, and the only recognized function of the Army doctor was to treat the sick. The use of military titles and forms by Medical officers was at this time was not customary, even in official correspondence, and . . . Hoff [was] much ridiculed on their use. Gradually it became obvious that in an Army military methods were necessary for good results.[4]

Hoff's obsessions ran beyond rank and command, to include the question of the medical officer's legitimacy and status. Members of the Medical Department, Hoff argued, "were in the army but not of it. They were without rank and had few rights that any one was bound to respect."[5] Overtasked and underpaid, denied the most basic military courtesies by a culture insistent upon proper form and respect, the Army medical officer was an essential adjunct to the line, but was nevertheless treated like an outsider.

Some medical officers could—and often did—break under such a stifling climate of indifference, leaving as their five year enlistment expired. Others lost themselves in the new field of microbiology, where they made a different name for the Army Medical Department. Hoff chose another course. Immersing himself in the branch's history, he made a strong case for promoting the communal identity of the medical officer as a point of *esprit de corps* distinguishing the military surgeon as a unique professional. Despite his eccentricities and prickly personality, Hoff gathered around himself a collection of like-minded younger medical officers who were no less vocal or eloquent in making their case alongside their patron.[6] Over nearly twenty years, from 1898 through 1917, Hoff pushed for greater respect, legitimacy, and status for Army medical officers.

Hoff needed all of his contacts, friends, and mentors, as he eventually—perhaps expectedly—overstepped his bounds. Over the summer of 1918, complaints mounted over the unequal rank between the Army and Navy medical heads, and the spillover problem of low respect accorded medical officers in the National Army. In July 1918, Hoff wrote an editorial criticizing a recent War Department decision to post reservists to duty with the General Staff. Caught up with his own sensitivity over the status of regular medical officers, Hoff unleashed a torrent of criticism: "Some might infer from this that the General Staff is ignorant of the fact that there are stupendous medico-military problems connected with war, requiring the advice and experience of experts who had devoted their lives to the study of such; but this is not our inference."[7] Hoff was formally reprimanded by Secretary of War Newton D. Baker.[8] Chastened, Hoff left the journal, disgraced and never to enter public life again. He died two years later.

Hoff's story serves as an introduction to the larger account of the Army Medical Department's Progressive public health policies and practices. Between 1890 and 1917, the quest for improved status, recognition, and acceptance by their uniformed peers was as important to medical officers as their medical, scientific, and sanitary accomplishments. Before we can understand the importance of science and sanitation to the Army physician, we must appreciate the role of status and how public health was seen as a means to obtaining the legitimacy so desired by men like Hoff.

THE ORGANIZATION OF THE ARMY
MEDICAL DEPARTMENT, 1818–1890

The Medical Department was established as an autonomous staff branch on May 14, 1818. Congress authorized a Medical Department under the direction of a Surgeon General, supported by two assistant surgeons general and an apothecary general, with a cadre of two assistant apothecaries, forty post surgeons, and one surgeon and two surgeon's mates for each regiment. This new department fit into Secretary of War John C. Calhoun's plan to bring the Army's senior division commanders under War Department control through an independent staff corps. This General Staff, including the Quartermaster Department, the Subsistence Department, the Office of the Adjutant General, the Ordnance Department, and the Medical Department, was charged with providing essential logistical and staff support, while remaining under War Department control.[9] Intended to provide elasticity for future Army expansion, Calhoun's structure survived three years. Claiming fiscal austerity, in 1821 Congress imposed stark reductions. Distinctions between post and field medical officers were eliminated, as were the apothecaries and the assistant surgeons general. The title of "surgeon's mate" was also eliminated, replaced with the title "assistant surgeon." In addition to the Surgeon General, the new establishment was set at eight surgeons and forty-five assistant surgeons. Since each of the army's garrisons, forts, and encampments required at least one medical officer, surgeons and assistant surgeons often served alone.[10]

Calhoun's scheme was resisted by line officers accustomed to managing their own affairs with minimal interference. The absence of centralized authority, save for occasional directives from Washington, and the way units were scattered across the country allowed the Army's commanders great latitude in their conduct. Indeed this independence was the impetus for Calhoun's decision to extend greater control over the military. Major General Andrew Jackson's recent occupation of Spanish Pensacola under the pretense of quelling the Seminole was a prime example of a line officer exceeding his mandate. Though reluctant to reprimand Jackson publicly, Calhoun used the staff to bring the headstrong General into line. Whenever Jackson ignored regulations by dealing directly with staff officers in his division as though they were loyal only to him, Calhoun countermanded his orders and reprimanded the General for neglecting the express orders of the War Department. For his part, Jackson had little use for the new staff arrangement, hardly surprising for a man who viewed staff officers as *"intermeddling pimps and spies of the War Department."*[11]

The Medical Department was soon the specific target of Jackson's disdain. As newly empowered members of the General Staff, medical officers were *ex officio* representatives of the War Department, required to make quarterly reports on the relative health and wellness of their associated commands.[12] This did not sit well with the imperious Jackson. Accustomed to ruling his command as a personal fiefdom, he ignored regulations and ordered all surgeons' reports be routed through his office before going to Washington. Surgeon General Joseph Lovell took notice and reported to Calhoun that while he expected some time was needed for most surgeons to learn the "proper form and regular manner" required in their reports, those in General Jackson's district had failed to observe even the most basic reporting requirements outlined in the department's regulations. "Some few surgeons chiefly at the South have as yet neglected all orders," he wrote, "and unless good reasons be assigned therefor, it will be necessary to adopt some means of enforcing obedience, or to supply their places with those who are disposed to be more attentive to duty."[13]

Calhoun quickly responded. "Both the publick interest and humanity towards the Army require an efficient medical staff, but it is not possible to render it efficient, unless by a rigid adherence to the laws and regulations," Calhoun wrote. "I am persuaded that no one is more deeply convinced of the truth of this proposition than yourself, and that it is only necessary to call your attention to the irregularities which I have stated to relieve me from the necessity of determining whether I shall permit the orders of the Government to be habitually neglected, or resort to the proper means of enforcing them. Should the alternative be presented I will not hesitate to do my duty." Jackson relented, acknowledging the General Staff's independence and unintentionally setting a precedent for staff autonomy.[14]

The 1821 reductions were only the first in a cycle of Congressional tampering. In 1832, four surgeons and ten assistant surgeons were added to the lists. In 1836, three surgeons and five assistant surgeons were added, as were another seven surgeons in 1837, bringing the department's established strength to eighty-three medical officers. While Surgeon General Lovell requested more surgeons and assistant surgeons to match the increase in the Army's posts (which had grown from thirty-five in 1826 to sixty-four in 1831), Congress ignored his requests. Instead, the increases of the 1830s were motivated by an immediate need in the field. The 1832 expansion was a response to the Black Hawk War, while the 1836 and 1837 increases came amidst the protracted guerrilla fighting in Florida against the Seminole Indians. Soon enough, Congress returned to its original form, slashing the numbers of surgeons and assistant surgeons to twenty and fifty, respectively, in 1842 as soon as the war in Florida ended.[15] As the call for volunteers for service in Mexico went out in 1847, Congress authorized an additional two surgeons and twelve assistant surgeons, plus another 135 civilian physicians as volunteer medical officers. Ten more assistant surgeons were authorized in 1849, followed by an additional four surgeons and eight assistant surgeons in 1856, bringing the Medical Department's total establishment on the eve of the Civil War to 107.[16]

The department achieved its manpower peak during the Civil War. The July 22, 1861 call for volunteers provided each regiment with an organic medical establishment: one surgeon, one assistant surgeon, and one hospital steward.[17] Serious expansion and reorganization followed an April 16, 1862 bill introduced by Massachusetts senator Henry Wilson. In addition to providing ten surgeons and ten assistant surgeons, twenty medical cadets, "and as many hospital stewards as the Surgeon General may consider necessary," the Wilson Bill also gave the Medical Department power over its own affairs.[18] According to Bonnie Blustein, the bill instituted "a new structure for the centralized direction and inspection of medical work in the army," going beyond the normal prospect of simply adding new personnel to the Medical Department. A formal structure for sanitary inspection, "whether in transports, quarters, or camps" as well as in hospitals was implemented, through a new Medical Inspector establishment. Inspectors had authority to report any volunteer or regular medical officer and contract surgeon who was "disqualified, by age or otherwise, or unfitted for the performance of his professional duties" for a medical review board.[19]

The Wilson Bill also revived the old position of assistant surgeon general. Since the assistant surgeon general's rank was set at that of a colonel of cavalry, the surgeon general was increased to a brigadier general, a level commensurate with other staff heads. Finally, on July 2, 1862, Congress extended the Regular Army's authority over the thousands of volunteer medical officers, ordering all brigade surgeons to be appointed medical staff surgeons of volunteers, "under the direction of the surgeon general." Congress authorized forty surgeons and 120 volunteer surgeons, as well as an additional assistant surgeon for every volunteer regiment in service.[20]

The Civil War also threatened the professional reputation of the Medical Department. Many volunteer surgeons and assistant surgeons were appointed on the basis of political allegiances and personal favors. As a result, well-trained physicians were joined by hundreds of quacks and pretenders. Accordingly, many soldiers looked askance at regimental medical officers, particularly if they had a penchant for drink. Even officers had their doubts. In his study of the Union Army, Bell Irvin Wiley recounts the comments of a captain in the Second Massachusetts Regiment: "'I pray the regiment may improve . . . but with our present surgeon I see no prospect of good medical attendance in case of sickness. He is a jackass—a fool—and an ignorant man—three quarters of the sickness could have been prevented by a good physician.'"[21]

Still Congress created a massive uniformed health infrastructure. By 1865, the Medical Department included forty-six surgeons and 110 assistant surgeons, seventeen medical inspectors, six storekeepers, seventy medical cadets, 547 volunteer staff surgeons and assistant surgeons, 5,991 volunteer regimental surgeons and assistant surgeons, eighty-five acting staff surgeons, and 5,532 acting assistant surgeons. This institutional empire was short lived. After the war, Congress began demobilizing the Union Army. On July 28, 1866, Congress set the Medical Department's established strength at 217 physicians: seven administrators (one Surgeon

General with the assimilated rank of brigadier general, one assistant surgeon general with the rank of colonel, five medical purveyors with the rank of lieutenant colonel); sixty surgeons with the rank of major; and one hundred and fifty assistant surgeons, at the rank of captain and lieutenant.[22]

Somehow the department made do. In 1869, for example, the Army consisted of 32,896 officers and men, stationed at 239 posts across the country and its territories, against the Medical Department's paper strength of 210 physicians. Despite Surgeon General Barnes' criticism that any change to the 1866 establishment "would prove prejudicial to the welfare of the troops and the efficient discharge of its duties," Congress barred all appointments and promotions throughout the entire service.[23] The effects of the freeze were dramatic. By 1873, there were sixty-three unfilled vacancies in the Medical Department, including five surgeons and fifty-five assistant surgeons. On June 23, 1874, Congress finally lifted the promotion freeze, but only after cutting three medical purveyors and ten surgeons. Likewise, the number of civilian contract surgeons was limited to no more than seventy-five. Congress removed this limitation after the Surgeon General's Office was forced to hire private physicians on a fee-for-visit basis.[24]

Constantly seeking more fat to trim from the Federal budget, Congress continued to target the Medical Department. In 1876, the number of assistant surgeons was reduced to 125 and the office of medical storekeeper was abolished. Exacerbating these actions was a Congressional oversight leaving the entire Army unfunded until November 1877, with all soldiers and officers going without pay for several months. Finally, in 1894, Congress reduced the number of assistant surgeons to 110.[25]

Matters were not helped by the peacetime necessity of contracting services from civilian practitioners. In 1828, Surgeon General Lovell noted while the number of forts, posts, and rendezvous had grown in the last seven years, the number of authorized medical officers had not kept pace, "so that it is now impracticable to furnish one Surgeon to a station, even if they should all be on duty."[26] His pleas, and those of his successors and supporters from the line and the War Department, were unheeded. As late as 1858, at least six posts functioned without a medical officer. Hiring civilian physicians was the only solution. Pay was low—between $20 and $30 a month—and conditions harsh, yet doctors still applied. Some, like one Dr. Goodrich retained to accompany a company of recruits from Vicksburg to Forts Smith and Gibson in the Cherokee Territory in 1835, were clearly unqualified. Goodrich was let go after seven days, even as cholera struck the column, "not because his services were not required, for the Cholera was prevailing to a great extent among them but because he was found entirely unfit to perform the duties required by his contract."[27] Still, the overall quality of contract surgeons was fair, thanks partly to the high competition for civilian practices at a time when there was a glut of physicians, eclectics, and homeopathic healers. Many contract surgeons were young graduates of regular medical schools, attracted to the prospect of regular pay.[28]

The antebellum Surgeons General accepted the services of civilian physicians begrudgingly. Contract surgeons challenged the medical officer's already tenuous identity and status as an essential military specialist. Surgeons-for-hire were considered a black mark by Surgeon General Thomas Lawton, who issued a stark assessment to the Secretary of War. "To enable the medical officers of the army *alone* to serve all the troops, the number of posts to be occupied must be reduced;" he wrote, "and as this proposition is not likely to be entertained, the question arises whether the medical staff of the army shall be increased to the wants of the service, or the present practice be continued of employing private physicians to perform the duties of a military surgeon." Lawson's proposal was not considered. The Army maintained its posts, and contract surgeons continued to be hired as the need arose.[29]

The number of contract surgeons increased dramatically during the Civil War. Over the course of the war, the Union Army retained 5,532 civilian physicians, who were only granted equivalent Medical Department grade in 1863. Thereafter the "Acting Assistant Surgeons of the United States Army" received the same authority and prerogatives over sick and injured soldiers, and the enlisted cadre of the Medical Department, as regular and volunteer medical officers. Despite this extension of impromptu grade, the status of contract surgeons remained very tenuous, their continued tenure at the Surgeon General's discretion.[30]

Contract surgeons remained essential after the Civil War. The Surgeon General's Office overcame its opposition to the civilian contractors in the face of Congressional indifference toward the regular establishment. This acceptance reflected resignation over the constant Congressional interference, as seen in Surgeon General Joseph K. Barnes' testimony before the House Committee on Military Affairs on January 23, 1869. Ordered to appear before the Committee, chaired by Congressman James A. Garfield, Barnes was asked if his department could fulfill its mission with its current established strength. "I could not possibly get along with the present force except by the aid of the contract physicians," Barnes responded. "Fill the army to the present standard contemplated by law and the present force would give you for duty with troops one regular physician to every 400 men, which is more than they could possibly do."[31]

RANK, STATUS, AND THE MEDICAL OFFICER, 1818–1861

Throughout the nineteenth century and beyond, the medical officer's professional and personal identity was comprised of a complex skein of conflicting elements. The basic components of this interwoven identity reflected the army doctor's two professional faces: physician and officer. For several reasons—the state of the medical arts and therapeutic practice, cultural friction points, the complexities of negotiating legitimacy within a closed hierarchical system, legislative indifference and fiscal restraint—the medical officer struggled to develop his identity. Unable to establish his legitimacy as a specialized member of the military arts and sciences, the American medical officer was subjected to insults, slights, and recriminations by other peer officers. Though some progress was made in addressing the apparent lack of respect and legitimacy, the uniformed physician remained an outsider within his chosen field.

The greatest mark of the medical officer's low esteem was the substitution of his title as "surgeon" or "assistant surgeon" for formal rank. Despite the individual respect from the general and junior officers of the line, army physicians were consistently denied the privilege of formal military rank, and all perquisites and status associated with it. Recognized in the Army lists and regulations only by their formal titles, they were "without military rank, . . . [and] not entitled to military command." Instead, they received assimilated rank. This scheme, with surgeons classed as majors, assistant surgeons with five years continuous service as captains, and junior assistant surgeons as first lieutenants, was used exclusively for administrative purposes, such as determining their pay, seniority, and right to housing.[32]

Though medical officers received formal Congressional recognition of their assimilated ranks in 1847, on the whole, the Army continued to treat its physicians as doctors-for-hire. As part of the act authorizing the Army's expansion for the war with Mexico, Congress ordered "that the rank of the officers of the medical department of the army shall be arranged upon the same basis which at present determines the amount of their pay and emoluments: *Provided,* That the medical officers shall not in virtue of such rank be entitled to command in the line or other staff departments of the army."[33] The question of rank and status for the medical officer in the officer community appeared to be resolved, but this was hardly the case. A year later, Congress abrogated the section of the 1847 act that included medical officer rank. Within the Army, regular officers of the line and staff also disregarded the act. Line officers accustomed to treating surgeons and assistant surgeons as consultants continued to do so, even when their own grade was junior to that of the physician attached to their command. Hopes of restoring physicians as full members of administrative committees and boards were also dashed when the Adjutant General advised the old system would remain in place, as the new act only created greater confusion.[34]

A joint Army and Navy board was commissioned to investigate and report on the issue of rank on July 18, 1850. Among the questions the committee was charged with was the order of precedence between non-military staff officers and the line and staff, and the extent of command authority between line officers and non-commissioned officers and the staff. In its concluding report, the joint board stated the 1847 act only applied to choice of quarters, service on administrative boards, councils, and courts, and the honors and privileges associated with their grade. Though they could claim high rank via the brevet system, surgeons and assistant surgeons were required to clear all absences, leaves, and temporary detachments from their posting through the commanding line officer, even if he was a brevet second lieutenant.[35]

The joint board's findings were the last word on the subject before the Civil War. For the most part, military physicians were treated with the appropriate respect due a fellow professional. Still, there were occasions when the point of the medical officer's lack of status was driven home. In 1850, shortly after the joint board released its report, Senior Surgeon Clement Finley was brought up on charges of disobedience of orders and contempt and disrespect toward Captain and Brevet Lieutenant Colonel Braxton Bragg. The dispute involved Finley's leaving the post without first notifying Bragg, who took offense and preferred charges against the surgeon. The ensuing court martial found Finley guilty of all charges and recommended his immediate release from the Army, a sentence commuted by President Millard Fillmore, who noted that "The law of 1847, expressly excludes them [medical officers] from command. Now the officers of that corps are not a distinct and independent body, but are a part of the army and as they cannot command it follows that when on duty they must be commanded."[36] The 1850 court martial, and President Fillmore's comments, reinforced the medical officer's position as a marginalized subordinate. Aside from gaining the right to append the formal title of their military grade to their name, the act of 1847 did nothing to increase the medical officer's position and respect within the institution.

The lack of lineal rank marginalized the Army's physicians for most of the nineteenth century. The keys to understanding the reasons for this professional isolation are the acculturation and self-legitimization processes experienced by officers themselves. As representatives of a professional army in a culture antithetical to a standing military, Army officers were quite sensitive regarding their unique abilities and social status. Their legitimacy constantly questioned by citizen militia advocates, and undermined by the wartime intrusion of both well-meaning amateurs and political aspirants, professional officers were extremely sensitive over their rank and the prerogative of command. In fact, the ability to command, which itself placed an individual within the hierarchy of officership, was considered the most essential aspect of rank, and the most jealously guarded component of the Army officer's legitimacy.[37]

Problems of grade and rank aside, other factors strained relations between medical officers and their commissioned peers. The Medical Department was viewed as an adjunct support branch by the regular line and staff establishments. Much of this was related to their own unique educational pathway to professional identity, as well as their interactions with civilian society after entering military service. Unlike line and staff officers, most of whom came from West Point, physicians and surgeons acquired their education through a tenuous and at times fragmented process of individual apprenticeships, formalized medical schools of differing quality, and long residencies—all at their own expense. Then there was the very nature of healing itself. Just as the military officer represented the masculine ideal, the physician, regardless of his training, practice, and own maleness, occupied a feminized role in American society. The language associated with healing was feminized—nurturing, succoring, nursing—reflecting a gender differentiation between the two professions. Even as physicians acquired a masculinized identity in antebellum society, military officers and laymen attracted to the military ideal retained this differentiation, lest the officer's own claim to privileged masculinity be diminished.[38]

Therefore, to many West Pointers, medical officers were not "real" soldiers, though they also wore uniforms. Certainly, the value of their services on post and in the field could not be ignored, yet line and staff officers did not see how military physicians could serve two professional masters— the healing arts and the military tradition—at the same time. They were educated, trained, and acculturated as doctors, not officers; therefore, the military physician had no legitimate claim upon a place in the command structure and culture of rank in the army. They were not seen as peers in arms, but due to their attempts to achieve social and command equality with the line and staff, were instead a challenge to the established order. Rather than "go along" with the traditional and charismatic-rooted authority of the line, by claiming their technological prowess excluded them from slavish devotion to the line's authority, medical officers were seen as challenging the line's privileged status as members of an exclusive social elite. As a result, even though members of the military establishment, army physicians were repeatedly denied full access to the social and professional communion of officership. Denied identity and status as an officer, the army physician was relegated to a peripheral status in the Army's command hierarchy, listened to only when his professional opinion did not seem to intrude upon the course set upon by post and field commanders.[39]

This ambiguous status had other effects as well. In 1830, Secretary of War John Eaton eroded the Surgeon General's control over his own department by rescinding regulations granting medical officers the right to choose their stations, instead reserving the task for his own office. He also restricted the Surgeon General's right to grant extended furlough beyond thirty days duration for his subordinates, routing all requests through his office.[40] Another sign of the medical officer's low status was his low pay and compensation for expenses. As of 1834, medical officer pay had not changed since the War of 1812: $45.00 monthly pay and $47.00 emoluments for surgeons, and $40.00 pay and $41.00 reimbursement for assistant surgeons.[41] Not only were medical officers paid less than captains and majors of the line and staff ($87.00 and $103.00 for captains, $127.00 and $143.00 for majors of the line and staff respectively), they were also paid less than their Navy counterparts.[42] The disparities in pay and emoluments were particularly stinging considering the duties, obligations, and circumstances of the medical officer compared with his line and staff counterparts.

Medical officers did not have the luxury of readily appointing a replacement upon their illness or absence, save at their own expense. Not that medical officers had free funds to use to hire temporary replacements; after subtracting their own living expenses, paying for extra medicines and supplies when necessary, and other expenses, the Army surgeon or assistant surgeon rarely had any money left to call his own.[43] Line officers took some pity on the medical officers' plight, issuing several petitions to Congress for a remediation of the disparity in pay. Still, action was not taken until 1834, when the medical officer's pay and emoluments increased to a level commensurate with cavalry officers: $50.00 a month for surgeons, plus rations and forage equal to the rank of major, while assistant surgeons received pay commensurate with their assimilated rank of captain or first lieutenant.[44]

Even the medical officer's uniform was subject to outside meddling. In 1839, a new medical officer uniform was designed, replacing the epaulettes that were the most visible signs of military rank with an aiguillette. Presented with the implication that army physicians did not deserve recognition as officers, Surgeon General Thomas Lawson exploded. "If under these circumstances the commanding general of the army could feel himself justified in putting me off with an aiguilette, a piece of tinsel on one shoulder," Lawson wrote, "while he decorates every brevet second lieutenant with an epaulette on each shoulder, and the staff lieutenant with an aiguilette besides, I must be satisfied without a military dress."[45] Lawson's letter had the desired effect. When the new uniform was authorized the following year, it included gold-trimmed epaulettes, with embroidery and a gold crescent and laurel wreath with "M.S." embroidered in old English characters in the center.[46]

Even the most basic military honor was denied to medical officers. On August 3, 1843, the Adjutant General wrote Lawson regarding proper salutes due to medical officers. Several surgeons complained about the lack of respect shown by enlisted men standing guard at posts. The Adjutant General determined that while surgeons possessed the assimilated rank of major, the honor was superfluous, intended only for pay and housing allowances. Salutes, a formal acknowledgment of command, were not covered in regulations, as medical officers did not have "the military 'rank' of 'field officers.'"[47]

The combination of regulated formality and cultural elitism only marginalized medical officers. Even though their responsibilities increased, the Army continued to treat physicians as non-combatant staff adjuncts to the line, entitled only to assimilated rank. While new positions were created to help manage the department's human and material resources, those assigned to them were still identified by their occupational title rather than by military rank. But though medical officers were treated as second-class citizens within the officer community, their treatment at the hands of their peers emboldened many, inspiring them to strive all the harder for recognition and legitimacy within the Army.

THE QUEST FOR LEGITIMACY, 1818–1890

Achieving social acceptance and professional legitimacy within the Army was the paramount concern of medical officers throughout the nineteenth century. Simple titles like assistant surgeon, surgeon, and chief surgeon failed to recognize the full range of duties expected of medical officers. The bedrock of military culture was the respect and obligations of rank. Without commensurate rank, military physicians were interlopers, "classed as aliens by those among whom they must pass their lives," a circumstance that only worsened when faced with officers who directed enlisted personnel to ignore the orders of medical officers.[48]

Efforts to win legitimacy were not helped by some physicians' preoccupation with achieving personal validation as officers by displaying their own martial prowess. Even Surgeon General Thomas Lawson sought line command during the Seminole War. His first attempt came in 1836, when he accepted the Lieutenant Colonelcy of a regiment of Louisiana volunteers bound for Florida. A year later, as Surgeon General, Lawson raised a regiment of Pennsylvania and New Jersey volunteers; despite his new role as chief of a staff branch, he did not return to Washington to assume his duties until 1838. When Major General Winfield Scott departed for Veracruz, Mexico in 1846, Lawson accompanied him as chief medical officer, his petition for line command denied.[49]

Legitimacy could be enhanced by brevet promotion. Many medical officers, including Surgeons General Thomas Lawson and Joseph K. Barnes, won recognition through the award of brevet rank, an honorific granted as a reward for meritorious conduct. For medical officers, honorary brevet rank was more than recognition; it established the Army physician in the fraternity of officership, transcending the limited rank structure imposed upon the Medical Department by regulations and strenuously enforced by the Adjutant General's office. Though brevets were given to the Medical Department since the Mexican War, the extent to which they were awarded during the Civil War was remarkable. In addition to Surgeon General Barnes, who was brevetted a major general at the close of the war, twelve surgeons were brevetted brigadier generals; fourteen surgeons and one assistant surgeon were raised to colonel; fifty-three surgeons and assistant surgeons were given brevet promotion to the rank of lieutenant colonel; sixty-three assistant surgeons to major; and eight assistant surgeons to captain.[50]

The distraction of crossing over into the line notwithstanding, Lawson and his successors recognized that the best way to achieve legitimacy was by establishing military medicine and hygiene as a highly specialized discipline, governed by a strict hierarchy of responsibility and knowledge. Three avenues were particularly critical in the quest for acceptance. First was creating a high professional standard for civilian physicians seeking Army employment. Second was establishing a permanent enlisted component, subordinate only to the medical officers. Third was building upon the experience of the Civil War to improve their own self-awareness as specialized professionals and to reinforce their own claims for acceptance as such.

The first step was the creation of stringent entrance qualification examinations and promotion boards for prospective and established Army physicians. First implemented on July 7, 1832, the Army Examination Boards required all candidates to stand before a board of three senior medical officers. The tests were significant as they were intended to limit access into the Medical Department to a very narrow section of the American medical community, privileging those who possessed a clinical knowledge of the body and whose practice conformed to traditional methods of therapeutic intervention. Candidates were tested on canonical knowledge available only through formal medical apprenticeship or training. Newly hired assistant surgeons would be tested again in five years. Ostensibly, the second exam was a prerequisite for promotion; but failure to pass the exam within two attempts constituted grounds for dismissal.[51]

Testing served two purposes. The circumstances of Army life dictated that prospective medical officers be above all else general practitioners, ready to handle any case, including fevers, fractures, gunshot wounds, childbirth, scorbutic taint, and epidemics. Equally significant was the boards' effect on limiting access to the department. By privileging regular clinical medicine and therapeutic practice, the examinations eliminated virtually all sectarian and non-traditional practitioners from candidacy. Between 1835 and 1861, 1,240 candidates were invited to appear for examination. Only 264 passed. The Medical Department's heads were not dismayed. On the contrary, they were proud of how the examination process culled the weak and incompetent from the start. Commenting on the passage of five candidates from a field of twenty-four applicants in 1839, Surgeon General Thomas Lawson pointed to this as proof of the Medical Department's high standards: "It may be that we have erected too high a standard of merit—that too much is exacted from the human intellect; we are not conscious, however, that more has been asked, than ordinary talents, a good primary education, and the actual study of the science of medicine can attain."[52]

Lawson blamed the national system of medical education for the low number of passing applicants. For him, anyone claiming expertise and professional title without the advantage of clinical instruction and participation in a dissection theater was a charlatan: "A knowledge of the science of medicine is not, like divinity and law, to be acquired by reading books in the closet, and listening to the reading of a course or two of lectures; it can only be attained by *seeing and feeling* [emphasis added]; in connexion with the knowledge acquired from books." Any so-called "medical school" that de-emphasized or rejected clinicalism and anatomy not only failed to produce adequate candidates represented a threat not only to the profession, but the nation itself. "The great multiplication of medical schools in every section of the country," he concluded, "together with the proverbial facilities of becoming licensed practitioners, has so lowered the standard of professional excellence, and so manifestly degraded the medical character of the United States, that the present system will be, it is to be hoped, by a more enlightened public opinion ere long put down."[53]

At a time when medical licensing was ineffectual and diminishing in relevance, the Medical Department entrance examinations constituted the most rigorous exclusionary barrier in American medicine. Medical licensure in America had more to do with regional interests and marketability than competency. Codes introduced during the colonial period and maintained in the early republic were mostly honorific, the state and local boards granting licenses given no real power to regulate access to the profession. If anything, medical licenses were a marketing tool used to attract paying clients to physicians trained in the regular system of health and therapeutics. By the 1820s, even these vaguely worded codes were being dismantled by state and local governments, responses to the loud and boisterous calls of the "common man," empowered by the egalitarian impulse to reject all symbols of preference and elitism regardless of their utility or merit.[54]

The nation's beleaguered community of regular physicians praised the Surgeon General's policy. At the inaugural meeting of the National Medical Association in 1846, the requirements of the Army Examination Board were identified as a key benchmark for the fledgling association's Committee on Medical Education. When the committee polled the Surgeon General on the Medical Department's position on the state of medical education, Acting Surgeon General Henry L. Heiskell in turn affirmed the support of the nation's regular physicians when he identified several factors that doomed unsuccessful applicants, in particular their "*insufficient preparatory education; a hurried course of professional pupilage; want of proficiency in practical anatomy*, in *pathology*, and in *clinical medicine*."[55] In 1849, the nascent American Medical Association adopted "the rules and requirements of the Army and Navy Boards of Examiners" as the model for its own proposal for a reconstituted state examining board, itself the foundation for a renewed effort at licensing health practitioners.[56]

Thanks to the Army Examination Boards, the Medical Department established its reputation as an elite collection of clinically oriented general practitioners and surgeons. The Medical Department became a model for physicians seeking to establish their own corporate identity amidst the intellectual and professional turmoil of the antebellum era. Even as regular line and staff officers strove to keep physicians out of their own cultural and corporate realms, by denying them access to the identity of officership, the Army Examination Boards gave medical officers an advantage in creating their own homogenous, intellectually secure, and robust corporate identity. Decades after the first board met in New York, medical officers pointed to their ordeal as evidence of the department's farsightedness. Allowed to set the parameters for entrance into its ranks, in 1832, the

Medical Department began its journey toward becoming an elite branch within the Army, even as its members were denied legitimacy by the officer community.

Another factor establishing credibility was the enlisted Hospital Corps. Medical officers long recognized the value of trained, non-commissioned stewards, not only as caregivers but also as administrative assistants. Prospective stewards came from line units. Occasionally the new steward's quality was questionable; obviously some line officers using the opportunity to be shed of troublemakers and malingerers. But most enlisted personnel sent to work in the post hospitals were eager and willing to learn as much as possible about their new job, even acting as post apothecaries or performing minor surgery when the surgeon was unavailable. No matter how good the enlisted stewards were at their new jobs, however, they could always be called back to their units. And even if they remained attached to the hospital, they were liable for the normal fatigue and guard duties of a line soldier.[57]

In 1853, Surgeon General Lawson proposed a permanent corps of hospital stewards as "supernumeraries in a regiment or corps . . . not specially attached to any organized company of the line of the army." Their duties would encompass all the tasks performed by temporary stewards. Lawson was convinced line officers would support any effort to create an independent cadre of enlisted personnel for the Medical Department, as it would eliminate the need for soldiers to be taken from line companies.[58] As for the stewards themselves, he was certain they would prove their worth tenfold. Knowing he was excused from the fatigues and routine duties expected from the soldier of the line, the steward "will feel proud of his station, and be disposed to devote the best energies of his mind and body to the duties of his office . . . reconciled to his avocation, and of course, in a better frame of mind to discharge faithfully the duties assigned to him in the hospital."[59]

In 1856, Congress finally authorized a permanent establishment of hospital stewards. The newly enlisted steward would never replace the medical officer, but he was a critical adjunct, relieving the medical officer of several medical and administrative duties. The hospital steward was also a potential check upon the otherwise unguarded contract surgeon, safeguarding against non-accepted therapeutic activities or unmilitary behavior. The steward also made it possible for medical officers to accompany field expeditions without having to contract out coverage in their absence, as the enlisted orderly could be left to manage the post hospital. Seen in this light, the campaign for the permanent hospital steward was not merely an attempt to reduce the influence of civilian physicians in the army, it was also a move toward creating a command structure for medical officers. The new Hospital Corps thus helped advance the arguments of medical officers seeking the formal award of lineal rank. By formally recognizing the dual structure of commissioned medical officers and enlisted hospital stewards, with tasks and obligations divided along lines of professional ability, training, and grade, the Army finally acknowledged the medical officer's prerogative to exercise command.

Both outcomes proved essential in the Civil War. The need for hospital orderlies, ambulance attendants, cooks, and nurses was at least as great as that for skilled physicians and surgeons. Congress gave the Surgeon General carte blanche to employ as many enlisted hospital stewards as he saw fit for the duration of the Civil War. At the same time, a corps of medical cadets was authorized "to act as dressers in the general hospitals and as medical officers alone." These cadets were incorporated as an intermediary step between the medical officer and the hospital steward, and were drawn from the nation's medical students.[60] By the war's end, 931 hospital stewards were in uniform, supported in hospitals by over 5,000 woman nurses and in the field by seventy medical cadets. For the most part, the hospital stewards were conscientious and highly skilled, many of them medical students who eagerly sought an opportunity to practice their craft while in the service of the Union.[61]

THERAPEUTIC PRACTICE AND THE ARMY MEDICAL OFFICER

Of all the staff branches, the Medical Department was charged with the most obvious duties and tasked with the most difficult of circumstances. The medical officer's chief duty was caring for the soldiers, officers, and families under their watch. Physicians entering the Army's service soon discovered the extent and nature of practice expected of them was very different from that in the civilian world. Unlike many civilian counterparts, medical officers enjoyed a permanent patient base. The size of the patient base varied between the different posts a physician would be assigned to, from a few dozen soldiers and a single officer at small frontier palisades to, in the case of a post like Fortress Monroe, nine artillery companies drawn from three different regiments.[62] During his assignment—which could last anywhere from a few weeks to ten years—the attending medical officer administered to what was essentially a captive community. Uniformed physicians possessed greater latitude in gauging the health of their charges. Placed in close proximity with their patient base, medical officers were well informed as to the different exciting factors—such as alcohol, food, exposure, crowding, overexertion—dictating the balance of health in an individual. This translated into a detailed knowledge of the individual patient's medical history. The close relationship between Army doctor and patient also facilitated closer interventional management, affording medical officers the ability to modify and adjust therapies as they observed the symptomatic progression of a disease and its treatment. Medical officers also had greater success than their civilian counterparts in terms of disease prevention. The preventive methods practiced by medical officers were largely environmental in nature, focusing upon moderation in diet, drink, physical exertion, and other activities. Still, the Army's hierarchical social networks rendered it easier for uniformed physicians to institute a range of institutional practices prefiguring later public health initiatives.

The medical officers' practice encompassed more than therapeutic management and sanitation. Army physicians administered the small post hospitals, managing all aspects of supply and equipment in their care. They acted as apothecaries, compounding and dispensing medicines with personal experience and handbooks of *materia medica* as their only guides. Before 1856, they also trained and managed the enlisted men detailed as orderlies by post commanders. Afterwards, they were assisted by a permanent establishment of enlisted hospital orderlies, who still required supervision and training. Medical officers also advised the line on the health of commands in garrisons and in the field, particularly on locations for campsites and new forts, the construction of barracks and hospitals, water supplies and drainage, and food. Medical officers accompanied expeditions into the field, medicine chest in tow, treating wounds, injuries, and illnesses in the field. Finally, they were required to make quarterly reports to the Surgeon General's Office in Washington on the general health of the communities in their care as well as the medical topography and climatic factors of their post. Between administrative duties and medical practice, army physicians were likely the hardest working members of a military garrison.[63]

When it came to the actual nature of their practice, Army doctors subscribed to the same knowledge schemas of understanding and treating disease as their civilian *confreres*. The body was a complex and delicate instrument, governed by a series of balances between normative states and external conditions. Ill health and disease was the result of an imbalanced internal environment, either resulting from the influence of immoderation in social and personal actions, or the onset of toxins from an independent external factor. In order to restore the balance, physicians paid careful attention to the progression of symptoms, measuring it against each patient's unique age, gender, body type, and other factors. This observation was in turn used to inform the physician of the particular therapeutic application—depletive, antiphlogistic, and stimulative—best employed. Empirical observation also informed the measure of therapy, ranging from a simple application of a mustard poultice to induce blistering to the administration of massive doses of mercurial calomel and copious bloodletting, releasing the disease entity's hold on the system through a heroic effort. This system of practice, what John Harley Warner describes as therapeutic specificity, was simultaneously flexible and highly personal. It allowed physicians to tailor treatment to a specific disease, requiring not only a careful touch and surety of knowledge between different substances and their interactions, but more than a level of passing familiarity between the practitioner and the patient. Army medical officers were ideally placed to develop such relationships. Not only were they the exclusive agent of healing for soldiers and officers in their charge, but they also enjoyed an exhaustive familiarity with their patient base.[64]

Public interest in wartime health and military medicine validates interpretations of the Civil War's centrality within the greater context of social change. The conflict itself exceeded its immediate political aspects of resolving the constitutional and moral crises associated with slavery. Historian George M. Frederickson summarized how the Civil War awoke Northern intellectuals to the possibilities of transforming American society in the wake of the conflict, using the rhetoric of a martial moral imperative combined with the rationalization necessitated by war. The military experience, he wrote, imbued professional elites and social reformers with the organizational and practical skills to promote a social agenda emphasizing the specialized expert's primacy as architect and guardian of change.[65]

At the center of this movement to cast aside the egalitarianism of the antebellum era was the medical profession. Bonnie Blustein has noted how the wartime activities of regular physicians were framed to resolve the decades-long crisis that plagued the medical profession over system, practice, and education. For regular physicians in the North, the Civil War was not only a struggle to preserve the political union, Blustein observes, but also to unite American medicine under a single dominant approach, dictated by those who privileged expertise acquired through formal education and a system that emphasized direct intervention. The Civil War, she writes, taught civilian physicians and administrators in the Sanitary Commission the merits of a practice valuing hospital management and public health administration as much as therapeutics, a scientific approach that "had come to encompass, even transcend, the values of efficiency, discipline, progress, national unification, and elite authority relationships so important to the [U.S. Sanitary Commission's] vision of America."[66]

Despite the efforts of the civilian relief agencies like the U.S. Sanitary Commission, the Army Medical Department was the primary agent of the changes that would shape the course of American medicine after 1865. Under the leadership of two Surgeons General, Brigadier General William Alexander Hammond and Brevet Major General Joseph K. Barnes, the Medical Department expanded its intellectual and organizational horizons to encompass medical science, hospital management, and education. Many recommendations possessed antecedents in the antebellum army. Nor did the Medical Department succeed in overcoming the well-worn pattern of peacetime Congressional indifference. Despite the rhetoric associated with the 1862 legislative act "to increase the efficiency of the Medical Department," such measures were only temporary expediencies. Still, the experience of the Civil War exerted a marked influence on the Medical Department for years to come, in both material and symbolic ways.

The experience of managing health through the vehicle of the extensive wartime medical system validated the regular medical officer's sense of purpose. For the first time the Medical Department was organized on a rational basis, with well-established chains of command and authority delineating the responsibilities and obligations of the medical officer and hospital orderly. Medical officers were empowered by their control of the vast depots of medical supplies and equipment, acquired through their own skills of negotiation, or from government apothecary suppliers under their own control. Even though the department exercised control and agency over its own affairs for only a brief four years, the memory of the experience would provide bittersweet inspiration for decades afterwards. Neglected and soon forgotten in the Army, the experience in field and general hospitals was nevertheless a foundation for future reform in the civilian worlds of public health and medical practice.

Many accounts of the Medical Department's Civil War activities focus on the drama of wartime military medicine. Combat surgery at the height of the age of amputation has captured the imagination in scholarly works, popular novels, and films. Portrayals of pus-oozing shattered limbs cut off willy-nilly by numbed surgeons, of gangrenous infection racing through the body, and of pigs rooting through piles of discarded limbs outside of tent hospitals are part of the stock narrative of the Civil War. Unfortunately for those on both sides of the conflict, the Civil War occurred just prior to the great revolution in medical knowledge and therapeutics. Germ theory was but a few years on the horizon. Surgeons in Europe groped toward aseptic surgery in the 1840s, but the method did not gain widespread acceptance until English surgeon Joseph Lister published a report on the use of carbolic acid in 1867. Ether and chloroform were well known as anesthetics, but the demand was so great and the supply so limited it was doled out sparingly. These factors help account for the readiness to amputate legs and arms shattered by soft lead projectiles and shell fragments.[67]

The Medical Department's greatest challenge was keeping the armies safe from disease. The diseases wracking the Union forces were little different than those faced by antebellum medical officers. The difference was the scale and scope of infection among the mass levies of volunteers and conscripts. Dysentery and diarrhea were the greatest complaints among soldiers, with 1,739,135 reported cases and 44,558 deaths reported. These "alvine fluxes," along with measles, typhus fever, the different intermittent malarial fevers, and a newly constructed disease, "typho-malarial fever," constituted the so-called "camp diseases." What distinguished these from other illnesses was their association with overcrowding, poor diet, and inadequate sanitation. The threat of disease was obvious; whereas 93,969 Union soldiers died of wounds sustained in combat, and another 400,000 were wounded, well over six million different cases of illness were reported between 1861 and 1865. Of this, 186,216 died as a result of sickness and disease. In the first two years of the war alone, 55,093 died of disease, as compared with 14,999 deaths from wounds and injuries.[68]

Vouchsafing the individual soldier's health, thereby preserving the overall health of the army as a whole, fostered a new interest in public hygiene and sanitation. While generally aware of the communal obligation to eliminate noisome health hazards, health and wellness were individual concerns. The image of thousands of young volunteers, regulars, and conscripts succumbing to childhood diseases, camp illnesses, and fever invigorated the hygiene movement. Wartime necessity made hygiene even more important. "In the military service, more than any other, a knowledge of the means of preventing disease and of facilitating recovery by methods other than the mere administration of drugs is necessary," Hammond opined. Just as the armed force was the guardian of the health and life of the state, so too was the individual medical officer the solitary defender of the force in his charge.[69]

While regular medical officers already understood his precepts, Hammond's 1863 military hygiene manual, *A Treatise on Hygiene with Special Reference to the Military Service*, was the first serious introduction to the subject of preventive medicine for many volunteer and contract surgeons. Hammond divided his manual into three sections: a discussion on the importance of close physical examination of recruits; a brief review of the innate factors—such as race, temperament, idiosyncrasy, age, morbid habits, sex, heredity, age, and constitution—generally accepted as responsible for health and disease; and the different exciting factors that also shaped the balance between wellness and illness.[70] Hammond's outlook on disease causation, prevention, and cure, though informed by his own delvings into physiological chemistry over the last fifteen years of his career, remained tightly bound to environmental and systemic outlooks informing the therapeutic specificity that defined the core of regular medical knowledge.

The most significant departure was how Hammond incorporated the latest thoughts on the importance of ventilation, cleanliness, and overcrowding into the preventive regimen. It was essential the different structures occupied by soldiers—especially hospitals and barracks—be constructed according to the best methods and designs used in the civilian world. "Unlike other habitations—with the exception of prisons—the inmates [of hospitals] are incapable of going out to obtain fresh air and light," Hammond wrote. "They must submit to the conditions in which they are placed, and if these are such as are inconsistent with the requirements of sanitary science, the evil falls upon them with much greater force than upon those able-bodied persons who, though they may reside in insalubrious habitations, are within their walls but a small portion of the day."[71] The chief concern in building hospitals was the patient's recovery. Urban centers, manufactories, graveyards, rivers, marshes, and canals were to be avoided, while hills or elevated points were to be sought out; the better to avoid inundation in stale, stagnant miasmas of decomposition. Other precautions included building on dry, sandy soil, avoiding the temptation to build cellars, applying liberal coats of white plaster to the walls, and ensuring the free flow of air through windows, grates, and doors. This last point was critical: "No duty is more imperative upon those having charge of hospitals than that of doing all in their power to insure, as nearly as possible, complete ventilation of the wards under their charge. . . . No better test of the professional fitness of a physician or surgeon to take the charge of a hospital can be found than the estimate which he puts upon the importance of providing an abundance of fresh air for his patients."[72] Borrowing a page from Florence Nightingale, Hammond equated unventilated hospitals with death. Filth was more than a tangible physical presence. The air itself was polluted with the filthy exhalations of illness, decomposition, and stagnation, leaving those confined in their beds ready prey for malignant hospital gangrenes, blood poisoning, typhus and typhoid fevers, and cholera.[73]

The centerpiece of the army's medical system was its general hospitals. Before the war, hospitals were relatively small affairs located at the army's larger forts, intended to facilitate personal care for the relatively small number of soldiers reporting for sick call at any given time. Regimental tent hospitals were the norm. Exposure to camp diseases among newly gathered volunteers and the experience of First Bull Run and subsequent engagements revealed the complete inadequacy of independent regimental hospitals to handle the volume of sick and wounded. As brigades and later divisions became the chief administrative and command structure in the field, the resources of the regimental hospitals were collected into larger field hospitals, where immediate sick care and surgery was dispensed in camp and in field. But even these facilities were inadequate according to the growing sanitary sensibility of the age, and permanent structures outside of the army command system, general hospitals, were requisitioned and constructed. Initially these were established in large buildings—warehouses, hotels, churches, factories, and schools—that could be commandeered by the military as the need arose. But the volume of patients and the erratic sanitary condition extant in the appropriated structures mandated the construction of large hospitals able to accommodate well over a thousand patients at a time.

After his appointment, Surgeon General William Hammond and his Medical Director of the Army of the Potomac, Jonathan Letterman, undertook a program of organizing, designing, and building new general hospitals throughout the North. All new hospitals shared a number of essential qualities. They were built as close to lines of communication, rivers and railroads especially, as possible, to facilitate the smooth transfer of sick and wounded from the field to the wards. All were self-contained institutions, equipped with their own kitchens, storerooms, laundries, offices, and where permissible, entertainment facilities. Wards were laid out in accordance with the latest sanitary reforms. Natural ventilation was incorporated to keep hospital infections at bay. The focus on ventilation and the need to move patients to and from wards and operating theater, clinic, or dining hall, led the Medical Department to move away from extemporized hospitals in existing structures to specially designed pavilion wards. The advantages of the single or two story pavilion design, with separate wards connected to a centralized administrative structure, were the ability to move patients smoothly from one area of the hospital to another and the establishment of distinct wards for each condition, thereby avoiding the possible spread of opposing infections or diseases. The actual design of pavilion hospitals varied, from circular layouts like that used for the U.S. General Hospital at Point Lookout, Maryland, to v-shaped buildings like Harewood Hospital at Washington, D.C. Between the converted hospitals and new ones constructed on the pavilion model, the Medical Department controlled a massive system of general hospitals, which in September 1864 peaked at 202 general hospitals with a capacity of 136,894 beds.[74]

The act of creating centralized facilities to manage the sick and wounded marked a significant transition in the social construction of disease and wellness. Before 1861, hospitals were an uncommon sight, existing only in America's largest cities. Then, hospitals fulfilled a specific, class-oriented purpose very different from that taken for granted in the twentieth century. In antebellum America, hospitals were often the sole access to medical care for the urban poor, and were considered beyond the pale for the middle and upper classes. Its clinics dispensed medicines and advice to urban day-laborers and factory workers who could not afford visits to or from practicing physicians. Other urban poor, including prostitutes, vagrants, drunks, and street urchins, were generally shunted off to the local almshouse for care, though more often than not, the chief distinction between the hospital and the almshouse were different entrances into the same building. Regardless of what it was called, the hospital represented an entire range of attitudes centered on concepts of deference and obligation that defined American social interaction in the antebellum period. Because hospitals served the urban poor, the middle and upper classes avoided them at all costs—although hospitals thrived as vistas where interested spectators could observe firsthand the wages of sin and effects of poverty upon the body. Hospitals also undermined the private transaction between healer and patient that was central to the therapeutic system. Most interactions between physician and patient took place in the privacy of the home, where the afflicted was most comfortable and had the support of family and friends. Open wards tore away the veil of privacy separating the sick from society, exposing the sick individual not only to the dangers of tainted miasmas emanating from other sick patients, but also the censure of social betters visiting the wards. Adding to the hospital's stigma was the growing number of unworthy poor gaining admittance into the wards as the differentiation between almshouse and hospital blurred. The presence of alcoholics, syphilitics, and the mentally ill in wards further tainted the reputation of hospitals, so that it became associated even among the working poor as the end of the line—the last resort of the dissipated and degenerate seeking a comfortable bed to pass their final days.[75]

The Civil War changed this perceptual bias, endowing the hospital with a socially acceptable mission. The care received by sick and wounded volunteers, grouped in wards specific to their condition, was not an absolute guarantor of survival but certainly ensured that many lived who otherwise would not. Conscientious yet frugal reformers witnessed the efficiency of economies of scale regarding medical care, and the great potential for safe-guarding the regular physician against eclectic practitioners by creating a holistic environment for health under one roof. The increasing success of surgery, particularly excisions and amputations, undertaken in hospitals provided another possible venue for transferring medical care for the worthy from the home to a centralized locale, where recovery could be guarded and managed more expeditiously.

Though much of the Medical Department's activities were restricted to the Army's uniformed community, medical officers had ample opportunities to engage in public health that crossed the line between the civilian and military spheres during the Civil War. As the Union Army extended its control over the South, civil-military public health was increasingly characterized by direct military intervention. The most often cited example of local public health intervention was Major General Benjamin F. Butler's quarantine of New Orleans. Even as Butler arrived in the city with an occupation force on May 1, 1862, he was concerned over the likelihood of a yellow fever outbreak which could result in the Confederate reinvestment of the city. By the end of May, Butler and naval Captain David M. Farragut quarantined New Orleans. The quarantine went beyond the usual commercial blockade to and from the Confederacy; instead it was intended to keep yellow fever from entering the city via the holds of any vessel on legitimate business. All traffic entering the city was routed through a quarantine station at Fort St. Philip, seventy miles below the city, "wherein thirty-two and sixty-eight pound shots should be the messengers to execute the health orders."[76]

On June 4, 1862, Butler took additional steps to keep New Orleans disease free. After considering the likely sources of the fever—in his own estimation, the piles of festering garbage, offal, and human and animal waste accumulating on streets, canals, and the shore of Lake Pontchartrain—Butler imposed a comprehensive sanitation program. Two thousand workers, drawn from the city's unemployed, were employed to clean up the city's streets, marketplaces, open sewers, canals, and river frontage. Civilian teamsters and soldiers of the Quartermaster Corps carted away household and business garbage, which was ordered to be placed in disinfected receptacles by the curbside. All unpainted houses, warehouses, and other structures were coated over with a whitewash of crushed limestone, alum, and salt. Butler himself acknowledged that the orders on their own would have been impossible to enforce, and based upon the experience of failed civilian attempts to enforce sanitation, he was correct. Yet his own disclaimer was rather ingenious, as he made inspection and enforcement duties of the occupation forces, and freely locked violators up in the parish prison for the slightest transgression.[77]

Butler's quarantine and enforced sanitation policy did not win him any favor in New Orleans, which remained sympathetic to the Confederacy throughout the occupation. Yet the results could not be overlooked. From

May 1, 1862, until the summer of 1867, long after the withdrawal of Federal troops from New Orleans, the city remained free of yellow fever. The connection between sanitation, quarantine, and the absence of fever was not lost on local physicians and medical officers. After leaving New Orleans in August 1862, Surgeon T. H. Bache, U.S. Volunteers, credited the quarantine with completely preventing the disease during his stay there, despite the fact that "the epidemic was 'over due,' as they say."[78] Bache's comments were later seconded by Assistant Surgeon George Miller Sternberg. Assigned there over the summer of 1863, Sternberg credited the quarantine as even more effective than the blockade in keeping yellow fever at bay, noting that while yellow fever appeared among the naval squadron stationed in the area, not a single case appeared in the city.[79] Over the course of the war, 1,223 cases of yellow fever appeared in the South, including the Department of North Carolina, the coastal islands of South Carolina and at Florida stations, of which 424 were fatal. But save for those cases at the quarantine hospital reported by Assistant Surgeon Sternberg, New Orleans remained free of the fever until after the end of the war.[80]

The Medical Department's activities in New Orleans were undertaken primarily to prevent the outbreak of diseases among Northern troops stationed there. Public health nuisances were abated by extending the direct coercive authority of the military medical structure over a civilian population. This blurring of lines between the distinct military and civilian cultural spheres was remarkable even against the backdrop of a predominantly egalitarian society undergoing its transformation into one more orderly and hierarchical through the crucible of armed conflict. Nevertheless, this process was emulated in the coming decades by civilian public health activists in American cities. When metropolitan public health boards assumed greater responsibilities in the 1880s and 1890s, their officials were armed with a range of inspection, quarantine, and enforcement powers similar to those exercised by Union medical officers. Indeed, by 1902, officials in the U.S. Public Health Service were attired in uniforms that bore a marked similarity to those worn by medical officers in the Civil War, down to their Federal blue frock coats and trousers, epaulettes, insignia, and pillbox caps. The adoption of the outward trappings of a military structure matched the desire to create an implied social necessity. When responsibility for public health shifted to the state in the late nineteenth and early twentieth centuries, civil servants willingly adopted a militarized perspective, seeing in the visage of a uniform and command hierarchy the full weight of the modern state they wished to serve and defend from an invisible enemy.[81]

WINNING AND KEEPING RANK AND STATUS, 1863–1890

The Civil War dramatically affected the question of formal rank and status for medical officers. As late as 1862, the Medical Department remained governed by the same antebellum-era codes, regulations, and perceptions preserving lineal rank as the exclusive social preserve for the West Point graduate in peacetime. Efforts to win recognition of their claims to rank and status were initially stunted by the erratic quality of volunteer physicians, whose reputations were unfairly applied across the entire uniformed medical service. But the reforms transforming the Medical Department from a small peacetime support bureau into a massive infrastructure of military public health soon changed the status of the Regular Army's medical establishment. By 1866, Congress accorded the medical officer the formal rank and place in the Army's command hierarchy sought throughout the antebellum years. The most surprising aspect was not the line and staff branches' willingness to accede to the opening of the community of rank to medical officers; rather, it was the length of time it took army physicians to acknowledge their new status.

The first indication that rank would be extended to medical officers occurred in the flurry of reform acts passed by Congress in 1863. For the first time, the Army's Regulations stated medical officers "by virtue of their commissions . . . may command all *enlisted* men, like other commissioned officers."[82] Still excluded from serving on Councils of Administration, the *Revised Army Regulations* of 1863 acknowledged the medical officer's unique command over general hospitals, which were recognized as the exclusive province of the Surgeon General.[83] Both developments were significant. Prior to this, exercising command outside of the Medical Department was not open for discussion. While post and field hospitals were accepted as the surgeon's domain, their control was not absolute. According to the line, hospitals were useful adjuncts to the business of military affairs. Yet, if left under the absolute control of the medical officer—an outsider to the Army's command culture—hospitals could become a haven for malingerers, shirkers, and other slackers in uniform. Colonel and Brevet Major General Emory Upton remarked on the purported corrosive influence medical officer command of general hospitals exerted on military discipline. "Malingerers and deserters, as well as deserving convalescents, had used the hospitals as half-way houses to their homes," Upton wrote, calling the grant of autonomy to general hospitals "undoubted proof of bad administration."[84] Unlike regimental or brigade hospitals, where attending surgeons had at least a passing familiarity with the individual soldier claiming sickness, medical officers attached to general hospitals were completely unaware of their charges' abuse. "In the large General Hospital the surgeon was forced to make up his mind from a few imperfect observations," Upton added, noting discharges for rheumatism were so abused they were banned in June 1862.[85]

Equally distasteful was the prospect of Medical Department authority over hospitals as part of a grander scheme to achieve command authority over non-medical personnel. Attempts to win control over general hospitals were seen as "a systematic course . . . pursued by the Medical Department to erect itself into a *military corps*, exercising all the functions of command, not only over the large number of patients and convalescents properly brought under it for treatment, but over all officers and troops stationed at general hospitals as guards, . . . claiming to be entirely independent of every other officer of whatever rank, except the Surgeon General."[86] Such attitudes only created conflicts with medical officers, who responded that line officers subverted the authority of army doctors over their patients. Petty challenges to the Medical Department's control over general hospitals mounted, forcing Surgeon General Barnes to request Secretary of War Stanton's intercession in the matter. Barnes wrote the Secretary on September 13, 1864, asking for clarification of the command issue through a general order stating that all general hospitals were under Medical Department command.[87]

On December 27, 1864, Stanton issued War Department General Order Number 306. General hospitals became the sole facility within the Army where the Surgeon General, through his appointed agents, exercised total control over all ranks and grades, regardless of their branch affiliation. Enlisted men assigned as guards, porters, and other positions were under the control of the senior medical officer in charge. Likewise, all patients, no matter their rank, were obligated to obey the orders and recommendations of the medical officer for the duration of their confinement.[88]

After the war, medical officers and their supporters strove to make the wartime changes permanent. As part of the July 28, 1866 act creating a new peacetime establishment, Congress ordered the Army to convene a special board to draft new regulations incorporating and recognizing the many executive orders and legislative statutes issued during the Civil War. The new regulations and articles of war that followed were codified in the 1868 *Army Regulations*, institutionalizing many of the clarifications with regard to rank, command, seniority, and departmental autonomy that had been made during the Civil War.[89]

The 1868 *Army Regulations* asserted the medical officer's legitimacy within the Army and his place within the official hierarchy and informal culture of officership. The most salient initiative extended rank to the medical officer. The old titles of "surgeon" and "assistant surgeon" were transformed into formal grades that still reflected one's occupation and relative status within the Medical Department. But physicians were also accorded rank to determine their place within the Army's command hierarchy. Whereas before the war, medical officers were entitled to address only by their title in all formal correspondence, they were now permitted to indicate their military rank, brevet rank, and departmental grade.[90] This formal usage of rank as title matched the extension of command authority to medical officers over enlisted personnel first described in the 1863 *Army Regulations*. The award of formal lineal rank also provided a solution to other problems. As members of the general staff, medical officers were obligated to obey orders from junior line officers, but the latter were enjoined by regulations "not to assume to give him orders not necessary for the efficient service of the post." Nor were senior medical officers expected to take his place at parades and formations as subordinates to the junior line officer.[91]

Lineal rank for medical officers, the extension of command authority over enlisted personnel, and the recognition of legitimate authority and autonomy over matters of health were all significant changes in the Army's institutional culture. Equally important was the general lack of opposition to the new regulations. Unlike the first time rank was extended to medical officers in 1847, the Adjutant General's Office offered no resistance. Congress also refrained from backsliding on the issue. While staffing levels and appropriations remained subject to revision, Congress only reaffirmed the medical officer's new status and responsibilities. The 1884 Army appropriation act, for example, followed the precedent of 1868: "That officers of the Medical Department shall take rank and precedence in accordance with date of commission or appointment, and shall be so borne on the official Army Register: *Provided*, That the medical officers of the Army and contract surgeons shall whenever practicable attend the families of the officers and soldiers free of charge."[92] In the end, the extension of lineal rank and command authority to the Medical Department was less divisive than many believed earlier.

Having achieved their place within the Army's culture of officership, medical officers acted with decorum. Unwilling to stir up resentment to their hard-won legitimacy, few flaunted their rank before the line establishment. Others sought to defend the new situation by painting the extension of rank and command as a redressing of past injustices. In July 1890, Major and Brevet Lieutenant Colonel Alfred Woodhull described the significance of rank and its distinction from grade as applied to medical officers. Accordingly, medical officer rank was not an intrusion upon the command prerogatives of the line, nor was it intended to unbalance the Army's command hierarchy, but was rather recognition of the unique and special staff function which only medical officers could fulfill—safeguarding the health and well-being of the Army in peacetime and war. Simple titles like assistant surgeon, surgeon, and chief surgeon were only descriptions—and often erroneous ones at that, failing to recognize the full range of duties medical officers were expected to undertake. Since rank was the bedrock of military culture, so long as they were deprived it, military physicians would remain interlopers, "classed as aliens by those among whom they must pass their lives," their recommendations for maintaining health in the field and at posts deprived of any weight if line officers chose to ignore them.[93]

By the 1880s, the issues of rank and status were hardly as controversial as they had once been. The line and staff establishments had little issue with parity in lineal rank and emoluments for medical officers. Some line officers remained skeptical of the abilities and moral character of certain medicos—for example, surgeons with "nothing to do but confine laundresses and treat the clap"—but such views had fallen into the minority.[94]

Colonel and Brevet Major General Emory Upton recognized the special professional qualifications of the medical officer, recommending in a March 7, 1872 letter to House Military Committee Chairman John Coburn that the Medical Department be preserved in the event of a staff reorganization: "In a special corps, like the Engineer or Medical Corps, officers are unquestionably more efficient who are educated, trained, and promoted specially for these services. . . . The staff corps to which officers should be specially confined are the Engineer, Ordnance, and Medical Corps."[95] According to Major General Winfield Scott Hancock, the shared experience of the Civil War, when medical officers worked closely with the line and administered to its sick, wounded, and dying, created a special bond between the combat arms and the Medical Department. "After many years of examination, discussion, and trial," Hancock reported to Secretary of War J. D. Cameron in October 19, 1876, "we have settled down to the belief that the best way of providing the members of the medical corps with what is due them, is through real military grades and rank. I do not recommend a change in this respect, although I do not know that I should advise that course as an original measure."[96] Fourteen years later, these opinions were echoed by Brigadier General and Brevet Major General Wesley Merritt. Recognizing the close relationship between the Medical Department and the line, Merritt took an apologetic attitude toward extending lineal rank to medical officers. "The neglect to give them their proper military titles results from habit rather than design," Merritt wrote, following that "I for one am willing to be cured of the habit," and "though I consider the professional designation a highly honorable one, I will cheerfully give the military title when I am sure it is personally desirable.[97]

Not all line officers were as enlightened on the subject. As the Civil War receded into memory and new calls for institutional and doctrinal reform were made in the hope to facilitate modernization, several traditional-minded officers rejected the change. Traditionalists exercised a vocal campaign against what they perceived to be a dangerous and demasculinizing intellectualization of the Army officer corps. These officers believed combat was the best instructor; too much book learning, the anti-intellectuals feared, weakened one's grip on the manly virtues—physical toughness, mental acuity, courage, and audacity—essential to the officer's character and ability.[98] They were not only concerned about the effects of intellectualization in the officer corps, however; they also jealously defended the line's prerogative as the guardian of tradition and discipline. Traditionalists like artillery Captain James Chester took offense to extending lineal rank to the uniformed physicians, and decried the policy as a sign of the dangerous erosion of the line's control of the Army's culture of command and discipline:

[A]n assistant-surgeon of less than five years' service, is legally invested with the rank of first-lieutenant, and has the right therefore to the title.

Now, while we admit the rank, as legal and indisputable, we maintain that its character is tainted by the statute which deprives it of the full function of command. It is not military rank proper, because of the limitations of the law, and was never intended to be. It is a kind of latent rank which legally adheres to certain commissions, and was put there, merely to protect the pocket and dignity of the officer, and not to confer on him either place or title in the hierarchy of command.[99]

Accordingly, the title of "Assistant Surgeon" was not confusing, but rather well-suited to the young physician's station. Enough that a young Assistant Surgeon receives the pay and emoluments—but not title—due the first lieutenant or captain; the actual rank itself should be reserved for a combatant officer.[100]

Chester's anxiety becomes clearer when he turned to the question of the virtues of the civilian title of "Doctor" as compared with military titles. Was "Doctor" not a noble title in itself, representing "the highest degree in any of the learned professions, and has been the goal of professional ambition for centuries"?[101] Granted, the honorific lost some of its sheen when appropriated by those who had not earned the right to use it, but no more so than when civilians claimed undue military rank as a title. "Think of the effect of saying 'Good bye, Major,' in almost any representative assemblage south of Mason and Dixon's line. Why! Almost every livery-stable keeper, publican and gambler, in certain districts, is a major; that is, he seems to have the social rank of major, if common consent can be accepted as sufficient credentials."[102] But was that reason enough to give up title dearly achieved? Absolutely not: "No; let us stick to our titles; they are ancient and honorable, and fairly descriptive, and they have been borne by too many distinguished men for us to be ashamed of them. . . . The doctorate cannot be disgraced by quacks and charlatans any more than military titles can be by bogus officers. To be addressed as 'Doctor' or 'Colonel' is an honor or an insult, according as the title is or is not rightfully due."[103]

Others were less acerbic than Captain Chester, but equally concerned over the issue. Colonel Thomas M. Anderson, commanding officer of the 14th Infantry Regiment, after lauding the accomplishments of military surgeons, was confused as to why the surgeon or assistant surgeon sought formal lineal rank. "It is surprising to meet medical men ashamed of their title of 'Doctor.' 'Doctor' means 'Teacher.' Applied to a man who can instruct us in the science of life and the rules of living, it is a high and honorable title."[104] The regular conference of rank and grade upon medical officers provoked more distaste when the Medical Department's scheme of advancement was compared with that employed by other line and staff branches. In March 1896, an editorial in the *Journal of the Military Service Institution of the United States* compared the legislated and average duration between promotion from first lieutenant to captain between the Medical Department, the Ordnance Department, Engineers, Cavalry, Infantry and Artillery. Whereas medical officers received automatic promotion to captain after five years (contingent upon satisfactory completion of an examination), ordnance and engineer lieutenants were promoted only after fourteen years' service. The average among the line branches, considering the last five captains in each regiment, was greater: 16.1 years for the Cavalry, 18.3 for the Infantry, and 23.9 for the Artillery.[105] The relative ease of promotion for medical officers was viewed as yet another abuse of the system by physicians. "Can any one imagine a better deadener of professional soldier pride and military spirit than such examples afford?" wrote the editorialist. "We cannot."[106]

Long after the "Old Army" faded into a dim memory, medical officers with a penchant for prose created the stock narrative that helped define the public image of the Medical Department in its first century. The self-created image of the nineteenth century Medical Department peddled by medical officers *cum* historians was one of selfless sacrifice and incredible forbearance, of a collectively constructed medical officer gifted with the patience of Job, forever subjected to mishap, indifference, and mismanagement. Gifted with skills in healing and administrative management, the medical officer was constantly ignored, insulted, and overtaxed by his peer officers and Congressional overseers. Save for the Civil War experience, the nineteenth century was an era of inadequate resources, shabby treatment, and by and large, a "day of small things in the United States Army" and by extension, its medical services.[107] A closer examination of the Army Medical Department in the nineteenth century reveals a different type of organization and circumstance. The antebellum medical officer was keenly aware of the relationships between wellness, physical and moral hygiene, diet, and temperance that became hallmarks of the public health movement later in the nineteenth century. At a time when the practice of regular medicine itself was in doubt in the United States, the army physician became the embattled profession's avatar of efficiency, skill, and legitimate authority within a clearly delineated social institution. The Civil War represented a brief era of newfound empowerment marked by several critical organizational developments. For all of its accomplishments, the Medical Department remained a subordinate branch whose fortune was tied to the fate of the Army as a whole. When the Army returned to its frontier constabulary role, the Medical Department suffered its familiar fate of being asked to do too much with too little.

But the antebellum and Civil War experiences offered hints to another possible outcome for the medical officer besides languishing at forts and posts, waiting for the next war to be reconstituted in a haphazard fashion. While surgeons and assistant surgeons plied their grim trade as bonesetters and sawbones, trying to salvage what they could of the human wreckage of battle, another path to professional legitimacy within the Army and in civilian society was being charted. The army doctor may not have been able to pin a precise name on what they were doing in preserving the health and wellness of the soldier on post and in the field, but their actions were the first steps toward a formalized system within the U.S. Army that would become a critical influence upon civilian and imperial public health in the progressive era. After 1890, a new mission for the medical officer took shape, one that not only transformed the shape and character of the Army Medical Department, but also resolved the question of status as members of the officer community once and for all.

2 The Medical Officer in "The New School Of Scientific Medicine," 1861–1898

The late nineteenth century was a special period for the professions in the United States. The Civil War invigorated public respect for the learned expert, validating claims of privileged knowledge and expertise in a host of fields, not least of which was medical practice and science. The shared experience of regular and volunteer medical officers, contract surgeons, medical cadets, hospital orderlies and stewards, civilian nurses, line officers, wounded and sick soldiers, and the surviving family members redirected perceptions of an impotent medical profession governed by an educated elite. For the first time in the collective memory, health and wellness transcended local and regional perspectives to become a matter of national interest. The effects of camp diseases and fevers were fully revealed; no one was immune to the illnesses rife in camp and hospital. Likewise, the sad victims of battle—the blinded, crippled, and maimed—did not disappear from society's view, but remained long-term reminders of the war, giving as much testimony to the ineffectiveness of surgical practice as to the cruelty of war itself.

In the end, American medicine became firmly wedded to science. By 1910, efforts to impose high uniform educational standards, emphasizing laboratory training and scientific detachment, bore fruit. Though the Army Medical Department profited from these educational reforms, in truth the institution was already far ahead of the rest of the American medical profession in setting high standards for membership in the corps. The antebellum Medical Department's examination boards created a cadre of highly skilled practitioners dedicated to empiricism and therapeutic specificity when such outlooks were out of vogue. Demands of practice and administration limited opportunities for practical research and experimentation, but medical officers were routinely engaged in scientific observation. And where the Civil War exerted slight influence on the growth of medical science in the civilian sphere, the conflict heralded a new awareness and appreciation for scientific methods within the Surgeon General's Office. The resulting infrastructures made it the national agent for promoting medical science. By 1895, forty years after the end of the Civil War, the image of the medical officer as scientific researcher *par excellence* dominated the public's imagination, not to mention the uniformed physician's sense of corporate professional identity.

The newly constructed identity of the physician in uniform as an active agent for preserving health and combating disease also created a more combative, masculine image of the medical officer. Before the 1890s, the medical officer was viewed as a passive figure, hampered by the practical restrictions of his knowledge base and the cultural isolation that kept him an outsider in his chosen professional spheres. But as the army surgeon's professional identity shifted, his utility increased exponentially. Medical officers increasingly identified themselves as *men* of action, soldiers who, though they did not wield a gun or lead troops in battle, were locked in mortal combat with an enemy as brutal as any their line peers would face. The "firing line" was extended beyond the field of battle, to the barracks, hospital ward, encampment, and line of march.

SCIENCE AND THE MEDICAL OFFICER, 1833–1890

Compared to Europe, American medical science experienced fitful growth during the antebellum period. Few physicians pursued empirical research. The fragmentation of American medicine into sectarianism not only retarded the development of the nation's medical schools. It also fostered ambivalence toward rationally oriented systems of health awareness emphasizing uniformity in the body's interactions with exciting or sustained factors and their complementary therapeutic methods.[1]

For its part, the antebellum Medical Department was ambiguous toward medical science. The department was the nation's chief agent for collecting and tabulating medical and meteorological statistics. Medical officers were required to maintain daily health logs and record the medical topography at their posts. However, aside from these purely empirical practices, Surgeon General Thomas Lawson believed the medical officer's chief obligation was medical practice in the field or the post. Original research only interfered with this duty. Medical officers were not expected to waste time and resources pursuing abstract theories that challenged the primacy of the department's accepted systemic foci. Even the sanitary and hygienic measures undertaken by medical officers reflected the primacy of practice. The Army's sanction of preventive medicine did not reflect a specific theoretical association of disease causation. Rather, it recognized the balance between wellness and system, and the negative influence of different exciting factors on soldiers engaged in strenuous activity under extreme conditions.

The exclusive association of the medical officer's identity with his practice of medicine created tensions. The majority of medical officers entered the service before the advent of the Army Examination Boards, and even those who stood before them possessed a framework of knowledge that remained rooted firmly in traditional systems. Shortly after they were first convened, however, the examination boards became the indirect cause of some of the department's tensions over therapeutic and theoretical solidarity. Though they championed examination boards as essential to maintaining a high professional standard—and as a way to exclude sectarianism from the service—Lawson and the senior surgeons of the Medical Department were products of a different age than the assistant surgeons who passed the boards. Many of the old guard belonged to a tradition emphasizing personal apprenticeship under an established practitioner. This sort of intellectual development privileged traditional approaches to medicine as a place where active therapeutic intervention and close personal interaction with the patient mattered more than the detached rationality coming into vogue among certain graduates of the newly established medical schools.

HAMMOND, BILLINGS, AND THE ORIGINS OF ARMY MEDICAL SCIENCE

Following Lawson's death in May 1861, the official line on scientific work changed. Under the two Civil War Surgeons General, William Alexander Hammond and Joseph K. Barnes, a new respect for clinical and laboratory science gradually hold in the Medical Department. Hammond initiated necessary infrastructural reforms during the conflict while also establishing medical science as one of the Medical Department's chief priorities. Indeed, when combined with the controversy surrounding his arrest and court-martial on January 17, 1864, and his subsequent (and unwarranted) lionization as a prescient modernist taking a brave stance against toxic calomel, these reforms secured Hammond's reputation as a medical reformer.

Hammond recognized the unique opportunities the Civil War presented for advancing medical knowledge, and he wasted little time establishing scientific inquiry as an essential component of the Medical Department's mission. On May 21, 1862, he issued a circular ordering medical officers to make precise reports on their activities, including the nature of all wounds and illnesses they treated, as well as any pertinent indicators or perceived exciting factors, the treatment given, and progression of recovery. Hammond also required medical officers to collect "all specimens of morbid anatomy, surgical or medical, which may be regarded as valuable, together with projectiles and foreign bodies removed, and such other matters as may prove of interest in the study of military medicine or surgery." [2] All the collected specimens were initially housed in the Surgeon General's Office, until their later placement in the Army Medical Museum. [3]

After his dismissal, Hammond's vision was preserved by his successor, Joseph K. Barnes. Even though Secretary of War Edwin M. Stanton viscerally disliked Hammond and everything he stood for, Barnes convinced him science was an entirely appropriate pursuit for medical officers. On June 24, 1864, Barnes ordered medical officers to preserve and forward to Washington specimens removed from wounded and dead soldiers, photographs of interesting cases, newly devised dressings and splints, and plaster casts of stumps after amputation.[4] Six months later, Barnes took a decisive step toward creating a permanent scientific establishment attached to the Office of the Surgeon General by summoning seven clinical-oriented medical officers to begin making sense out of the warehouse of reports, letters, specimens, photographs, and etchings that had accumulated since the war began.[5]

Over the next twenty-five years, medical officers attached to the Office of the Surgeon General set about establishing the Medical Department's reputation as America's primary medical science institution. Cataloging the specimens collected by medical officers was the first priority. When Hammond ordered physicians to collect anatomical specimens "and such other matters as may prove of interest in the study of military medicine or surgery," in May 1862, it was with the intention of setting the materials aside for future study and display in a museum.[6] Following President Lincoln's assassination, the Army purchased Ford's Theater on West Tenth Street, and set aside the third floor for a new museum. There it remained until 1887, when the collection was moved into a brick fire-proof building adjacent to the Smithsonian Institution, at 7th and B Streets, SW. By 1872, the museum collection included: 6,093 surgical specimens, plaster and wax casts, and surgical instruments; 1,125 preserved lesions and disease specimens; some 6,000 microscopic slides; nearly 1,000 skulls representative of different Indian tribes and various medical deformities and curiosities; thousands of complete animal skeletons; untold thousands of photographs and sketches, including over 1,000 photographs in four quarto volumes of Civil War patients recovering in civilian and military hospitals; hundreds of thousands of official reports filed by medical officers during and after the war; and representations of the current state of medical and surgical practice, including complete ambulances, litters, splints, artificial limbs, and field medical kits.[7]

Regular Army and National Guard medical officers continued sending prepared specimens to the Office of the Surgeon General for inclusion in the collection, while unique objects and curiosities were purchased or donated from admiring physicians at home and abroad. In 1890, for example, Surgeon General John Moore reported the museum collection had grown to 29,285 objects, including seven skulls exhumed from sixth-century Frankish graves near Worms, Germany, a collection of human embryos at various stages of development, and a skeleton of a woman who was bedridden for twenty years, exhibiting osteomalacia.[8] These specimens, along with curiosities of the Civil War—such as the steel breastplate taken from a dead Confederate at Gettysburg, the proof of its failure in the bullet hole through the center, and the amputated right leg of Major General Daniel E. Sickles, U.S. Volunteers, delivered in its own miniature coffin—ensured the Army Medical Museum was a popular tourist attraction for years. The museum was also welcomed as a marvel by physicians and medical officers from around the world. Expecting a quaint collection of medical curiosities inside a "simple red brick building" adjacent to the Smithsonian Institution, visiting dignitaries were amazed by the scope of the museum's collections: sectioned and preserved organs, embryos, and tumors; wax models of skin diseases in their different stages; pathological human specimens and preserved animals from all over the world; as well as displays of medical corps uniforms from throughout the world and historical artifacts, including coins, medals, microscopes, and medical instruments.[9]

Even though Secretary Stanton assented to collecting the material, some worried if the monumental task of cataloging, collating, and publishing could proceed without interruption. As soon as the war ended, the rush to demobilize the Union armies threatened to cut off any funding for tasks not seen as immediately relevant to the health of the soldiers remaining in uniform. To preserve funding for the Army Medical Museum, Joseph Janvier Woodward appealed to the memory of those lost in the recent war, linking medical science directly to national security:

What was the direction these efforts took—what were the results attained—why our soldiers died, and how this can be best and most economically prevented in future wars—are questions upon which the experience of the present struggle, as recorded in the official reports and documents, can throw a flood of light. Such a publication, therefore, becomes one of the most important duties of the Medical Department of the army; a duty the evasion or neglect of which would be a grave crime against the army of the United States, and against every American citizen who, in future wars, volunteers in the defence of his country.[10]

Woodward's appeal to preserve a record of the Medical Department's wartime accomplishments played to the emotions of militia advocates, but his message was aimed at preserving the prerogatives and autonomy of the professional medical officer. By reserving for his department the obligation to preserve, record, and analyze the historical experience of its wartime service, Woodward committed the Surgeon General's Office to furthering its own identity as a distinct elite within the twin spheres of civilian and military professionalism.

Compiled from the vast collection of wartime reports, photographs, and specimens, *The Medical and Surgical History of the War of the Rebellion* was an impressive effort. The collection's size alone meant the series would be divided into three parts, released over an eighteen year period. The first part, in two volumes, was a comprehensive statistical abstract of disease and combat injuries with extracts and excerpts from volunteer and regular medical officer reports from every theater. The second and third parts, in three volumes each, presented the most extensive account of military medicine heretofore published. Part II examined the different diseases that followed the Union Army throughout the war, with special attention given to the "alvine fluxes"—dysentery and diarrhea—and the different malarial fevers, including a new etiological condition, "typho-malarial fever." The third part was devoted to surgery and battlefield injuries. Completing the history were detailed discussions on the Army's general hospitals and its battlefield evacuation scheme.

In the second part, Woodward adapted the medical classification scheme introduced by British physician William Farr in 1855 for the British Army's study of the Crimean War. This version categorized the diseases and conditions of the Union Army into five distinct classes: zymotic diseases (miasmatic, enthetic, and dietic illnesses); constitutional (diathetic and tubercular) diseases; parasitic diseases; local diseases specific to a system or body part; and violent diseases and deaths (including homicide, suicide, and "execution of sentence"). Even though the last volume in the second part appeared in 1888, well after the relationship between microbes and disease was identified, Woodward remained skeptical. He was suspicious of germ theory, viewing such reports as at best tomfoolery, and at worst, quackery: "When we consider the number and variety of the organic germs which can be detected in the atmosphere by this microscope at all times, and when we remember that it is precisely those lower forms which have been best studied that are most abundant, we shall not be surprised that pretenders have found here a fit field for charlatanism, or that many well meaning but incautious persons have fallen into error."[11] Woodward dismissed notions that disease was caused by a bacteriologic agent. "For it must be admitted that up to the present time no vegetable forms have been observed, in the dysenteric stools, which differ morphologically from those observed in healthy individuals, and that no reasonably convincing evidence of any intrinsic difference, not morphologically expressed has been brought forward," Woodward concluded, describing germ theory as a mere revisitation of the fanciful seventeenth-century "doctrine of animicular contagion."[12]

The Medical and Surgical History of the War of the Rebellion was welcomed as a landmark in medical publishing. American reviewers praised the series eloquently, describing Part II as "the foundation-stones upon which the practice of army surgeons will be built, . . . [proof] that America now holds the surgical sceptre of the world," and "a valuable contribution to the literature of the fluxes; in fact, the most valuable with which we are acquainted."[13] Foreign reviews were equally praiseworthy. Rudolf Virchow himself writing that the series could proudly boast "The greatest exactness in detail, careful statistics even in the smallest matters, and a scholarly statement embracing all sides of the medical experience."[14] The review in The Lancet acclaimed Part I as a major scientific and moral accomplishment, noting so long as the medical and organizational knowledge accrued during the war was used "for the future benefit of mankind, an additional compensation will be made for the calamities which the war occasioned."[15]

Woodward's younger peer, John Shaw Billings, represented the final link in the transformation of the medical officer from the empiricist of the older age to the scientific rationalist of the modern age. Billings was aware of how his profession changed during his career; as he shared in an address before the 1903 Army Medical School's graduating class. When he joined the Medical Department at the start of the Civil War, he entered a world of therapeutic practice dominated by the empirical holistic system. Thermometers were considered interesting toys. Hypodermics were so new that one of his first official duties was to instruct the head of his examination board in their use in a clinical environment. Had he been so bold as to suggest that germs caused disease, and that some illnesses could be treated through the administration of antitoxins, Billings wryly noted, he would have been sent to an asylum for a much-deserved rest. Yet, within a decade, Billings and his associates were reaching toward a new scientific world, staining tissue sections and discovering the minute animiculites present in the blood of the sick.[16]

Over his thirty-three-year career, Billings was the Medical Department's intellectual representative both with the general public and the medical community. For one thing, Billings's expertise was a highly desired commodity. In 1869, he helped the Treasury Department reorganize the Marine Hospital Service along the model of the Army Medical Department, creating the structure that ultimately became the foundation for the U.S. Public Health Service. In 1879, he was appointed vice-president of the short-lived National Board of Health. Following this, he was sent as the head of a commission to control yellow fever raging in Memphis, Tennessee, where he championed a centralized sewage and streets system. Billings also co-founded the American Public Health Association, serving as the organization's president in 1880. Recognized as an expert on modern hospital design, Billings helped plan several facilities, including the Hospital of the University of Pennsylvania in Philadelphia, Johns Hopkins Hospital in Baltimore, and Peter Bent Brigham Hospital in Boston. He also assisted the Census Bureau in compiling mortality statistics for the 1880 and 1890 census.[17]

Medical literature was where Billings had the greatest influence, however, in a series of monographs and reports in the tradition of the Army's pre-war *Statistical Abstracts*. In 1870, Billings issued his first comprehensive sanitary survey, the Surgeon General's Office Circular Number 4, *A Report on Barracks and Hospitals*. This was followed in 1875 with a more comprehensive survey, Circular Number 8, *Report on the Hygiene of the United States Army*. The two circulars provided a well-detailed overview of the hygienic condition at the Army's 235 posts and the general health of the American soldier during the heyday of the frontier army. Both reports dealt with the material aspects of the soldier's life, including barracks, quarters, guardhouses, and hospitals, foodstuffs and rations, clothing, and medical supplies. The two circulars also combined meteorological and mortality statistics with first-hand accounts from medical officers serving across the country, a model established in the Army's 1840 *Statistical Report*. They also reveal Billings' own thoughts on public health and hygiene, and his continued association with the connections between environment, morality, and overall health.

Billings reserved his most scathing critiques for the condition of base housing. "Air-space," the extent of personal space per man in his lodging, and ventilation were singled out by Billings as the cause of most of the disease plaguing the army. Comparing the effects of consumption and other respiratory diseases on soldiers versus the civilian population of the United States, Billings concluded that a white soldier serving in the Army was on average twice as likely to be discharged or die from tuberculosis than had he remained in civilian life, and nearly four times more likely to fall victim to pneumonia, influenza, catarrh, or some other respiratory illness. "I think it is no exaggeration to say that the service loses by death and discharge on account of overcrowded and badly ventilated barracks and guard-houses, about 100 men every year," he concluded.[18] Billings also attacked the lack of proper bathing facilities in barracks as proof of neglect. "Next to fresh air and food," he wrote, "personal cleanliness is the most important agent in preserving the mind and body in proper working order, and it is not only a duty, but necessary facilities."[19] Failure not only promoted disease and poor discipline, but eroded the high morality of the soldiery. "A dirty man will, in most cases, be a discontented, disagreeable, and dissolute man; for the condition of his skin has much more to do with a man's morals than is generally supposed."[20]

Billings' work as a bibliographer and librarian established him as one of America's leading intellectuals. But before he took on the task of creating free urban libraries across the country, Billings transformed the small collection of books and folios in the Surgeon General's Office into the massive Army Medical Library, creating what would become the world's largest collection of medical literature and ultimately, the foundation for the National Library of Medicine and the cornerstone of the National Institutes of Health. For decades before the Civil War, the library of the Surgeon General's Office was a small collection of books, mostly devoted to clinical practice and surgery, literally housed in the Surgeon General's Office. When Billings took over responsibility for the library in 1865, it had grown to some 1,800 volumes, large enough to warrant a permanent overseer.

Over the next thirty years, Billings acquired new texts and journals, classic tracts and folios, and rare volumes with a dogged zeal that bordered on the maniacal, prompting his friend Oliver Wendell Holmes to warn only half in jest, "Dr. Billings is a bibliophile of such eminence that I regard him as a positive danger to the owner of a library, if he is ever let loose in it alone."[21] Always seeking new acquisitions, Billings subscribed to medical journals from around the world and retained book agents on private contract throughout Europe and the United States, sending them lists of books to be purchased at auction. He also maintained close contacts with other librarians, all for the purpose of exchanging recently published books and journals for like material as it appeared. When he retired from active service in 1895, the Army Medical Library was one of the world's largest collections of medical literature. In thirty years, the library's holdings had grown from 1,800 volumes to some 117,000 books and journals, and another 193,031 pamphlets and theses.[22]

The reverse side of Billings' passion for acquiring new materials for the Army Medical Library was the problem of cataloging the holdings. He could have simply created a listing of the collection, but Billings saw the opportunity to use the Army Medical Library as a springboard for a comprehensive reference bibliography. The resulting *Index-Catalogue of the Library of the Surgeon General's Office, United States Army* was the largest and most exhaustive index of medical literature created up to that time. Ultimately, the first series of the *Index-Catalogue* would comprise sixteen volumes, each over 1,000 pages long. Working from index cards, Billings and his assistants cross-referenced the thousands of books and tens of thousands of medical journals according by subject keywords and author's names. Because of the long time of production and the ever-constant march of medical literature, Billings recognized his work was obsolete as soon as it appeared in print. To remedy this, he envisioned successive revisions of the *Index-Catalogue* every few years, which in turn would be supplemented with monthly updates in the form of an *Index Medicus*. Between the two indices, a running commentary on the state of medical literature was established, the eventual foundation for the American Medical Association's Quarterly Cumulative Index Medicus (QCIM), and in turn, the National Library of Medicine's *MEDLINE* index.[23]

Billings' works reveal an amazing breadth as an administrator, bibliographer, and sanitarian. Yet, though he possessed a remarkably clear vision of the future rationalization and centralization of the medical profession, his view of scientific medicine remained tied to his original training in clinical physiology. It fell to other medical officers to explore the new scientific currents driving the direction of the profession. During the last months of the Civil War, Assistant Surgeon and Brevet Lieutenant Colonel Woodward began experimenting with natural-light photography of microscopic slides. These early attempts, and subsequent efforts using magnesium and electric lights, saw the birth of a new process of capturing detailed and accurate images of tissue samples; cellular structure; and, though Woodward remained skeptical of their importance in disease causation, the bacilli responsible for typhoid, dysentery, and other diseases.[24] In the winter of 1878, Assistant Surgeon George Miller Sternberg began his first experiments with disinfectants, work marking the start of a fascination with the nascent germ theory elaborated by Robert Koch and Louis Pasteur that set him on the path toward becoming the premier American bacteriologist of the late nineteenth century.

Though many in the Medical Department—including for a time Billings himself—remained skeptical on the subject of germ theory, the system gained new converts when a direct connection was made between hospital gangrene and erysipelas and microbes in 1892. Conventional wisdom held that the act of combustion and the natural frictions created by the bullet's travel through the atmosphere to the point of impact sterilized firearm projectiles. Ensuing infections were blamed on other factors, such as miasmatic hospital air or poisoned bullets, since the heat-sterilized bullet created an aseptic wound. The first public challenge to this theory was made by Captain and Assistant Surgeon Louis A. LaGarde in October 1892. Later acclaimed as an originator of modern ballistic forensics, at the time Lagarde wished to determine whether the act of firing a gunpowder weapon rendered the projectile aseptic. Firing bullets infected with anthrax into wood boards, and later, live rabbits, he discovered the spores survived and could cause infection. LaGarde concluded, "The heat developed by the act of firing is not sufficient to destroy all the organic material on a projectile, the cherished notion of three centuries and more to the contrary notwithstanding." Thus, "a septic bullet *can* infect a gunshot wound."[25] Later experiments with tetanus, ricin, and curare only further validated LaGarde's 1892 observations, leading him to observe "that all forms of bacterial life and animal poisons may be conveyed into wounds made by firearms, and that the clinical evidence of poison in the case of bacteria depends on the variation of the factors already mentioned."[26] LaGarde's work did not provide a direct association with public health and contagious disease, but it did offer further evidence microbes caused infection, giving greater credence to the arguments raised by surgeons and physicians for making the hospital an antiseptic environment.

GEORGE MILLER STERNBERG AND "THE NEW SCHOOL OF SCIENTIFIC MEDICINE"

On May 30, 1893, President Grover Cleveland chose the replacement for the recently retired Surgeon General, Charles Sutherland, a forty-one-year veteran with "a most amiable disposition and [who] was a delightful companion," but had little other effect on the Medical Department.[27] Surprising many long-term officers and civilian observers of the Army, Cleveland selected Colonel George Miller Sternberg, a fifty-five-year-old physician and veteran of thirty-two years' service, over the heads of many senior medical officers. Many acclaimed the move as evidence the old days of superannuation were over.[28] Prior to Sternberg's appointment, senior Medical Department personnel were unfairly judged as self-serving general practitioners who valued rank over the Army's needs. Indeed, by 1893, the office was a political prize, shared out to those with influential patronage. Sternberg's appointment was thus seen as a break with the old habits of "stand-pat" medicine and business as usual administration.

The medical profession also saw Sternberg's appointment as a signal victory for scientific medicine. "He is a member of many learned and scientific bodies and has contributed largely to medical literature," reported *The Medical News* on Sternberg's promotion. "By virtue of his scientific attainments and original investigations, as well as of active service in the field, the appointment of Dr. Sternberg will receive the cordial approval of the medical profession."[29] Likewise, the *Texas Medical Journal* acclaimed Sternberg's appointment, applauding President Cleveland on "the very first instance, so far as we know, where the appointment has been made in recognition of any other claims than party fealty and party service."[30] Equally impressive were comments in the popular press of the day, which hailed Sternberg as the ideal of the American man of science. "No man among Americans has studied the micro-organisms with more profit or has contributed more to our knowledge of the nature of infection, particularly of that of yellow fever, than Dr. George M. Sternberg, of the United States Army," reported *Appleton's Popular Science Monthly* in November 1899. "His merits are freely recognized abroad, and he ranks there, as well as at home, among the leading bacteriologists of the age."[31]

Just as the public press lionized Sternberg as an example of the American scientist conquering the hostile frontier of microbes and bacteria, the medical press likewise elevated the man into a scientific icon, though for a different purpose. By 1893, the controversies dividing the medical profession in the United States for most of the nineteenth century were winding down, and proponents of medical practice based upon formal education and training, chemical and surgical intervention, and public health were winning the day. But while "regular" physicians were claiming primacy in the profession, challenges and dangers still threatened their growing professional hegemony. Homeopathy remained appealing to working- and middle-class Americans, so much so that the regulars accorded legitimacy to the craft's practitioners in 1901 as part of their own quest to expand the authority of the profession.[32] Millions of Americans still eschewed the acclaimed professional advice of the regulars in health, latching on to unconventional treatments, patent medicines, and dietary fads. And even among the regulars, tensions existed between those who ascribed to a more holistic, environmental approach and the advocates of the new scientific medicine. Acclaimed as the "father of American bacteriology," Sternberg provided reformers a powerful icon for winning influence and prestige. As Surgeon General, Sternberg became something even greater—the embodiment of a public commitment to follow the direction of scientific reform.

The new Surgeon General recognized his power as an iconic figure in American medicine. During the June 1898 meeting of the American Medical Association, Sternberg was elected president of the association. Though his election was due as much to a wartime burst of patriotic fervor as it was to recognition of his accomplishments as a researcher and physician, Sternberg made clear that his allegiances lie with the reformers. "The medical profession in this country has suffered more from the ignorance of some of its members who hold diplomas from regular schools of medicine than from the attacks of those whom we call irregulars or quacks," he said in the address read before the assemblage by Colonel Alfred A. Woodhull:

> Scientific medicine, being founded upon demonstrable truths, must in the end maintain itself and secure the confidence of the people. . . . There are those who still speak of us as "old school physicians," ignorant apparently of the fact that scientific medicine is to a great extent of very recent origin. . . . While, therefore, we still have with us some "old school doctors," who have fallen behind the procession, the profession as a whole has been moving forward with incredible activity upon the substantial basis of scientific research, and if we are to be characterized by any distinctive name, the only one applicable would be *"the new school of scientific medicine."*[33]

Sternberg's appointment in late May 1893 and his reception were clear signals regular practice and laboratory-oriented science now dominated the medical profession. In the late nineteenth century, the Army Medical Department was highly respected for its scientific and civil-military activities because for decades it was the sole federal agent capable of practicing health on a national basis. In the absence of a strong civilian agency responsible for public health and medicine, the Army Medical Department and its Surgeon General were the *de facto* watchdogs of American public health and medicine. Capable leadership during the Civil War and immediately afterward established the department's future scientific and sanitarian missions. More significant was the presence of well-motivated and inspired medical officers who kept the Medical Department focused on science and sanitation during its years of uninspired leadership. George Miller Sternberg's appointment was testimony of the nation's willingness to place its trust in these advocates of scientific medicine and organized public health. Under Sternberg's direction, the Army Medical Department would take great strides to establish itself as the most professional branch in the military services, with the highest standards of formalized educational training and advancement keyed on raw ability rather than attenuation. Sternberg's actions also made the Army Medical Department the public embodiment of elite medical practice and laboratory science, the very model of "the new school of scientific medicine."

CODIFYING LEGITIMACY THROUGH SPECIALIZATION

Establishing a science-oriented culture within the Army Medical Department was not the only challenge facing the institution at the turn of the twentieth century. In their quest for legitimacy, intellectual empowerment, and professional identity, the Army's medical officers followed the same pathway taken by other professional groups throughout American society. In the late nineteenth century, groups of highly educated and skilled trades-men, professionals, and workers pursued formal organizational structures for asserting common identity and legitimate authority in their fields. In her study of the Army officer community's own quest for professional legiti-macy, historian Carol Reardon notes that Army officers were no different in seeking out public recognition of their claims to elite knowledge and status: "Like a chemist or a social worker or a member of any emerging specialized field of knowledge at that time, the army officer demanded that others recognize his authority in matters dealing with his unique service: national defense."[34] To this end, the Army officer followed the example of the burgeoning civilian professional in the 1880s and 1890s, creating what Samuel P. Huntington has charted as the three chief conduits for estab-lishing a professional corporate identity: graduate programs and advanced degrees in specialized sub-sets of applied knowledge; specialized journals for publicizing new developments in their fields; and professional associa-tions to defend their status from external challenges.[35]

By 1890, specialization was nothing new in the American medical pro-fession. For the previous two decades, as a resurgent clinical practice-oriented medicine began turning the tide against eclectics and sectarians, like-minded practitioners began identifying with each other on the basis of their interests and expertise. The American Medical Association recog-nized medical specialization in 1866.[36] Seen in this light, the move toward specialization by military physicians was part of a broader trend in Ameri-can medicine, evidence of the profession's growing maturity.

The Medical Department's quest for legitimacy extended corporate recognition within the Army. In the 1890s, the Regular medical officer faced a new challenge to his status from the citizen-soldiers of the National Guard. Born in response to the Great Railroad Strike of 1877, the National Guard represented a new stage in the state and local militias. Since the early days of the republic, the militia was as much a social fraternal network for middle- and upper-class males as it was a defensive military organization. The specter of labor unrest combined with romanticized memories of the Civil War to lend a new political dimension to the American militia after the 1877 strike. Militia advocates joined together in 1878 to create the National Guard Association, a lobbying group dedicated to making the state militias a well-funded and trained national reserve. The 1878 Posse Comitatus Act in turn provided the new organization with a mission, mak-ing the state militia the primary agent of dealing with civilian unrest.[37]

The Guard soon tired of its strikebreaker role. By 1889, its leadership was promoting the National Guard as a real militia, tying it to the romanticized vision of the militia espoused by political figures like Illinois Representa-tive and former Major General John A. Logan. State Adjutant Generals and other senior militia officers called for a reevaluation of the nation's military policy. On January 23, 1884, New York State National Guard Association President, Brigadier General John C. Graves, argued:

> The demand of the day is for an adequate number of our best citizens organized under the law into tactical bodies, furnished with the best arms and most complete equipments, well officered, drilled and disciplined. Such bodies acting under proper orders in accordance with the laws of the land can, as a National Guard, repress the riotous element in our communities, assist in maintaining the laws, ward off petty invasions, and form the nucleus of a great army in time of war, by furnishing, in conjunction with the Regular Army of the United States, the officers and trained men required to properly organize and fit for service the great body of volunteers which must always form the bulk of our armies.[38]

Others also pitched a dynamic defensive role for the Guard. In 1885, Ohio Adjutant General E. B. Finley lauded the performance and changes in his state's militia, which had gone from "an expensive amateur organization . . . more ornamental than useful," to Ohio's first line of defense against anarchists and rioters. The Guard's role as a guarantor of domestic order proven, Finley argued, it was time for Congress to recognize its accomplishments in wartime and to follow the lead of other great powers by establishing the National Guard as a regular standing militia.[39]

Efforts to legitimize military medicine as an independent professional specialty were equally motivated by the desire to assert the Army Medical Department's authority over its National Guard counterparts. Just as other Regular officers needed to establish their primacy as the chief agents of military affairs, the medical officer had to ensure his status as an expert in his own specialized practice. Without such recognition, their authority would be eroded by misinformed civilian physicians who believed their own expertise granted sufficient ground for commission and authority.

However, unlike the Army's more radical Uptonians who preferred eliminating the militia entirely, medical officers proposed the Guard in fact be established as a ready military reserve. This defense of the Guard was not exactly apostasy; the number of true Uptonians was never that large in the Regular Army, and most reformers saw a reserve as an essential component of a modern army.[40] More interesting was the extent Regular Army intellectuals avoided deliberate confrontation with the National Guard medical establishment. Unlike the Army's other branches, the Medical Department was the only organization which possessed a direct professional counterpart in the civilian community. Antagonizing the American medical profession which had supported it throughout the long struggle for legitimacy would only hurt the Medical Department.[41]

This sensitivity led Army physicians to emphasize what Carol Reardon describes as the inherently "safe leadership" of the Regular officer.

According to Reardon, new technology transformed warfare. Commanders could no longer control all aspects of the battle, but needed to delegate many tasks to subordinate staff and line officers. Military institutions thus followed the same path toward modernity as civilian commerce and industry, with highly specialized practitioners taking responsibility for individual components of a single system. Accordingly, the Army's intellectuals emphasized specialization and cooperation within the officer community, with each branch and department making contributions based upon its own expertise for the sake of the whole. Medical officers embraced the concept of safe leadership, seeing within it the implicit acknowledgment that they were essential to the function of the institution as a whole.[42]

The shared professional knowledge of civilian and military physicians was another factor. National Guard medical officers were not as familiar with military culture as their cousins in the Regular Army, but their medical expertise could not be discounted. One issue affecting regular medical officers was the constant change in medical knowledge. Medical officers could not practice their craft in a vacuum; every component of military medicine—sanitation, bacteriology, nutrition, surgery—was affected by new scientific and practical developments defined by civilian physicians. The Medical Department thus had to acknowledge that the Guard medical officer, unlike militia officers in other branches, was not always a dilettante playing soldier and decorating his breast and shoulders with gold ribbon, but a professional peer who could make valued contributions.

Acceptance and status within the Army achieved, specialization became the new grail quest for Medical Department officers in the 1890s. Securing claims as guardians of a highly specialized practice would guarantee the Regular medical officer's primacy in the field while also institutionalizing the knowledge that came at such high cost in the Army's recent history. As an essential component of the medical officer's identity, specialization was a natural extension of earlier struggles for status and establishing a scientifically grounded practice and administration. Two vehicles in particular—the Association of Military Surgeons of the National Guard of the United States, later the Association of Military Surgeons of the United States, and the *Journal of the Association of Military Surgeons of the United States (JAMSUS)*, later *The Military Surgeon*—became vehicles for preserving this specialized knowledge, establishing the primacy of regular physicians of the Army, Navy, and U.S. Public Health Service over part-time medical officers, and securing recognition for military medicine as a specialized practice in its own right. In combination with the Army Medical School, incorporated in 1893, the Journal and Association established the foundation for professional specialization, corporate identity, and legitimized identity for the members of the Army Medical Department.

THE ASSOCIATION OF MILITARY SURGEONS
OF THE UNITED STATES

The professional association of the military physician, the Association of Military Surgeons of the National Guard of the United States, was the brainchild of Illinois Guard Surgeon General Nicholas Senn. He pioneered in abdominal surgery at a time when wounds and injuries to the digestive tract constituted a death sentence. His innovations in this area, including introducing hydrogen gas into the digestive tract to gauge the state of wounds there, as well as his interests in surgical pathology and bacteriology, won him acclaim as one America's preeminent surgeons. From the 1880s until his death in 1908, Senn dominated the medical education scene in Chicago, where he was appointed to the teaching faculty of four city medical schools. In June 1897, the esteem Senn's peers held him in was reflected in his election as president of the American Medical Association.[43]

After graduating from Chicago Medical College in 1868, Senn split his time between a lucrative private practice and perfecting his surgical skills on animals. His research interests led him to Germany, and a second M.D. from the University of Munich in 1878. However if surgery and teaching were Senn's avocation, military medicine was his passion. In 1882, the thirty-eight-year-old Senn was appointed surgeon general of Wisconsin, with the rank of brigadier general in the Wisconsin National Guard. A year later, when he moved to Chicago, he was immediately appointed surgeon general of the Illinois Guard, which he remained until his death in 1908. In this role, Senn sought to bring the Guard's standards up to those of the Regular Army. Particularly keen on improving the caliber of the Guard's officers and enlisted men, he instituted stringent physical examinations for all recruits, as well as intellectual assessment testing for officer candidates and promotion examination boards that were copied by other states.[44]

Following the example of progressive reformers in the Guard, Senn hoped to promote a greater sense of professionalism among Guard officers. This was particularly true for the medical officers of the state services. "I have every reason to believe that most, if not all of these officers are good physicians," he observed, "but we must all admit that few of them possess the requisite qualifications and training to satisfactorily perform the manifold duties required of a military surgeon."[45] Without a uniform standard of training, or even a forum in which to compare methods used by the individual state guards to prepare physicians for military service, there was little hope of elevating the standards of National Guard medical officers. Not only would their tenuous status as professional military medical practitioners suffer in the eyes of the public and the regular establishment, they would be subject to the same ambiguous relationship with the state line officers the Medical Department experienced for much of the nineteenth century. "I have often heard the complaint made that the line officers do not show proper respect for the military surgeon, and do not treat him with becoming courtesy. How could it be otherwise?" Senn asked, pointing out that for many Guard medical officers, their commitment was based upon a flashy uniform and the title it carried rather than practicing military surgery, hygiene, or hospital administration.[46]

The answer was organization: "It is apparent that something must be done to raise the standing and usefulness of the medical service. I know of no way of accomplishing this object except by concerted action. . . . The stimulus imparted by the work and success of others is the motor which impels individual effort, and comparison of the results realized become either a source of gratification or acts like a lash that arouses the latent force to renewed action."[47] As the embodiment of the citizen militia concept, the National Guard represented even more than the Army Medical Department the nexus of the two professional spheres of identity. Not only would the Guard medical officer acquire new opportunities to better his knowledge of military medicine and administration, he would gain a measure of legitimacy denied regular medical officers. As part-time soldiers, members of the Guard were also freer to organize a professional association, as opposed to medical officers in the Regular Army, for whom lineal rank was considered suitable recognition of their professional qualifications.[48]

Senn took the first steps toward establishing a corporate voice for National Guard medical officers when he invited sixty-three state surgeons general and medical officers from eleven states to meet in Chicago on September 17, 1891. The group styled itself "The Association of Military Surgeons of the National Guard of the United States," appointed a committee to draft a constitution and by-laws and design insignia.[49] Though Senn founded the Association around the Guard, he wished to open membership to Regular medical officers. In 1893, the association's constitution was amended to admit active duty personnel from the Army, Marine Hospital Service, and Navy as members in full-standing. The newly reconstituted "Association of Military Surgeons of the United States" was flooded with regular medical officers; by 1898, approximately one third of the membership was associated with the regular uniformed health services. After membership was opened to the regular services, Army medical officers dominated the association. In 1895, Surgeon General Sternberg was elected president of the Association, and immediately strove to bring the Guard and Regular medical services closer together. Sternberg pointed out the mutual affiliations between the two and the unique opportunities the Association of Military Surgeons offered for expanding professional and intellectual horizons. Moreover, he observed how the association promoted the exchange of practical medical knowledge between National Guard and Regular Army medical officers in a wide range of areas, including surgery, antisepsis, evacuation of the wounded, sanitation, and field hospital administration.[50]

The Association of Military Surgeons of the United States provided a venue for regular and state medical officers to join together in defense of their occupation and profession. By the winter of 1897, the association had grown from sixty-three state medical officers to 391 life and active members and forty-eight associate and corresponding members, from all of the uniformed Federal medical services and the various state militia branches.[51] The organization was on the verge of even further expansion. Plans were announced to incorporate regional chapters of the Association, expanding the influence of the regulars over the organization and the state militias.

THE JOURNAL OF THE ASSOCIATION OF MILITARY SURGEONS OF THE UNITED STATES

Despite its importance as a symbol of the medical officer's identity and legitimacy, a regularly serialized journal did not appear until 1901, ten years after the founding of the Association of Military Surgeons. During its first nine years, the association relied upon proceedings volumes from the annual meeting to communicate the organization's mission and accomplishments. As the annual transactions increased in size and scope from year to year, a growing number of members of the association lobbied for a serialized monthly journal. Advocates, including Colonel Senn, Surgeon General Sternberg, and Captain Charles E. Woodruff, argued a regular journal was the missing component of the medical officer's legitimacy. Compared with the other trades and professions, advocates argued, "Military medicine and surgery, alone, is unrepresented" by a professional journal. In a heartfelt appeal made at the 1895 meeting, proponents linked the issue to the old problem of intra-service identity and legitimacy. While the three line branches and many state National Guard organizations had their own journals, "the medical department, in which change and progress are more constant factors than in any of [these] others, has none."[52]

An independent journal for the uniformed health services finally appeared in 1901, in the form of The Journal of the Association of Military Surgeons of the United States (JAMSUS), under the direction of the Association's secretary, retired Captain James Evelyn Pilcher. Like John Shaw Billings, Pilcher was a respected man of letters in the medical and library professions, having edited the Annals of the Anatomical and Surgical Society, the Columbus Medical Journal, and the Proceedings of the American Medical Editors Association, as well as collaborating in the Dutch medical history journal Janus. When selected as secretary by the Association of Military Surgeons, he was living in Carlisle, Pennsylvania, where he taught economics and sociology at Dickinson College and was editing the twelve-volume Fourth Series of Pennsylvania Archives.[53]

From its inception, JAMSUS was to be the chief forum for medical officers in the Regular Army and Navy, the National Guard, and public health officers of the Marine Hospital Service (after 1902 the Public Health and Marine Hospital Service) to discuss issues related to combat medicine and the preservation of public health in the uniformed services. In this regard it was not very different from other American military service journals. Unlike these other professional journals, however, *JAMSUS* entertained a more global outlook that would have satisfied Emory Upton. According to Russell F. Weigley, the nineteenth-century line journals avoided considering the possibility of war with the great powers, so recent and potent was the experience of the frontier Indian-fighting army and so unlikely the event of foreign invasion: "The soldiers who had tested their vision and judgment against the distances and dangers of the Great Plains while the Indian wars lasted were mostly too farsighted and realistic to believe that 'relations to foreign powers' of the sort that sustained European armies could provide a substitute reason for being for the American army in any predictable future."[54] Instead, literary-minded officers wrote on issues much closer to their own particular branch needs or personal interests. A brief survey of the artillery and cavalry journals between 1895 and 1898 provides some insights into these interests and how they reflected the professional focus of the authors' branches. Each of the line journals obviously represented the interests of their specific branch, but also promoted a generally progressive line regarding modernization and professionalism within the service as a whole. For the most part, the essays in the artillery journal were more technically oriented—emphasizing ballistics, engineering, and new technologies—than the cavalry journal's focus on veterinary care, administration, and horsemanship.[55]

Historical and biographical studies and reminiscences also were more prevalent in the cavalry's journal. Cavalry officers writing for their journal were motivated by cultural and practical factors. When writing about great cavalrymen of the past, authors promoted the cavalry's primacy over the Army's other line and staff branches. At the same time, contributors sought to preserve tactical lessons acquired during the Civil War and the Indian Wars.[56]

The activities of the great powers were not ignored, however. Each journal regularly posted news on foreign military affairs. Reports from American military attaches on foreign maneuvers, campaigns, and equipment appeared frequently, and both journals published occasional reprints from other national military journals. But any presentation of foreign military services was not to provide information on a perceived future adversary. Instead, the content was intended to assist the ongoing rationalization and modernization of the American service. In the June 1896 issue of the *Journal of the Cavalry Association*, for example, First Lieutenant Charles D. Rhodes wrote a glowing assessment of the German cavalry system. By describing the training regimen, regulations, equipment and clothing, and remount system of the German cavalry, Rhodes hoped "to broaden our views in regard to what should constitute the proper organization, equipment and training, to secure the greatest efficiency in the cavalry arm of the present day."[57] *The Journal of the United States Artillery* observed a similar perspective in using foreign case studies to promote domestic military reform. English, German, and French essays highlighting gunnery training

and ballistics were frequently reprinted in the pages of the artillery journal. Reports comparing foreign methods and results with those used in the
United States appeared as well. In all cases, the journal's intent was not to
present a foreign threat, but rather to support reform.[58]

Even on the cusp of the First World War, officers writing in their professional journals viewed foreign militaries as benign influence, not potential
adversary. In the March 1913 issue of the *Infantry Journal*, Captain William Wallace, 7th Infantry Regiment, equated civilization and morality with
militarism. Accordingly, the West's desire to avoid another annihilative war
on the scale of the Napoleonic contests a century before brought about a host
of global conventions to restrict war. Yet, paradoxically, Wallace wrote, the
"great truth" of international relations was: "*That the maintenance of these
rules is only possible where war is being conducted by nations whose people are military and whose armies are highly disciplined.*"[59] Modern killing
technology and the attendant brutalization of warfare made it impractical
for war to be entrusted again to amateur citizen soldiers, who Wallace felt
would quickly descend into anarchy. Pointing to the German armies occupying Paris in 1870 and the relative lack of looting and other violent acts,
Wallace found his own model for American martial excellence:

> Only a military people can produce a disciplined army, and a disci-
> plined army only can be depended upon to carry out the established
> humanities in its activities. As for the conduct of an unmilitary people
> it is a fact that, whatever their peace virtues, they naturally grow hys-
> terical when war treads close, and become rankest cowards or perpetu-
> ate fiendish acts which invite retaliation and are certain to turn the war
> into legitimate massacre.[60]

Wallace's proposal was extreme, even by the standards of the most devoted
Uptonian. Nonetheless, it reflected a deep admiration for the influence of
the German example in some quarters of the American military.

The few essays describing perceived threats to national security paid more
tribute to intra-service branch rivalries for funding than a cohesive national
defense policy. Looking toward their own mission, artillerists focused on
coastal defense against a seaborne invasion. In turn, cavalry officers examined more local threats. Tactical studies were drawn almost exclusively
from the branch's recent history in the Great Plains and American Southwest, and presumed small unit operations against resurgent Indian tribes.
The only external threat taken seriously was Mexico. In 1897, First Lieutenant A. L. Mills, of the First Cavalry Regiment, wrote a comprehensive
military assessment of Mexico presuming an American offensive deep into
the country in the event of war.[61]

But despite his confidence of American success in any conflict, Mills'
essay was more of a casual exercise than a direct call for planning. In fact,
not until the eve of the First World War did American officers writing in

their branch journals seriously countenance war planning against a European power. In the eyes of the artillerists, America's transoceanic isolation, her strong navy, and the network of coastal artillery forts presented a hard nut for any invader.[62] Others were even more casual in dismissing the possibility of war with a European power. Brigadier General James Parker captured this sentiment in an essay on "The Value of Cavalry as a Part of Our Army" that appeared in the July 1914 cavalry journal. Assessing the need of a mounted regular force in the Army, Parker discounted the possibility of a war with Europe: "We are, fortunately, not in contact with the great military powers and they have little to gain by attacking us. But to avoid concrete instances of what is possible, our history shows us to have engaged in several wars with contiguous nations on this continent in the last seventy years."[63] The more likely threat was domestic in nature: "We in this country are not altogether free from the fear of civil disturbances, and while it is assumed the States are in a position to cope with these, history shows many instances when they have been obliged to call upon the general Government for assistance."[64]

For their part, Regular and Guard medical officers submitting papers to the Association of Military Surgeons' professional meetings and journals followed a similar path. Many papers dealt with various practical medical and surgical issues: the effects of small arms projectiles on both soft tissue and bone; new techniques in combat and emergency surgery; the relative physical condition of new recruits and veteran soldiers; the role of the Hospital Corps and different methods of combat evacuation and first aid treatment in the field.[65]

Other essays mirrored the same path taken in the line journals to establish legitimacy and autonomy. Historical studies and biographic sketches lauding the traditions of the Medical Department appeared frequently, as did evaluation summaries and reports of maneuvers and encampments. Contributors spent as much time on foreign conflicts and individuals as on the more recent experiences of the American Civil War and frontier wars. Such long-term ruminations on the validity of military medicine were essential, however, as the department's own struggle to acquire legitimacy within the Army was still so recent. Thus, essays on the history of the tent field hospital, placing its lineage firmly with the work of Ambrose Pare in the late sixteenth century, the medical and surgical equipment and accoutrements of an expedition against the Turks by the Duke of Burgundy in 1457 and others made regular appearances.[66]

Another area where the Medical Department's intellectual development appeared more advanced was in the contemplation and preparation of mass armed conflict with the Great Powers. Line officers focused extensively on tactical solutions best suited to small units pursuing irregular forces in the wilderness, coastal artillery defenses, or how the United States was culturally indisposed to making serious attempts to improve military readiness under the direction of the Regular Army. Medical officers, on the other hand, paid more attention to the armed capabilities of the European and Asian powers, and made direct links between military medical organization and the ability to wage mass war. For them, the successful administration of large general hospitals, supply trains, trained orderlies, ambulance corps, and a scheme of corps, divisional, and brigade personnel was evidence of their importance as legitimate members of the Army as an institution. There was far less to be gained in terms of influence and prestige for the Medical Department as a peripheral adjunct to a small constabulary force than as a large, well-organized and administered organization. This vision of the department and the medical officer as Uptonian professional was elaborated upon by Lieutenant Colonel Charles R. Greenleaf, assistant medical purveyor for the Army Medical Department, in 1892. "Imagine, if you please," he wrote, "that we are to-day at war with a foreign nation and have an army of occupation in the field of one hundred thousand men. . . . The efficiency of that army, the care of its sick and wounded, and your own reputation, depends upon your doing the right thing, THEN AND THERE."[67]

THE ARMY MEDICAL SCHOOL

The idea of an Army school devoted to military medicine and public health was first articulated during the Civil War. As early as 1862, Surgeon General Hammond planned to open an Army medical school in response to the great need for skilled military surgeons. The school would first be attached to one of the larger general hospitals, but would later be incorporated with a permanent facility in conjunction with the medical museum. Such a facility, "in which medical cadets and others seeking admission into the corps could receive such instruction as would better fit them for commissions and which they cannot obtain in the ordinary medical school, is a great desideratum."[68]

Hammond's planned school fell victim to his personal feud with Secretary of War Edwin M. Stanton. In September 1863, while the Surgeon General was in the field on one of the inspection tours Stanton forced upon him, Brigade Surgeon John Hill Brinton proposed a course of lectures on military medicine and surgery be given at the Army Medical Museum building. Brinton set about preparing a small lecture room in the museum and selected a curriculum and cadre of instructors. Among others, Surgeon Richard H. Coolidge was to lecture on the Army's culture and military-medical ethics, Assistant Surgeon William Thomson would give a course on ophthalmologic surgery, Assistant Surgeon Joseph Janvier Woodward would teach military medicine, while Brinton reserved for himself the course on gunshot wounds. The preparations made, Brinton invited all physicians, surgeons, and medical cadets serving in the capital. All that remained was official approval from the Secretary of War, which never came. Convinced students would shirk their duties, Stanton ordered the school closed before it ever opened.[69]

Hammond's failed effort lingered with medical officers. In 1890, Major and Brevet Lieutenant Colonel Alfred A. Woodhull pointed to the need for an Army Medical School. It would instruct new officers in military protocol and etiquette and a uniform system of military medicine, replacing the existing system of ad hoc education at the side of an older, and perhaps jaded, military physician. Woodhull also observed that the realities of military service in isolation at distant posts left many medical officers in the dark with regard to new techniques, therapies, and other knowledge. "Medicine is a progressive science," he wrote, "and those out of the current must be caught in the eddies and lose progress, or sometimes be stranded on the bars or entangled against the banks."[70] To ensure Army physicians remained as current as possible with the rapid changes in medical practice and science, Woodhull recommended the Army provide ready and frequent paid leave opportunities for medical officers to attend post-graduate education at established medical schools in the United States and Europe. Just as line officers enjoyed the opportunity to study at their own special schools, so should the officers of the Medical Department.[71]

Illinois National Guard Surgeon General Nicholas Senn also had a scheme to promote a national military medical school. Accordingly, new medical cadets would remain in school for five years, their education split among medical, administrative, and military courses. In the interest of national unity, Senn proposed the academy be placed in one of the midwestern medical centers, either Chicago or St. Louis. After all, Senn offered: "The East has the academies at West Point and Annapolis, let the West have the third National military educational institution." But the national military medical school envisioned by Senn would fulfill a mandate far exceeding the naval or military academies. Unlike the existing schools, Senn's proposed institution would be a true university, providing post-graduate courses for veteran medical officers and surgeons from the National Guard. The benefits were twofold. First, all physicians enrolled in post-doctorate courses would keep abreast of the latest changes in their field—thus furthering the mutual corporate identity of medical officers. Second, volunteer and militia medical officers who never received formal instruction in military medicine would gain tremendously from courses informing them of the current state of military hygiene, surgery, and sanitation. They would also acquire a greater sense of professional obligation and duty, thus elevating the quality of the state services closer to that of the regular establishment.[72]

Senn's appeal was seconded by other medical officers. Colonel John Van Rensselaer Hoff looked toward the example of the British Army Medical School at the Royal Victoria Hospital in Netley. Established in 1860, the British military medical school, established as a post-graduate program, was renowned for its sanitary curriculum and the tremendous clinical opportunities for young surgeons. As the centerpiece military hospital for the British Empire, the Royal Victoria Hospital received patients from all over the globe, giving students there an opportunity to observe rare conditions and injuries they would never encounter in a domestic civil institution. According to Hoff, an American school could follow the British example. Instead of admitting passed candidates directly into the service, the examining board's role would change to being the gateway for prospective students into a post-graduate academy, where candidates would be considered probationary officers while taking a course of instruction in military medicine and the duties of the medical officer. Not only would this increase the overall level of professional quality of first lieutenants entering the service, it gave senior medical officers serving as instructors an opportunity to gauge their character and mettle, reducing the high turnover of dissatisfied junior medical officers before their fifth-year examination. A regular course of instruction would also impose uniformity in practice and ability where, in the existing system of new officers being sent directly to their first postings, there was none. Veteran medical officers would benefit as well, since their service as instructors at the school would help them stay acquainted with the most recent advances in medicine.[73]

After he was confirmed as the Army's new Surgeon General in 1893, Sternberg was free to act on the question of a national post-graduate military medical school. Though the Medical Department always selected highly qualified candidates for the limited openings in its ranks, capability and skill in general practice and surgery did not always translate into success as a medical officer. Civilian medical schools were unable to prepare aspiring physicians for the various duties of administration and command expected of them. But more important to Sternberg was the general lack of proficiency in preventive medicine and sanitation among new medical officers. Before 1893, medical schools paid only lip service—if any attention at all—to the problems of hygiene and public health. For too many years, young assistant surgeons had to learn preventive medicine and sanitation through painstaking trial and error, at times at great expense to the institution and the individuals under their care.

Though perhaps unavoidable for much of the prior seven decades, by 1893 Sternberg felt the Army's indifference in ensuring its medical officers shared uniform expertise and training was inexcusable. "During the past twenty years the prevention of disease has made infinitely greater progress than its cure," Sternberg wrote. "A special education is needful to prepare a medical man to undertake the responsibility of protecting the public health. . . . The course at the Army Medical School will prepare him to cope with the question of practical sanitation that will be presented to him at every turn in his military career . . . all bearing upon the preservation of the health of the military community under his sanitary care."[74] As a service branch school, the Army Medical School would convey the medical officer with greater legitimacy as a member of the Army community. But for Sternberg, the school would do more than bridge the gap between the physician's and officer's spheres of identity and professional obligation. It would be an exemplar of formal education in sanitation, hygiene, and preventive care—in short, the first national public health school.[75]

The school also changed how candidates entered the Medical Department. Before 1893, the Army Examination Boards were the sole gateway into the department. But though new candidates still faced an examination board, the focus of the testing shifted, from the deciding factor in commissioning new medical officers to becoming a preliminary screening board. The testing was still rigorous. First was a comprehensive physical examination. Next candidates advanced to the written and practical examinations. The first round of written tests covered general knowledge, including mathematics, geography, history, literature, and Latin—all considered essential to the education of all aspiring professionals. More daunting was the medical knowledge examination. Applicants were tested across a broad spectrum, including anatomy, physiology, histology, chemistry, physics, materia medica, therapeutics, surgery, general practice, and obstetrics and gynecology. The questions themselves ranged from simple identifications of the sort routinely given to first-year medical students—"Describe the spinal cord," or "Give the anatomy of the spermatic cord," for example—to more detailed problems, such as the surgical treatment for abdominal gunshot wounds, or the causes and symptoms of aortic insufficiency. Failure to score at least 80 percent in the written examinations resulted in disqualification.[76]

The final stage was the practical exams, in which a medical officer observed the candidate's technique on rounds and in the operating theater. Candidates were taken to the United States Soldiers Home, where they were challenged to diagnose individual cases. If successful, they were sent to the Army Medical Museum to perform surgery under the eye of Major Louis A. LaGarde. Again, if the candidate scored at least an 80 percent score on the practical exam, then he received his commission as an assistant surgeon with the grade of first lieutenant in the Medical Corps and orders to report to the Army Medical School at the start of the next term.[77]

The course of instruction was a whirlwind tour through the latest developments in scientific practice and sanitation. The centerpiece was the morning clinical pathology and bacteriology lab. Though Captain Walter Reed was listed as instructor of record for the course, he was frequently joined at the lectern and the lab by the eager Surgeon General. Under Sternberg's and Reed's watchful eyes, officer candidates practiced tests, screens, and procedures they learned in their weekly lectures. They prepared their own cultures and tissue stains, discovered how to isolate and identify bacteria on slide samples, and learned how to test serum on live animals. Using the resources of the Army Medical Museum, Sternberg and Reed also introduced many students to the new worlds of tropical bacteriology, helminthology, and entomology, highlighting the different plasmodia, trichomonas, and trypanosomes that were spread by biting insects, as well as the many types of exotic parasitic worms that were now within the boundaries of the

American medical regime. For most students, these courses were their first exposures to these new avenues of medical knowledge. Sternberg's emphasis on microbiology was calculated to serve another purpose beyond improving the medical officer's diagnostic and therapeutic skills. By introducing aspiring military physicians to bacteriology and microscopy, Sternberg nurtured a cadre of scientific researchers to follow his example and elevate the Army Medical Department into the first rank of medical research, on the same level with the Pasteur Institute and the Koch Institut in Berlin.[78]

Sternberg's and Reed's lectures dovetailed perfectly with the courses on military sanitation and hygiene. Every Friday afternoon, candidates attended John Shaw Billings' lectures on sanitation and social and physical hygiene. As curator of the Army Medical Museum, Billings drew upon the specimens and case studies in its collections, as well as his own extensive experience as a medical officer, physician, bibliographer, and administrator, in lectures on the long and deadly association between armies and disease. After laying out the history of military hygiene, Billings mentored his students on the many different aspects of military sanitation and public health, including the causes of disease; disposal of waste and sewage; the distribution, purification, filtration, and aeration of drinking water; the preparation of food; and the extent of sanitary jurisprudence and the course of relations real and anticipated between Army medical officers and civilian public health officials.[79]

Military surgery and medical practice were the third focus of instruction at the Army Medical School. On alternating Mondays and Tuesdays, led by Major Charles Smart, the class reviewed diseases prevalent within the soldier's community in peace and war, with special attention given to typhoid fever, malaria, and venereal disease. The intention was to so familiarize prospective medical officers with the causes, symptoms, and etiology of the more common ailments to facilitate quick diagnosis, setting the course toward treatment and prevention. Like the Sternberg and Reed lectures, the military medicine course was accompanied by a dedicated laboratory exercise period. Daily from 1:00 p.m. until 2:50 p.m., candidates worked in a chemical laboratory, where sanitary considerations like water analysis, poisons and heavy metals testing, and the study of pharmaceutical compounds were the chief subjects.[80] Military surgery lectures were chaired by Lieutenant Colonel William Forwood. Beginning with a review of the origins of military medicine, he led students through a course of fourteen lectures and clinical rounds at the Soldiers' Home Hospital. Lectures focused primarily on the effects of gunshot injuries, using live-fire experiments on cadavers and the many specimens collected since the Civil War for the Army Medical Museum.[81]

Though the Surgeon General was inclined to emphasize instruction in medical practice and science, another important reason for the military medical school was preparing new medical officers for mundane aspects of the service. This was facilitated through a fifteen-part course on the duties

of medical officers, taught by Colonel Charles Alden. Various administrative and non-clinical aspects of a medical officer's work were covered,
including the examination of new recruits, the nature of their relationship
to the line and staff branches, sanitary and medical inspections, managing
supplies and hospitals, field duties, and how to detect malingering. Combined with the Saturday morning exercises at the Hospital Corps School of
Instruction and the horse-riding exercises across the Potomac River, these
courses were a structured yet gentler immersion into military culture for
new medical officers.[82]

No less important was the school's part in establishing the case for
military medicine as a legitimate medical specialty. Medical officers long
considered their practice to be different from their civilian counterparts.
Specialization became more appealing after 1898. Medical officers pointed
toward the public spectacle of mismanaged hospitals at the Army's volunteer camps as proof for specialized training in military medical administration. Whereas civilian physicians were bound by the limits of their
practice and their patient base, medical officers were not only expected
to provide a full range of medical care to thousands of sick and wounded
soldiers, they were expected to advise and instruct officers and enlisted
men in rudimentary sanitation, while also establishing regimental, field,
and divisional hospitals. They had to know how to identify hygienically
sound hospital sites with good drainage, ventilation, and access to clean
water close enough to the battlefield to facilitate quick evacuation of the
wounded, yet not so close as to be at risk from errant fire. They had to
devise and implement schemes of evacuation, transportation, and resupply,
all while performing their medical duties. The experience of 1898, regular
medical officers like Captain Edward L. Munson claimed, proved military
medicine was not easily mastered by trial and error, that regardless of their
merits or intentions, "a good doctor was not necessarily a good medical
officer . . . we must have trained men with troops, and that the doctor does
not answer the purpose."[83]

Between its opening in 1893 and its closing on account of the War with
Spain, twenty-four newly commissioned first lieutenants graduated from
the Army Medical School. With the exception of the 1894–1895 term,
when Congress froze new appointments, courses were held every year
between 1893 and 1898. Though closure was unavoidable, on account of
the size of the regular establishment in 1898 and the need for senior medical officers in the field, Surgeon General Sternberg wished it could continue
the course of instruction during the war.[84] When the school reopened on
November 4, 1901, it welcomed the largest class in its short history. Twen-
ty-three first lieutenants were admitted to the school. To accommodate the
increased enrollment, the school was moved to the General Hospital at
Washington Barracks, sharing the facility with the Hospital Corps Company of Instruction until a new school was built. In 1904, Congress finally
approved $300,000 for a new general hospital in the District of Columbia,

including space for the Army Medical Museum and Library and the Army Medical School. When the new facilities opened in 1909 at Walter Reed General Hospital, the school's laboratories, x-ray equipment, and lecture halls were again brought together under one roof, in immediate proximity to the museum, library, and patient wards. The school remained at Walter Reed until 1916, when increased enrollments on the eve of American entry in the war in Europe overwhelmed the facilities there.[85]

Aside from a new home and the inevitable faculty changes, the program of instruction changed little until October 1904, when the course of study was increased to eight months. New subjects included tropical medicine, ophthalmology and optometry, and roentgenology, reflecting recent changes in medical science and the new duties of medical officers serving in the Philippines and Caribbean. New candidates were no longer guaranteed a commission; instead they were hired as contract surgeons for the duration of the course, and were commissioned as first lieutenants after graduation. The new policy resembled the old system of retaining passed candidates on contract until an opening appeared. The Army Medical School thus became a venue where the suitability of candidates was tested before they were commissioned, eliminating the potentially embarrassing dismissal of a first lieutenant upon failing the course of instruction. The status of the students changed again in 1908, with passage of the bill creating the Army Medical Reserve Corps. Candidates attending the school were redefined again, now commissioned as first lieutenants in the Medical Reserve. And again, this shift in the status of students helped to resolve a potentially troublesome point, since graduates retained their reservist status until a vacancy appeared.[86]

THE CHALLENGE OF SPECIALIZATION

Even as they promoted military medicine as a unique specialty, medical officers were not blind to the effects of the Army Medical School when it came to promoting greater professional differentiation within their own corporate identity. By privileging medical research, sanitation and hygiene, and general practice, surgery, and administration, Sternberg and his successors fostered a cultural split among medical officers on the basis of their own specialized interest. Almost imperceptibly at first, three different cliques of professional interest took form in the twenty years after the founding of the school. Tensions between the three were minimal at best, restricted for the most part to the pages of the department's professional journal and the annual meetings of their professional association. Yet the delineation of medical officers between research scientists, sanitarians, and practitioners/surgeons was very real and exercised no small influence over the Medical Department's direction and identity between 1890 and 1920. Though they often viewed this sub-specialization as representative of demographic influences within the Army as a whole, young medical officers like Captain Edward B. Vedder recognized how specialization was affecting their corporate identity. The time when the medical officer could be a generalist, accomplished in general practice, surgery, sanitation and hygiene, obstetrics and gynecology, and nutrition, were passing. Changes wrought in invasive surgery by advances in bacteriology and antisepsis, the growing importance of the Army Medical Laboratory's work in bacteriology and parasitology, and the recent need for medical officers skilled in tropical municipal hygiene and sanitation made a persuasive argument for specialization.

Yet, Vedder noted, the circumstances of American military medicine that set it apart from civilian practice—particularly the need for any medical officer to be dispatched to the field in the event of war or other national emergency—would not permit the specialist to be completely divorced from general practice. Therefore, Vedder wrote, what the Medical Department needed was "the development *not of specialists, but of military surgeons who have a specialty.*"[87] After graduating from the Army Medical School, medical officers would devote the first ten years of their career in field service. At the end of this period, if the officer wished to pursue a specialized branch—bacteriology, surgery, diseases of the eye, for example—he would take a practical aptitude examination designed to demonstrate his fitness for specialized study. If eligible, the officer would then be posted to a general or brigade hospital to learn his new specialty from expert senior medical officers.[88]

Though Vedder seemed to advocate sub-specialization in the Medical Department, close reflection indicates the exact opposite. At the core of the medical officer's identity was the premise that he was at heart a generalist, who could be sent into the field to attend to a command's immediate needs. This was of course the traditional role of all medical officers since the department's creation in 1818. For nineteenth century medical officers specialization meant the assertion of a specialized legitimacy as expert practitioners of *military* medicine, nothing more. While the medical officer might practice another specialization—surgery, sanitation, or nutrition, for example—only he could claim authority in military medical affairs. Vedder, however, spoke toward another problem that would vex the Medical Department until 1917: Could military medicine be even more specialized, without affecting the primary responsibility of the medical officer toward the command in his care?

This intellectual shift was made easier by the perception that professional advancement in the corps pivoted upon the medical officer's chosen avocation in the field of medicine. By 1890, they already considered themselves as a corps of elite practitioner-officers who were the line's intellectual superiors. Where other Regular officers were prepared for their administrative duties and combat by the state, medical officers had to pursue an education at their own expense and survive a grueling ordeal before the

Army Examination Board to win their commissions. Line and staff officers enjoyed a career-long process of mentorship under superiors and peers. New medical officers had to learn their way around the Army's maze of administrative details and the delicate minuet of officer culture on their own. The self-confidence enjoyed by medical officers manifested itself in a growing consciousness of their especial corporate identity, distinct from civilian practice. Beginning in the 1890s, establishing military medicine as a specialized branch of medical science replaced achieving status and command authority as the chief objective of professional identity development for the officers of the Medical Department. Winning recognition for the legitimacy of military medicine in turn was assisted by the practical experiences of the Spanish-American War. The impact of the fever camps disaster on the self-identity of medical officers as specialized practitioners was profound, establishing the context for further specialization that would determine their institutional development and public identity for the next twenty years.

3 The Other War of 1898
The Army Medical Department's Struggle with Disease in the Volunteer Camps

Sim Goddard left Pierre, South Dakota on May 11, 1898, a hearty young man eager for adventure abroad. When he reported to the Sioux Falls recruiting station for his physical examination, he was so afraid of being rejected as overweight, he fasted for the next twenty-four hours, spending most of the time in a steam bath to lose seven pounds and pass the examination. A week later, Private Sim Goddard, Troop E, Third U.S. Volunteer Cavalry, boarded a train to Camp George H. Thomas in North Georgia, to begin his training as a soldier.[1]

Like many other new recruits, Goddard had the usual complaints. On May 29, he wrote, "I caught three or four heavy colds since I left and have had a soar [sic] mouth and throat but I am coming around all right now."[2] Days later he contracted a light case of measles, but was otherwise healthy. The young private reassured his mother he was well and in no imminent danger. "I don't think it is likely we will go to Cuba very soon because we are not in shape, we haven't any arms nor saddles nor half enough horses and we have only got apart of our clothes, and we have had no mounted drill yet," he described, "but still there is no telling what we may do."[3] Goddard wrote he would apply for the regimental band. "If I get into the band and we have a battle I won't be in the fighting part of it but will join the hospital corps for the time being and help take care of the wounded," he wrote, adding, "but of course it isn't bullets that kills the most men anyway."[4]

Army life agreed with Goddard throughout June and July. He was appointed trumpeter for Troop E, and passed the days in mounted drill, marching, and practice with "the 'crack-*something* guns.'"[5] Goddard continued writing reports of his good health, and how much he enjoyed his adventure. In mid-July, however, he fell ill. Laid up in his tent, he went an entire week without eating. The regimental doctor came by daily to check on him, but to little effect. "Our doctor don't know beans," Goddard wrote home on July 26, 1898, "he just gives me some little white tablets every day. I tooke [sic] them until they got to hurting my stomach, and now I throw them away as fast as he gives them to me."[6] Three weeks later, he was on the mend. "I am getting over my sick spell about as fast as any body could. My appletight [sic] is bigger than my stomjacket [sic] and I feel good in every way only I am so weak. I cant begin to get on my horse bareback and he is a small horse too."[7]

Private Sim Goddard was one of the lucky ones. The Medical Department's post-war review of the Army's training and mustering encampments shows typhoid fever reached epidemic proportions in the summer of 1898. At least 20,738 cases of typhoid fever—over 19 percent of the 107,973 Volunteer soldiers assembled—were identified. Of these, 1,580 would die of the illness. But survival did not mean a return to health. Thousands of soldiers, like Private Clarence N. Beach, Third U.S. Volunteer Engineers, just barely survived. Bedridden for six months after first contracting typhoid fever at Jefferson Barracks in St. Louis, Missouri, Beach remained an invalid for life.[8]

The Medical Department's response to the epidemic was controversial. To many, the Army's reaction was scandalous. For many sick soldiers' families, medical officers became scapegoats for the epidemic's rapid spread and the ineffectual response. Volunteer soldiers and officers joined the chorus of outrage, claiming mismanagement and incompetence by Surgeon General George Miller Sternberg and his department. These attacks were bolstered by sensationalized accounts in local and national newspapers. Immediately after the epidemic, the public's estimation of the Medical Department sank to unheard of levels, as alluded to by Lieutenant Colonel John Van Rensselaer Hoff three years later:

> A lady was passing through the wards of an overcrowded military hospital when she suddenly encountered two men sawing and hammering on some boards. She looked at them in some surprise and wondering asked:
> "What are you doing there, my men?"
> They looked up at her and one of them said:
> "What are we doing? Why, we are making a coffin, that's what we are doing."
> "A coffin?' she asked. 'For whom are you making a coffin?"
> "For that fellow over there in that bed. Don't you see him?"
> The lady looked in the direction indicated and saw a man apparently in good condition and watching the operation with great interest.
> "Why, that man is not dead, and indeed he does not look as if he were going to die. Can't you postpone this work?"
> "No," the men said, "we can't postpone it. The doctor told us to make the coffin and he knows what he gave him."[9]

The point of the story, Hoff explained, was to highlight how low the Medical Department's reputation had fallen after the training camps debacle. The department's first order of business was to reform itself and repair its damaged image.[10]

To their credit, Sternberg and his subordinates heeded the critiques leveled against them. While they did not accept the charges of incompetence or favoritism, they acknowledged much was mishandled during the summer of 1898. Fourteen years later, Lieutenant Colonel Francis A. Winter looked back with dismay. In a paper presented to the 1912 Army War College class, he argued much of the shameful debacle could have been avoided. All that was painstakingly achieved during the Civil War, from battlefield evacuation schemes and echeloned hospital care in divisional field hospitals, to the establishment of a well-oiled machine of hospital supply distribution, had disappeared: "Certainly, it is amazing, almost unthinkable, that the lessons learned during the Civil War had been so completely lost."[11]

The Spanish-American War was thus an important watershed for American military medicine and public health. Lieutenant Colonel Winter recognized the importance of the war as a catalyst for change within the Medical Department. "I may say, I think, that the Spanish War has been, of all other factors, the one of greatest potency in bringing about the conclusion that the Medical Department has no obligation more pressing than that expressed in its contract to provide for sick and wounded in time of war."[12] His conclusion that the typhoid outbreak was not due to any failings by the Regular Medical Department and that the epidemic prompted critical institutional reforms continue to be validated. For example, historian Vincent J. Cirillo notes that the Medical Department was well informed and worked hard to stem the typhoid epidemics in the volunteer camps. Regular medical officers were well acquainted with the germ theory of disease, and the role of sanitation in preventing camp diseases. The problem resided within the Army's own institutional culture, specifically its traditional emphasis on the primacy of line officers over their medical counterparts. Yet the tragedy brought reform. After a post-war Congressional investigation, the Medical Department's influence and importance within the Army grew, as seen in the post-1898 institutional reforms: the resurrection of a medical supply depot system and the creation of the Army Nurse Corps in 1901; the release of the Army Typhoid Board report in 1904; the establishment of the Department of Military Hygiene at the U.S. Military Academy in 1905; the creation of the Army Medical Reserve Corps in 1908; and finally, the discovery of a viable antityphoid vaccine in 1911.[13]

Such reforms were certainly important. Yet the department's status within the Army was not the sole outcome of the Spanish-American War. When the outcry over the typhoid epidemics subsided, the Medical Department's image underwent a dramatic revision in the eyes of the American public. First castigated as responsible for the epidemic disease that killed and crippled thousands, the professional medical officers of the Army Medical Department became noble heroes. More than any other public health crisis, images of healthy young men falling victim to an easily preventable, yet deadly disease so close to large population centers brought home the vital importance of public health. The awareness that the Regular Army physician understood the unseen dangers attending disregard for sanitation and hygiene validated the public health messages of civilian reformers.[14]

The volunteer army's experiences in the summer of 1898 also produced a subtle change in the mission of the Army Medical Department. The uneven ratio of casualties from disease versus combat trauma—nearly 7.44 to 1—heightened awareness of the importance of hygiene, sanitation, and microbiology.[15] Likewise, the training camps crisis cemented a growing trend toward specialization. At the war's onset, the ideal medical officer was a well-rounded generalist. The public spectacle of the typhoid fever epidemic transformed the department's own approach toward professional specialization. In the epidemic's wake, Regular medical officers aligned their future professional identities and careers along three distinct paths of practice. At the same time, specialization prompted the creation of a rough hierarchy within the department, as the lessons of the Army's war with disease took priority over its medical response to combat in Cuba and the Philippines.

PREPARING FOR WAR

One area historians have agreed upon is the government's haphazard response once war was declared on April 25, 1898. The Regular Army, a force of 2,143 officers and 26,040 enlisted soldiers, languished in virtual insignificance since 1869. Tasked with frontier pacification and domestic security, the Army was ill-prepared for war against even a second-rate European power like Spain. Just as in the war with Mexico and the Civil War, citizen soldiers, either members of the state militia and National Guard or short-term volunteers, were called upon. President William McKinley drew from both sources in two executive proclamations. The first, for 125,000 men, was issued on April 23, 1898, after Congress had passed a joint resolution authorizing the use of force in Cuba. A second request for 75,000 men went out on May 25. In turn, Congress increased the Regular Army to 61,000 men, and extended its own call for 10,000 volunteers to make up sixteen regiments of so-called "immune" volunteer troops, capable of serving in tropical campaigns without fear of contracting yellow fever.[16]

The Regular Army looked with dismay at the mass of volunteers. Many regular officers disliked the prospect of having an untrained rabble of volunteers thrust upon them. Three weeks after the President's first call for volunteers, the *Army and Navy Journal* reported on the state of the early arrivals:

A majority of the recruits have never handled a rifle, and are not even clothed. Although in camp with other troops, and notably in the New York camps these recruits have had no instruction in the manual of arms, because there are not rifles enough on hand to arm them with, and they have merely been assembled with other troops, unarmed, and unprovided for in almost every respect. To suppose a force of this character can be shipped off to Cuba, or Porto Rico, instantly at the pressing of an electric button, as the mass of our citizens have been led to believe, is the height of absurdity.[17]

Civilian newspapers were equally disappointed. "The plain truth is that, in spite of all the hurrying and pushing that has been done from the Adjutant General's office," the *New York Times* reported on May 13, 1898, "the volunteer army is not ready for the field and can not be made so without considerable further delay. No appreciable portion of the 125,000 men who have offered their services to the Government are prepared for campaigning in this country, much less are they prepared for the vicissitudes of outdoor life in a hostile country."[18]

Regular medical officers were likewise critical of the volunteer force. Save for a few states—such as Massachusetts, New York, and Pennsylvania—the National Guard was more of a political club than a quasi-military organization. Officered by local politicians and influential citizens, the quality of the various state militias was erratic. Guard troops were often retained on regimental rolls even though physically unfit. Parades, monthly drills, and the rare deployment to maintain order was the normal routine for guardsmen, leading the Surgeon General to observe that "service in the State military forces in time of peace is a wholly different matter from service in the Army of the United States against an active enemy, with all the possible incidentals of fatigue, hard fare, and exposures of every kind."[19]

Sternberg pointed toward the high number of disabilities reported among regiments serving with the Seventh Army Corps in Tampa. Soon after mustering, troops reported to sick call boasting a host of infirmities—hernias, epilepsy, syphilis, heart disease, hemorrhoids, and physical deformities—that should have been revealed by physical examination. Seven hundred and forty-seven men were immediately discharged when their conditions were discovered. By mid-July, the problem of physically unfit troops was so great the War Department issued a general order establishing medical examination boards staffed by regular and volunteer medical officers to review all proposed disability-related discharges forwarded by regimental medical officers.[20]

Nevertheless, the majority of the young enlisted volunteers were of good physical condition and sound character. Drawn from all sectors of American life, their raw potential for soldiering was not unnoticed. The *Army and Navy Journal* of August 20, 1898, noted many militia and Guard volunteers were "the very men the Army will value most. They are strapping young fellows, mostly recruited out of the streets, to whom the pay and livelihood is an object, and who have no business cares awaiting their return. . . . It would have been well for us if we had had them alone and allowed the organized members of the National Guard to continue in their employments at home."[21]

Their age was another issue. President McKinley's call-up extended the minimum age of volunteers to eighteen, a decision Sternberg felt was mistaken. "All military experience shows that young men under 21 years of age break down readily under the strain of war service," he later wrote, "and the regiments of our Volunteer Army had many of these boys in its ranks."[22] More at issue were Victorian notions of physical and emotional maturity. Teenagers were considered less immune to the hardships of wartime, so their premature use risked the vitality of the state as an organic entity. State and national volunteer recruiters, Sternberg warned, operated under "the mistaken principle that in time of war anyone is good enough to be food for powder. To accept the man best fitted for the service to be required of him is one thing. To accept a man who may fire a musket or stop a bullet if he be assumed to be in his place in the line is another. In warfare which requires only the manhood of a nation to conquer, the best men should be selected."[23]

THE MEDICAL DEPARTMENT ON THE EVE OF WAR

The call for 200,000 volunteers left the Surgeon General scrambling to provide sufficient medical support. After considering the number of vacancies and medical officers assigned to administrative, scientific, and teaching tasks, as well as those detailed to general hospitals and garrisons, only 100 medical officers were available for field duty. The first call for volunteers included eight corps surgeons, at the rank of lieutenant colonel, and 110 division and brigade surgeons, all majors. Most of these positions—three corps surgeons and seventy-four division and brigade surgeons—were filled by direct presidential appointment or were hired as contract surgeons at the monthly rate of $150.00.[24]

The situation was different with the volunteer regiments. Each was allowed a senior surgeon with the rank of major, supported by two assistant surgeons with the rank of captain or first lieutenant. Many state militia regiments reported with a full medical complement. Regular medical officers were not impressed by their volunteer counterparts. "The organization of the medical department of the volunteer regiments was very incomplete and unsatisfactory, bringing with them the organization employed in the State service," according to Lieutenant Colonel Louis Mervin Maus, Chief Surgeon attached to Seventh Corps.[25] Many volunteer medical officers, he observed, may have been distinguished physicians, but they lacked the basic administrative skills necessary to function as military surgeons. "The majority of the regimental services mustered into the volunteer service were entirely inexperienced in the duties of a military surgeon," Maus noted, "and few were even required to pass a professional examination."[26]

Others shared Maus' outlook. Charles B. G. de Nancrede, volunteer surgeon with the Michigan National Guard, observed many volunteer medical officers were convinced patriotic fervor counted more than practical knowledge, so they ignored advice offered by regular medical officers. Yet Sternberg considered the majority of state medical officers to be quite competent in matters related to surgery and field medicine, but woefully ignorant of hygiene and sanitation. The Surgeon General reserved his criticisms for a failed medical education system: "Unfortunately, hygiene and practical sanitation are subject which receive little attention in our medical schools or from physicians and surgeons engaged in the practice of medicine."[27] Even if the volunteer medical officer was well informed in camp sanitation, his recommendations meant nothing if his line counterparts ignored him.

The contract surgeon experience was different. There was no shortage of applicants for service with the Medical Department. The outbreak of war brought over 2,000 applications for a commission to the Surgeon General's Office. The Surgeon General initially rejected any who were not immune to yellow fever, but the circumstances of rapid mobilization led him to reconsider his policy. The Medical Department was generally enthusiastic about the abilities and skills of the contract surgeons. Many were recent medical school graduates, trained in the latest sanitary and surgical methods. Regular medical officers were impressed by their commitment and drive. As outsiders to the military medical service, free of the political hubris many volunteer surgeons used to win their commissions, contract surgeons held no formal rank save the title of "acting assistant surgeon." When these same contract surgeons took ill with the diseases they were treating in their charges, they were not even entitled to paid sick leave.

There was another dimension to the regular medical officer's enthusiasm for the contract surgeon. Uniformed state medical officers were often more concerned with preserving control over their own supplies and personnel than the soldiers in their care. This selfishness stung medical officers who sought to consolidate regimental resources into a single system to accommodate the needs of an entire brigade, division, or corps. By comparison, the young contract surgeons exemplified the values espoused by the regular establishment. Lieutenant Colonel Alfred C. Girard, chief surgeon of Second Corps, praised their attention to detail and professionalism, noting "by their zeal and efficiency raised themselves in the esteem of the volunteer medical officers, who, in the early days of the war, did not consider them good enough to share in their mess."[28] Lieutenant Colonel Maus spoke for many when he reported to the Surgeon General, "In my opinion these officers are as fully entitled to any consideration resulting from war service, as the commissioned medical officers of volunteers."[29]

Finding enough medical officers was not Sternberg's only challenge; the call for volunteers also failed to provide a volunteer Hospital Corps. Few states took the need for trained hospital support staff seriously, leaving regimental medical officers to rely upon line officers to detail privates as litter bearers, orderlies, and nurses. The enthusiasm and quality of such men was suspect. According to Maus, "It was the exception to find any of the hospital attendants qualified for nursing and first-aid assistance. None knew anything about litter drill, or the various methods of carrying the wounded."[30] On May 31, the Adjutant General's Office authorized transferring volunteer orderlies into the Hospital Corps, elevating all serving

Hospital Corps privates to the grade of acting hospital steward. A month later, the number of Hospital Corps stewards was set at 200.[31]

More than the Spanish fleet or army in Cuba, the twin specters of yellow fever and malaria worried the War Department. Major General Nelson A. Miles, Commanding General of the Army, was especially chary of landing in Cuba during the rainy season. On April 18, 1898, Miles explained his reservations to Secretary of War Russell A. Alger, pointing out that history conspired against a successful invasion of Cuba during the rainy season. Endemic yellow fever and malaria made Cuba a pesthole. Miles noted the island was occupied by 80,000 acclimated and immune Spanish troops—the survivors of an original force of 214,000. His concerns were validated by an April 19, 1898 joint army-navy board report. The report by Lieutenant Colonel Arthur Wagner, the head of the Army's Military Information Division, and naval Captain Albert S. Barker presented a plan for joint service operations. Both men noted that a rainy season invasion would decimate an American invasion force.[32]

Miles' doubts were fueled by Surgeon General Sternberg. Taking stock of his own experiences with the 1879 Havana Yellow Fever Commission, Sternberg warned Cuban cities were cesspools of pestilence. Virtually every city was rife with yellow fever, including Matanzas, Cardenas, Cienfuegos, Sagua, and Santiago. None of these cities compared with Havana, however, where 11,897 deaths were reported in the military and civilian population between 1870 and 1879.[33] This recent data, combined with the historical record of epidemics since 1648, painted Cuba as the graveyard of American forces sent there during the sick season.

Miles instead decided on a gradual deployment of American troops in the Caribbean. Rather than send Americans to the fever islands, it was better to allow the Navy freedom to demonstrate against the Spanish fleet and institute a blockade of Cuba and Puerto Rico. Aside from the opportunistic seizure of the Isle of Pines and the sea port city of Nipe, the Army would spend the summer training and equipping for battle in the fall. Miles felt if all went well, "we can compel the surrender of the army on the island of Cuba with very little loss of life and possibly avoid the spread of yellow fever over our own country."[34]

The realities of political pressure and the news of the U.S. Navy's Asiatic Squadron's success in Manila Bay forced a change in Miles' strategy. Overriding the Commanding General's plans, President McKinley and Secretary Alger accelerated invasion timetables. The Army's Fifth Corps, under the command of Major General William R. Shafter, was to embark for Santiago as soon as the 25,000 volunteer and regular troops comprising the force were assembled. Numerous delays in organization and loading the ships delayed Fifth Corps departure until June 14, 1898. Moreover, an expeditionary force consisting of some 20,000 men was dispatched to take control of the Philippine Islands. Commanded by Major General Wesley Merritt, the first elements of Eighth Corps left San Francisco on May 25,

1898, on a thirty-six day journey to Manila. Deprived of the opportunity he expected was his due as the head of the Army to lead the main invasion, Miles pleaded to be allowed to invade Puerto Rico.[35]

CAMP GEORGE H. THOMAS, CHICKAMAUGA, GEORGIA

When the War Department divided the mass of volunteer regiments into seven corps in early May 1898, volunteer training camps were established throughout the South. First and Third Corps were assembled at Camp George H. Thomas near Chickamauga, Georgia. Second Corps was sent to Camp Russell A. Alger in Falls Church, Virginia. Prior to its dispatch to Cuba, Fifth Corps encamped outside of Tampa, Florida. Two other corps were assembled at multiple locations: Fourth Corps at Mobile, Alabama, and Fernandina, Florida; Seventh Corps at Jacksonville, Miami, and Panama Park, Florida.[36] This work will consider the experiences at Camps Thomas, Alger, and the Florida camps.

Established on the site of the Civil War battle of Chickamauga in North Georgia, Camp George H. Thomas was home to the First Army Corps and elements of the Third and Sixth Corps—in total over 60,000 men.[37] At the time, the consensus was the camp was well placed and fulfilled all the basic requirements for a large cantonment. Bisected by the Chickamauga Creek, the terrain was a gentle rolling plain, interspersed with woods and covered with a firm clay-based soil. Standing surface water was not a serious concern thanks to the grade of the terrain and the natural drainage afforded by the creek. The camp was also well situated near railroads and other thoroughfares, ensuring ready supply and easy access for arriving regiments.[38]

On May 15, advance elements of the First Ohio Cavalry Regiment detrained in Chickamauga and marched to its campsite on Dyer Field. Other regiments followed, laying their tents in serried rows alongside marked-out parade grounds and in the pine woods. At first, many were taken with the prospect of pitching camp on the famous battlefield. Boyish awe and excitement soon turned to ennui and boredom as the routine of military camp life set in. In between drill, rifle training, inspections, and more drill, men found relief wherever they could.[39]

Boredom soon translated to a near-universal disregard for the sanitary precautions essential to a large military encampment. Anticipating this, Sternberg issued his first wartime circular on April 25, 1898. First laying out the medical officer's responsibility to the troops under his care, the circular outlined a series of recommendations. All encampments "when practicable" should be laid out on high and well-drained ground. Company latrines were to be covered with earth, quicklime, or ash three times daily, and covered over when filled to within two feet of the ground surface. Kitchen waste was to be burned, not buried. All drinking water was to be boiled, filtered, or brewed as tea or coffee. Similarly, care was to be exercised in permitting soldiers to eat local produce. Ripe fruit in moderation was considered acceptable, "but green or overripe fruit will give rise to bowel complaints."[40]

Sternberg followed with six more circulars. Save for Circular No. 3, outlining the Medical Department's table of organization, all these documents reinforced the sanitary guidelines outlined in Circular No. 1.[41] Sternberg had good reason to issue frequent reminders. While many volunteer medical officers understood the Army's sanitary policies, they had little influence over line officers and enlisted men. Captain Harry L. Webber, regimental surgeon with the 8th Massachusetts Infantry Regiment, observed the men's reluctance toward taking appropriate precautions: "Digging and caring for sinks did not appeal to the men as heroic soldiering. They hated and shirked this duty and as a result the sinks of many regiments were so repulsive that the men refused to use them, and polluted territory surrounding the camp."[42]

Within weeks, typhoid cases appeared in regimental hospitals. Early cases were limited to recruits who reported sick to their mustering camps, or acquired the disease there. Every regiment reported several cases of typhoid fever within two weeks of arriving at Chickamauga. Many initial cases were misdiagnosed. The favored diagnoses of the Civil War—"remittent fever," "typho-malarial fever," and "Acute Diarrhea"—were generously applied by regimental surgeons.[43] Either way, the presence of typhoid and the sorry state of public sanitary hygiene were a dangerous combination. Even when privy pits were used, failure either to cover or disinfect the daily wastes created a "center of infection from which the disease was likely to be propagated and an epidemic possibly developed."[44] The danger was exacerbated by the placement of the pits. For example, after the 1st West Virginia Volunteer Infantry Regiment arrived from Charleston, West Virginia, its men dug out shallow latrines and sinks in the rocky knoll above the regiment's tents. The limestone rock was so prevalent that the average sink was no deeper than fifty inches; far less than the eight feet mandated by First Army Corps. These sinks quickly filled to capacity, and during the summer rains overflowed, flooding the campsite below with its noxious contents.[45]

Though many volunteer officers acknowledged typhoid was in their units, they also sought to deflect responsibility, blaming the local environment and inhabitants.[46] One officer with the 12th New York Infantry reported typhoid was rife among local sharecroppers after meeting a destitute family afflicted with the disease on the camp's outskirts. Such reports were expected, as typhoid was considered a rural disease, a byproduct of placing privies and manure heaps near wellsprings.[47] Nevertheless, a thriving trade in food, candies, soft drinks, and alcohol flourished around the camp as local farmers and merchants set up shops and refreshment stands around Camp Thomas. Northern and Midwestern volunteers cast merchants as callow speculators selling tainted wares at exorbitant prices. Acting Assistant Surgeon Charles B. Craig told reporters, "There is no doubt but that the men have dissipated a great deal during their stay here, and dissipation is calculated to breed sickness anywhere in the world. They ate and drank almost anything that came along, and as a result they would become ill."[48] One soldier from the 2nd Wisconsin Infantry was less polite. "Yesterday I read in a Kentucky paper that six men of the Second regiment had died from eating poisoned pies, this was quite untrue. However, the doctors say the 'nigger pies' are the cause of some of the illness in camp."[49] On June 8, all shops were declared off limits: "The native fakirs have been ordered off the grounds by Gen. Brooks. This is a good thing for the boys, as the fakirs sold turn-overs, and after a fellow ate one he turned over, not once, but several times."[50]

The real crisis began with the late-summer rains. Camp Thomas sat along the flood plain of the Chickamauga Creek, with no thought given to the summer thunderstorms that swept through the region in late June and throughout July. According to James E. Payne, Captain with the 5th Missouri Infantry, the storms did "not begin in a gentle shower and get you accustomed to it. On the contrary, it just lets go and comes flooding down in an unceasing torrent for hours at a time. If it holds up for a spell or a day, you may depend upon it that it is only getting ready for a renewal of hostilities, and intends to never let up until the ground is full as a sponge, streams all overflowing, adjacent lands submerged and patience drowned out or washed away."[51] Existing sinks were quickly flooded, the noxious contents spread all over the surrounding areas. Flooded sinks provided some amusement—one soldier walked unknowingly into a five foot deep slop hole covered with kitchen refuse—but also created a real hazard. Standing water evaporated in the hot sun, leaving behind a layer of polluted dust covering everything in sight. Soldiers tracked the dust into mess tents and their own bedclothes. No place was safe from the dust—not even the water barrel carts bringing fresh water into the camp from the outside. On one occasion, a soldier snuck out of camp hiding in one of these wagons as it left camp for a fresh supply of water. According to the official report, "A subsequent inspection of the camp site of the regiment to which this man belonged showed it to be almost an impossibility for his shoes not to be free from defilement."[52]

The July deluges had other ill effects as well. Latrine and sink runoff contaminated water springs throughout the camp. Orders to boil all drinking water drawn from the springs and creek were ignored. According to one observer, the average volunteer considered such orders an infringement upon their own common sense and personal rights. "Now it is one thing to give an order that a certain water must not be drunk, and another to enforce that order, and when the men are untrained, healthy young fellows who have never been ill, never seen any illness, never realized the necessity of paying any attention to hygienic rules and unaccustomed to obedience in any form, it was well nigh impossible at first to have such an order carried out."[53] Even when barrels of boiled water were stored on ice, soldiers refused it. Concepts like the germ theory of disease did not make sense to the body of volunteers. The possibility that disease-carrying microbes existed in otherwise clear water was unknown—or at least, ignored—throughout the encampment. An incident involving the Eighth Massachusetts illustrates this. A spring adjacent to an outpost near the Chickamauga Creek was flooded during the storms, leaving behind a coating of slime after the creek subsided. Acting upon the suggestion that germs floated, "they plunged a canteen to the bottom of the spring, with the opening stopped by the thumb against the entrance of bacteria. When the canteen was on the bottom, the thumb was removed until the canteen was filled, the opening was then plugged with the thumb, and the supply brought to the surface."[54] Every person who drank from the spring came down with typhoid shortly afterward.

Meanwhile, the flooded sinks were a breeding ground for a massive swarm of flies. They were everywhere, harassing men lounging in the shade and marching on the parade grounds, and lighting on everything in the camp. Clouds of flies were routinely seen around the latrines and kitchen sinks. Every regiment was overrun by the pests, which quickly covered any food left in the open. Quick-thinking officers purchased wire screens and cheesecloth dish covers to keep the flies away from the food, but this did little to prevent spoilage in the Georgia sun. Some regiments sought to control the number of flies in their camp by burning latrine and kitchen sinks as they were filled. Such effort was wasted, however, as other regiments allowed their own waste to linger.[55]

The outbreaks were enhanced by the hospital system. Initially each regiment maintained its own tent hospital. Here regimental medical officers and orderlies watched their charges, treatments often colored by a general distrust of those reporting sick. Orderlies excused their callousness on the grounds they were discouraging malingerers. Volunteers formed a different opinion. One Wisconsin volunteer noted that "were it not for the friends of boys calling on them, while in the hospital and seeing that the details are looked after, such as drinking water and meals, many a poor fellow, I am afraid, would not pull through."[56] The regimental system was soon abandoned. In June, Lieutenant Colonel Rush Huidekoper ordered the formation of three divisional hospitals and a reserve hospital in First Corps, with a total capacity of 726 beds. Lieutenant Colonel John Van Rensselaer Hoff followed suit in Third Corps, establishing two division hospitals, with 120 and 285 beds respectively.[57]

Even though the hospitals were established in June, a struggle for control over regimental resources continued through the summer, and remained unresolved when the typhoid epidemic erupted. By late July, after the rains had wreaked havoc with the camp's rudimentary sanitary system, First Corps' hospitals were overwhelmed with sick. Many were turned away and sent back to the regimental tent hospitals for treatment. When the First Division was dispatched to Puerto Rico on July 23, 1898, its divisional hospital was left behind to care for 153 sick men[58] To help resolve overcrowding and supply problems, two divisional hospitals at Chickamauga were redesignated general hospitals. And still the sick came, prompting the construction of

Sternberg Hospital, a new 1,200 bed general hospital, at Wilder Tower Hill on August 15, 1898. As soon as the wards were standing, fifty-six patients from the Third U.S. Volunteer Cavalry and the Third Corps, Second Division hospital were sent over, with more following until 553 men were admitted.[59]

By early August it was apparent Camp Thomas had to be abandoned. The camp's original design as a temporary summer encampment only compounded problems. On August 15, the healthy members of First and Third Corps were entrained to smaller winter quarters in Knoxville, Tennessee; Huntsville, Alabama; and Lexington, Kentucky.[60] Sanitation was a priority at the new camps. The War Department issued a General Order on August 10, 1898, putting all line and staff officers on notice that they were responsible for enforcing "proper sanitary conditions in camp and strict cleanliness of the person."[61] Despite precautions, typhoid cases appeared immediately after the move. Fortunately, these were proven to be latent cases who had not yet exhibited full symptoms. Soon the disease rate dropped, signaling an end to the epidemic. During its run, typhoid fever decimated the two corps. Out of an aggregate strength of 47,975 men in First and Third Corps and the attached Cavalry Brigade, 10,339 probable cases of typhoid fever were identified; 21.55 percent of the total strength being afflicted with the disease. Of these, 752 died of typhoid.[62]

Meanwhile, every effort was made to empty the general hospitals at Camp Thomas. On August 9, all ambulatory sick in general and field hospitals were granted a month-long furlough, after which anyone unfit for service was granted an indefinite furlough for the duration of their anticipated recovery.[63] In response to the furlough order, concerned citizens chartered trains to evacuate sick soldiers to local hospitals near their families. The arrival of these trains sparked a new controversy. In Philadelphia, for example, the first train from Camp Thomas was greeted by hundreds of friends and loved ones. The warm welcome soon turned into shocked silence as the train pulled into Chestnut Street Station. An hour after it arrived, the first sick soldier, Private Frank Coon, Company E, Ninth Pennsylvania Volunteer Regiment, was carried off the train:

> As the litter, borne by three white uniformed members of the Episcopal Hospital staff, emerged from the door of the baggage car through which all of the sick soldiers were carried hundreds of heads were uncovered and the deep hush that had marked the scene became deeper still. It was almost as if the soldier were dead instead of only seriously ill. . . . From then on until nearly 1 o'clock stretcher after stretcher was borne through the long aisles of the cars into the baggage car and from there across the wide platform to the waiting ambulances. . . . To those who gazed upon them in the flickering light of the old depot many of the stretchers, although they contained the forms of what were once, strong, lusty men, appeared to be empty. This was because of the emaciated condition of the sufferers.[64]

Nothing conveyed the realities of the epidemic at Camp Thomas quite like the mercy trains. Experienced physicians recoiled at the emaciated, unconscious, and feverish young men lolling listlessly in filth-covered stretchers on the trains. Governors and wealthy citizens sent hospital trains to Chickamauga to bring their sons home regardless of the cost. Over the next two weeks, the rails between Chickamauga and the rest of the country were filled with chartered trains bringing sick soldiers home. The furlough order emptied the Chickamauga hospitals of most of its patients, yet the worst cases remained behind. For these poor souls, the ordeal was not over. To alleviate overcrowding at the Chickamauga hospitals, 180 sick patients, many in the late stages of typhoid fever, were moved from Camp Thomas to Fort McPherson, just outside of Atlanta. The relocation was poorly handled. Clad only in nightshirts for the train journey, many patients suffered a relapse during the move; ten men died soon after arrival. Orders from the Surgeon General's Office followed, prohibiting all premature transport of the gravely ill.[65]

Many volunteers blamed the War Department. Staff departments—particularly the Adjutant General, Quartermaster, and Medical Departments—received the most criticism. Echoing charges leveled by militia advocates since the 1820s, critics attacked the Adjutant General's Department as a collection of pencil pushers with little experience in soldiering. "Officers who were experienced in campaigns, as Miles, Wilson and Merritt, were ignored," wrote Colonel Robert W. Leonard, 12th New York Volunteer Infantry, "and the Adjutant General's office was allowed to try its "prentice hand.'"[66] Captain Harry E. Webber, 8th Massachusetts Infantry, split blame between the Quartermaster and Medical Departments. Every article his regiment needed—tents, lumber, disinfectant, and water barrels—was in short supply. Unfilled supply requests forced the regiment to turn to local vendors, accelerating the epidemic. The Medical Department failed in the most basic preparations for the gathering troops. Volunteer medical and line officers identified shortages in supplies, medicines, and trained hospital attendants, and attacked the decision to abolish regimental hospitals. In short, the Medical Department was a hidebound institution, its officers incapable of exercising the managerial and professional skills needed in wartime.[67]

As the epidemic reached its high point, Acting Assistant Surgeon Charles F. Craig was ordered to investigate the epidemic's potential connections with malaria. One of the bright young contract surgeons so admired by Surgeon General Sternberg, Craig's microbiology training made him the ideal choice for the study. In the course of his investigation, Craig examined ten corpses and tested the blood and urine of over 315 patients. Widal examinations proved typhoid existed throughout the camp, afflicting 80 percent of the cases in the hospital. Water surveys from wells and springs throughout the camp revealed bacteria at all the sites, but no typhoid, leaving no question the Chickamauga Creek was fit for domestic use before the arrival of the volunteers. He also identified a link between the flies infesting the camp and the spread of typhoid. Flies placed on sugar cubes impregnated with the bacillus were examined, and typhoid was found within their digestive systems. "There is nothing in the climate, ground, or water that would have originally caused typhoid fever," he concluded. "There might have been some slight illness on account of the change of climate, but if the system of the men had not been weakened by dissipation there would have been very little serious sickness."[68]

Craig's report was welcomed by the Chattanooga press. His announcement of the region's previously salubrious condition and general good health of the inhabitants was heralded by city fathers eager to preserve their reputation and the pace of economic development. According to an editorial in the *Chattanooga Daily Times*, the exoneration of the region was no small matter:

[P]eople have been led to believe that Chickamauga Park was a veritable den for the typhoid germ, its home, as it were, whence the poison is Scattered over the country. . . . The government has no right to force Chattanooga and the section contiguous to Chickamauga Park to rest under the imputation of being neighbors to a "pesthole." An official declaration . . . based on irrefutable evidence, should, in justice to our people, be made by the department, locating once and for all the blame for the typhoid epidemic.[69]

The insistence for a formal apology points toward a sensitivity regarding regional identity obscured by the rush to proclaim the war an act of national reconciliation. Even as many observers saluted the war's healing effect on the rifts that had separated North and South since 1861, Southerners remained vigilant over any challenges to their own honor and self-image. The breakdown at Camp Thomas presented just such a threat, provoking feelings of persecution at the hands of callow Northerners who projected their own failings on the region as a whole.

Surgeon General Sternberg acknowledged these concerns. In his 1899 annual report to the Secretary of War, he pointed to the physical and moral quality of the volunteer soldier as the primary factor in the typhoid outbreak. The "immature constitutions" of the young and the poor condition of older volunteers was the most significant cause for the epidemic, forming "the basis of a sick list which necessarily increased in proportion to the hardships, privations, and exposures of camp life, to the recklessness and the ignorance of youth . . . , and to the want of that company and regimental discipline which in the Army represents the household virtues, the domestic economy of the family, and the police system of civil communities."[70] The breakdown of sanitary conditions, from the failure to maintain privy pits to the abuse of the surrounding woods for personal relief, could be traced to this one issue. Other factors, including the quality of food, the climate, and the influence of alcohol and venereal disease among men visiting the saloons and brothels of Chattanooga, were nowhere near as important.[71]

CAMP RUSSELL A. ALGER, FALLS CHURCH, VIRGINIA, AND CAMP GEORGE G. MEADE, HIGHSPIRE, PENNSYLVANIA

The 23,000 men of the Second Army Corps gathered at Camp Russell A. Alger, west of Falls Church, Virginia. As regiments arrived in May and June, they set up camp wherever they found a convenient spot. The resulting chaos caused terrible overcrowding; troops pitched tents on meadows better suited for parade and drill, or scratching out clearings in the dense brush amidst the thick pine and oak woods. Overcrowding was briefly alleviated when the Third Division was ordered on June 23, 1898, to join the Fifth Corps in Cuba to take part in the invasion of Puerto Rico. Their abandoned sites were quickly filled by new regiments. Supply deficiencies were also a problem, adding to the overcrowding. It was not uncommon for five or six men to share a three-man pup tent, with blankets as the only cover from the hard clay beneath.[72]

The faults at Camp Alger were quickly apparent. The tramping of over twenty thousand pairs of feet stripped away grass and topsoil throughout the camp, exposing a substrata of hard yellow clay over solid rock. A thick cloud of dust soon covered the site, "which made the air of the neighboring camps almost irrespirable in sultry weather." Conditions and tempers were not improved by the scarcity of water throughout the camp. Originally planners felt the small creek bisecting the camp, and the area's artesian springs, would prove adequate. Such hopes were misplaced, however, particularly as the creek was contaminated by surface pollution after the evening rains. Efforts to restrict the use of local water were ignored—even after Berkefeld and Maignen water filters were distributed and twenty-nine deep wells were drilled to service the regimental camps.[73]

Soon after taking charge of Second Corps' medical affairs on May 20, 1898, Lieutenant Colonel Alfred C. Girard ran into trouble with the volunteer surgeons under his command. A student of European hospital and evacuation schemes, Girard was considered an expert on military hospitals. Girard impounded all regimental supplies, with the intention of setting up three 200-bed divisional hospitals as the primary level of medical care in Second Corps. He had not counted upon resistance from volunteer medical officers, however. Regiments with ample supplies were reluctant to share their own materials with other less-prepared units. Enlisted hospital stewards joined the outcry, claiming Girard's plans for consolidating state medical services under Medical Department control would cut their own pay to the lower federal rate. In order to stem an open revolt, Major General William M. Graham, Second Corps commanding officer, allowed a two-bed dispensary for each regiment.[74]

These problems affected Girard's opinion of the volunteers for the remainder of his career. Stung by the rebukes to his expert judgment from subordinates, not to mention having his authority undermined by the corps commander, Girard focused his ire upon the entire volunteer establishment.[75] In reports on the condition of the camp, Girard repeatedly cited the state volunteers' ignorance of basic sanitation: "Every one seemed satisfied with the *beauty* of his camp," he wrote, "but apparently no one ever looked after the dejecta."[76]

Girard had a point. Throughout the camp, companies set up field kitchens and mess tents adjacent to open pit latrines and cesspools. Many mess areas were little more than lean-tos constructed from cast-off wood scraps and canvas. The sinks were too few and too shallow, and casual indifference resulted in their "constantly reeking with fresh and uncovered excreta, and so near to the kitchens and company streets that the fecal odor was everywhere perceptible."[77] On routine sanitary inspections commanders agreed with Girard's findings and implemented his recommendations, only to allow their companies to lapse back into sloth a few days later. Girard later complained his career and his professional reputation were destroyed by the ignorant volunteer physicians under his charge, to the extent that the "papers cannot remedy the harm they have done me."[78]

The unlicensed and uninspected vendors surrounding the camp created other problems. Merchants set up crude stands to sell everything imaginable, including lunches, soda, candy, vegetables, fruit, lemonade, milk, and alcohol. Soldiers began calling the area "Shantyville" or "the Midway." According to a soldier from the 8th Ohio Infantry, many flocked to places like the Metropolitan Restaurant and the Delmonico Hotel after dark, "when they were ablaze with the glory of gasoline lamps, and exchange their good money for vile circus lemonade, green apple pies, black cigars, and unripe bananas, after which they would wind up the banquet with a dish of ice cream containing all the elements of that toothsome delicacy except cream."[79] The following day regimental surgeons were busy attending to the distressed revelers, who couldn't understand why they were so sick.

Other regiments suffered similar fates. Typhoid struck the 65th New York Infantry Regiment's E Company hard, with seventeen cases appearing between July 10 and August 2. This company of society boys from Jamestown, New York, kept a very rich mess, supplemented by daily care packages from home. The company also contracted with a local milkman to deliver three gallons of milk a day. The regiment's senior medical officer, Major Albert H. Briggs, suspected the milkman adulterated his wares with water drawn from contaminated pumps, but was unable to verify his suspicions. Briggs concluded a more likely source of illness was three train cars of food delivered to the regiment, courtesy of the Buffalo Evening News. "These cars ... contained food of various kinds, such as boiled hams, fowls, canned stuffs, cakes, pastries, etc. The following morning 154 men presented themselves at surgeon's call, all suffering with diarrhea. Company E lived riotously for a few days." Not surprisingly, the first cases of typhoid fever in E Company followed a week later.[80]

The attention paid to unscrupulous merchants reflected the general feeling that the typhoid outbreak was local in origin. Observers emphasized the disease appeared only after individual soldiers broke discipline and drank the local water. Girard described several incidents in which soldiers from four different regiments became sick after imbibing local water or milk, including an outbreak in the First New York Cavalry Regiment in which men fell ill despite the regiment's issue of bottled Hygeia and Apollinaris water.[81] Girard's suspicions were validated by a sanitary inspection of Second Corps. Six regiments in the First Division brought infected soldiers with them into Camp Alger, for example, while only two regiments in the Second Division imported typhoid to the Virginia site.[82] Taken together with overcrowding and the problems with privy sanitation, these factors were accepted as the epidemic's sources in Second Corps.

Camp Alger remained relatively healthy through June. The majority of sick cases were for relatively normal camp diseases. Only twenty-seven typhoid cases were reported during this period. In early July, however, the typhoid rate exploded. Just like Camp Thomas, the combination of filth, poor sanitation, flies, and the summer heat transformed the site into a fever pit. The only substantive difference between the two camps was a summer drought, which saved Camp Alger from the floods of ordure that plagued Chickamauga. Nevertheless, the disease quickly took hold in Falls Church. After July 10, the number of cases rose. By July 31, 779 men—3.5 percent of the Second Army Corps—were sick with typhoid fever. When possible, the worst cases were removed to the Army's general hospital at Fort Myer, Virginia. Otherwise they were treated in regimental and divisional tent hospitals.[83]

The true extent of the typhoid epidemic at Camp Alger was doubtlessly understated. Many early cases were miscast as malaria or an indeterminate gastrointestinal complaint. The investigating board's report highlights many cases were very short in duration—frequently under twenty-four hours—with over a third of the afflicted returning to active duty within forty-eight hours. When combined with the discovery that many alleged malarial cases later displayed immunity to typhoid, misdiagnosis was clearly the norm. The same was seen in the diarrhea cases. A statistical analysis of 3,894 cases of intestinal disturbance revealed only 174 men—4.4 percent of the total—later contracted typhoid. Conversely, a review of the 1,951 typhoid cases reported at Camp Alger determined 1,777, some 91.9 percent of the total reported cases, had no prior history of diarrhea or intestinal disturbance. The Typhoid Board concluded "in addition to the occurrence of a large number of recognized cases of typhoid fever of average duration and severity, there were a still larger number of milder infections appearing as simple diarrheas or as fevers of short duration."[84]

As sick rolls mounted and the first victims were buried, morale in Second Corps plummeted. While volunteers waited for the disease to strike their encampment or mess, news from Cuba and Puerto Rico made it clear the war would be over before they arrived. Reasoning that the greatest danger they faced was disease, many volunteers openly expressed their regrets and hatred for the camp. "Camp Alger!" one trooper would recall, "The hot, the dusty. The place where the tents turned yellow with dust, and the ground cracked open with heat; where water was scarce, and typhoid fever lurked in the air."[85] Even volunteer officers who once eagerly looked forward to war, worried for the safety of their men and their own lives. Many commanders relocated their regiments to new camp sites to outrun the disease. Some followed the 1st New Jersey Volunteer Infantry Regiment's example of posting guards around regimental camps to prevent men from frequenting the food vendors. Others took a decidedly interventionist route in enforcing personal hygiene. The 12th Pennsylvania Volunteer Infantry Regiment, for example, posted a guard at every privy. His duty was to ensure every occupant covered his own wastes with fresh dirt upon leaving, after which he stood watch to ensure the soldier washed his hands.[86]

The spectacle of a deadly epidemic so near to the capital was a tremendous embarrassment to the McKinley administration. In mid-July, a team of officers left to scout a location for a new camp. After reviewing several other sites along the Susquehanna River, the committee selected a ten-mile long site at the Thoroughfare Gap, between the towns of Highspire and Middletown in Pennsylvania. Medical officers were given a broad fiat in the location and layout of the camp. Potential water supplies were surveyed, and artesian wells were dug deep into the aquifer. Water was in turn pumped into storage tanks and then piped to individual campsites via iron mains laid before Second Corps' arrival. A general order required each company to maintain water filters, while the regimental camps' placement received special attention. Company campsites were separated by wide streets, with kitchens and privies placed at opposite ends of the camps. Lastly, all tents were floored, to keep the soldiers' sleeping areas clean. Elements of the Second Division started leaving Camp Alger in mid-July, setting off on a long march in the midst of heavy summer storms. In the last days of August, the remaining elements of First Division also broke camp, but pursued a different course. Save for three Pennsylvania units—the 8th, the 12th, and the 13th Volunteer Infantry—the division's five remaining regiments were sent back to their home states, the men given a thirty day furlough. Rather than disband First Division, however, the War Department replaced the furloughed regiments, with new, ostensibly healthy, organizations.[87]

These steps were taken in the hope the typhoid epidemic had run its course at Falls Church. Though the new site was better planned than Camp Alger, relentless summer storms soaked men and equipment alike. Dirt streets tramped out by the new arrivals became mud wallows, with daily run-off flooding tents pitched next to streets and parade grounds. The outbreak continued, this time no regiment was immune. Regiments left Camp Alger with existing, yet unpresented cases percolating in their ranks, while new regiments arrived with their own typhoid cases. Soon after arriving at Camp Meade on September 17, the 35th Michigan Volunteer Infantry was hard struck with typhoid fever. By month's end, 216 cases were diagnosed, with another 128 following in October. The 202nd New York Volunteer Infantry suffered a similar fate. Before departing from Hempstead, New York, over a dozen cases of typhoid fever were diagnosed among the men there, with a number of other reported cases of malarial remittent fever. After arriving at Camp Meade on September 14, the typhoid and malaria rate skyrocketed; 108 likely cases of typhoid being reported for the entire month, with an additional fifty-nine in October. Eight of these patients would die of the disease.[88]

The worst outbreak involved the 15th Minnesota Volunteer Infantry Regiment. Called to service in July 1898, the Fifteenth Minnesota saw its first typhoid cases appear at the state mustering camp at Camp Ramsey, outside St. Paul. Initially labeled "ephemeral fever," medical officers changed their diagnosis to typhoid only after consulting with the St. Paul Department of Health. Afraid these cases were the first signs of a broader epidemic, the Department of Health sampled the company's water and ice supplies. Their analysis revealed no typhoid bacilli, but a follow-up analysis revealed the water cart used to fill company water barrels was contaminated. On August 9, orders were issued to boil all drinking water and ban all ice shipments to the camp. These instructions were generally disregarded, thanks to the summer heat. Realizing the futility of the earlier orders, the camp was connected to the city water mains. Even with filtered water, however, uninfected members of the Fifteenth Minnesota risked contracting the disease. Minneapolis and St. Paul drew their water directly from the Mississippi River, below the point where the Twin Cities' sewage entered the river. Even though typhoid was not epidemic at the time of the encampment, chief regimental surgeon Major William A Dennis reported "they have the disease there the whole year round."[89] By August, 602 men, nearly 50 percent of the regiment's full establishment of forty-six officers and 1,279 enlisted men, were stricken with "bowel afflictions." On August 21, 180 men were reported absent, confined to St. Paul hospital wards. The Fifteenth Minnesota left for Second Corps on August 23 with forty sick men still on their muster rolls, all dispatched to the First Division hospital after arriving at Camp Meade.[90]

The resurgence of typhoid cases among new regiments created a new crisis. The daily influx of new patients rapidly overcrowded the divisional hospitals. There was also the problem of yet another move for Second Corps, this time to a warmer Southern site in the early Fall. Fearful for the sick who could neither be moved nor left to recuperate in a temporary encampment, Girard assented to send sick men home on the civilian trains that began arriving at Camp Alger in late August. Soon afterward, Girard transferred all of the remaining typhoid cases to hospitals across central and eastern Pennsylvania.[91]

Soon after Second Corps arrived at the new site, medical officers scouted out Southern locations for winter quarters and oversaw the construction of pavilion hospitals at new sites in Augusta, Georgia, and Greenville, South Carolina. Tents, beds, and hospital supplies were sent ahead of Second Corps to Athens, Georgia, so a fully equipped and staffed hospital would be ready when Third Division arrived. By early November, the new sites were ready, and Second Corps entrained for the move, the Second Division arriving at Greenville on November 10, and the First Division reaching Augusta on November 19.[92]

SEVENTH CORPS IN MIAMI AND JACKSONVILLE, FLORIDA

Comprised of 31,000 men in three divisions, Seventh Corps initially encamped near Tampa, Florida, the port of embarkation for Cuba. In early May, it was divided and sent to summer training camps. First Division was dispatched to Miami, while Second and Third Divisions were moved to Camp Cuba Libre, near Jacksonville.[93] Again, no one considered the possibility of a typhoid epidemic. The Jacksonville encampment in particular was considered secure, as it was supplied with fresh water piped in from a thousand-foot deep artesian well. The selection committee overlooked the hundreds of small, ten to fifteen foot deep wells scattered throughout the surrounding poor neighborhoods. Smallpox was considered the greater threat, prompting wholesale vaccinations in early June. Though successful—only four cases appeared in Seventh Corps—the vaccination program was soon forgotten.[94]

The first cases of typhoid in Jacksonville appeared in early June, amidst the Second Division's 4th Virginia Infantry Regiment. Within ten days of arriving at Camp Cuba Libre on June 7, five men died of typhoid fever, indicating they brought the disease from Richmond. There, men from several companies drew water from an old well, soon identified as the source of a dysentery outbreak. By July 31, twenty-seven definite typhoid cases were reported, with another four probable cases observed. Many more cases of "long malaria" were reported—sixteen different cases between June 17 and July 31—as well as an additional eighty-three reports of diarrhea, dysentery, and other intestinal complaints. In all, 232 probable typhoid cases and 191 other intestinal disorders, with twenty-one typhoid fatalities, were reported in the 1,274 man strong regiment before it mustered out in December 1898. And even this total was incomplete. A later review of the Fourth Virginia determined dozens of men who reported sick on the regimental sick rolls did not appear on the divisional hospital reports.[95]

Following these first cases, several men from the 2nd Illinois Infantry Regiment fell ill. The Second Illinois outbreak was initially traced to a supply of allegedly tainted meat provided to Company F on May 29, 1898. After eating the meat, the entire company was stricken for nearly two weeks with violent diarrhea, vomiting, and other signs of food poisoning.

Immediately after this, the company reported twenty cases of typhoid. The regiment's remaining eleven companies initially were considered disease free, although closer review later revealed the Second Illinois was not quite as free of typhoid as earlier reports indicated. Between May 17 and May 29, seven men were admitted to the regimental hospital for typhoid-related conditions. Before the year's end, 344 cases of typhoid and typhoid-like malarial fevers were recorded, as well as another 316 intestinal disorders. Unwilling to dismiss the connection between the "tainted beef" and the disease outbreak in Company F, the Typhoid Board noted the illness already existed throughout the regiment, and its spread was due to other factors.[96]

The disposal of the Second Illinois' infected latrine waste provided the impetus for typhoid's spread within the camp proper. Like other regiments, Second Illinois utilized the tub system in its latrines. Human waste was collected in large half-barrel tubs, frequently made of old whisky barrels, and was emptied daily into wagons that hauled the ordure out of camp. "The contents of these tubs were rendered partially liquid by the admixture of urine," the official report described, "and there can be no doubt but that a considerable portion of their contents were splashed along the road and thus became intermingled with the dust."[97]

This accounted for the appearance of twenty cases of typhoid among two companies in the 1st Wisconsin Infantry Regiment in July. Companies C and H of the First Wisconsin were encamped astride one of the access roads used to haul goods into the camp and for removing the latrine tubs in the evening. Captain Leverett N. Persons, the commanding officer of Company C, described how this process affected his men:

> The disposal of fecal matter from the sinks was by hauling in tubs, filled to overflowing and constantly slopping and spilling along this (shell) road within 20 feet of our tents, and generally at mealtime. It was impossible to keep the dust out of our food, and the passing of these filthy and vile-smelling wagons while the men were eating was almost in itself cause enough for sickness, even had infectious germs been absent from the loath-some loads.[98]

Persons complained to the regimental commander, who permitted the company's tents to be moved on July 12, after the first cases appeared in his command. Soon, men in other companies became ill with typhoid, remittent fever, and various intestinal complaints. Accordingly, the dryness of the season, which produced a thick layer of dust along the road and all nearby surfaces, meant it was "very probable that the infection was conveyed by the dust while the men were resting or sleeping in their tents."[99]

Events were compounded by the situation in the Third Division. Located at Panama Park, four miles northeast of Jacksonville, the Third Division encampment was laid out similarly to the Second Division camp. Again, the water supply was considered safe, drawn from artesian wells and pumped into the camp from a treatment plant. An early culprit in the spread of typhoid there was the 2nd Mississippi Volunteer Infantry Regiment. When the Second Mississippi detrained in Jacksonville in early June, the regiment was already stricken with numerous cases. Within two weeks, forty men were sent to sick call, all afflicted with typhoid. To outside observers, the entire regiment was pre-disposed to typhoid. "When they came here they had the parchment, yellow-pumpkin complexion, and you could have identified a Mississippi man abroad on the streets of Jacksonville by his peculiar appearance," the Second Corps' chief surgeon, Lieutenant Colonel Louis Mervin Maus reported, "They came from the swamps of Mississippi; in fact, they called two or three companies of this regiment 'swamp heads from Natchez.'"[100]

As typhoid took hold in the Seventh Corps camps, Maus struggled to identify the epidemic's origins. Only a few state regiments brought the disease into camp. In the end, two primary channels of infection were identified. First was the complete disregard of basic hygiene among the volunteers. Several regimental kitchens, mess rooms, and latrines were tended by soldiers who, though sick, were ambulatory enough to be assigned light duties by their commanding officers. Throughout all of Seventh Corps, even such basic measures of cleanliness like washing hands after using the latrines were absent. Unlike Chickamauga and Falls Church, the Florida camps enjoyed better sanitation from the onset. In Miami, the First Division's latrines were piped directly into the city's sewer network. At Jacksonville, the Second Division used the aforementioned tub system. Twice daily, the camp's waste barrels were emptied and disinfected with carbolic acid or lime. In the evening, the day's waste was carted out to the city crematory. The Third Division relied upon the more traditional pit system, but here more attention was given to covering the day's accumulations with a layer of quicklime.[101]

This lack of personal hygiene was compounded by the prevalence of flies throughout the camps. According to individual accounts, flies were everywhere, traveling in swarms "back and forth from sinks to kitchens, and at times [they] fairly covered up the food, prepared and unprepared. As the tubs containing fecal matter were being carted away, they left a trail of flies through the camp, whose feet were no doubt fouled with feces."[102] Not until September 1 were orders issued to erect screens around company mess rooms and hospital tents and to place mosquito nets over every cot in the hospital wards. Under Maus' direction, tubs of carbon water, a byproduct of the city gas house, were used in the Second Brigade, Second Division hospital, where they proved effective in driving flies out of the area. No other hospital made use of this crude chemical repellent, however.[103]

In both camps, infected water was a problem. In Miami, the city water supply "had a disagreeable taste and odor," was colored by bits of decaying organic matter, and was lukewarm. Maus learned the water was drawn directly from the Everglades and from a local shallow well, and was contaminated with sewage and decaying vegetable matter. Despite orders, many soldiers preferred the cooler water from local wells. During drill and rifle training, many quenched their thirst from the shallow wells of nearby farmhouses, often located near outhouses and septic fields. Seeking to halt the disease's spread, commanders ordered the pump handles removed from the wells.[104]

Maus also found issue with the local vendors. In both Jacksonville and Miami, the roads leading into camp transformed overnight into a carnival-like avenue of food sellers, taverns, restaurants, and general stores. The quality of the food and drink left much to be desired, the sellers themselves allegedly perennial typhoid victims. In Jacksonville, milk sellers were especially suspect. Daily local dairies sent milk carts into the camp, where their goods were quickly snatched up by the soldiers. The sudden rise of typhoid incidents among the milk drinkers drew attention to the dairies' practices. Following an inspection of some dairies in the Jacksonville suburbs, Maus determined it was general practice to rinse the milk cans in water drawn from shallow six-foot deep wells near residential privies. Other dairies were found to dilute their milk with water from the same source. Despite these discoveries, the sale of milk continued.[105]

During his July inspection tour of the Miami camp, Maus expressed particular concern over local sutlers and their product. He wrote to Sternberg: "When not on duty the men were constantly drinking or eating between meals articles of this class, and as the lemonade, etc., were made and sold by the negro element, it is fair to suppose that the water used for its manufacture was taken from infected wells."[106] On July 26, 1898, Maus' concerns resulted in a General Order requiring division commanders to inspect all vendors near the camps, and restricting soldiers from doing business with those who failed the inspection. Similarly, "Peddlers and vendors of lemonade, pies, etc., will not be allowed to enter the regimental camps, the soft drinks furnished by them being in many instances stale and generally productive of sickness."[107]

Maus identified one last indicator for the disease in Seventh Corps: the immoral tendencies of the volunteer soldier. In particular, Maus felt alcohol use left the imbiber unable to resist disease in the tropical Floridian climate. According to Maus:

> The excitement incident to army life, together with absence of home environment and its influences, led many of the men to indulge freely in whisky, beer, and other concoctions who otherwise were of temperate habits. . . . On every hand peddlers and vendors of such wares were to be found. The saloons of Jacksonville did a thriving business during the presence of the Seventh Army Corps, and at the expense of the men's health. The use of alcohol in the tropics is of itself a sufficient cause for gastric and hepatic derangement to the unacclimated, without taking

into consideration the disturbances liable to result from camp cooking and the irregular eating, so common among the volunteer troops, who have but recently been called out.[108]

Maus' cautions against alcohol usage were not really relevant; a few regiments in Jacksonville or Miami maintained a canteen that sold light beer, to no ill effect. Indeed, in the Typhoid Board's final investigative report, no link was made between alcohol use and typhoid, save to point out previous beliefs that sudden or dramatic dietary changes induced typhoid were "founded upon false conclusions arising from erroneous conceptions of the etiology of the disease."[109]

REACTION TO THE TRAINING CAMPS EPIDEMICS

The Volunteer camp epidemics were the paramount crisis of the Spanish-American War for the McKinley Administration. The spectacle of rampant disease in the encampments cast a dim shadow over the unexpectedly easy triumphs in the Caribbean and the Philippines. The reality of the War Department's poor preparation was matched by rumors of inefficiency, incompetence, and profiteering at all levels. As reports leaked home, civilian fears for the lives of their sons and husbands began to mount.

Newspapers fed the hysteria as reporters detailed the horrific progress of the camp epidemics. Accounts of "pest-holes," often including the names of the latest fever victims, inflamed and outraged anxious people at home, while grisly stories of depraved medical incompetence fueled their fears. On August 30, 1898, *The Atlanta Constitution* published an interview with Captain Samuel S. O'Connor, 9th New York Volunteer Infantry, describing how he discovered the dissected corpse of one of his sick soldiers in the Second Division hospital. According to O'Connor, the soldier fell sick on Monday the 20th, and died five days later. The fate of the unfortunate volunteer was only revealed when O'Connor went to the hospital to visit his charge. There he found the private, naked on a cot, his abdomen laid open and vivisectioned. Asked his opinion on the hospitals, O'Connor concluded, "the division hospitals are rotten—utterly rotten in every way. I would never expect to see a sick man of mine alive again if he were sent to one of those horrible places."[110] Such accounts were eagerly consumed by readers.

An angry public searched for a scapegoat to blame for the disaster. Not surprisingly, Surgeon General Sternberg and the regular medical officers of the Army Medical Department were early candidates for the public's wrath. Many volunteer officers vilified the Medical Department's decisions to consolidate regimental hospitals and supplies into larger division and corps organizations under its immediate supervision. One medical officer attached to the Second Division Hospital at Chickamauga expressed disdain for the regular establishment in a story printed in *The New York Herald* detailing the horrors at Camp Thomas. Every sort of callous indifference was exhibited by the medical staff to the patients there, he recalled, describing how sick soldiers were left sprawling on the ground underneath canvas hospital tents, the essential medicines and supplies either in short supply or non-existent, having been sent to the newly established Sternberg General Hospital.[111]

The most vicious attacks against the Medical Department were launched by the "yellow press" houses—specifically the Pulitzer- and Hearst-owned news organizations. Both papers devoted extensive editorial and news column space to the mismanagement of the Medical Department by Surgeon General Sternberg. The Hearst organization focused on the Surgeon General's role in approving the poorly designed camp sites. On September 2, 1898, The New York Herald printed an editorial on the selection of Camp Wikoff. The editor continued, "If the Surgeon General is equally responsible for the selection of other camp sites and is equally accountable for their sanitary regulation he will be kept busy for a long time to come in making exonerating explanations before the public will be inclined to shift the blame on other shoulders."[112]

The Chicago Daily Tribune was even more strident. The low point came on September 2, 1898, after the paper printed the names of 1,299 soldiers who died in the training camps. Under the headline "Harvest of Death in Camps," the *Daily Tribune* not only disputed the official investigative report of Camp Thomas, it also accused the War Department of covering-up the truth. According to the news story, the official tally of 198 dead at Camp Thomas through August 22 was off the mark by over 150 men. Claiming the camp's hospitals kept no mortality records, the *Daily Tribune* also noted regular and volunteer officers kept reporters from seeing existing records.[113] The next day produced a call for Sternberg's removal. Calling his wish to defer formal investigation of the Medical Department until the end of the crisis an example of "the trite and ancient dodge of every incompetent who wishes to stave off an investigation," the *Daily Tribune* called his excuse "all rot. ... Imbecility never changes for the better, and it is always on hand with its feeble excuses, dodges, and deceptions, concealing the truth. Dr. Sternberg's answer to his critics is an insult and should be considered paramount to an admission of his own conscious incompetency."[114]

Other newspapers tried to defend Sternberg and his department. *The New York Daily Tribune* championed his offer to hold an open investigation and the conduct of the Medical Department as evidence of his own selfless devotion to duty and service at the expense of his own reputation.[115] The paper blamed the volunteer militia. "Typhoid fever is one of the most unnecessary of diseases," the editor wrote on September 7, 1898, stating that the outbreak was a hallmark of ignorance and carelessness, and not caused by some external environmental cause.[116] Yet calls for restraint and careful investigation were lost amidst the drumbeat of charges and counter-charges in the sensational dailies.

In their quest to defend Alger and President McKinley, Republican papers like the *Philadelphia Inquirer* followed the lead of the Hearst and Pulitzer presses in attacking the Medical Department. "Secretary Alger's War Department has given a magnificent account of itself;" read an August 25, 1898, *Philadelphia Inquirer* editorial. "Now let it turn its attention to the hospital service and bring order out of chaos. The sick must be cared for, and there is no excuse for a medical department when, with unlimited money at its command, it fails to grasp the situation in a peaceful camp with all the resources of the world at its very doors."[117]

Editorial cartoonists were no less caustic. Two motifs soon emerged. First, Secretary Alger and the War Department—including Surgeon General Sternberg and his medical officers—were cast as incompetent bureaucrats and sycophants. A cartoon from *The New York World* reprinted in the August 31, 1898 *Atlanta Constitution*, showed a chorus line of department heads, from Secretary Alger to Surgeon General Sternberg, Subsistence Department Chief Brigadier General Charles P. Eagen, and Quartermaster Department Head Brigadier General Marshall I. Lodington, all pointing fingers at each other, echoing the same refrain: "It's His Fault!"[118] Other newspapers drew both Alger and Sternberg in a harsh light. *The New York Herald* transformed Secretary Alger into a bumbling fool, sheltering under an umbrella held by President McKinley against the storm of public indignation, pondering a straw-filled effigy of himself in response to the direction to "investigate himself."[119] *The Chicago Daily Tribune* portrayed Alger as a modern-day Nebuchadnezzar, interrupted in his banquet of glory and victory with cronies Sternberg, Eagen, and Lodington by Illinois State Surgeon General Nicholas Senn, who points toward Camp Wikoff as proof of "the Handwriting on the Wall."[120] Perhaps the most vicious attack on Secretary Alger and the War Department's purported hidebound bureaucracy appeared in the September 10, 1898 *New York Herald*. A haggard Uncle Sam sits wearily, caught between the rising sun of Bryanism and the foul stench of incompetency emanating from a pile of moldering skulls. Labeled "Algerism," the miasma is crowned with the beady-eyed and disheveled head of the Secretary of War, as the caption reads: "Are there not some things worse than the bad dollar?"[121]

The second theme running through editorial cartoons focused upon the suffering of the common soldier. The *Minneapolis Journal* portrayed the sick volunteer as a pathetic, gaunt shell of a man, no better than the starved prospectors returning from the Klondike gold fields.[122] Another cartoon from *The New York Herald* showed an injured, bedraggled soldier greeted by a foppish Secretary Alger. In response to Alger's question, "Say, haven't I been a good war secretary," the soldier is shown knocking over the Secretary, screaming "No! No! No!"[123] The *Chicago Daily Tribune* printed a facsimile of a recent feature at the Paris Salon, showing a moribund soldier lying in the tropic sands, the sphinx-like figure of "Fever" sitting over him, claws clutching the victim's breast.[124] One of the most bitter cartoons responded to allegations that several Army physicians were practicing veterinarians. Appearing in *The New York Herald*, the cartoon illustrated a horse-headed medical officer, "Appointed for the war," with his veterinary school diploma sticking out of his back pocket, administering to an emaciated dying soldier in a camp hospital. Surrounded by various patent medicines, including a bottle marked "Spavin Cure," a box of "Condition Powders" to be used "For Blind Staggers," and another box labeled "Sure Thing for Heaves," the dying patient and the (in this case literal) horse doctor sit beneath a crude picture of Secretary Alger, "The Soldier's Friend."[125] More than the angry tone of the stories and editorials appearing in all papers, these editorial cartoons clearly marked the growing public outrage over the training camps.

Yet the first official response to the public outcry over the camp crisis came from Secretary Alger, when he asked the President to establish a board to investigate allegations of War Department incompetence and graft. An executive commission of twelve men, chaired by Grenville M. Dodge, retired Major General of Volunteers, Iowa Republican congressman, and railroad entrepreneur, was convened on September 24, 1898. The board, soon known as the "Dodge Commission," set to work immediately, visiting all existing Corps encampments and general hospitals and collecting testimony from some 495 witnesses, from the Secretary of War and Commanding General to privates and contract civilian employees. On February 9, 1899, the Commission issued its final report absolving Secretary Alger and the War Department of any deliberate wrongdoing or intentional neglect. The Army was not found completely blameless. The current system of an autonomous commanding general sharing control with the Secretary of War was faulted as an obstruction to the Army's efficient operation and the principle of executive civilian control. In a direct affront to Major General Miles, the Dodge Commission recommended abolishing the position of Commanding General, returning full civilian control of the Army to the Secretary of War by transforming the Army's uniformed head into an advisory general in chief.[126]

Criticism of the Army's performance was not restricted to its commanding general. According to the report, the typhoid outbreaks resulted equally from poor planning, accident, and indolence. Contrary to the claims of individual state boosters, typhoid was brought into the training camps by infected volunteers. Once there, the poor design of the camps—particularly with regard to the placing of latrines and sinks and the lack of wood flooring for tents—created a perfect environment for an epidemic.[127] The decision to disband the regimental hospitals in favor of larger brigade and divisional infirmaries was also cited as a factor. In the absence of a localized treatment capacity, most cases instead chose to "tough it out" rather than seek assistance, ultimately with deadly consequence.

Regarding the Volunteer Army, the board recommended future state and militia regiments be commanded by either active or retired regular officers. Schools of instruction were also proposed, so new volunteer officers could learn the basics of military protocol and procedure as well. The Quartermaster's Department came in for special censure, as it was considered "neither physically nor financially prepared for the tremendous labor of suddenly equipping and transporting an army over ten times the size of the Regular Army of the United States." Despite the efforts of individual officers and enlisted personnel in the Army's supply depots, the Quartermaster's Department was held responsible for the failure to move essential supplies to the field and training camps as the typhoid epidemic spread. The Dodge Commission recommended establishing a separate transportation branch, thus relieving the Quartermaster's Department of the burden of managing supplies and seeing them distributed to the field.[128]

The commission's report was kinder to the Medical Department. Many problems were deemed systemic of the Army's traditional ambiguity toward the branch. Attention was called toward the Medical Department's chronic peacetime understaffing and underfunding. Regular medical officers were acclaimed as "faithful, earnest workers, and to their unresisting efforts to properly and skillfully care for the sick and wounded, often in the midst of adverse conditions, is in large measure due the unusually low mortality rate indicated in the returns." By comparison, the volunteer medical officer was a poor substitute. "It is to be regretted that due provision by law was not made for the commissioning of surgeons and assistant surgeons, U.S. Volunteers, on the general staff of the army as are the medical officers of the regular establishment. There would have been thus obtained competent men in full number and the best interests of the sick beyond question served." Here especially the commission called for schools of instruction, as civilian physicians appointed as regimental surgeons were particularly uninformed of the nuances of military culture and protocol. [129]

In all other matters, the Medical Department was absolved of wrongdoing. The chronic shortages of medical supplies and equipment were the Quartermaster Department's fault. The typhoid outbreaks were blamed on the poor discipline and ignorance of the enlisted volunteers and their officers, including obstinate regimental surgeons. The commission recommended the Medical Department be immediately expanded and given full control over managing and transporting a full year's supply of supplies and equipment for a field army four times the size of the peacetime cadre. It also recommended maintaining a reserve corps of volunteer nurses and orderlies and reducing the department's administrative paperwork, thereby freeing medical officers to attend to their patients and other medical affairs. Finally, the commission called upon the president to introduce legislation giving medical officers in charge of hospitals, transports, and other medical commands full control over Subsistence Department funds for the purpose of purchasing food for the sick. Though the Dodge Commission's overall findings were intended to satisfy the public's desire for fixing blame for the epidemic, its recommendations for expanding the fiat of the Medical Department were taken to heart by Surgeon General Sternberg and his subordinates, and would play a major part in determining the course of reform over the next two decades.[130]

Sternberg anticipated his critics by ordering an internal scientific inquiry into the epidemic. On August 18, 1898, he summoned three medical officers—regular Major Walter Reed and two volunteer medical officers, Majors Victor C. Vaughan and Edward O. Shakespeare, each noted bacteriologists—and assigned them the task of visiting the camps, reviewing the sick reports of each regiment, and identifying the origins and course of the epidemic. Between August 20 and September 30, the three inspected the major volunteer encampments, as well as Camp Wikoff, the Fifth Corps' quarantine encampment on Montauk Point. They also visited the Medical Department's two general hospitals at Fort Monroe, Virginia, and Fort McPherson, Georgia, where the most serious cases were sent from Camps Alger and Thomas. The committee visit left no detail unexamined: personal hygiene; water supplies; camp topography; the disposition and placement of tents and outbuildings; the layout and maintenance of kitchens; food storage and preparation; the placement of sinks and latrines vis-à-vis kitchens; and the disposal of human and kitchen wastes were all reviewed. The board followed the Surgeon General's example and ordered all hospital patients undergo Widal tests and microscopic blood examinations to determine the true nature of their disease. After their inspection tour, they examined the monthly regimental sick reports of the 92 regiments—a total of 107,793 men—who never left the United States. Where possible, the committee followed the history of each infected enlisted man and officer diagnosed with mild diarrhea to determine if he exhibited future immunity to typhoid fever—a sure indicator of a misdiagnosed infection.[131]

The Typhoid Board Report was a landmark study in disease etiology. The report consisted of two volumes: the first incorporating the board's reports and findings, the second containing graphs and tables charting the data collected on each regiment. For the first time, typhoid fever was revealed as an infectious contagious disease in its own right, not merely a form of malarial fever. Specificity transformed how the disease was perceived and treated. Most noteworthy was the conclusion that typhoid was also transmitted by direct and indirect human contact, not merely via environmental factors such as infected water or miasmatic influences. Likewise, the report offered the first conclusive links between typhoid and an insect vector. Houseflies were now recognized as transmitters of disease. The findings of the Typhoid Board launched a thousand "swat the fly" campaigns across the nation, and invigorated the nascent insecticide industry. It also introduced a Medical Department obsession with latrine design that lasted through the First World War. The report also broke down many of the behavioral assumptions related to disease in general. Contrary to the assumptions held by the three board members and their assistants, typhoid did not just affect those with physical predispositions to illness. Typhoid struck the robust and healthy young male just as readily as the slight-framed neurasthenic. Indeed, the report indicated those very types presumed more susceptible to disease had a better chance of surviving the illness or only suffering a minor form of infection than stronger and younger volunteers. They were exposed to typhoid at some point before joining the militia, and were thus less likely to experience the full ravages of the disease in the camps. The most remarkable facet of the Typhoid Board Report is its reflection of the scientific model championed by Surgeon General Sternberg. It attests to the relatively advanced state of medical practice and science among the regular officers in the Medical Department, the young contract surgeons hired by Surgeon General Sternberg, and the well-informed science-oriented physicians of the National Guard.[132]

The final report contained fifty-seven chief findings. According to the report, typhoid fever existed in every single regiment in the Regular and Volunteer Army assembled in the Eastern United States, including the expeditionary force sent to Cuba. Moreover, typhoid appeared in over 90 percent of the volunteer regiments within eight weeks of their arrival at one of the assembling camps. This was no surprise to the Board; typhoid fever was so widespread throughout the country, it was inevitable some would arrive at the encampments already sick. Similarly, the Board pointed out that since typhoid was a classic "camp disease," it was more concerned with the failure of the camps' medical officers to recognize the disease in its early stages and the rapidity of its spread.[133]

From the beginning, many soldiers afflicted with typhoid were misdiagnosed with malaria or some other "remittent fever." According to the Typhoid Board, Volunteer and Regular Army surgeons diagnosed approximately 50 percent of the real and probable cases—10,428 men—with typhoid from the start. In all cases, diagnosis was facilitated by the seriousness of the affliction—it was easy to identify typhoid if the patient presented the classic later symptoms. In cases where the symptoms were not violent or were short-lived, malaria became the diagnosis of choice. Many physicians still clung to the nosology of a single "typho-malarial fever" developed during the Civil War by Brevet Major Joseph Janvier Woodward. Such a classification, based upon the visual identification of symptoms and post-mortem intestinal examinations, failed to account for the presence of two distinct biologic agents. Nevertheless, it remained popular among physicians unskilled in the methods of microbiology. Likewise, the 1890s marked the boundaries of a great knowledge shift in therapeutic and diagnostic practice. Many physicians continued to associate health and illness with external factors—including miasmatic and pythogenic theories—and their diagnostic acumen was influenced accordingly. For several physicians, for example, it was inconceivable their regiments were afflicted with typhoid fever. After all, they reasoned, typhoid was a miasmatic condition.

The encampment of soldiers in relatively dry, open fields was not at all conducive to a miasmatic disease. It was more likely that the reported illnesses were "camp diarrheas" and other spontaneous pythogenic ailments common to military life.[134]

Such conclusions, the Typhoid Board concluded, were bunk. The overwhelming evidence—physical examinations, the monthly sick reports, medical officer reports, and the daily observation of camp life—pointed toward a specific disease origin. Likewise, Widal tests and follow-up histories of cases with miscellaneous diarrheas and intestinal complaints showed typhoid fever was more widespread than believed.

Miasmas and internal combustion were not the only factors linked with the disease. Many sought to identify typhoid as a preexisting environmental condition native to the camp areas. Others claimed the disease was nothing more than a tragic part of the acclimatization process—as Northern volunteers entered an unfamiliar environment, their bodies were more susceptible to intestinal complaints. The individual's response was a mark of another, hidden factor, be it the manifestation of a hitherto secret physical condition, or the result of squandering one's moral vitae in the pursuit of a dissipative lifestyle. The members of the Typhoid Board immediately rejected these theories as baseless. Accordingly, the Board presented a multi-faceted explanation for the spread of typhoid fever in the camps. Given the nature of the encampments, with the gathering of thousands of young men from across the country, typhoid was inevitable, regardless of the sanitary precautions undertaken. Since typhoid fever was by nature gastrointestinal, obviously the disease spread through the transfer of infected fecal matter. The actual mode of transmission, however, differed from case to case, confirming the theory of disease specificity. Likewise, the progress of the disease and the nature of its rapid and simultaneous spread indicated the importance of collective public sanitation. When the system of waste disposal broke down, the disease accelerated to epidemic proportions. At this point, several environmental factors came into play. Flies in particular acted as a living vector of the disease, transmitting the typhoid bacillus wherever they lighted. When the summer rains flooded the shallow sinks and latrines, the polluted waters contaminated all surfaces it came into contact with.[135]

These factors were outside the range of human control; the ability to take measures to reduce them or lessen their impact was not. And the Typhoid Board was most critical of human indifference and ignorance. "Camp pollution was the greatest sin committed by the troops in 1898," the report concluded, noting there was no legitimate reason for this to have occurred. [136] Frequently, the advice of the medical experts regarding camp locations was ignored by superior line officers. In its summary of the failings of the line establishment, the report continued, "it appears to us, that line officers were to some extent responsible for the condition of the camps under their command. The medical officer can only recommend; the line officer can command."[137] The message could not be clearer for those aware of the Medical Department's struggle for legitimate authority; incorporating volunteer elements into the Army jeopardized the progress made by the regular establishment over the last eight years.

The Typhoid Board made several recommendations to prevent future embarrassments. Some dealt with the application of sanitary and hygienic methods: including waste disposal; the disinfection of water for bathing, cooking, and drinking; the enforcement of personal sanitation among the enlisted members of a command; the regular relocation of campsites; and that the sanitary policing of a campsite. The most significant conclusions, however, dealt with the medical officer's legitimacy and the responsibility of the line officer for the good health and well-being of his command. Line officers had to be better informed in military hygiene. More importantly, the entire relationship between line and medical officers needed to be reexamined. "In our opinion," the report stated, "it is of the greatest importance that more authority be granted medical officers in all matters pertaining to the hygiene of camps."[138]

The Typhoid Board's findings were hailed by Sternberg and civilian public health advocates. The Surgeon General's fears about the general failings of the volunteer and militia establishment were validated. Critics who blamed the epidemic on perceived inefficiencies and failures in the Medical Department could be dismissed out of hand. The general ignorance of both volunteer line and medical officers with regard to sanitation and hygiene sealed the fate of the victims of the epidemic more than any other factor, Sternberg noted. No matter how learned and experienced a medical officer may be with regard to sanitary science, his advice would be for naught if the legitimate authority did not heed their recommendations. Even in the civilian sphere, sanitary experts were consistently ignored or misused by politicians and legislators. "Perhaps it was too much to expect that typhoid fever should be excluded from our camps," Sternberg noted, "unprovided with sewers and occupied by new levies of troops, having for the most part inexperienced officers both of the line and in the staff departments."[139]

A second outcome of the camp epidemics and the resulting inquiries further cemented the Medical Department's reputation as an organization of expert modernity. The experience of rampant disease in an increasingly modernizing society was a tremendous embarrassment to the American public. After the initial outrage over the epidemics faded, participants and observers alike reassessed the debacle. The result was a new appreciation of public health and sanitation. Even at the height of public outrage over the camp crisis, detached observers noted the greatest challenge of the affair was whether or not the volunteer soldier would remember the degradation of rampant disease and consider how to avoid it. Americans across the country became more open to the ideas of community hygiene in the wake of 1898. The idea that such squalor and degradation as seen in the training camp not only could, but *did* happen here opened the eyes of many of those Americans who remained skeptical of the deadly power of microbes and their insect carriers. The Spanish-American War did not transform American attitudes toward public health, but it provided evidence of the hazards in denying that public health required public vigilance.

At the same time, a new hero emerged from the experience: the regular medical officer and sanitarian. Just as the erratic performance of the volunteer soldier in the short war with Spain reinforced the need for expert leadership and guidance in modern war, so too did the training assert that citizen-soldiers faced danger in many different guises:

> The most formidable enemy an army ever has to face is disease, and the fitness of an army to meet another army depends upon the care of its physical condition. Battles are fought in mess-kettles. Soldiers are made ready for battle by the brains and consciences of their quartermaster and medical departments. Surgeons, nurses, cooks and commissaries must be as great as drill-masters, colonels and generals or the battle is lost.[140]

By January 25, 1899, the three medical officers investigating the camps were prepared to make their preliminary report to Surgeon General Sternberg. The typhoid epidemic, they concluded, was "incontestably due to the natural but faulty operation of some of the provisions of the present laws and customs regulating the sanitary service of the army."[141] Immediate action was warranted to enforce full compliance with future sanitary regulations, the report continued, lest similar epidemics exhaust the Army in its future actions in similar situations and climates while conducting its new mission of colonial administration.[142] Such defense necessitated expanding the regular medical establishment, increasing sanitary training, and providing the "proper *material and mechanical* means of prevention."[143] The preliminary report called for nothing less than redirecting the energies and mission of the Army Medical Department, with military sanitation taking over as the chief responsibility of the medical officer:

> The *conservation* of the full fighting strength of the army is the economic basis—the fundamental principle—upon which the sanitary and medical service should be organized. . . . To provide and properly equip and supply hospitals and to adequately man them—or to make the most ample provision for the care of disease—is at best but a slipshod means of conserving the fighting strength of an army. That most important end is to be secured most certainly, most promptly and most economically through *the prevention of disease*. . . . To keep the soldier out of the hospital is incomparably the greatest, most economical and most humanitarian service which the medical corps of the army can possibly render the country.[144]

The elevation of sanitation and preventive medicine bore the unmistakable stamp of Surgeon General Sternberg. He used the preliminary report's findings to validate his defense of the regular Medical Department. What mattered most was the presence of a clear benchmark of failure and disaster. Before the camp crisis, predictions of the anticipated costs of indifference were only hypothetical worst-case scenarios. The epidemics provided exactly the sort of distressing event needed to promote increasing the Medical Department's legitimacy and power.

For this reason, the January 25, 1899, preliminary report is more influential than previously suspected. Without laying out specific findings, the report carried the immediate recommendations for reform that would be used over the next two decades. Trends that had directed modernization—the pursuit of legitimacy and rank; the rise of laboratory science and scientific practice; the ongoing move toward specialization—all came together at this point to determine the Medical Department's direction until the First World War. By claiming disease prevention was a paramount strategic issue affecting national defense, the Typhoid Board's preliminary report provided the manual by which Surgeon General Sternberg and his successors would keep the Medical Department in the forefront of Army-wide reform.

Following Sternberg's direction, Major Reed laid out four recommendations for improvement: increasing the number of medical officers; redirecting their functions to focus on sanitation; incorporating a rigorous training course emphasizing military hygiene; and giving greater weight to their recommendations with higher rank and more authority over the line and staff establishment with regard to sanitary affairs.[145] Since the number of medical officers was insufficient for safeguarding the peacetime army in domestic posts, it would be more difficult to provide adequate care for a larger force deployed across the globe. While unwilling to project an actual number, Reed advised there was an "absolute necessity for a material increase of the numbers of the medical corps relative to the numbers of enlisted men."[146] Considering the growing importance of sanitation, reordering the practice and scientific priorities of the Army physician was essential. Whereas hygiene and epidemiology were previously considered a tertiary concern of the medical officer, behind administration and medical practice and surgery, it was time to reconsider this hierarchy of knowledge. Transforming the medical officer from a general practitioner into a sanitarian required a new focus on sanitary education. Hitherto relegated to a secondary place in the curriculum of medical schools across the nation, hygiene and sanitation would now be elevated in priority. This would be undertaken in the same way the Army Medical Department "saved" regular medicine decades earlier—under the aegis of the Army Examination Board. If new candidates were required to demonstrate expertise in hygiene as part of their qualifying examination, the nation's medical schools would in turn follow the Army's lead by increasing their own course offerings to ensure their graduates were not excluded from access to this prestigious career path. Furthermore, hygiene would become a major component of the five year exam, ensuring that young military officers did not neglect the study or practice of military sanitation.[147]

Major Reed recognized it was neither practical nor desirable to transform the Medical Department into a Sanitary Department. What he sought in his recommendations was the creation of what he described as "'a strong sanitary arch.'" The walls of the arch would be the well-informed and trained regimental surgeons, all with a demonstrated expertise in military hygiene. The keystone holding the arch together, however, was a permanent cadre of specially trained sanitary inspectors. Charged with safeguarding the health of the Army, these sanitary officers would serve as "the keen eyes by which the vision, not only of the chief surgeon on the staff of corps, division, and brigade commanders,—but also that of the surgeon general of the army—may be able to penetrate clearly at any and all times into the hidden recesses where the germs of disease are most likely to flourish and menace the health of the troops."[148] Here was the call for further specialization anticipated since the Army Medical School was opened. A clear delineation of responsibility and specialization appeared, with sanitarians, laboratory-oriented microbiologists, and general practitioners and surgeons each claiming autonomy and legitimacy. The shakeout of a hierarchy of privilege and power among these three specializations within the Medical Department would follow.

The lessons of the fever camps extended to the civilian sphere as well. Much of the remaining skepticism regarding the germ theory of disease causation was swept away in the aftermath of the camp epidemics. The public inquiries of the Medical Department's typhoid investigative board and the Dodge Commission, well reported in newspapers, brought the new science of microbiology into the parlors of middle-class America. The chief result of these inquests was to bring home the signal importance of personal hygiene and public health as bulwarks against disease. Disease was suddenly recognized as a preventable condition. Tell Arminius Turner realized as much in his account of the 15th Minnesota Volunteer Infantry Regiment:

> The question of army sanitation has never before engaged public attention as during the last war, and the secret of this popular interest is out. It lies in the conviction that somebody is accountable for the larger part of the sickness. It is no longer a visitation of providence; it is a visitation of ignorance or indifference. It will no longer suffice to tell the public that disease and death are the fortunes of war and must be accepted as a natural consequence. The public has learned better and proposes to hold someone besides providence responsible for the havoc and death wrought by epidemics.[149]

This was nothing new—American public health reformers had championed active hygienic intervention since the 1840s. However the combination of a well-documented epidemic among healthy males from across the nation and the field-tested conclusions of expert microbiologists, under the Surgeon General's direction made the difference.

Figure 1 Colonel John Rensselaer Van Hoff, Assistant Surgeon General, U.S. Army Medical Department, 1906.
Source: U.S. Army Heritage and Education Center, RG112S-MM.154.

Figure 2 Regimental Tent Hospital, Camp George H. Thomas, Chickamauga, Georgia, Summer 1898.
Source: National Archives II, College Park, Maryland, RG 165, U.S. Army Signal Corps Photograph 83833.

Figure 3 Chow line for dinner at Camp Thomas, Summer 1898.
Source: National Archives II, College Park, Maryland, RG 165, U.S. Army Signal Corps Photograph 85584.

Figure 4 Midday scene at Camp Cuba Libre, Jacksonville, Florida, Summer 1898.
Source: National Archives II, College Park, Maryland, RG 165, U.S. Army Signal Corps Photograph 84826.

Figure 5 "Scene at Big Springs—three miles from Camp Alger, VA." July 12, 1898.
Source: National Archives II, College Park, Maryland, RG 165-SW-5A-6.

Figure 6 Interment ceremony, Arlington Cemetery, Virginia, September 1898.
Source: National Archives II, College Park, Maryland, RG 165, U.S. Army Signal Corps Photograph 84902.

DR. SENN READS THE HANDWRITING ON THE WALL.

Figure 7 "Dr. Senn reads the handwriting on the wall." Illinois National Guard Surgeon GeneralNicholas Senn cast in the role of Daniel, warning of imminent disaster at Camp Wikoff to a disbelieving cast of War Department and Army staff heads dining on the glories of victory. Secretary of War Russell Alger is in the foreground; the three other seated figures, from left to right, are: Surgeon General George Miller Sternberg; Commissary General Charles Eagen;and Quartermaster General Marshal Ludington. In his hand, Senn clutches his letters warningof conditions at Camp Thomas in Chickamauga.

Source: Chicago Daily Tribune, September 1, 1898.

ALGER.—"SAY, HAVEN'T I BEEN A GOOD WAR SECRETARY?"

Figure 8 "Say, haven't I been a good war secretary?" Secretary of War Russell Alger greeting and rebuffed by an injured and emaciated veteran.
Source: New York Herald, September 22, 1898.

APPOINTED FOR THE WAR

Figure 9 "Appointed for the War, (special attention given to dogs)." A caustic commentary on the conditions in volunteer training camps in the United States. The horse-headed physician is a response to news that some volunteer medical officers alsopracticed veterinary medicine.
Source: New York Herald, September 23, 1898.

Figure 10 "The wanderer's return." A fanciful meeting between a Yukon prospector (Joe Klon Dike) and a volunteer soldier (Will Volunteer).
Source: Minneapolis Journal, September 5, 1898.

Figure 11   Colonel Louis Mervin Maus with Moro tribesmen on Jolo, Philippines, 1903.

Source: U.S. Army Heritage and Education Center, RG 92S-1.6.

Figure 12   Colonel Louis Mervin Maus, 1905.

Source: U.S. Army Heritage and Education Center, RG 92S-1.119.

JUST OUTSIDE THE GATE

Figure 13   The wages of a night on the town, in the "Good-Fellow's Grotto."
Source: "Just Outside the Gate," *Uncle Sam's Magazine.* XV:3 (July, 1909), 65.

AND UNCLE SAM PERMITS IT!

"Along the military reservation it was the custom of three or four miserable saloons to establish themselves, expressly and exclusively for the purpose of furnishing liquor to the soldiers—liquor of the worst kind—and not only furnishing liquor, but furnishing everything that makes for iniquity."—*Archbishop Ireland.*

Figure 14 Columns of soldiers, descending into a vale of iniquity, prey to the liquor interest "monster."

Source: "And Uncle Sam Permits It!" *Uncle Sam's Magazine.* XV:3 (July, 1909), 73.

Glass Point-Loaded.

TO PREVENT DISEASE

Always urinate at once after withdrawing at end of connection. Pull cotton out of glass tube. Shake out tablets and capsule.

1.   TO GUARD AGAINST CLAP

Hold glass tube in right hand, point downward and on thumb; fill nearly full with water (hot or cold) and drop in one tablet. Place second finger over top and shake until tablet is dissolved; holding the penis in left hand, end slightly open, pointing downward, place point of glass tube into penis, the thumb being removed; holding tube in 3 fingers bring tube and penis up and removing second finger from top of tube the fluid will run into the penis; hold so a moment.

2.   TO GUARD AGAINST SYPHILIS AND SORES

Pull apart capsule pressing out contents and rub in gently but thoroughly over entire penis, especially over head.

Wrapper used on "Packet."

Appearance of Packet when issued.

Figure 15   The multi-purpose "K-Packet".

Source: William Lyster, "Venereal Prophylaxis in the Army—The Necessity of Cooperation with Line Officers," Military Surgeon. 29:1 (July, 1911), 67–72, 68.

4 Making the Tropics Fit for White Men
Army Public Health in the American Imperial Periphery, 1898–1914

The war with Spain signaled the United States' arrival on the imperial stage. Army medical officers were soon engaged as the primary agents of American imperial administration. As others struggled with the subtle nuances of the imperialist game, the Medical Department took on the immediate task of reconciling an alien indigenous people with their new overseers. Thanks to their rising status as experts in identifying the disparate causes of disease, the Army's medical personnel were America's primary contact with its new imperial subjects. Were Americans to reside in a potentially hostile environment, interacting with a distinctly different people who might carry dangerous diseases, then it was the Army Medical Department's job to clear the way.

In the process, these medical officers validated a worldview based upon racial superiority and nationalist chauvinism. The resulting verification of the Anglo-Saxon social order and the apparent triumph of American civil administration held a greater message than changing the standard of living. Combined with their sensitivity over status and renewed legitimacy as guardians of the Army's health after the fever camps, the Medical Department's new role as *de facto* imperial proconsuls of health and wellness established the institution as one of the Army's most visible branches.

Tropical service also put American servicemen and female nurses into closer contact with new cultures and ethnicities. Experiences in the Philippines, Cuba, Puerto Rico, and, after November 18, 1903, the Panama Canal Zone, followed different courses. Many viewed their imperial service as a civic evangelical mission, bringing the material benefits of American medicine to a benighted population. Their work, intended to palliate the tremendous suffering afflicting so many of the Republic's new charges, was partly intended to bring the fruits of American scientific progress to bear on populations considered biologically and socially inferior. American civic and scientific know-how would provide the inhabitants of these tropic locales the basic requirements—health, education, and sanitation—necessary for political and commercial development. Public health measures and new infrastructures—especially road networks—were essential for the proper commercial development of these tropical lands.[1]

Public charity and rudimentary civic development were not the sole motivators of Army physicians abroad. Public health activities were also undertaken with an institutionally focused motive: American soldiers living in primitive sanitary conditions risked contracting debilitating diseases, threatening the delicate balance of imperial control. Medical officers were critical members of the imperial system, acting as defenders of political order. Some viewed their service abroad as a life-altering experience, their encounters with Filipinos, Puerto Ricans, Cubans, Panamanians, and others expanding their own awareness of human diversity. This minority of medical officers took time to learn the languages, customs, and cultures of the people they served. They learned to accept them, if not as equals, then as a people deserving of more respect than American racial ideology offered.

For the most part, however, American medical officers saw their role as concerned yet detached observers. Educated in the "new" methods of microbiology, sanitation, and tropical medicine, Army medical officers also saw their service abroad as an opportunity to test their knowledge in a venue relatively free from civil interference. In the imperial periphery, Army medical officers not only had greater liberty to act, they were often the sole actors responsible for the health of an entire district.

Tropical service immediately challenged the foundation of the medical officers' professional knowledge. Americans soon discovered the rules governing disease in the United States no longer applied. Common diseases in the tropics, including smallpox, tuberculosis, malaria, and typhoid fever, were hardly recognizable. Major Azel Ames, a brigade surgeon in the U.S. Volunteers who served in Puerto Rico with I Corps, described the puzzlement he and his peers shared in dealing with smallpox on the island:

> For the first time in the cognizance of American sanitary officers, the spectacle was presented of the non-populous regions feeding the disease to the cities and towns, a condition of things which it will readily be seen, greatly increased the difficulty of control. Where, as in the United States, the usual primary centers of the contagion are a few large cities or manufacturing towns, the task of restricting it is obviously much easier, and its spread is much less rapid, than when a score or two of small and scattered communities, without sanitary regulation, are sending it daily to the market-towns and cities about them.[2]

Ames echoed observations made by leading tropical disease experts. Malaria expert Sir Ronald Ross likewise noted the peculiar virulence of common disease in the tropics. When villagers and military personnel survived grim tropical living conditions, Ross observed, the very quality of life exerted a degenerative effect upon the survivors. The threat of disease not only kept civilization at bay; it also led to the physical and social degeneration of the human resident. Western medical science, Ross noted, needed to turn back the tide of darkness in the tropics and reset the balance in favor of civilization over nature run amok.[3]

"THE WHITE MAN IN THE TROPICS IS AN EXOTIC:" TROPICALITY AND THE VALIDATION OF WHITENESS

In short, the tropics could be tamed, and American military physicians were up to the task. Even as medical officers claimed successes, Americans arriving at their new posts wrestled with various schemes to define and project power over indigenous subjects. Even the most benevolent acts associated with Western civic and social reform were subordinated to critical power relationships developed by imperial administrators. While medicine and public health were obviously no exceptions, the extent to which the imperial interlude transformed American medical science and the norms of practice was remarkable. The "colonial/tropical medicine" specialty itself was a tool to facilitate the hierarchical and paternalistic relationships between colonizer and colonized. What better means of asserting control than by creating a specialized knowledge that legitimized the primacy of Western institutions and also marginalized the identity of the subjects' most personal possession—their own bodies.[4] Colonial authorities used sanitation and public health to contextualize Western dominance. Indigenous explanations for disease and ritualistic therapeutics were dismissed as superstition and further evidence of an innate inferiority, especially when compared with Western accomplishments. By making their own cultural standard the yardstick for measuring how "civilized" different societies were, the West could consign virtually all non-whites as inferior, validating the imperial project itself.[5]

At the center of this discourse was the concept of *tropicality*. For present-day observers of the imperial project, the most pressing analogue for tropicality is orientalism. Compellingly described by Edward Said, orientalism represents a series of cultural and literary tropes which have reduced the societies and inhabitants of the Mid- and Far East to an infantilized and effeminate reverse of how Western Europeans imagined themselves. Latent and overt orientalist schemes of thought justified an imagined occidental cultural superiority by imbuing its subjects with a sense of "otherness" that translated into moral and physical weakness.[6]

Unlike orientalism, tropicality confers upon the physical environment the alluring exoticism and physical and moral dangers that reside within the indigenous peoples and cultures Westerners came into contact with. As historian David Arnold describes:

> It can be argued, however, that alien landscapes were often imbued with as much importance as peoples or cultures themselves. Landscapes, and other aspects of the physical environment, such as climate

and disease, were endowed with great moral significance. Environments . . . were widely believed to have a determinating influence upon cultures: savagery, like civilization, was linked to certain climatic or geographical features. Nature, at least beyond the privileged shores of Europe, dictated culture. . . . Part of the significance of 'tropicality' lay in its deep ambivalance—Edenic isles set in sparkling seas—the tropics also signified an alien world of cruelty and disease, oppression and slavery.[7]

In contrast to the "Orient," where the languid dissipation of the inhabitants was played out on the physical environment, the "Tropics" were a place where climate and topography exacted a moral and physical regression on its residents.

Tropicality was hardly a new device constructed by Americans. Since the first voyages of European exploration, participants recorded their observations in literary forms intended to convey the sense of alienation they felt in new lands and among strange peoples and cultures. Separated from home by long journeys across hazardous seas, dislocated travelers sought to validate their sense of normalcy and rightness in comparison with the peoples and places they saw. Simultaneously, these exercises in difference explained how beautiful and exotic people and locales concealed a mortal threat to the lives and souls of Europeans who ventured there. Over time, an explanative trope came to dominate European perceptions of the tropics, in which paradise and pestilence were two sides of the same coin.[8]

In the tropicalist scheme, nearly all health problems in the colonial world were derived from the dangerous environment. Disease was more likely to occur in the hot and steamy tropics, but the very nature of humanity was corrupted by prolonged exposure to the climate. Westerners believed the indigene exerted a degenerative force on "healthy and superior" Europeans, his lax morality and heathen religious and social practices corrupting white intermediaries. After the acceptance of germ theory and the concept of the healthy vector, the native population itself became an infectious agent capable of spreading disease and corruption to the outside world. The superiority of Western medicine was self-evident; left alone, indigenes would be decimated by "tropical" epidemics. Meanwhile, they constituted dangerous centers of pathogens that could escape the imperialist cordon and wreak havoc in the West. In this light, even basic humanitarian actions served a dual purpose. On the one hand, acts of environmental and physical intervention to halt disease, they also represented a scheme of cultural intervention facilitating Western control at the expense of the traditional cultures. In this context, Western medicine and sanitation took on a much larger perspective: Western science offered a means to purge indigenous cultures of their reliance upon superstition, ritual, and fear, replacing them with a scientific Christian sensibility.[9]

The Americanized concept of tropicality became part of a pan-Atlanticist exegesis of racial supremacy and imperial control; yet it was not just lifted from existing European definitions. It was instead derived from a variety of familiar themes and concepts. These disparate elements of an American imperial discourse were glued together by the active and passive contributions of Army and Navy medical officers. These military physicians projected upon the imperial project a veneer of respectability derived from their own legitimate authority and scientific expertise.

The first theme was the concept of a moral civilizing impulse. Many Americans claimed the United States needed to fulfill a broadly defined civilizing imperative prior to the Spanish-American War. America's mission centered around democratizing its new possessions. And as President William McKinley observed in 1899, America's civil obligation was wedded to its Christian ethos. In an interview with a group of Methodist preachers, McKinley described the American mission in the Philippines: "[T]here was nothing left for us to do but to take them all, and to educate the Filipinos, and uplift and Christianize them, and by God's grace do the very best we could by them, as our fellow men for whom Christ also died."[10] Notions of an American-sponsored Great Awakening in the new imperial periphery were soon laid to rest in the face of a robust Roman Catholicism. The civilizing impulse did not abate, however. Americans were even more convinced the United States must exercise direct control over its new subjects. Otherwise the new colonies would slip into anarchy, and be quickly snapped up by other, less "benign" imperialists. Even where the United States did not directly take over an island as a commonwealth, as in Cuba, it so dictated the course of the country's civic and economic affairs as to make it in fact a protectorate.[11]

Racial ideology was another factor at play. In 1900, the American world view was defined by race. Racial stereotypes suffused American culture. Racial consciousness also extended beyond the black/white dichotomy that was a product of America's legacy of slavery. Racial hierarchies and the supremacy of Anglo-Teuton whiteness were realized in nursery rhymes and grade school primers long before historians and ethnographers elaborated on them in sophisticated texts by historians and ethnographers. By the turn of the century, many American intellectuals were even moving beyond racial classification to impose a fluid Darwinism on individuals and communities that would take shape as eugenics, and which exposed the supposed dangers of racial degeneration.[12]

Long service abroad in the American imperial periphery reinforced existing attitudes and biases among soldiers and officers. Filipinos, for example, were reduced in crude soldiers' songs to a primitive, subhuman other, "cross eyed kakiack ladrones," immoral residents of a "land of dopey dreams" where "Social customs there are few, all the ladies smoke and chew/And the men do things the Padres say are wrong."[13] Other songs challenged the political rhetoric associated with the American imperial mission:

I'm only a common soldier-man in the blasted Philippines
They say I've got Brown Brothers here, but I dunno what it means
I like the word Fraternity, but still I draw the line
He may be a Brother of Teddy R—but he ain't no friend of mine.[14]

Other accounts further dehumanized the Filipino. A February 15, 1901 article compiled from military officer reports compared their subjects to monkeys, noting: "They can run up the long branchless trunks of the cocoanut trees, using both their feet and hands, almost as quickly as a monkey."[15] Negative comparisons abounded between the Filipinos and the crudest images associated with African-Americans, with labels like "nigger" bandied about freely.[16] Even African-American troopers used racial epithets to describe the indigene. "We haven't had much fighting here because it is hard to catch the 'gugues' together in sufficient bunches," described Captain Frank R. Steward of the 49th Infantry, U.S. Volunteers, in a letter published in *The Bee* of Washington, D.C. on April 6, 1901. Continuing his description of the "gugues," whom he identified as "members of the 'bolo' people," Steward concluded "The 'Gugu' is a fleet-footed animal. I had one musician slightly wounded. I got three Insurgents killed and I don't know how many were [wounded]."[17]

Many Americans adopted the rhetoric and discursive lens of tropicality to describe the cultural differences they experienced abroad. Colonel Louis Mervin Maus, the first American Commissioner of Public Health in the Philippines, portrayed the entire population of the Philippines as a simple-minded people, bowing to the superior knowledge of their new American masters. "The watchword of American activity in Cuba and the Philippines was 'Cleanliness,' . . . Indeed, such an impression was created in the minds of the simple-minded natives over 'Limpieza,' the Spanish word for cleanliness, that they regarded it as a new tutelary god added to the long list of saints before whom they had bowed for centuries."[18]

Hospital Steward Kenneth Fleming's encounter with a Filipino family offers an example of how enlisted personnel viewed their circumstances through a tropicalist lens. After arriving at the Manila suburb Pasig in 1898, he became acquainted with a local woman who sold milk to the regimental hospital. Fleming's initial description of the woman imbued her with a sense of near-whiteness. "This Milk Maid was a short and very stocky build, probably 5' 2" tall, square shouldered and not black of complexion [sic], just a dark chocolate and very heavy bust," Fleming wrote home. "She had a beautiful disposition and I'm sure if she had been white and dressed in style, she would have attracted attention in any town in the U.S."[19]

Fleming's assessment soon turned. When the milk seller's mother was sick and in need of medicine, he was sent to deliver a prescription to the family. Climbing the five foot ladder into the shack, Fleming gave the young woman's mother the pills she needed. He also made an unanticipated discovery:

Thee Milk Maid was sitting in some kind of a bamboo chair and a naked Philippeano [sic] boy was laying on her lap holding a cocoanut shell and she was holding a big black tit in one hand and milking herself with the other into the cocoanut shell. I asked here where was her cow—she said 'no got'!! Of course, I knew then she was selling her own milk to the boys.[20]

Though disgusted, in the end Fleming kept silent, noting that despite its source, the milk bolstered morale among the sick in the ward. More significant than the shock and acceptance over the peculiar source of the milk, however, was the dichotomous portrayal of the Filipinos he interacted with: beautiful and eroticized, yet still less than normal (read by Fleming: white) and degenerated. The "Milk Maid's" donation itself becomes a sort of tainted offering as well. Certainly helpful if not essential for the recovery of the sick and injured soldiers in Fleming's care, it nevertheless was dangerous—almost as if the milk would literally transform the imbiber into a member of a lesser race itself.

Another factor was the doctrine of *acclimation*, the gradual acquisition of a protective immunity to the effects of the tropical climate. Some believed acclimation was possible, if proper precautions were taken. Clean quarters, good food, boiled water, careful attention to personal hygiene, and moral habits were all ascribed as factors facilitating acclimation.[21] Some went further, ascribing the readiness with which American soldiers appeared to rebound from so-called tropical disorders to the robust superiority of the American physique. Not only were Anglo-Saxon's materially and spiritually superior, proponents argued, they were also well-suited for survival in the tropical periphery despite the hazards of sun and clime.[22] Acclimation became a mark of racial and ethnic superiority, and a prerequisite for social and economic progress. Having proven their ready adaptability in all climates, white Americans were poised to share the promise of American civilization with their new subjects. Sojourns to the new American tropics would rejuvenate constitutions made frail by "dissipation, hardihood and exposure" at the same time local infrastructures were being improved. "At the decline of the century, when excessive social pleasures exert a marked tendency to deterioration of the race, caused to a large degree by exaggerated and excessive artificiality in living, an outdoor life away from the turmoil of the city would rapidly transform physically devitalized manhood into men worthy of their peers."[23]

Others were less sanguine. In their opinion, while visitors from temperate climates to the tropics learned precautions to avoid most illnesses, the climate nevertheless continued to wear some down. Over time, even the healthiest males would feel the accumulated effects of the tropic climate. American medical officers paid particular attention to the French and British reports from India, Africa, and Southeast Asia. The incessant barrage of harsh light and tropic heat broke down the more sensitively attuned constitutions of white Europeans and Americans by overstimulating the nervous system. Headaches, irritability, lack of appetite, sexual excitement, heat exhaustion, and disinterest in duty and social activities were all symptoms of an imminent, aggressive degeneration, labeled *tropical neurasthenia* by physicians.[24]

Tropical neurasthenia became a great concern for all the nation's uniformed medical services.[25] The concept of neurasthenia itself was nothing new, first described by New York neurologist George M. Beard in 1866. Along with Philadelphia surgeon Silas Weir Mitchell, who examined links between nervous exhaustion and diet, the two launched a Western obsession with neurasthenia as a by-product of industrialization that lasted into the First World War. Mitchell concluded the increasing incidence of nervous collapse was related to America's rapid urban and industrial growth. "It has long been believed that maladies of the nervous system are increasing rapidly in the more crowded portions of the United States," Mitchell wrote in his 1871 treatise, *Wear and Tear, or Hints for the Overworked*:

> Neuralgia is another malady which has no record there, but is, I suspect, increasing at a rapid rate whenever our people are crowded together in towns. Perhaps no other form of sickness is so sure an indication of the development of the nervous temperament, or that condition in which there are both feebleness and irritability of the nervous system.[26]

Overwork, poor diet, lack of physical and intellectual stimulation, and anxiety over one's livelihood and status all combined to wear down the new urban American male.[27]

Just as smallpox, tuberculosis, and other diseases were accorded greater power in the tropics, tropical neurasthenia was considered a more dangerous form of the familiar domestic condition. No Americans serving in the tropics were safe, though the condition's severity varied: "Comparatively few individuals entirely escape if they live in the tropics for any length of time. In many persons the manifestations are slight and they are taken as a matter of course, due to climate. They do not consider themselves really ill, but commonly explain: 'The climate is getting onto my nerves.'"[28]

Aside from the tangible threat of infectious disease, informed medical officers were concerned with the environment's debilitating effect. Individuals accustomed to temperate climates were in grave danger. Army physicians carefully monitored new arrivals for any sign of tropical neurasthenia. "Life in the tropics has a pronounced depressing effect on the man from the temperate zone," wrote Major Henry P. Birmingham in 1903, "and this is particularly the case for one who is subjected to hard service or unwonted conditions."[29] The condition was considered the handmaiden of other conditions, notably malaria, dysentery, and "soldier's heart," a form of degenerative tachycardia plaguing veterans that was linked to too much time in the field. Those suffering from chronic illnesses, particularly tuberculosis, were likewise at great risk.[30]

A consensus developed that the condition especially targeted those at either extreme of military age. "Immature youth"—those between seventeen and twenty-one—were most susceptible to tropical neurasthenia, as were men over forty. The Medical Department used tropical neurasthenia as justification for limiting the length and frequency of tours by white soldiers. "The white man in the Tropics is an exotic," an 1899 account stated, noting that where possible, "black troops should be used in places where high temperatures prevail, almost exclusively." Reports recommended limiting deployment to veteran white soldiers, between the ages of twenty-five and thirty-five, and preferably from the American South.[31] Major Charles Francis Mason, a surgeon with service in both Puerto Rico and the Philippines, stated "I do not believe a soldier should be kept continuously in the tropics longer than three years; two years would be better."[32]

Another factor placing the middle-aged soldier at risk reflected the Regular Army's anti-volunteer bias and the popular consensus of the soldier's identity. Anyone who entered military service later in life was suspect: "[T]he fact of a man's presenting himself as a recruit after middle age is presumptive evidence that his life has been more or less a failure," reflecting either a neurotic disposition or a predilection for strong drink. Using anecdotal observations of the sick rate among volunteers sent to the Philippines between March 3, 1899, and June 30, 1901, Major Birmingham concluded such men were more likely to be afflicted by tropical diseases and neurasthenia due to their weak constitutions. "Very few of these men were ever returned to duty," he concluded, "they either died or were sent home."[33]

Even as tropical neurasthenia became a factor limiting the effectiveness of whites in the tropics, some believed too much was made of climate's role in the onset of tropical neurasthenia. They agreed the region's torrid humidity and harsh sunlight exerted a gradual atonic effect, especially on those who avoided strenuous activity and used alcohol as a rejuvenative. But other factors were more significant, especially the greater challenges and exertions involved in transporting modernity and civic order to the new American frontier. The Isthmian canal project was a primary example of how overwork in the tropics magnified the effects of nervous exhaustion. An observer explained: "The American goes the pace according to his previous habit, and while his physical and mental capacities may be able to stand it in the States, it is entirely too strenuous for his new environments. He either drops more or less into the pace of the country or breaks down. What may be normal work in one place is overwork in another."[34]

The challenges of overwork without distraction, rest, or proper diet remained the chief causes of tropical neurasthenia. Typical American amusements—theaters, parks, sporting fields, concert halls, and even a close circle of friends—were few. The same applied to diet, which was described as bland, monotonous, and unvaried for months at a time. Faced with such boring monotony, the white American in the tropics walked a tightrope of wellness, facing certain peril on either side of him. On one side was the danger of boredom, and the "great liability of drifting into alcoholic or sexual excesses," a choice that not only signaled the onset of neurasthenia but also accelerate the degeneration of the individual. The other side promised the gradual onset of serious nervous collapse, as seemingly uneventful bouts of homesickness and irritation grew into a full-fledged physical and mental breakdown.[35]

A more extreme thread of tropicality considered climate and topography as factors setting the lines of ethnographic division in humans and helping establish a racial hierarchy that privileged whites of Northern European descent. The chief proponent of the racialized climate was Lieutenant Colonel Charles E. Woodruff. A member of the Army Medical Department since 1887 and brigade surgeon attached to General Wesley Merritt's Philippines Expedition, Woodruff styled himself an expert on the effects of the tropical climate, authoring numerous controversial essays, articles, and several books on race and eugenics. Considered a crank and a hypochondriac by his peers, Woodruff was allegedly obsessed with vindicating his failure to serve out a complete tour in the Philippines by turning to abstract explanations focusing on the combined effects of light, color, and race. Woodruff reiterated a theme dear to American society: the degeneration of whiteness in the face of immigration, assimilation, and now, imperial expansion.[36]

According to Woodruff, the earth was divided into environmental zones bordered by isothermal boundaries. Animal species were extremely limited insofar as their capacity to survive and flourish across these zones. Natural selection exerted its toll on species that strayed from their native habitat. "Living species are thus found to be like glaciers—rigid and apparently unchangeable," Woodruff wrote, "generation to generation, yet molded like clay if the forces are sufficient; for heredity holds a form to its parental type, and yet, by the selection of variations in any given direction, it takes a new form."[37] The same was true in the case of man, who evolved from a series of anthropoid types into current ethnic and racial norms. Indeed, all racial signifiers—skin color, body frame and size, hair color and texture, eye color, shape and size of the nose—were examples of biological variations evolving in response to environment.[38]

Despite these variations, individuals and groups alike frequently visited and occupied different climatic zones, seemingly without ill effect. Even recent history demonstrated races flourishing in zones seemingly at odds with Woodruff's classification: Northern Europeans lived and worked in all environments; immigrants arrived daily from a variety of climates in the United States over decades; white Americans spread across a continent encompassing several different environmental and climatic zones; and the descendants of Africans brought against their will to the Western Hemisphere. In all these cases, Woodruff's theories were tested and found lacking. Woodruff disagreed, noting any visible successes critics pointed toward were temporary. As a "true scientist," Woodruff looked toward the historical precedent. Humanity's innate intelligence gave it a great advantage over other species in compensating for the effects of hostile and unnatural climates. But ultimately all racial types residing out of their proper environmental zone were doomed to extinction:

> Man's intelligence permits him to appreciate the dangers of a climate and avoid most of them by proper protection, so that he survives longer than other forms out of their zones, even as long as two generations in the case of white men in India, but here, with all his care, a third generation is unknown. In lesser changes he survives longer still, as in the case of the case of our negroes, but here extinction is inevitable, for we know that the lesser change from the Soudan to Egypt is always fatal in the long run—that is, in a few centuries.[39]

Woodruff believed the moderately temperate clime of the continental United States was more suited to the dark-haired Mediterranean ethnic type, dooming both the blond-haired, blue-eyed Nordic Aryan and Negroes residing there. Over time, both ethnicities faced extinction, either through an inevitable birthrate decline or through assimilation with the ever-increasing waves of Southern and Eastern European immigrants. Despite this conclusion, Woodruff had little use for the so-called "melting pot":

> The pleasing dream of the low types flocking here that America is a "melting pot" destined to make an alloy of all races, has no scientific basis and is sheer nonsense. The hybrids could not breed true to type anyhow, and if they could it is evident that even if they were adapted to one place they would not be to any other. Types unfit for the environment must disappear, and as elsewhere explained, though we might develop as diverse types as in Europe, there cannot possible be an American type fit for every place.[40]

Woodruff offered a grim outlook for America's new tropical possessions. Acclimatization was a myth. Harsh and prolonged sunlight, the never-ending tropic summer, and the twin extremes of incessant rainfall and humidity would erode the actinic and neurasthenic health of Europeans in the tropics.[41] Yet the geopolitical realities of imperial stewardship forced upon the United States left no alternative. Woodruff offered a list of precautions to ensure young men sent abroad would survive their tour of service without jeopardizing the imperial project. Ideally, no blondes should be sent to the tropics, but rather swarthier brunettes, all between twenty and thirty-five years old and of a slender, yet fit, physique. To avoid cellular damage from the sun's ultra-violet light, whites should be clothed in dark, opaque clothing, and fitted out in wide-brimmed hats. Where possible, Americans should live in well-ventilated, open houses on hillsides, and follow the local habits of midday siestas. Woodruff also proposed restricting whites to supervisory positions in all but the most sensitive areas, leaving hard labor for the local inhabitants. Finally Woodruff recommended short tours for Americans in the tropics. "We can never expect all men to serve two or three years in the tropics without damage," he wrote, noting exceptions to the rule resulted more from individual compliance with his precautions than any other factor.[42]

The discourse of control evolving in the new American Empire borrowed from the disparate elements of race, religion, and civic authority. This imperial discourse also incorporated a "scientific" element that bore the imprimatur of the Army Medical Department. This contribution validated tropicalism as a definitional and validational tool, establishing the context of white American civil and social control. Much work conducted by American medical officers in the 1900s in the Philippines and Caribbean may be viewed as part of a much larger project aimed at defining how an entire portion of the globe was not only culturally different—and hence inferior to—the white inhabitants of the Northern temperate zones. It also conferred a significant measure of hazard to this region that threatened the health of any white who dwelled there too long.

The effort by American military physicians to promote tropicality as a linchpin of an evolving imperial ideology was not surprising. Since 1818, individual medical officers recorded their observations in anthropology, ethnology, and the physical topography of their stations. The individual reports of medical officers serving throughout the American West are filled with accounts of cultural and topographic difference—both positive and negative—from the Mexican borderlands to Puget Sound. The difference between these and the essays and books written by medical officers in the early 1900s was the methodology and exactitude applied to their claims. Sternberg's medical officers enjoyed the advantage of a post-graduate education that privileged numerous subjects that would prove beneficial to practice on the ground of the new empire. After resuming classes in 1901, the Army Medical School expanded its training in tropical bacteriology, helminthology, and parasitology, bringing in instructors from the medical school at Johns Hopkins University and experts from the U.S. Public Health Service. The medical officer's interest coincided with their increased status and self-awareness as legitimate experts within the Army. Taken together, these aspects of expertise provided the Army's medical officers a claim to special privileges they had never enjoyed previously.[43]

SANITATION TO THE RESCUE: GORGAS IN HAVANA

After grappling with the logic of the mosquito vector, the momentum of discovery passed to the Army's sanitary-focused medical officers. For the past decade, the *modus vivendi* of the Army Medical Department centered upon the microscope. Identifying the germ was the first step toward disease control. Yellow fever was different. Since the germ causing the disease was too small to be observed with the state of lens technology available at the time, there was no real hope of developing an antitoxin or a vaccine. The emphasis, therefore, shifted from cure to prevention: "For our purpose," wrote Major Valery Havard, Chief Surgeon of the Department of Cuba, "the mosquito is the enemy, and all our efforts must be directed against it."[44] For the first time, the Medical Department mounted a comprehensive campaign to control a disease, with the ultimate goal of complete eradication.

Army sanitarians realized a successful yellow fever eradication campaign in Cuba would bolster their influence within the Medical Department. Since yellow fever was introduced into Cuba in the eighteenth century, the island became the epicenter of annual cycles of disease that directly threatened the United States. Hence, the immediate benefits of managing an efficient eradication effort in Cuba were tremendous for the sanitarians. Not only would it elevate their prestige, giving them a greater say in the direction of the Medical Department's organization and mission, success would provide a tremendous boost for American hygienic and public health science. The British might have been first to crack the mystery of malaria. The Germans may have advanced the cause of public hygiene and sanitation in urban planning. American success in eradicating yellow fever in Havana would assert a superior applied hygiene that was lacking in the purely clinical approaches of the European sciences.

Eradication was no simple matter. When the United States took control of Cuba, the appalling sanitary state of Havana came under public scrutiny. Shocked American officers discovered scenes of urban destitution long gone in the United States. Open sewers running alongside the city's narrow cobblestone streets, overflowing with garbage, animal corpses, and fetid ordure were the rule.[45] The Army's chief sanitary officer in Havana, Major William Crawford Gorgas, noted how despite the best efforts in the two years since the end of the war, yellow fever remained endemic. In the winter of 1899–1900, an outbreak struck Havana, Santiago, and other Cuban cities isolated by years of blockade and war. Fueling the new epidemic was the arrival of some 12,000 Spanish immigrants, virtually all of them non-immunes. By the end of the fever season in 1900, some 1,400 cases were recorded in Havana alone, despite the Sanitation Department's efforts. Indeed the fever seemed worse in cleaner neighborhoods, those which had benefited the most from new sewers and where Americans resided and worked.[46]

When Reed read his preliminary notes on yellow fever before the Pan-American Medical Congress in February 1901, Gorgas was there. Though he accepted the board's results, Gorgas was initially unsure that vector eradication could actually succeed on its own. Other as yet undiscovered factors, including casual transmission between infected and non-infected persons, had to play a role. Nor was it guaranteed any control campaign would be completely successful.[47] Gorgas and his aides evaluated their options. An estimated 40,000 non-immunes remained in the city, in constant danger.

Quarantine and fumigation, the traditional response to yellow fever, was insufficient. "Even with the truth of the mosquito theory granted, it seemed impossible, under any system of killing mosquitoes, to avoid leaving a sufficient number to carry on the infection," Gorgas said. "No mosquito work in the Havana houses could possibly destroy all of these insects and a considerable number must always escape; and these, it was thought, would be enough to keep up the infection."[48]

In January 1901, Gorgas began a study of the stegomyia in Havana, and learned the insect was an urban creature that had adapted well to life with humans. Equipped with short wings, stegomyia was capable only of short flights at any given time. Though a diurnal creature, the mosquito shunned direct sunlight, preferring to rest in shaded areas until disturbed or made aware of a potential food source. The female required still water for her eggs, which hatched in three days. The larvae, "yellow fever wigglers" according to Gorgas, would emerge from the water after five to six days as full-grown mosquitoes.[49] Gorgas's surveyors discovered the mosquito in virtually every household in Havana. Every family collected rain water in clay pots, barrels, and large cisterns; all perfect breeding grounds for *stegomyia*. Likewise, the city's cesspools and outside privies—some in continuous use for over 400 years— served as nurseries for eggs and larvae. Since nearly every household in the city either collected rain water or maintained an open cesspool, no place in Havana was safe. Finally the city was ringed by vegetable gardens and farms, irrigated by miles of open ditches that, though overgrown with weeds and filled with refuse of every imaginable type, provided a breeding ground not only for *stegomyia* but also the malaria-carrying *Anopheles* mosquitoes.[50]

Gorgas decided upon a three-tiered sanitary plan to exterminate the mosquito in Havana: remove its breeding grounds; deny adults the opportunity to enter the city's dwellings; and exterminate those mosquitoes still present in the city. He concluded the mosquito was a domestic pest that did not venture far from where it was bred. "I believe that, practically, in a city such as Havana, the mosquito is bred within the house which he troubles," Gorgas observed, "and that the yellow fever mosquito—the Stegomyia— generally breeds in the rain water barrel and receptacle."[51]

Three different squads of mosquito workers were created, each with different responsibilities. The "Stegomyia Brigade" ensured every water supply and cesspool in the city was mosquito proofed. Havana was divided into seven districts, each overseen by an inspector and an assistant. City ordnances gave inspectors enforcement powers in matters relating to mosquito control, ranging from issuing fines for non-compliance to authority to destroy any unprotected receptacles discovered on subsequent inspections. The inspectors and assistants visited every residence and business in Havana. Initial inspections revealed virtually every house in the city had *stegomyia* larvae in water receptacles and cesspools. Offenders were ordered to mosquito-proof their water containers, while assistants poured a pint of oil into cesspools. Any found to have ignored the inspectors' orders on a second inspection were fined ten dollars, and all non-compliant receptacles were destroyed.[52]

The suburbs, farms, and swamps ringing the city were assigned to an "Anopheles Brigade." Though the less congested environs surrounding Havana presented little threat from *stegomyia*, the area was perfect for the hardier *Anopheles* mosquito. Years of irrigation saturated pastureland outside the city to the point where the grazing cattle left behind holes wherever they paused, which in turn filled with water, making ideal breeding pools. Also divided into sections, the Anopheles workers had the laborious task of clearing and draining irrigation ditches and other depressions, and oiling areas which could not be drained. Aside from the old quarries northwest of the city, the Anopheles Brigade encountered little problem. There two different solutions were adopted, pumping water out of the larger quarry, while the second one was dug deeper, revealing a porous aquifer that absorbed the standing water.[53]

A third squad, the "Yellow Fever Brigade," was dispatched to the homes of newly infected victims. Here the old system of quarantine and fumigation was employed with a vengeance. After screening the patient's room, every other portal of the house was sealed with thick paper, securing it from the outside world. The house was then fumigated with pyretheum powder, a pound for every 1,000 cubic feet in the residence; on average, 150 pounds per house. Two hours exposure was considered sufficient for the average house, the fumes either killing or intoxicating any mosquitoes present, which were then swept up and burned. Once the infected house was fumigated, the process was repeated on all neighboring buildings. A second solution was discovered that damaged fabric even less; a mixture of one part camphor to three parts carbolic acid, which in turn was vaporized by a spirit lamp. In the city's tobacco warehouses another agent had to be used. Sulphur, pyretheum, and even camphor would spoil the tobacco. Experimentation revealed smoke from burning tobacco stems was just as lethal to mosquitoes as sulphur, and did not affect the leaf tobacco at all.[54]

Gorgas' vector eradication scheme was a large scale exercise in urban sanitary engineering. At no stage in his project did the medical establishment play a part, save to care for disease afflicted persons. The chief roles were reserved for sanitary inspectors and the managers leading the squads of mosquito workers. In its logical distribution of labor and clear-cut responsibilities, as well as the division of labor into organized teams, the Gorgas plan was influenced by its author's status as a military officer. The *stegomyia* mosquito was effectively portrayed as a cold, ruthless enemy of humanity; the response in turn was portrayed as mankind's long-awaited counter-offensive in the age-old war between man and microbe. In Gorgas' case, the militarized rhetoric of "war against disease" was not inappropriate; the entire project was organized and conducted as a military exercise, a point not lost to observers. One contemporary physician observed that the Spanish-American War and the yellow fever projects were linked, and that the combination of Reed's discovery and Gorgas' response alone were well worth the war's cost in money and lives. Furthermore, the Army medical establishment alone commanded the ability, resources, and commitment required to effect full eradication.[55]

At the same time, the *stegomyia* eradication scheme represented a novel and uniquely American response to the problem of disease. The Gorgas project was predicated upon transforming the environment. In essence, the ideal of the frontier was shifted to the microcosm of the intersection of human civilization and nature. The vector eradication response promoted by Gorgas entailed a drastic transformation of several environments simultaneously. First, the social environment of the individual and community was subjected to immediate change. Certain behaviors and habits were no longer deemed safe or acceptable, and the censorious powers of the state were employed to effect a change in the household environment. Though the full weight of the state was never directly exploited, the *potential* for its use was implicit. It was not insignificant that the first employment of the Gorgas scheme was conducted outside of the boundaries of the American core, nor that the military was the primary agent of change in these areas. Even after 1898, large sectors of the domestic American populace remained misinformed and skeptical about germ theory, not to mention the role of the insect vector. This, coupled with the innate resistance to government interference in personal affairs, would have made the first employment of the Gorgas plan far more difficult in the United States than in Havana, part of the new American imperial periphery and subject to different standards of coercion, control, and persuasion. Responsible for colonial administration, the military was the natural actor for implementing the scheme. And it did not hurt that its author was a member of one of the more professionalized corps within the Army, globally recognized as a model of scientific and practical expertise.

At a time when many privileged intellectual elites favored the general parameters of the Frederick Jackson Turner's frontier thesis as a rationalization of the unique American spirit and its manifest destiny, the idea of changing the environment to eliminate threats to Euro-Americans, thus facilitating the advance of white civilization, was well taken. The act of *changing* nature to fit the physiology of Americans seemed in itself innately American and well in keeping with the tradition of homesteaders and settlers taming the Western frontier. Gorgas expressed his work in these terms, as he stated in a paper read before the Medical Society of the District of Columbia on March 18, 1903. "This mosquito work in Havana is of particular importance as demonstrating the possibility of freeing an infected tropical city from yellow fever, and of greatly decreasing the amount of malarial fever . . . ; and if these two diseases, yellow fever and malaria, can be eliminated from the tropics, I do not see why the Caucasian cannot enjoy as good health there as in the more temperate regions."[56]

Four years later, writing from Panama, Gorgas further outlined his work in the context of conquering the tropicality construct. When the United States first arrived in Panama in 1904, the area was rife with malaria, yellow fever, dysentery, and smallpox. "In fact," Gorgas wrote, "the conditions were more favorable for producing a high mortality upon the introduction of a large force than they had been at any time in the past. Into this region the Canal Commission has introduced the largest force ever before present on the Isthmus, some forty thousand persons, ten thousand of whom are white nonimmunes."[57] Within three years, the general state of health on the Isthmus improved: yellow fever was eradicated, and malaria infection rates were brought under manageable control, thanks to the sanitarian, Gorgas argued.

I think the sanitarian can now show that any population coming into the tropics can protect itself against these two diseases by measures that are both simple and inexpensive; that with these two diseases eliminated life in the tropics for the Anglo-Saxon will be more healthful than in the temperate zones; that gradually, within the next two or three centuries, tropical countries, which offer a much greater return for man's labor than do the temperate zones, will be settled up by the white races, and that again the centers of wealth, civilization and population will be in the tropics, as they were in the dawn of man's history, rather than in the temperate zones, as at present.[58]

The Gorgas plan provided a solution to the one of the problems contained in the tropicality construct—the innate lethality of the tropics to Northern temperate zone whites. By transforming the tropical environment, it was finally possible for whites to live in the tropics without fear of imminent death from disease.

Within months of its implementation, Gorgas' scheme proved a tremendous success. The January 1901 survey indicated Havana was awash in *stegomyia* larvae, concentrations being found in over 26,000 different residences and businesses in the city. An inspection conducted a year later discovered only 200 sites within the city limits, which were immediately targeted for eradication. The corollary indicator was the rate of disease within the city. Between 1890 and 1901, the average yellow fever death rate in Havana was 511; in 1901, the rate had fallen to 151, and by September 26, 1902, the city was declared free of yellow fever.[59] Gorgas was quick to claim credit for his new method. "I think it is evident that the disappearance of yellow fever from Habana was due solely to this mosquito work," Gorgas reported. "Remember that it was an every-day disease in Habana, and had been so for more than a hundred years, just as consumption in New Orleans, a city of about the same size as Habana."[60]

Even as his flying squads were completing their first year's work, Gorgas considered a second opportunity to highlight his eradication methods.

Gorgas proposed going to Panama. Sternberg agreed, and ordered Gorgas to return to the United States in the Fall of 1902 in preparation of his departure. After a long delay prompted by Congressional debates over the funding for the proposed canal, Gorgas was appointed chief sanitary advisor to the Isthmian Canal Commission in March 1904. Three officers—Navy Medical Director John W. Ross; Major Louis La Garde, Surgeon; and Major Cassius E. Gillette, Corps of Engineers—were designated his assistants. As chief sanitary advisor to the Isthmian Canal Commission, Gorgas was charged with determining if his method of mosquito eradication could be brought to the site of the proposed Trans-Isthmian Panama Canal.[61]

For centuries, the narrow tropical Isthmus was recognized as one of the most unwholesome environments on earth. Visitors to the Isthmus quickly discovered the effects of the tropical climate on those dwelling there. "The first impression of the Isthmus when seen from the sea is pleasing, the land being mountainous, rugged, beautifully green," recounted one observer. However, the picturesque vista soon gave way to a more sinister landscape as one came ashore at the town of Colon. "The city is small, having only about three or four thousand inhabitants, chiefly negroes, who live in a state of squalor, surrounded by puddles of water and every kind of filth. . . . The surroundings of the city are low, marshy, and extremely unattractive."[62]

Conditions were no better inland. A trip across the narrow Isthmus on the Panama Railroad took but a few hours, time enough to enter a primeval world. Dense impenetrable tropical forests lay on either side of the track. Occasional villages dotted the line of the railroad, occupying small clearings cut from the forest, the huts sitting upon stilts to prevent flooding from the constant rainfall. For several miles, the track paralleled the dangerous and unpredictable Chagres River. A choppy and swift torrent during the best of times, the Chagres frequently flooded its banks after heavy rainfalls. Across the Isthmus was the city of Panama. Described as a "quaint old Spanish city whose stately churches, pretentious residences, and massive ruins tell of antiquity and historic vicissitude," the small city had changed little since the 1700s. Without a public water system, the people of Panama collected rain water in cisterns for personal use. The city also had no sewers save for open ditches running alongside the streets into cesspools. Garbage collection was also non-existent, refuse merely tossed into the streets for the dogs and buzzards.[63] Even during the dry season, daily rainfall was normal. In 1904, the Isthmus experienced 160 inches of rain throughout the year. Compounding the discomfort was the narrow temperature range, with average temperatures ranging from 85 to 96 degrees Fahrenheit in the shade over the course of the year.[64]

In such a damp, humid tropical climate, it seemed only natural that disease would flourish. In 1859, William P. Buel, a surgeon employed by the Pacific Mail Company, observed "Panama has the reputation of being a place of extraordinary insalubrity—a sort of hot-bed of disease—where the fever which bears its name reigns with undisputed supremacy."[65] For much of the nineteenth century, the climate and topography were reckoned as the base source of the diseases—malaria (identified here as "Chagres Fever"), typhoid fever, yellow fever, dysentery, and various skin infections—prevailing there. The tropical environment produced various miasmas, byproducts of rotting vegetable and animal matter in the sultry heat, and spread their organic poisons throughout the Isthmus. The end result—"The climate is not friendly to the white races"—was indisputable.[66] Panama was not just a dangerous tropical environment, it was the archetypical "green hell."

Yet, its geography, constituting a narrow fifty mile wide finger of land separating the Atlantic and Pacific Oceans, made the place irresistible to Europeans and Americans. The promise of a shortcut between the two oceans brought speculators, investors, and adventurers to Panama for centuries. In 1881, the latest venture, the *Compagnie Universellé du Canal Interoceanique de Panama*, began work on a sea-level canal running from Colon to Panama. Headed by French engineer Ferdinand de Lesseps, the company expected to complete the project within six years, at an anticipated cost of $127,000,000. The forty-eight mile long canal between Colon and Panama, was to be essentially a big cut, 29.5 feet deep and 72 feet deep, across the Isthmus.[67] The project soon foundered, thanks to graft, bribery, and most of all, yellow fever and malaria. Between 1881 and 1889, 22,189 workers were recorded as dying of yellow fever, malaria, Chagres fever, and other diseases. However, as James Thorington, chief resident surgeon of the Panama Railroad Company in Colon, noted in a December 15, 1910 letter to Colonel Gorgas, there was a tremendous discrepancy between the reported mortality figures and the actual death rate in the Isthmus. "The constant coming and going of white railroad employees to and from New York and New Orleans and their indiscriminate dwelling here and there in Colon made it utterly impossible to keep any reliable percentage of the mortality rate," he wrote Gorgas. Thorington also noted he was told by Gonzales Echeverria, chief resident physician at Colon Canal Hospital, that the French were unlikely to publish any such statistical record, noting that "Dr. Echeverria said to me when discussing this subject 'to publish such statistics would be to kill it' (meaning the work on the Canal) and to leave it unpublished gives it a chance to go on."[68]

From the beginning of the American effort, sanitation and mosquito eradication were considered the most essential conditions for the project. However, the challenges Gorgas faced in Panama were far greater than in Havana. Neither Colon or Panama City possessed sewer or water systems; open sewers, cesspools, wells, and rainwater cisterns were the order of the day. Greater challenges faced the Americans as they moved inland. Across the swath of land comprising the Canal Zone, over forty camps and villages housing at any given time over 50,000 laborers and their families were built along the path of the canal excavation. The malaria-carrying *Anopheles* was considered the greatest threat. Early surveys conducted by the American commission revealed over 70 percent of the 12,000 inhabitants along the line of planned construction were infected with malaria. "This means that practically every female Anopheles mosquito that bites a human being along the line of the canal becomes infected, and our examination has further shown that there is no lack of Anopheles mosquitoes," Gorgas wrote.[69] The entire zone was ideal breeding ground for both *Anopheles* and *Stegomyia* mosquitoes; over a third of the land surveyed for the canal was swampland, with the remainder hills broken by streams and ponds. With an average rainfall of over one hundred inches, major excavations and small ditches became breeding grounds for mosquitoes within hours of their creation.[70]

From the very moment he assumed charge of the cleanup of the Isthmus, Gorgas ran into trouble. Though he had taken the precaution of ordering over $50,000 worth of supplies, including eight tons of pyrethrum powder for fumigation, the Canal Commission's reception of the request was mixed. Despite Gorgas's public success in eradicating the disease in Havana, several members of the commission were unconvinced that insects spread the disease. They questioned Gorgas's requests for supplies, funds, and personnel to carry out his plan.[71] Another problem was the immense scope of the project and the drastic differences in climate compared with Havana. At first glance, Panama appeared an easier task than Cuba. The population of the entire area was less than that of Havana—for example, in 1904, the city of Panama held some 20,000 inhabitants, compared with Havana's 250,000 residents. Yet the true nature of the challenge facing Gorgas's sanitary teams lay in the rugged terrain and constant rainfall. No amount of sulphur or pyrethrum, it seemed, could completely eradicate the mosquitoes plaguing the Isthmus. Any progress made on fumigating buildings was outweighed by the standing water in puddles, ponds, and rain barrels throughout the construction site and the surrounding jungle.

The Commission's skepticism was buttressed by a crippling yellow fever outbreak during the first six months of 1905. The disease quickly spread among the non-immune workers gathering in Panama and Colon. Panic set in when two men died of yellow fever, causing a mass exodus of white employees. The sporadic progress made to date came to a complete halt, and it looked as if the American effort would follow the de Lesseps venture into ignominious failure. By June 1905, the Commission demanded Gorgas's replacement.[72] Fortunately, he had the support of President Theodore Roosevelt. When slow progress caused Roosevelt to shake up the standing Commission in July 1907, he retained Gorgas as Chief Sanitary Officer.[73]

Just as in Cuba, Gorgas outlined the primary mission of the sanitary inspectors as eliminating the mosquito disease vector and destroying all local breeding grounds. In short, the Havana plan was brought to Panama. The Canal Zone was divided into twenty-five districts, each under the administration of a chief sanitary inspector, who was supported by three assistants. Each district inspector was given charge of forty to fifty laborers, a smaller force of carpenters, and two dispensary workers.

The laborers began clearing brush and grass around dwellings and along drainage paths. Unlike Cuba, however, the extra step of placing tile drains along the drainage courses was taken. Where the drainage course was too wide or deep for tile, a concrete causeway was poured. After the drains were installed, laborers returned periodically to mow the grass around them and sweep the drains clear of any obstructions.[74] In the temporary camps, pools created by construction, and other areas where drainage was impractical, the laborers poured oil and sulphate of copper, killing all mosquito larvae and rendering it unsuitable for further breeding.[75]

Meanwhile, sanitary inspectors were busy inspecting and fumigating every house and standing structure in Colon and Panama. Over the course of a month, inspectors visited every single building in the two cities. This preliminary smoking-out of mosquitoes was followed up by a second and a third fumigation over the first year of American activity in the Canal Zone. The original eight tons of insect powder Gorgas requested was soon exhausted, prompting numerous sulphur and pyrethrum requisitions from the United States. By March 1905, the Army was shipping two tons of each material every week to the Isthmus, where it was quickly used. By the end of the year, Gorgas reckoned over one hundred and twenty tons of pyrethrum and three hundred tons of sulphur—the entire annual output of the United States prior to 1904—were burned to clean out the cities on either side of the Isthmus.[76]

Carpenters screened all windows and doors of houses, offices, and other structures in the zone. Recognizing screening purchased by the Commission was flimsy, Gorgas instructed the carpenters to replace all screens regularly, annually if need be. Finally, a new corps of dispensary workers managed the supply of quinine for the district. Here the limits of the Sanitary Department's intrusive authority were met, as even Gorgas acknowledged he could not compel the Commission's civilian employees to take the prophylactic dose of quinine. However, every effort was made to keep the medication ever present. In every dining hall and mess table a supply of three-grain pills was placed for any who wished to take it. Dispensary workers also traveled throughout villages and camps daily, offering quinine to any who wanted it.[77]

As in Havana, the field sanitary inspectors' work was supplemented by a maritime quarantine of the Canal Zone's four principal ports—Ancon, Panama, Colon, and Cristobal—to prevent new cases of yellow fever or malaria from entering the area during the cleanup. Since the zone was under direct American administration, Gorgas' board was also charged with establishing a modern health infrastructure in the zone. Medical Director Ross established two new general hospitals in Colon and Ancon, a convalescent hospital at Taboga Island in Panama Bay, and twenty-five small hospitals along the canal. Modeled on a military evacuation scheme, the small hospitals were temporary stops for sick and injured workers en route to one of the general hospitals.[78]

As the 1905 outbreak slowed in September, work on eradication increased its pace. In Colon, fumigation teams eradicated the existing mosquito population. Carpenters screened every building. Laborers cleared a half-mile surrounding the town of all brush and dug canals to drain the town and neighboring marshes. In the city of Panama, similar efforts were undertaken, with the result that within a short time, yellow fever was completely eradicated in the Canal Zone. After December 1905, only a single case was reported on the entire Isthmus, Gorgas proudly reported in May 1907. The Isthmus of Panama, formerly doomed as a "pesthole," was free of yellow fever.[79]

Progress against malaria was much slower. For the first two and a half years of construction, malaria infection rates were horrific, reaching a high point of 821 cases per thousand workers in 1906.[80] The more robust nature of the *Anopheles* mosquito precluded total eradication: unlike *stegomyia*, *Anopheles* bred in the wild and could easily fly over three miles in search of a host. And unlike yellow fever, malaria is a chronic condition, providing mosquitoes a potential source of infection for years after the initial onset of the disease. Still, Gorgas pointed toward a declining rate of malarial infection as evidence of success in control, if not eradication.[81]

Between the mosquito eradication campaigns in Havana and Panama, and the subsequent successful application of his model in New Orleans and Rio de Janeiro, Colonel William Crawford Gorgas was showered with praise and rewards by a grateful world, including gold medals from the Liverpool School of Tropical Medicine and the American Museum of Safety. In 1907, he was elected head of the American Association of Tropical Medicine, and two years later was elected the president of the American Medical Association. On January 16, 1914, Gorgas received his greatest honor when he was appointed Surgeon General. Amidst the hoopla, Gorgas forgot his earlier misgivings over the practicality of total eradication, crafting a personal narrative that ascribed yellow fever eradication as a strategic mission of the United States and increasingly presenting himself with a clear vision of ultimate success from the start. Gorgas's speeches and academic papers positioned himself as humanity's champion against a dread scourge."[82] As Gorgas' version took shape, his own championing of vector eradication took center stage as the greatest scientific accomplishment of the day, demoting Walter Reed to a supporting player in the struggle.

PUERTO RICO: DIFFERENT DISEASES AND DIFFERENT APPROACHES

When I Corps landed in Puerto Rico, medical officers discovered smallpox there. Despite the vaccination of all Americans, Army physicians were concerned. There was a slight chance of infection among individual soldiers whose vaccination was faulty. The scope of the disease also threatened future economic and political development, a threat realized in the fall of 1898 when the island was quarantined by neighboring countries.[83]

Smallpox in Puerto Rico followed a different etiology than in the United States. Whereas back home the locus of infection was the urban industrial core, in Puerto Rico the disease resided primarily in small rural villages. The overall population density of the island—an average of 264 persons per square mile—combined with the overwhelming poverty, poor sanitation, and local fears of isolation and quarantine to generate a constant cycle of infection. Medical officers soon determined newly infected victims routinely carried the disease into the market places of neighboring towns and cities from their villages.[84]

As the Army doctors planned an intervention, they discovered numerous factors—a poor transportation network; rural and urban overcrowding; a shortage of native physicians; the inaccessible hill country; the difficulty in bringing and storing variola to the island—all threatened to derail any campaign. The paternalism and racism of the island's new imperial masters was another limiting, if unrecognized, factor. Major Azel Ames, architect of the forthcoming smallpox control effort, described his own concerns over "the great difficulty, even with plenty of virus, of vaccinating these hundreds of thousands of unregistered people, mostly ignorant and scattered, speaking foreign tongues, and unused to sanitary control."[85] Ames never considered, of course, just *who* was the foreigner, nor how a newly conquered people would respond to a vaccination campaign.

Despite the problems, several conditions contributed to success. The island's geography was the most significant, as a stringent inspection system would prevent smallpox from returning to Puerto Rico after eradication. The recent transfer of control to the U.S. Army was another positive. As long as the military directly administered the island, the Medical Department had privileged access to a readily available coercive means for enforcing public health policy. Puerto Rico was also home to several large cattle ranches, which provided a ready host for producing home-grown variola. Finally, the virulence of smallpox among the indigenous population was an unseen blessing; the majority of the adult population had already survived their own infections, thus the only group needing immediate vaccination were young islanders.[86]

The Army's smallpox eradication effort began on January 3, 1899, with a General Order from the newly appointed military governor, Major General Guy V. Henry, to the island's local mayors (*Alcaldes*) introducing mandatory vaccination.[87] This order marked the Army's first co-operative civil public health program. Previously, any Medical Department's interaction with civilian populations was either on a singular, *ad hoc* basis, was subordinated to a clear military operational need, or was facilitated by the temporary activities of investigative commissions. Puerto Rico's smallpox campaign was different. Undertaken in the name of the civil government, under direct local supervision and funded by the Insular Department, all field and laboratory work was directed and performed by the Army's medical officers and enlisted orderlies. Success offered a model for future disease control campaigns, as it proved possible for the military, through the medical expert branch, to act in cooperation with local civilian governments and agencies without subverting their authority.

In the six months after the order was issued, smallpox eradication was the occupation regime's highest priority. On January 7, 1899, Ames opened a smallpox vaccine farm near Coamo Baths with the ultimate goal of producing one million glass-filled vaccine points.[88] In February 1899, the vaccination program began. In four months, over 860,000 people were vaccinated out of a total population of 960,000. Those not vaccinated were considered immune, having already contracted the disease. Shortly thereafter, Puerto Rico was declared free of smallpox. The ease with which the effort was completed surprised many. Whereas in February 1899, 3,000 new cases were reported, two and a half years later, the mortality rate dropped to two cases per year.[89]

Still, Puerto Rico retained a reputation as an unwholesome and sickly place. Visitors left believing the island's environment characterized both the best and worst aspects of the tropics. On the one hand, the warm, humid trade winds created a sort of garden paradise, lush with green vegetation and wildlife.[90] At the same time, it was reputed as a hotbed of sickness. The unusually virulent smallpox was only one example: malarial fevers, yellow fever, chronic dysenteries and diarrheas, syphilis, filariasis, and the so-called "mazamorra," or "ground-itch," a topical dermatitis affecting those who went barefoot, were all endemic. No place on the island was safe. Even the highlands, where the altitude and breezes dissipated fever-causing miasmas, were dangerous. The daytime tropical heat, humidity, and direct sunlight combined to break down the physical structure of unacclimated whites, not to mention the inevitable nervous collapse. The fresh and abundant fruit, if eaten hastily, could ferment in the stomach, creating discomfort and sickness. The island's water was also risky. Virtually every well and stream was polluted by raw sewage. When the warm temperature of the water and the abundance of silt—the "rich vegetable pabulum"— were factored in, local water became a "culture medium *par excellence*" for diseases, worms, and parasites.[91]

For the new American occupiers, these factors posed a serious threat. After yellow fever, the greatest fear for white Americans was tropical neurasthenia. As early as September 1899, officers in the Caribbean and Philippines advised against sending soldiers to the tropics for tours longer than a year. In his report to Washington, reprinted in the September 30, 1899 *Army and Navy Register*, the military governor of Havana, Brigadier General William Ludlow, cautioned:

Experience has also shown that it is not advisable to maintain men of northern races continuously on service in the tropics. Not only are the losses from disease severe, but the entire body of men becomes greatly deteriorated from climatic and other effects. It is believed that if garrisons of American troops are to be maintained in the tropics, these facts should be taken into account, and permanent dispositions made with reference to their exchange between home and foreign stations.[92]

Other officers agreed, framing their arguments in the context of tropicality. The poor health of indigenous Puerto Ricans bolstered such claims. Between the effects of generations of exposure to the tropical miasmas, heat, and sunlight, and the intermingling with the island's surviving Indians and imported Negroes, the racial stock of the current population was believed to have degenerated. Considered least fortunate were the *jíbaro*, the island's poor laborers descended from the original Spanish colonists. Early nineteenth-century accounts described them as lazy and indolent, content to "swing themselves in their hammocks all day long, smoking cigars and scraping their native guitars. . . . Their children, isolated from the cities, without education, live in social equality with the young negroes of both sexes, acquiring perverted customs, only to later become cruel with their slaves"[93] Even native Puerto Ricans accepted the twisted logic of a racialized tropical environment. In September 1903, Captain José Lugo-Viña, assistant surgeon with the recently raised Porto Rico Regiment, affirmed the notion that his own people were victims of the cruel environment:

> Thus it will be seen that we have not only to seek for the micro-organisms that impoverish the blood of our people, but also to try to improve our ways of living and the conditions by which we are surrounded. We are descended almost exclusively from one European nation, which, though strong and vigorous on its own soil has bequeathed to us through the influence of a tropical climate, an enfeebled constitution. We have lived for centuries without sanitary laws that might in part have remedied the evil, and without schools or religious ideas, lost amid the waters of the Caribbean Sea.[94]

Evidence of racial degeneration was seen in the chronic tropical anemia afflicting the island's native population. In 1901, retired Colonel Charles H. Alden, a former Assistant Surgeon General, described Puerto Rican anemia, or "tropical chlorosis," as the greatest mortal disease afflicting the island, ascribing over sixteen percent of Puerto Rico's average annual death rate between 1890 and 1900 to the condition.[95] Only the most prestigious elites were free from the condition, which appeared most virulent in the island's large coffee plantations. Poor laborers and their families working and residing there all displayed the same symptoms: sallow complexions, distended abdomens, and physical exhaustion. Tropical chlorosis was so endemic it was labeled "the lazy disease" by Americans, a pejorative "angrily resented by press and people of the Island, where they do not fail to feel keenly the cruelty of the jest that would make laziness with them a disease."[96]

Even as the island's new masters sought to turn the climate and environment into factors delineating threats to their own racial superiority and power, Army medical officers began deconstructing myths of tropicality used to buttress white American exceptionalism on Puerto Rico. Unlike Cuba or the 1899 smallpox eradication effort, less attention was given to work undertaken in Puerto Rico. Yet the work undertaken in Puerto Rico by First Lieutenant Bailey K. Ashford between 1899 and 1906 transformed the field of public health. Ashford's discoveries not only paved the way for what would become the first American, and then global, public health philanthropy. They also heralded the beginning of a new relationship between the Army Medical Department and the private civilian sector.

Ashford arrived in Puerto Rico as part of Major General Nelson A. Miles' invasion force on July 25, 1898. The twenty-five year old first lieutenant, a graduate of Georgetown University's medical school, was part of the last pre-war graduating class of the Army Medical School. Within a few days of landing at Guanica, the Americans established a rough field hospital near San German. There Ashford tended to wounded American and Spanish soldiers brought in following the few brief yet spirited engagements on the island. After the fighting ended, Ashford joined other medical officers in the campaign against smallpox.[97]

No sooner had the smallpox eradication effort ended than Puerto Rico was struck by a devastating hurricane on August 8, 1899. Over 2,200 people were killed by flooding, which destroyed most of the island's plantations, driving the rural poor into cities and towns for food and shelter. All the island's coastal centers were hit hard, and the entire population faced the prospect of famine and epidemic disease.[98] Ashford was ordered to establish a hospital near Ponce, where the civilian hospital was devastated by the storm. He was shocked to discover three-quarters of the patients he treated were afflicted with what he first diagnosed as anemia. Ashford came to doubt his assessment as patients failed to respond to an improved diet with iron supplements. Over the next three months, various diagnoses, including malaria, dysentery, and racial degeneration were each considered and rejected, until Ashford conducted tests to determine if pernicious anemia was the agent. The results of the blood work revealed a high percentage of eosinophiles, a white blood cell associated with parasitic infections.[99]

Ashford still needed physical proof of a parasite from a patient. The next day, November 24, 1899, microscopic examination of fecal samples revealed eggs, which he identified as *Ancylostomum duodenale*, a parasite native to northern Italy and Switzerland. Certain he discovered the cause of the anemia, he notified San Juan of his discovery.[100] The island's chief surgeon, Colonel John Van Rensselaer Hoff, responded immediately, instructing Ashford to prepare a pamphlet detailing his findings, and to return to

Washington. The resulting bilingual pamphlet, "Anemia, Its Causes, Treatment and Prevention," was issued in early 1900 by the Superior Board of Health in San Juan to all physicians and pharmacists.[101]

Nevertheless, Ashford retained doubts that hookworm was responsible for the fatal Puerto Rican anemia. At the Army Medical School, Ashford attended a seminar on helminthology by the Department of Agriculture's parasitologist, Charles Wardell Stiles. In December 1899, Ashford called on Stiles, but was forced to hand his samples over to Stiles' assistant, Dr. Albert Hassell. Upon receiving the samples and observing that the eggs were large for the typical *Ancylostomum duodenale*, Hassell agreed they deserved greater study and promised to pass them on to Stiles.[102]

By the time he returned to Puerto Rico, Ashford was convinced of the link between the "Puerto Rican Anemia" and the hookworm larvae. Upon his arrival, he persuaded the U.S. Public Health and Marine Hospital Service's Walter W. King to join him in a thirteen-month study of ninety-nine patients in Ponce's Tricoche Hospital. Each patient was subjected to repeated purgatives over a two-day period. On the first evening of treatment between thirty to sixty grains of magnesium sulfate was administered to each person. The next morning, patients were given a strong dose—two grams, or thirty grains—of thymol, followed by a second dose two hours later. Usually this was sufficient to cause the dramatic expulsion of the worms from the patient's bowel. If the patient did not void the worms by noon, a second dose of magnesium salts was given to the patient. Following the purging of the hookworms and their ova, the patient was given large doses of iron carbonate in commercially marketed pills to increase their low hemoglobin levels. Sent home after the first treatment, the patient was subjected to follow-up thymol treatments until microscopic examination revealed stool free of hookworms or ova. Even after discharge from the hospital, patients were regularly evaluated to gauge their full recovery. Ashford noted recovery often began quickly and was marked by an increase in eosinophiles and an overall improved emotional disposition. Remaining symptoms subsided over the next three to six months, with the heart murmur generally last to go.[103]

Upon completing the study, Ashford was confident he had discovered the cure for the anemia plaguing Puerto Rico. Of ninety-nine patients treated, fifty-seven were completely cured. Another thirteen were still under hospital observation, and another twelve were convalescing at their homes. Ten patients died, though Ashford quickly distanced his test from the causes of their deaths, noting they were either too far advanced for treatment or suffered from other conditions, namely tuberculosis and malaria. Only five failed to show any progress. Here again Ashford sought to clarify a secondary reason for the results, noting three were tubercular.[104]

With a successful trial behind him, Ashford considered therapies and environmental control. Unlike other diseases in the Caribbean, uncinariasis was a chronic condition; successful treatment of an infected victim did not mean that the individual would remain free of the disease. Unless efforts were made to address the behavior of the exposed population, in essence transforming the very culture of the rural Puerto Rican, repeat infection was inevitable. Thus, any projected effort to eradicate hookworm in Puerto Rico entailed a three-pronged approach of therapeutic intervention, cultural reeducation, and environmental transformation.

In some ways, the therapeutic angle was the easiest of the three to address. Unlike other diseases, uncinariasis was parasitic. There already existed a body of folk knowledge from rural Southern Europe and the American South that could be tapped into, as well as a number of commercially available nostrums and tonics in the United States touted as vermifuges. When tested in Ashford's controlled environment, however, almost all of these remedies proved worthless. The same was true of several treatments commonly used by physicians, including eucalyptus extract and chloroform. The three most viable vermifuges were soon narrowed down to male fern extract, thymol, and beta-naphthol. Male fern extract was quickly ruled out as unstable in tropical humidity and as being frequently adulterated by unscrupulous vendors. Beta-naphthol, a chemical used in the dye industry, worked admirably in irritating the worms and forcing them to release their hold on the intestinal wall, but was generally ineffective against worms lodged deeper in the intestinal folds. Thymol, a topical antiseptic and preservative, proved more effective but required careful administration. Highly toxic in its pure state, thymol provoked the desired result if administered in small doses mixed with wine or liquor. Nevertheless, it could cause great harm in severe cases. Testing the two vermifuges on small control groups—forty patients treated with thymol, and thirty with beta-naphthol—revealed either one served the desired purpose. By the fifth weekly dose, thymol expelled 99.79 percent of all worms from the patients, while beta-naphthol removed 98.73 percent of the infestation in the individuals.[105]

With a therapeutic response in hand, Ashford next considered the issues of cultural reeducation of the rural Puerto Rican poor and environmental transformation. Earlier, he identified links between the high reported incidence of anemia and rural poverty. The condition was virtually unknown among those who could afford shoes. The rural poor, especially those living and working on coffee plantations, were not so fortunate. The island's plantations were densely packed with coffee bushes, the ground beneath the shrubs remaining moist due to the dense shade beneath the foliage. Tenant farmers and day laborers worked long hours in these fields, voiding their waste where they stood. The combination of the microenvironment, total ignorance of sanitation, and abject poverty allowed hookworm to flourish.[106] Hookworm disease was thus related to human behavior. Though possible to treat exclusively through therapeutic intervention, without a simultaneous campaign of sanitary education, reinfection was inevitable. And unlike diseases investigated in Cuba, the Philippines, and elsewhere, the medical topography of hookworm precluded a massive environmental remediation. The vector in this case was not a mosquito or fly, but the afflicted themselves.

The solution was to bring the news about hookworm directly to the people. In 1904, Ashford and King established their first field hospital in the Bayamon district. Within six weeks, 931 cases were treated at the cost of a single fatality from a lethal misdosage of thymol. The results were quickly tabulated, with the district of 32,000 inhabitants witnessing an immediate 20 percent decline in mortality. The field hospital moved next to the Utuado district, where 1,500 cases were treated in a six-week period.[107] In the traveling hospital's first year of operation, 5,490 people received treatment. As reports spread of the Americans' success in eliminating "*mazamorra*," more came seeking treatment. In the clinic's second year, an additional 18,865 were treated. Soon Ashford began predicting total eradication, noting 50,000 people were treated in 1905 alone.[108]

From the beginning, the hookworm clinic was more than a treatment center. While waiting for treatment, patients received information about the condition. Sanitary lectures divulged the secrets of *la mazamorra*. Families were given an opportunity to see the "little worms" that entered their bodies while they were working barefoot in the fields, and how they traveled through their bloodstream to take up residence in their bowel. Explanations were given freely to basic questions, such as why the disease was so rife among coffee pickers and their families, how the "ground-itch" was an indicator of future sickness, and why it was important to cover one's waste. Patients could watch the laboratory screening of their blood, from the initial test for infection to the hemoglobin counts following successive treatments. They were also present for the post-purge stool examination, witnessing with their own eyes the wriggling mass of worms that came out of their own bowel. This act of making patients active participants in their own treatment was essential. "Every sanitary lecture we gave was repeated and discussed by thousands of lips between sunrise and sunset, because the people were vitally interested. The station was not feared, but sought out, not the subject of jest, but of great respect," Ashford later recalled.[109]

The transaction between the American field hygienist and the peasant farmer created a greater appreciation for public works and good government, something completely alien to them. According to Ashford, hookworm disease had a far broader effect on Puerto Rican society beyond public health. The physical exhaustion accompanying infection struck at the core of civil and social life on the island. So long as the population remained in the grip of the disease, Puerto Rico would never achieve its full economic and political potential. The vast majority of islanders, a "refined, gentle, respectful, law-abiding, and an intensely patriotic people," would remain mere peons, incapable of exercising their political franchise or advancing their economic status.[110] Hookworm eradication removed the immediate cause of their dissipation, but it was the act of direct participation in their cure that promoted civic development of the island. For Ashford, shepherding the Puerto Rican along the pathways of civic and economic improvement was an inseparable aspect of his public health work. Unlike Gorgas, Ashford sought to improve the lot of the indigene as a prelude to cultural and economic autonomy. "Our problem is not to make it possible for physically inferior races to live in the tropics despite the menace of parasitic invasion," he wrote near the end of his career, "our real problem is to fortify, by proper nutrition, a race of tropicalists that can successfully compete with their brothers of the temperate climates, really less favored by Nature than themselves."[111]

By June 1906, little doubt remained regarding the link between hookworm and anemia in Puerto Rico. On the basis of the proven success of Ashford and King's traveling clinic, the Puerto Rican legislature authorized a permanent commission to eradicate hookworm infection throughout the island. Under the direction of one of Ashford's colleagues, Dr. Gutierrez Igaravidez, the commission organized and opened thirty-five uncinariasis dispensaries throughout the island. Between July 1906 and June 1909, 247,901 patients were treated in the clinics, leaving Ashford to estimate that in the ten years since he discovered the link between the hookworm and the Puerto Rican anemia, over 300,000 persons were treated, with 426 fatalities, most likely from a toxic reaction to the vermifuge.[112]

Meanwhile, the Puerto Rican Legislative Assembly established a special Tropical and Transmissible Diseases Service within the Island's Department of Health, Charities, and Corrections. Ordered to open four permanent dispensaries in each of the island's seven sanitary districts, as well as any others deemed essential, the new organization soon operated fifty-five clinics. A bacteriological laboratory was also established in San Juan, where specialized testing could be conducted for less common diseases. Soon the new Tropical and Transmissible Diseases Service was operating along the same lines as the Army Medical Department, with a highly specialized cadre of laboratory microbiologists. The organization's structure was highly regimented, with a hierarchy of responsibility and command extending from the director to the individual laboratory assistants and visiting nurses. Identified as "medical officers," the civilian physicians of the Service stood apart from other local physicians as an elite corps of investigators with full power to intervene in local medical practice as needed. Focused on their primary mission of eradicating hookworm disease, the Service and its laboratory nevertheless existed as "the foundations for a campaign for the prevention of transmissible diseases, which should be the object of every modern sanitary organization."[113]

Ashford's success was not lost on local Spanish physicians. Unlike the case of yellow fever and Carlos Finlay, there was no indigenous visionary to point the way for Ashford to follow. The discovery and the resulting therapeutic response was exclusively American. One Spanish physician, Dr. Alonzo Sañudo, noted that after receiving a copy of Ashford's first pamphlet he felt "profound bitterness when he saw that an American had studied this matter while the Spaniards during our domination had done nothing in this direction."[114] Likewise, Dr. Jose Condina Castellví, in an address delivered in Spain in 1906, asked "[I]s it not shameful that after having been ours so many years . . . we come now to know, and only now, that 90 per cent of that anemia from which the rural population is suffering and which we limited ourselves to calling tropical is nothing more than the anemia of ankylostomiasis!"[115]

While Ashford's work was roundly praised by Puerto Rican and Spanish physicians, he was denied the acclaim showered upon his peers. Two and a half years after he visited Washington with samples obtained from his first patients, Ashford's former mentor, Charles Wardell Stiles, revealed his own discovery of a new species of hookworm, *Uncinaria Americana*, at the American Gastroenterologic Association's annual meeting on May 1, 1902. While Stiles recognized that "Dr. Bailey K. Ashford in Porto Rico" had collected samples of the newly discovered species, he offered no other acknowledgment of the medical officer's work.[116] Granted, Stiles was the first to identify the difference between the Old and New World species, and accounts of "chalk-eaters" were features in travelers' accounts in the American South even before the Civil War. But Ashford's omission by Stiles and the latter's subsequent acclaim as the sole discoverer of hookworm disease is one of the greatest misappropriations of scientific recognition.

Stiles' desire for sole recognition only grew as he grasped the opportunities available to him as the champion of hookworm eradication. By 1902, Reed and Gorgas' work in Cuba established a precedent for the success of American medical and sanitary science. At the same time, however, their discoveries and the attendant acclaim effectively muted Ashford's work in Puerto Rico. Yellow fever was the great scourge. Hookworm disease, while no less significant in holding back development, and more widespread than yellow fever ever was, was far less glamorous and exotic in comparison. Only later did the potential of Ashford's discovery and his therapeutic methods become clear. Having made his name as the "discoverer" of the New World hookworm, Stiles became the lone champion for hookworm eradication in the American South. However, his one-man crusade produced little result save polite ridicule by a skeptical public until his work reached the attention of Frederick T. Gates, the general manager of the philanthropic activities of the Rockefeller family in the spring of 1909. Appointed the Scientific Secretary of the fledgling Rockefeller Sanitary Commission, Stiles traveled the country delivering lectures on hookworm infection and touting the new organization's project in treating hookworm victims in the Southern United States. The ensuing campaign reached every corner of the American South in the next five years, and ultimately eradicated hookworm infection in the United States.[117]

Denied credit as the primary discoverer of hookworm disease and the architect of the therapeutic response, Ashford missed his chance to stand alongside Walter Reed and William Crawford Gorgas as one of the Army

Medical Department's great "men in khaki." In his 1934 autobiography, *A Soldier in Science*, Ashford attempted to set the record straight. Noting he preceded Stiles' 1902 announcement of hookworm infestation in the United States by publishing his own article in the *New York Medical Journal*, Ashford also observed how he intended to consult his former instructor on the feasibility of the parasite cycle he observed in Puerto Rico. Stiles' claim that he suggested Ashford examine the stools of his patients to find the hookworm there was also false. Recounting Stiles's own self-aggrandizement, Ashford recorded:

> He [Stiles] stated that he had emphasized the prophecy that hookworm would be found in American territory in connection with a clinical picture similar to that which I had encountered. But I have already recounted how I was directed to examine the feces of my first patient. Indeed, for that matter, as far back as 1881 Hirsh, author of a reference book on medical geography much used in Europe, had insisted that, from clinical histories published by American histories, hookworm must exist in the United States.[118]

Stiles, Ashford continued, did not show any sign of understanding a connection between hookworm and anemia in the Western Hemisphere before receiving Ashford's specimens. "So there was no connection whatsoever between the discovery of hookworm disease in Puerto Rico and Dr. Stiles," Ashford concluded.[119] Moreover, the photos Stiles provided as evidence of his alleged work were actually taken by Ashford. The first photo, allegedly a sick Georgia farmer being carried to hospital, was taken by Ashford in Utuado, Puerto Rico. The second photo, taken from a microscopic slide showing a hookworm with its head buried in a section of intestinal membrane, was created by Ashford at the Army Medical Museum during Ashford's 1900 visit to Washington. Ashford recounted that while he had never sent the photos for future publication, "the only way they could have reached the hands of the newspapers must have been through someone with whom I was communicating by letter at the time."[120] That someone, Ashford concluded, was Stiles.

Granting that advances in medical science often were the result of multiple threads of research converging at a single point, Ashford nevertheless claimed an exception in terms of hookworm:

> [O]ne fact was truly discovered in Puerto Rico, and in Puerto Rico only: hookworm as a scourge of the agricultural laborer in tropical and sub-tropical countries could be successfully treated and exterminated in a comparatively short period of time. This practical find completely revolutionized the treatment of the problem, and Puerto Rico furnished the first solution in the world through its Porto Rico Anemia Commission and their seven years' labor.[121]

Ashford bore little bitterness toward the Rockefeller philanthropy. After a 1910 visit to Puerto Rico, Rockefeller Sanitary Commission Director Wickliffe Rose was convinced of Ashford's foresight in identifying the link between hookworm infection and anemia. After inspecting Ashford's clinics in action, Rose left determined to bring the Puerto Rican model back to the United States. In his notes for a projected history of the Rockefeller International Health Division, Lewis Hackett recorded Rose's outlook, noting that "Dr. Rose left Puerto Rico a changed man, fired by new ambition and a new mission. . . . After he had reached home, it did not take long to organize the Rockefeller Sanitary Commission for work in the South on exactly the same lines as those laid down for Puerto Rico."[122] After their 1910 meeting, the two became close colleagues, with Ashford signing on with the Rockefeller International Health Board as a tropical disease expert. For the next two decades, they maintained a regular correspondence, and Ashford made frequent trips to Latin America on behalf of the Rockefeller philanthropies.

Ashford never forgave Stiles for claiming the discovery of hookworm disease as his own. Nor would Stiles withdraw his own claim as its primary discoverer. After leaving the Rockefeller Sanitary Commission, Stiles pressed his own case as the sole visionary who connected the physical evidence collected by Ashford with hookworm disease. Stiles' account painted himself as the lonely prophet of the potential for hookworm disease in the absence of real evidence of the parasite in humans. In all his lectures at Georgetown Medical College and the Army Medical School—including purportedly that attended by Ashford—Stiles claimed to have issued the caution: "'Gentlemen, if you find cases of anemia in man in the tropics or sub-tropics, the cause of which is not clear to you, consider the possibility of hookworm disease."[123] Accordingly, Stiles described Ashford as an uncertain acolyte who asked his mentor for direction after uncovering the first specimens of hookworm in humans.

Stiles clung to his version of the hookworm discovery narrative for the rest of his life. When Lewis Hackett started writing a history of the International Health Division for the Rockefeller Foundation, he followed Stiles point of view. Taking credit for putting Rose and Ashford together for the first time in 1910, Stiles recounted how the young medical officer fit into his own narrative of hookworm disease. "'Mr. Rose returned opposed to the plan of a clinic which he did not think would work in the South and it became necessary to convert Rose to the idea of a clinic by showing him that they already existed and that the idea was not a new one,'" Hackett credits Stiles as saying. Though cautiously skeptical of Stiles' version of events, Hackett hedged. "It does not appear from any subsequent reference to the Puerto Rican mission how much truth lay in either contention and the exact extent of Mr. Rose's indebtedness will probably never be known," he concluded.[124]

EMPIRE'S INFLUENCE ON THE ARMY MEDICAL DEPARTMENT

America's interaction with the tropical environment was different from other imperial powers. When the United States acquired the Philippines and its Caribbean possessions, the two chief models for imperial administration were France and the United Kingdom. While the focus was on identifying analogies to recommend an imperial policy, the differences in their systems of cultural and civil administration were equally significant. In the French case, great importance was assigned to assimilating the indigenous elites through language, education, and graduated civic responsibility. By making the local inhabitant—or at least the educated and property-owning elites—more "French," the indigene shared a stake in the success of the imperial system. The promise of the French system of assimilation was a global community built upon the ethos and values of the Second Republic; the reality was an increasingly disillusioned indigenous elite who shared unequally in the exploitation of their culture and geographic wealth. The British system was less concerned with importing the ideology of transnational pride than with the establishing grounds for civic reform and free trade. Never losing sight of the potential for economic development attending good government, British imperial administrators emphasized creating civic infrastructures—schools, police and military institutions, courts, and hospitals—that would benefit all subjects. But these institutions were also intended for facilitating control, and ensuring the ongoing segregation of subject from imperial overlord.[125]

Unlike the British and French, American military officers and imperial administrators sought to transform the environment and the indigene into a safe and recognizable form. Progressive colonial administrations in the Philippines, Cuba, and Puerto Rico offered chances to conduct social and civic engineering on a broad scale, transforming not only the native inhabitants' perceptions of themselves, but also by changing their physical environs. Secretary of War Elihu Root captured this sentiment in his October 7, 1899 address to Chicago's Marquette Club. Speaking on the topic of "The American Soldier," Root noted the civic impulse of American volunteer and regular soldiers serving in Cuba, Puerto Rico, and the Philippines, ascribing their works to a uniquely democratic ethos. Root described recent activities in Cuba and Puerto Rico to his audience as an example of this mission:

> Poor Cuba, torn by years of war and dissension, with her people gathered starving in her towns, with no knowledge of the art of government, almost forgetful of the arts of peace, has had her wounds bound up, her people returned to their homes, the tillage of the soil recommenced, the industry of her factories, the activity of her commerce, all the arts of peace revived, under the kindly tuition of the American soldier. He goes with the sword, with the bayonet, with the cannon;

but the moment that the enemy ceases to fire he is ready with open hand, with the spirit of John Howard and Florence Nightingale, to heal the sick, to succor the poor, to teach the ignorant, to set up the arts of peace and to turn the scene of warfare into the smiling land of plenty.

The soldiers of the United States in Porto Rico, when that island was swept by the frightful hurricane of the eighth of August, turned into a hospital corps every one, from general down to private. I am prouder of Wood in Santiago and Wilson in Mantanzas and Ludlow in Havana, cleaning the streets and disinfecting the pest holes and teaching the Cubans how to live cleanly and orderly lives, teaching them the simple elements of civil government; teaching them how to go back to work, to earn their living; teaching them how to become self-governing citizens of a free state, than I ever could be of a hero on the ramparts amid the hail of shot.[126]

In a broad oratorical stroke, Secretary Root linked the environmental transformative process and the Medical Department's sanitary mission directly to the military mission of the Army. The new progressive Army's *raison d'être* was not solely to fight and defeat the nation's enemies in the field, but to also transform defeated former enemies and subject peoples into friendly modern states, capable of self-governance and preserving a quality of life in our own image. And the Medical Department was the point of the spear the Army's new nation building mission.

This process gave new meaning to the concept of Americanization. Not only did it capture the American character, with its acclaimed need to "tame" the frontier, it also reflected American obsessions with cleanliness and health. After their experiences from the Civil War, rapid urbanization, and the more immediate case of the 1898 fever camps, Americans realized sickness *was* avoidable. American colonial administrators used sanitary reform to clean the filthy environment in the nation's new empire. When that failed, they turned to the scientific methodologies championed by the Army Medical Department. Sanitary reform was not abandoned; it was renewed with a vengeance after the discovery of the insect vector and the healthy carrier. Ultimately, the American imperial experience not only ensured the primacy of scientific medicine well into the next century, it also meant filth retained a prime place in the thoughts of a nation enamored with a "gospel of germs."[127]

Equally important was the imperial mission's effect on the institutional culture of the Medical Department. During the heyday of tropical medicine and sanitation in the department, from 1899 to 1914, professional advancement and promotion came far more readily to sanitarians and laboratory scientists working in the tropics than any other group. Not only were medical officers saving lives—by the millions if their reckoning is accepted, they were also transforming the deadly tropical environment into a pleasure garden, ready to accept the civilizing seeds sown by white Americans.

The successful collaboration of research-oriented medical officers and uniformed sanitarians in Cuba, Puerto Rico, and Panama solidified the informal triad of legitimacy based upon specialization. After 1900, sanitarians were increasingly in the ascendancy insofar as their influence in the department. The message of military sanitarians—that infectious disease could be prevented, provided proper hygienic measures were observed—was championed since the Civil War. The fever camp debacle of 1898 brought their message home with a renewed vigor. The message ultimately validated the Medical Department as the Army's resident expert on disease despite the virulence of the epidemic.

But it was the success of medical officers in implementing their practical visions of sanitation abroad that signaled a formal hierarchy within the Medical Department. The twin methods—Gorgas' environmental and cultural transformative war of eradication against the insect vector and Ashford's combination of therapeutic intervention and benign cultural education—brought sanitarians to the fore in the department.

5   The Ascendance of Sanitation in the Army Medical Department and the Quest for Preparedness, 1901–1917

"Lack of training on the part of troops is the most important pre-disposing cause of disease in armies. *It is the duty of all officers, of whatever rank or branch of the service, to endeavor to overcome this defect, for which they are mainly responsible.*"

Major Percy Moreau Ashburn, 1909.[1]

On February 2, 1901, Congress passed its first efficiency act for the Medical Department since the Spanish-American War. The act sought to rationalize the entire Regular peacetime establishment by limiting all future surgeons general following Surgeon General Sternberg to a four year term. Beneath the surgeon general, a hierarchical structure was established: eight assistant surgeons general with the rank of colonel; twelve deputy surgeons general with the rank of lieutenant colonel; sixty surgeons with the rank of major; and 240 assistant surgeons, with the ranks of captain and first lieutenant.[2]

After Sternberg retired on June 8, 1902, he was replaced by his chief assistant, William H. Forwood. A member of the Medical Department since 1861, Forwood served for three months, when his mandatory retirement after forty-one years service took effect. Forwood's brief tenure justified a rider to a June 30, 1902 Army appropriations act forbidding the appointment of future staff bureau chiefs with less than four years active service remaining before mandatory retirement.[3]

After Forwood, the appointment devolved to the department's most senior qualified medical officer, Robert Maitland O'Reilly. A veteran of the Civil War, O'Reilly served as a medical cadet. After the war, he attended the University of Pennsylvania's medical school so he could return to the Medical Department as an Assistant Surgeon on May 14, 1867.[4] O'Reilly's contemporaries described his tenure as one "marked by judgment, liberality, progressiveness, and energy," making him in spirit if not fact the successor to George Miller Sternberg. According to Mary Gillett, a key to O'Reilly's reputation was his policy of surrounding himself with young junior officers as subordinates. This led an entire generation of medical officers to admire him for his conscious effort to forego the seniority system.[5] There was more to O'Reilly than an easygoing nature. After his appointment, he set out to accomplish two objectives: implementing the Dodge Commission's recommendations and expanding the Medical Department. He methodically addressed each of the Dodge Commission Report's seven reforms: reorganizing the medical corps, establishing a ready hospital reserve, organizing a female nurse reserve, compiling a stockpile of medical supplies, creating a supply transport system, simplifying paperwork, and giving hospital commanders authority to provide adequate nutrition for the sick in their care.[6]

O'Reilly also confronted the staffing problems facing his predecessors since the establishment of the Medical Department in 1818. By 1900, it was clear the Medical Department was not attracting the highest caliber of medical graduates it once had. Low pay was not the whole issue; first lieutenants in the Medical Department earned a higher salary than over half of the country's doctors. While Mary Gillett notes "Medical Department salaries were too low to attract the best doctors," slow promotion, the prospect of dangerous foreign service, and rising opportunities in the growing domestic sphere should also be considered.[7] Medical school graduates eager to pursue scientific medicine or public hygiene had ready opportunities to practice their skills in burgeoning public health departments. And those interested in traditional practice and surgery also enjoyed new opportunities for advancement, because their skills and reputations as acolytes of the new scientific medicine were in great demand in urban hospitals. Weighed against the enticements of steady, well-paid employment, the opportunity to influence public policy and the newfound respect for the medical profession in American society, the Army Medical Department was no longer an alluring prospect for new physicians. In response, O'Reilly sought to increase the professional tenor and prestige of the Medical Department. He made the entrance examination more demanding and required candidates to have at least one year's experience as "attending surgeons in the principal medical centers of the United States." New officer candidates were hired as contract surgeons during their tenure at the Army Medical School, commissioned after graduation. These efforts were hamstrung in 1903, however, when Congress refused to extend the enlistments of volunteer surgeons. The sudden loss of two hundred volunteer medical officers left the department incapable of fulfilling its basic mission of safeguarding the wellness of the Army. In response, O'Reilly pled with the War Department for expansion, pointing out that while line regiments were officered in peacetime for a wartime expansion to a force of 100,000 men, the existing Medical Department staffing was sufficient only for a total force of 42,000 men. If, as O'Reilly noted, "Other nations, including so poor a nation as the Japanese, are willing to pay the cost of increased efficiency in the shape of a large and well organized medical service," how could the United States do otherwise?[8] The subsequent February 1904 appropriations request sought an increase in the department's establishment of twenty colonels, twenty lieutenant colonels, one hundred and ten majors, and three hundred captains, and the creation of a Medical Reserve Corps.[9] Congress took no action on the expansion bill for three years, sparking a fervent campaign on the Medical Department's behalf by the Roosevelt administration. Appeals on behalf of the Medical Department become a regular feature of the Secretary of War's reports to Congress. On January 9, 1905, President Theodore Roosevelt issued a special message to Congress in support of O'Reilly's plan for a Medical Reserve Corps.[10] Nevertheless, the bill remained in committee through 1907, causing O'Reilly to grouse: "This office is constantly embarrassed by demands for medical officers that can not be supplied, and little can be done in the way of preparedness for great emergencies with a personnel that is not sufficient to meet the little emergencies that occur in peace."[11]

On April 23, 1908, Congress added 123 new positions, including six new colonels, twelve new lieutenant colonels, forty-five majors, and sixty new captains and lieutenants, all collected in a new Medical Corps, an organizational entity distinct from the department's other branches. By making over half of the new positions senior appointments, Congress freed up the logjam of junior officers that had developed since the Army's 1901 reorganization. The act also strengthened Medical Department standards through mandatory examinations for all promotions up to lieutenant colonel, stipulating mandatory retirement for failure to pass the examination after two attempts. Surgeon pay was raised to a level equal to that enjoyed by senior physicians in the private sector, with the added bonus of a retirement pension set at three-quarter annual pay after forty years service. Lastly, the act finally eliminated the long-standing and problematic practice of assigning occupational labels to medical officers as complements to their rank. Medical officers were no longer identified as "Surgeon" and "Assistant Surgeon"— their formal title would reflect their grade as an officer in the U.S. Army.[12] The second component of the 1908 Efficiency Act addressed O'Reilly's 1904 recommendation for a ready medical reserve. Intended as a permanent solution to the contract surgeon dilemma, members of the new Army Medical Reserve Corps were to be between twenty-two and forty-four years old, graduates of a reputable medical school, and engaged in an active medical practice. After passing their entrance examinations, candidates were commissioned as reserve first lieutenants, and were eligible to be called up as the War Department deemed necessary. A substantial number of the initial candidates were contract surgeons when the act took effect, and 160 of those who applied were immediately passed into service as first lieutenants. This freed most of the other 204 physicians who enlisted in the Reserve Corps' first year from being detailed to service in the Philippines or Caribbean, though they were still liable to be called upon to replace local post surgeons who were dispatched in their place. Though failure to report carried no penalty other than the immediate forfeiture of commission, the new reserve enjoyed a satisfactory record of retention in its first year, with only six physicians vacating their commissions.[13]

The Surgeon General's Office welcomed the Army Medical Reserve Corps as a landmark development. For years, the Medical Department touted the foresight of Surgeon General O'Reilly, who retired shortly after the act took place, for promoting a reserve corps that was the model rest of the Army followed eight years later. A year after it was created, the department's new head, Surgeon General George H. Torney, lauded the effect the new branch had on recruitment. The ever-growing legitimacy of scientific medicine in the civilian sphere had restricted the pool of potential candidates for the Medical Department. The new Reserve Corps resolved this problem. It attracted higher quality recent graduates with the appeal of part-time military service and appealed to the patriotism of many physicians who had entertained military service but were unwilling to give up their practice or teaching positions. "The list of these gentlemen, now on the inactive list of the Reserve Corps, contains many names which are well known in scientific circles throughout the world," Torney wrote in his 1909 report.[14]

Not all were as enthusiastic. Some saw the Medical Reserve Corps as a pool of well intentioned but hapless civilians who created a greater drain on scarce resources in wartime. Even reserve officers felt this in the early years. In an address given before the Association of Military Surgeons, Medical Reserve Corps Lieutenant Harry C. Cox of New York admitted that, patriotism and zeal notwithstanding, the actual utility of the reservist physician remained untested. "We are essentially an unknown quantity in time of war," he said, "far more than our worthy confrères in the Militia."[15] His solution was to extend to Medical Reserve Corps members an invitation to attend the National Guard's camps of maneuver. Though simplistic, his proposal revealed a serious flaw not accounted for in the original Medical Reserve Corps scheme. After authorizing the reserves and filling them with new candidates, little effort was put into their practical training. Yet even here there was resistance. In this case, the culprit was not personal disdain on the part of the Regular establishment, or jealousy from National Guard medical officers, but War Department inertia. Citing the original 1908 Act and General Regulations, the War Department informed Cox it would call up the Reserve Corps only in times of national emergency. Naturally, Cox and others present at the Richmond meeting objected, noting participation in maneuver camps could only increase the readiness of the Military Reserve Corps to at least the same level as their National Guard and Militia counterparts.[16]

O'Reilly's replacement was George H. Torney, at fifty-nine the youngest appointee since George Miller Sternberg and the first since 1861 with no Civil War service. A graduate of the University of Virginia Medical School, Torney entered the Navy as an Assistant Surgeon. He resigned from the Navy on June 18, 1875, to accept a commission as Assistant Surgeon in the Army. Torney had little experience in the Indian Wars, serving as post surgeon at Fort Wood, New York, Key West, and Fort Monroe, Virginia before being stationed at Fort Brown, Texas. The commander of the Army's hospital ship, *USS Relief*, during the Spanish-American War, Torney served a brief tour as commanding officer and chief surgeon of the Army and Navy General Hospital at Hot Springs, Arkansas, before he was sent to the Philippines. In 1908, after returning to the United States, Torney commanded public attention during the San Francisco earthquake. As Commandant of the Presidio General Hospital, he promptly directed the humanitarian response to the disaster, an opportunity *The Military Surgeon* later argued "doubtless formed the controlling factor which contributed to his elevation to the Surgeon Generalcy, to which he succeeded on the 14th of January, 1909."[17]

Torney sought few changes in the administration and direction O'Reilly established, though a long-simmering controversy over charges of favoritism in the Office of the Surgeon General finally came to a head. Since the 1840s, the surgeon general kept favored medical officers in Washington as members of his personal staff. Since the time of William Hammond, this prerogative was used time and again to keep skilled researchers and scientists like John Shaw Billings and Joseph Janvier Woodward in Washington where they could work on independent projects. This policy, though resented by many less favored medical officers, went unchallenged until the Spanish-American War. After the war created a new slate of foreign duty postings, those who did not win exemption were more resentful. By Torney's appointment, the outcry against the retention policy provoked the direct intervention of the Army's Chief of Staff, Major General Leonard Wood. In response to claims of favoritism, Torney claimed he needed to keep a cadre of officers in Washington, since rotation would adversely affect the Army Medical School. He also argued the Army's recent successes against yellow fever and other diseases could only be realized by the retention of skilled microbiologists as permanent members of the Surgeon General's staff. Rotating such men out of Washington would have a negative impact upon the Army's future medical science research. In December 1912, Wood ordered all medical officers not attached to the Army Medical Laboratory abroad, regardless of Torney's arguments otherwise.[18] Despite the controversy, Torney was appointed to a second term in January 1913. In December 1913, however, he contracted pneumonia, dying on December 27. The position next passed to William Crawford Gorgas. By the fall of 1913, Gorgas was basking in the adulation showered upon him by a grateful medical community and the world's imperial powers. In 1908, he was elected president of the American Medical Association, and received numerous honorary degrees. Other honors soon followed in the wake of these awards, including offers to take over several university presidencies. Gorgas continued his work in Panama as the Canal Zone's Chief Sanitary Officer, determined to complete his career with the Army Medical Department before entering the civilian world.[19]

Gorgas' appointment signaled a new age in the Medical Department. Under the leadership of Forwood, O'Reilly, and Torney, the department underwent a dynamic period of transformation, in which the influence of the sanitarian grew over that of the microbiologist and the general practitioner/surgeon in the institution. Far more than the traditional struggle to win Congress over to the expansion of the department marked the period between 1902 and 1916. It also witnessed the rise of sanitary thought as the driving force behind the expanding mission and scope of the Medical Department.

THE RISE OF SANITARY TACTICS IN
AMERICAN MILITARY MEDICINE

In the two decades between the Spanish-American War and America's entry into the First World War, hygiene and sanitation became the centerpieces of the Medical Department's internal intellectual direction. Ever mindful of the fever camps, Army sanitarians took advantage of the accomplishments of medical officers in the imperial periphery to promote a sanitation-oriented mission for the department. The lessons of this interwar period indicated the future of military medicine lay in overcoming the microbial threat in camps and in the field, where armies traditionally suffered their greatest losses. Or, as Illinois National Guard Captain Gustavus M. Blech summarized, the Spanish-American War taught the "bitter lesson that in war, bullets are not the only things to be reckoned with for casualty lists, and that even the most patriotic force of young men in uniforms will not avail if they have not been properly trained to withstand the rigors of a campaign, and if their sanitary, supply and engineering services are not properly organized."[20] Progressive medical science and practice not only offered the greatest potential for saving lives, it also promised swift decision in future conflict. In an age where warfare was driven by new technologies of killing, military hygiene gave the nation with the best sense of sanitary order the advantage of bringing more healthy troops to the field than its opponent. The militarization of public health and sanitation that followed came to be known as *sanitary tactics.*

Though a topic of debate among medical officers since the American Civil War, sanitary tactics moved to the forefront of American military discourse after the Russo-Japanese War, the first war in which combat fatalities outnumbered those from disease. American observers validated the long-standing arguments about the importance of clearly delineated medical and line officer responsibilities. Two Army medical officers, Colonels Valery Havard and John Van Rensselaer Hoff accompanied the Russian Army, while Major Louis L. Seaman joined the Japanese forces. In addition, the American military medical attaché to the Tokyo mission, Major Charles Lynch, traveled across Japan to observe and report on military medical preparations.[21]

Reports on the Russian medical system revealed alarming deficiencies. Created around a peacetime cadre system, the Sanitary Department of the Russian Military Establishment was fleshed out with reservist physicians upon mobilization.[22] Enlisted orderlies and attendants (*"sanitats"*) were pulled directly from the ranks, and received no training. During combat, many orderlies abandoned their posts, leaving physicians alone to care for the wounded. Real nursing was provided by 5,000 volunteer female nurses. The Russian Sanitary Department was quite large: after calling up reservists, the Russian Far East Army had over 3,000 physicians, and when volunteer nurses and enlisted *sanitats* were factored in, the Sanitary Department was approximately 75,000 strong.[23]

Hoff was amazed at how Russian medical officers persevered amidst such primitive organization. "This unusual condition of affairs, for Russia is now almost the only nation . . . that has not a distinct military Sanitary Corps officered by medical officers with a fixed military status, must not lead to the inference that the physicians employed are not highly educated in their profession or that Russia in any way falls short of other nations in the care of her soldiers, for this would be a mistake."[24] Nevertheless, Russian soldiers suffered horribly. The Russian Army lay at the end of an extremely long logistical path back to Moscow, with the result that many Sanitary Department supplies never arrived. Sanitary conditions in China were primitive. For centuries, Chinese villagers in Manchuria lived in wretched medieval conditions: open sewers; livestock stabled at night in villagers' houses; human waste collected for fertilizer allowed to sit in open pots and dung heaps until used. During the summer of 1905, typhoid fever became pandemic throughout the Russian Far East Army, threatening an already over-stretched logistical and medical system. An estimated 230,000 soldiers contracted the disease—far more than the official Russian reports of 17.033 cases and 2,077 deaths.[25]

Unlike the Russians, the Japanese maintained a large peacetime medical corps, well trained in bacteriology and sanitation by German medical advisers. The peacetime regimental complement of ten surgeons was reduced to six in wartime, as regular physicians were shared with reservist units. The Japanese Army also maintained a medical reserve corps, well trained in military administration, discipline, and medicine, and considered equal to regular army physicians. Orderlies and enlisted personnel were also of high caliber, and were selected for service only after serving a year in the line. Once chosen, orderlies received six months training in a civilian hospital before returning to their regiments.[26]

Even more impressive was the Japanese Army's attitude toward its physicians and the relationship between the medical department and civilian relief organizations. Medical officers had full control over all military medical matters and were consulted in operational planning. Unlike its American counterpart, the Japanese Red Cross was established primarily as a wartime auxiliary force. Its Board of Governors included military representatives, and yearly reports were made to the Ministry of War. During peacetime, the Red Cross Society managed civilian hospitals in Tokyo and other major Japanese cities. All of these hospitals were modern, well-appointed plants, laid out on the pavilion model, all with a 500-bed capacity and supplemented with dispensaries, surgical units, laboratories, x-ray units, and other facilities. In wartime, the Red Cross hospitals, along with their medical personnel and nursing staffs, were placed at the disposal of the government, providing a ready reserve of base hospitals and sanitary trains.[27] The Japanese Red Cross also established Supplementary Red Cross Hospitals, or Relief Detachments, each with a 100-bed capacity and staffed with two physicians, a pharmacist, a clerk, two chief nurses and twenty junior nurses. In 1904 and 1905, seventy-eight relief detachments joined the Imperial Japanese Army. Of these, thirty-two went to Korea and Manchuria, while thirty-eight were assigned to hospital ships.[28]

While observers reported on the comparative systems of medical surgery, field medicine, and evacuation on both sides, Major Seaman's reports on Japanese medical hygiene captured the public's imagination. According to Seaman, the Imperial Japanese Army's medical infrastructure adopted in full the Dodge Commission's sanitary recommendations. Seaman was so convinced the Japanese had worked a miracle in military hygiene that after returning to the United States he traveled across the country extolling Japan's accomplishments. "Too much praise cannot be bestowed upon the medical department of the army and navy for their splendid *preparatory* work in this war," he wrote after returning to the United States. "The Japanese are the first to recognize the true value of an army medical corps. Care of the sick and wounded consumes but a small part of their time. The solution of the greater problem, preserving the health and fighting value of the army in the field—by preventing disease, by careful supervision of the smallest details in subsisting, clothing and sheltering the units, is their *first* and most important duty."[29]

Seaman used his experiences and observations to lobby the War Department to follow the Japanese lead in making military hygiene a paramount element of military science. As a volunteer medical officer (Seaman was chief surgeon of the First Volunteer Engineer Regiment), he felt at greater liberty to push the limits of his reporting obligations. Seaman offered two reasons for copying the Japanese. First, he explicitly linked military success and hygienic practice. Japan defeated the much larger Russian Empire thanks to the integration of its military medical services with war planning. In his 1908 book, *The Real Triumph of Japan: the Conquest of the Silent Foe*, Seaman elaborated on three aspects of this integration:

> First, thorough preparation and organization for the war, such preparation as was never made before; second, to the simple, non-irritating, and easily digested rations of the Japanese troops; and third, to the brilliant part played by the members of the Medical Department in the application of practical sanitation and the stamping out of preventable diseases in the army, thereby saving its units for the legitimate purposes of war—the smashing of the enemy in the field.[30]

His second reason targeted the perceived neglect of the lessons of 1898. In his opinion, the traditional neglect of hygiene and sanitation that characterized American actions in the last century had not abated. Even though the War Department committed itself to modernization, Seaman attacked the failure to appoint a military representative to the General Staff as a sign of the ignorance endemic in the line establishment. But then, he added, what else was to be expected of an institution that still considered military hygiene to be a secondary matter? Again Seaman compared American attitudes and practices with the Japanese:

> The killing departments—the cavalry, ordinance, infantry, etc.—and today Japanese officers are laughing in their sleeves at our senseless failure to have representatives on what they consider to be their three vital points [Medical, Commissary, and Transport Departments], whilst the only weak, comparatively burlesque feature of their army, its cavalry, is considered of sufficient importance to be worthy of special study. Certainly 'it is to laugh.' But what can be expected of a government that after its terrible lessons of 1898–9 still insists—especially in the tropics—of subsisting its army on a ration so rich and elastic (lovely term, that elastic), so elastic that when in the emergency of war its elasticity is tested, it bursts its bands and is found to consist of pork and beans and fermenting canned rubbish that in six weeks prostrates 50 per cent of its 250,000 units with intestinal diseases, and sends 3,000 to their last homes, to say nothing of the enormous number invalided and the 75,000 pension claims.[31]

Seaman's solution was to reorganize the Army and Navy medical services on the Japanese model. He also recommended incorporating courses in hygiene and sanitation at all federal military schools, including the service academies and the Staff and War Colleges.[32] The Association of Military Surgeons accepted Seaman's recommendations and adopted two resolutions aimed at reforming the Medical Department on the lines he advocated. First, it lobbied Congress to reorganize the medical departments of the Army and Navy to a level equal that of those nations "most advanced in sanitation." Second, it petitioned President Roosevelt to order the immediate inclusion of courses in sanitation and health at all military institutions and schools. Such instruction would ensure new officers "can be prepared to guard [their men] against the silent foe which scored 80 per cent of the deaths."[33]

After Seaman's speaking tour, accolades for the Japanese system grew. Nagasaki was a regular port of call for American officers serving in the Philippines in need of leave. Americans could not help be impressed by the bifurcated Japanese culture. Nowhere else could Americans witness modernity coexisting alongside a society that, in their eyes, was still medieval. Medical officers often took advantage of their visits to observe for themselves the vaunted Japanese sanitary scheme. Among the most important observations were the notes taken in 1907 by two medical officers, Captain Percy Moreau Ashburn and Lieutenant Charles F. Craig. During their tour in Manila, the two men took a month-long leave to Japan to recover from the tropical climate, and to study Kedani fever, a form of scrub typhus, and beri-beri. After a five-day sea journey to Nagasaki, the officers arrived in Japan. In Tokyo, the men were entertained at the Imperial Institute for Research on Infectious Diseases, several Imperial Japanese Army facilities, and Tokyo's Red Cross Hospital. At the Institute, the two were apprised of research to develop a remedy for dysentery, for example, while the Japanese Army Medical School was rated as "being a very good and very useful institution," organized on a basis very similar to that of the U.S. Army's own school.[34]

Not everyone in the Army accepted Seaman's glowing portrayals of Japanese military medicine. Critics were quick to attack Seaman's fervor as a self-appointed apostle of the Japanese. Challenging his pronouncement that disease was virtually absent among the Japanese Army, one *Register* column described Seaman's claim as sheer bunk.

> Dr. Seaman is equally reckless in his statistics, especially where he reports, as a result of the claims made by those 'conversant with the facts,' that the 'loss from preventable disease in the first six months of this terrible conflict will be but a fraction of one per cent.' . . . Any one who knows anything about military and naval sanitary conditions will appreciate how far fetched is the claim that the Japanese casualty, in time of war, in the class described is but one per cent. The rate is higher than that on board ship, where the conditions are well nigh perfect, in time of peace, and in a good climate.[35]

A more balanced critique of Japan's military medical scheme was offered by Ashburn and Craig. They considered Japanese military medical depots to be less well stocked than American facilities, and Japanese military hospitals to be overcrowded.[36] More significant was the virtual absence of commonplace sanitation in Japanese civil life in both the country and city. The practice of collecting night soil for use as fertilizer astounded Ashburn and Craig, who noted that "With few exceptions, the water closet is unknown in Japan . . . throughout the surrounding farming district[s], the smell of feces and ammoniac urine could not be escaped at any time of the day."[37] They also noted that typhoid fever, dysentery, and intestinal parasites were common throughout Japan.[38]

Disagreements over Japan aside, the campaign to promote sanitary tactics was achieving results. In professional journals, young line officers added their voices to the dialogue regarding questions dealing with hygiene and sanitary tactics. Indeed, formal recognition of this new openness to the subject was reflected in the creation of the Seaman Prize by *The Journal of the Military Service Institution of the United States* in 1900. Established by Major Louis L. Seaman, the $100 prize was awarded to essays addressing topics on military hygiene and sanitation as they related to the line.[39]

In 1905, the Seaman Prize was awarded to Captain Peter E. Traub of the Thirteenth U.S. Cavalry Regiment, for his essay "Military Hygiene: How Best to Enforce Its Study in our Military and Naval Schools and Promote its Intelligent Practice in Our Army." Traub, who later commanded the 35th Infantry Division in the First World War, described the current state of military hygiene instruction in the Army. Aside from the Army and Navy Medical Schools and its recent inclusion at the Infantry and Cavalry School, instruction in the subject was woefully deficient, limited to a mere ten hours recitation by young officers at their post garrison school for their career. Traub felt such preparation was inadequate: "It did not need the war with Spain to demonstrate the fact that a clean camp and the observance of a few common-sense, hygienic laws, will prevent much sickness, but it does seem to have needed the war with Spain and the experience of camp life gained therein to demonstrate to the officers of the line of the army that upon their shoulders *finally* rested the grave responsibility of preserving the health of their men."[40] Blame for 1898 rest not only among the untrained volunteers that crowded into the camps, but also with the Regular Army's line officers. Their failure to acknowledge the legitimate authority of the Medical Department, their disregard of medical officers attached to their commands, and their unwillingness to acknowledge and correct their mistakes was scandalous:

> Woe to the line officer, one would think, who failed to carry out to the letter and in the spirit intended, the plain precepts of his medical adviser. Yet, does one ever hear of a line officer's being tried for tolerating camp pollution and for making not only possible, but absolutely certain, the deaths of from three to ten men from disease—preventable disease—to one from bullets?[41]

Medical officers acclaimed Traub's essay. From Princeton, New Jersey, retired Brigadier General Alfred A. Woodhull wrote: "Captain Traub starts with the postulate that the practice of military hygiene is essential for general military efficiency, hence it should be taught in common with other military studies." Noting the current policy of merely failing the student in the General Services and Staff College's hygiene course, Woodhull added, "As the essayist suggest, it would be better to drop such an officer incontinently, than later to fill graves with innocent victims of his accumulated ignorance."[42]

Most important, Traub's essay sparked new interest in military hygiene among his peers of the line. Major D. H. Broughton, Eleventh U.S. Cavalry Regiment, agreed with the captain's proposed changes but offered a caution. "It will not be difficult to institute a study of military hygiene in the army," Broughton wrote, "but even then its principles will not be rigorously enforced unless our superior military commanders take an active interest in the matter." Broughton extended this to the War Department, proposing a category dealing with military hygiene should be made part of the promotion examination for all senior officers, not only second lieutenants.[43]

The Medical Departmant's strategic relevance was validated by the May 1904 appointment of Captain Charles Lynch as the Surgeon General's representative on the General Staff.[44] Medical officers supported the General Staff even before it was established on February 14, 1903; with its creation, the Medical Department gained access to a forum to present the case for including medical matters in Army planning and operation.[45] Lynch used his new position to proselytize the Medical Department's secular gospel of health, extolling the inherent modernity of the department's public health activities and the promise it held for the Army. "Sanitation is a new science," he wrote in 1908, comparing the high mortality rate of 68 deaths per thousand during the 1832 Black Hawk War to the post-1898 Army.[46] Quick to distance the modern state of medical practice from an earlier, "wholly empirical" age, Lynch praised the Army's current health, writing that "Today there is no infectious disease to which the troops of the United States are liable . . . of which knowledge of the methods of spread is not available to him who desires to make a study of the subject. Therefore, ignorance can no longer be taken as an excuse for the spread of preventable disease in our army and our navy."[47] Lynch put the Medical Department on equal footing with the line branches. Just as soldiers and officers needed to study tactics and military science to win battles, they also needed to study hygiene to remain healthy enough to wage war itself.

Others also emphasized the increased relevance of health, sanitation and the medical officer to the Army's overall efficiency. "It is becoming recognized more generally and more clearly than formerly that the physical vigor of an army, upon which so much of its efficiency depends, is mainly contingent upon conditions which we may modify," wrote retired Brigadier General Alfred A. Woodhull in 1908.[48] No longer bound by traditional camp diseases like typhoid, dysentery, and pneumonia, Woodhull promoted the idea that "morbidity, or sick-rate, is an important index of military efficiency and may be more effective in controlling operations than the mortality, or death-rate."[49] Employing a grim calculus of the debilitative effects of disease in large communities, he averred chronic camp diseases presented a greater drain upon military commands than acute diseases like cholera and yellow fever. Sick men required lengthy medical care, constituted an ever-present threat of infection to others in a camp, and necessitated a drain on resources not only at the expense of the healthy soldiers in a command but on the very mobility of the force itself. "These two principles should be thoroughly inculcated: that disease is extraneous and abstractly needless, and that the sick enfeeble the command without, as the wounded may be supposed to have done, having inflicted proportionate disability upon the enemy."[50]

PROMOTING SANITARY TACTICS: OFFICER EDUCATION
AND THE ARMY MEDICAL DEPARTMENT

After 1905, sanitary tactics was the new watchword for medical officers. While the support of new line converts like Captain Traub and Major Broughton was promising, the matter of how to inculcate sanitary tactics into the line officer's professional mindset remained. Two prolific advocates of sanitary tactics, Brigadier General Woodhull and Major Lynch, advocated further integration of medical officers into both the military's culture of officership and the development of tactical and strategic doctrine. Lynch proposed a course of instruction focusing upon hygienic training, while also incorporating sanitary science into the standard military history curriculum so as to draw attention to the influence of hygiene on the outcome of military affairs.[51] Woodhull sought a more dynamic course. It was not enough that the line officer receive basic instruction in sanitation and be encouraged to follow the advice of his Medical Department counterpart attached to his command. Something more was needed:

Command is a military function, upon whose exercise may depend the ultimate success of the operations for which the officer entrusted with it is directly responsible or in which he may be participating. . . . The object, then, of teaching military hygiene to cadets and midshipmen is to supply them with one more qualification for command, with one more agency of success, when they recognize that there is such a science of preventive military medicine, totally distinct from clinical medicine; and particularly that they may be familiarized with fundamental sanitary principles so that, avoiding their gross violation, they also may accept the technical advice of their medical officers even should they fail to appreciate the premises in detail.[52]

Woodhull recommended adding a didactic course in hygiene and military medicine at West Point and Annapolis. Such a course, he added, would not only educate future officers in the elements of military hygiene, it would also create a new understanding of what their Medical Department counterparts were. In turn, they "will recognize the medical staff of the two services as specialized comrades, heralds, and if need be, aggressive fore-runners to proclaim and mark out a route of military success, engaged in unobtrusive but hearty coalition in the more conspicuous work."[53]

By 1907, the War Department responded, including medical officers in the teaching faculty at the Army Staff College in Fort Leavenworth, Kansas, and the Army War College at Washington Barracks in the District of Columbia. A year later, instruction in field medical problems was included in the curriculum of the School of the Line at Fort Leavenworth. A Department of Military Hygiene was established at West Point, with instruction given to cadets by the post's senior medical officer. The intention was to eliminate the old attitude that medical officers were not equal in status, rank, prerogatives, and responsibility to their line and staff counterparts. "Not uncommonly it is believed that the duties of the medical officer are merely medico-professional and that these require no special knowledge of military affairs, but may be equally well performed by civilian physicians," explained Professor of Military Hygiene Lieutenant Colonel Frank R. Keefer. "This opinion is rather firmly fixed in the minds of unprogressive officers, conservatives in the sense that they resist all advance in the military profession and believe that 'Whatever is, is best.' . . . Of course these do not represent advanced thought but rather an extreme and harmful conservatism."[54] Seeking to dispel misconceptions as to the place of the medical officer in the Army, Keefer emphasized that "the prime function of the medical officer in time of peace and war, is not the *cure*, but the *prevention* of disease."[55]

Sanitary tactics education freed medical officers to further set the agenda by writing the military hygiene textbooks used at the four Army Service Schools and the Army War College. One author was Woodhull; his hygienic manual was originally published as an abstract of an 1889 lecture delivered to the Infantry and Cavalry School on Military Hygiene. Circulated for years as a practical guide to hygiene, Woodhull rewrote *Notes on Military Hygiene for Officers of the Line* as a full-fledged manual in 1909.[56] This new edition examined virtually every aspect of hygiene recognized at the time of its printing, and included chapters devoted to military clothing, food, housing, water, disease prevention, and the conduct of military sanitation and hygiene in different settings. Throughout his hygienic primer, Woodhull expressed the maxim that good health followed the insistence of a unit's commanding officer:

> When the medical officers invite attention to the physical causes of ill-health, especially to such as are obscure, their opinions should receive respectful consideration. But every officer of the line should possess among his qualifications for command not merely appreciation of the importance to the troops of vigorous health, but a general knowledge of the ordinary conditions which interfere with it. Because an army is a vital machine, its effective operation demands careful and constant recognition of whatever may affect that vitality.[57]

Woodhull's manual was immediately adopted as the centerpiece of all garrison school courses on hygiene and sanitation. Critics, however, objected to Woodhull's empirical approach. Thus, when it was time to select the core text for the School of the Line's new course in practical field hygiene offered at the beginning of the 1909 academic year, Woodhull's text was considered unsatisfactory.[58] The nineteen-day long class, called "Troops in Campaign," was the opening course for new students, consisting of lectures, conference roundtables, practical problems, and culminating in a field exercise. As the new course focused on real-world problems rather than theoretical applications, the Army sought a textbook more suited to this need.[59]

In 1910, the Army selected Major Ashburn's new book *The Elements of Military Hygiene, Especially Arranged for Officers and Men of the Line*, as the core text for the "Troops in Campaign" course. Ashburn focused upon three key areas: the personal hygiene of individual soldiers and companies; the causes of infectious and venereal diseases; and prevention. Drawing upon the public image of the 1898 volunteer, he warned of the costs that would accrue from a general failure to acknowledge the strategic value of military sanitation. "The child or the man who is trained to reason, to obey, and to conduct himself properly, is in much less danger from infectious diseases in camp or elsewhere than is the reckless, disobedient, or headstrong individual who knows no law but his own will and appetite," he wrote.[60] Such lack of individual training and discipline created the disease that plagued the volunteer camps in 1898, Ashburn commented. Moreover, he added, "It is this same lack of training that constitutes the greatest weakness and the greatest evil of our military system to-day, and gives origin to the fear that when we again mobilize an army of a quarter or a half million of men,—more than the regular medical staff can oversee,—the conditions of 1898 may be repeated."[61]

Major Edward Lyman Munson's *The Principles of Sanitary Tactics* was equally important. Munson, senior hygienic instructor at the School of the Line and assistant commandant of the Field Service School for Medical Officers, was approached to create the text that would serve the practical needs of the "Troops in Campaign" course. The result was a short primer in sanitary tactics intended to introduce the line officer to the prospect of close interaction with medical officers in the field, supplemented by thirty-five map problems that introduced sanitary tactics on varying levels, from detached battalion and squadron to the infantry division. The problems themselves ranged from medical officer specific problems, such as identifying the ideal location for a field hospital or the evacuation of wounded from an established position, to questions aimed at the line officer, such as the disposition of sanitary personnel in a larger force tasked with occupying a defensive position or the employment of a division's sanitary assets during action.[62]

More important than the presentation of tactical problems, however, was Munson's introduction of the concept of strategic hygiene to a broader audience. In his preliminary discussion of tactical education for medical officers, Munson stated his case:

That the work of sanitary transportation and relief by the Medical Department shall coordinate and operate in entire harmony with that of all other branches of the service is not only essential to its own high efficiency but is demanded in the interests of the military force as a whole, considered as a tactical unit. The Medical Department cannot be regarded or administered as a dependency or excrescence of a properly organized military force, but as one of its absolutely essential constituents, and there must be coordination in purpose and effort by all the departments and branches of an army.[63]

Line officers, Munson further noted, were also linked to sanitary tactics by basic military necessity. A unit's ability to fulfill its mission was contingent upon their general state of health and hygiene. And while it was the medical officer's primary duty to guarantee the wellness of the troops in his command, it was also the line officer's obligation to allow the medical officer this prerogative.[64]

The evolution of the hygienic primers between 1904 and 1909 reflected the growing influence of sanitary tactics on the Army's professional education system. But not everyone in the medical establishment believed sanitary tactics was the cure-all for the Army's anticipated wartime mission. For example, Medical Corps Major Harry L. Gilchrist felt too much emphasis was put on sanitation at the expense of the medical officer's traditional role as surgeon and general practitioner. The aftermath of a modern battle not only presented the greatest medical challenge to physicians, but also offered a rarely acknowledged influence on the prosecution of a military campaign. Amidst the chaotic debris of broken men left behind after battle, immense strategic needs remained:

> [E]verybody in authority is endeavoring to get order out of chaos; and the Commanding General is anxious to push on to secure the fruits of victory, or to withdraw if defeated. He realizes that his greatest impediment are his wounded; and he wants them gotten rid of at once. In other words, he wants his command, that is those physically fit, to continue the work, without delay and those who are, from any cause physically unfit, taken immediately off his hands.[65]

Gilchrist argued it was this aspect of the medical officer's duties that was in danger of being undermined and rendered useless. "There is no question but that the knowledge of medicine and surgery, the prevention of diseases, and the care of the sick and wounded are the essential functions of the Medical Officers," Gilchrist wrote. But without instruction and practice in other areas, their value was severely diminished. "In fact to be successful military doctors surgeons must be medical specialists in the art of military science," he concluded.[66]

Gilchrist's plea for medical officers acquiring expertise in military science was echoed by in the militia and the reserves. As the nation accepted military service as an independent profession after 1898, reservists and National Guard medical officers quickly asserted their own right to the profession's privileged knowledge. Captain Gustavus M. Blech identified the link between the medical and sanitary services and line efficiency to promote more education for all Regular, Guard and reserve medical officers:

Army organization, for the purpose of preventing disease and properly evacuating the sick and wounded to institutions on the lines of communication, is a science in itself and must be thoroughly studied. To be a cog in the great wheel of army organization the medical officer, like his comrades of the line, must know something of the great machine he is to serve. As he is likely to be called on to undertake certain sanitary-tactical moves he must know about the physical aspects of modern warfare. He must be able to make and interpret maps, to read and carry out military orders, to guard the interests of the army, the government and the injured or disabled in a spirit of equity, and finally he must know the minutest details of the organization and equipment of all medical stations and institutions in the field.[67]

Explicit recognition of military hygiene and sanitary tactics soon followed. The description of Medical Department personnel was amended in the Army's new 1910 Field Service Regulations, relabeling them as "sanitary troops."[68] The new title was quickly seized upon by medical officers as a redefinition of their responsibilities. "The very sound, sanitary troops, conveys and implies a new meaning, a new function and a new relation of the Medical Department," wrote Captain Henry D. Thomason. "It implies a radical departure from the conceptions of the past pertaining to the function of this Department."[69] Merely safeguarding his troops' health was no longer enough for the medical officer; sanitation became the core of his identity and existence. In 1910, the sanitarian had risen to dominate the professional identity of the Medical Department.

Promoting a higher degree of sanitary awareness imbued medical officers with a new strategic role. Sanitation-minded medical officers successfully recast the very meaning of military hygiene, transforming it from an adjunct of field operations into a necessary object of strategic planning. By claiming a strategic aspect of sanitation and asserting their primacy in this area, military hygienists asserted for themselves a coeval status to line officers in future war planning. But one question remained unanswered: How ready was the Medical Department for its new tasks?

MEDICAL PREPAREDNESS IN THE REGULAR
ARMY AND NATIONAL GUARD, 1903–1916

Preparedness became the watchword for the Medical Department in the decade leading up to the First World War. The 1903 creation of the National Guard created much concern over its readiness. Regular medical officers cited the performance of the Volunteer medical staffs in 1898 as evidence of the problems that lay ahead. The arguments advanced by the Medical Department were linked to the Uptonian perception that a standing army was the preferred agent of active national defense. Citizen soldiers had only the barest perception of what lay ahead. "It is not surprising, when one considers the uncertainty that has existed with regard to the strength and personnel of the U.S. Army Medical Department, that the corresponding department of the state forces should be in a more or less chaotic condition," one observer commented on the matter of the National Guard medical establishment.[70]

The questions raised about National Guard readiness were not unfounded. By 1907, no Guard medical department could field an organization larger than a regimental dispensary. No provision at all was made for base, reserve and field hospitals, or ambulance companies as stated in Army Regulations, despite annual apportions of two million dollars for supplies to each state and regular extra appropriations, such as the 1908 $200,000 award for supplies.[71]

Federal money was little help. In 1909, Medical Corps Captain Henry D. Thomason was assigned to the War Department's Division of Militia Affairs as liaison between the Regular establishment and the state militias. One of his roles was to assess the material needs of the National Guard's medical services in the field and along the lines of communication. Upon completing his review, Thomason had little good to say about the state of the Guard. By 1910, the level of militia recruitment had reached 141 infantry regiments, enough for fifteen infantry divisions. The total medical support for fifteen divisions, set by a November 10, 1910 Division of Militia Affairs circular, was sixty-one ambulance companies and sixty-one field hospitals. The Guard, Thomason determined, could only field twenty of each. In his annual report for 1914, the Chief of the Division of Militia Affairs, Brigadier General A.L. Mills found trouble throughout the Guard. In addition to a lack of armories, drill halls, equipment, instructors, and general support from the states, Mills also identified "insufficient personnel in the medical department itself of the Organized Militia."[72] Several Southern states warranted particular mention. Both Kentucky and Tennessee were given equipment to organize a field hospital; with no instructions, the equipment had gone to waste. North Carolina's medical department was so poorly equipped and organized Mills recommended it be mustered out of service. The Mississippi Guard had also been given a field hospital after the Governor certified sufficient troops existed to manage it. Inspection revealed no such organization existed save for a squad of hospital orderlies, and that the equipment had been dispersed, lost, stolen, and even sold.[73]

As Europe slid into general war in 1914, the matter of material readiness continued to vex the War Department. The Army Medical Department was ordered to ready supplies for a potential mobilization, and by 1915, had stockpiled enough supplies and equipment to outfit thirteen infantry divisions, each with four field hospitals and four ambulance companies. The Medical Department continued issuing orders for field chests and non-perishable field medical supplies through 1916, with the aim of outfitting the medical support for sixteen divisions in total. Supplies were also stockpiled for 200 recruiting stations, 427 horse-drawn ambulances, twenty evacuation hospitals and forty-four field hospitals.[74]

Many Regular officers felt preparedness equaled mandatory military education and drill among the nation's civilian males. With the war entering its first winter in Europe, members of the Association of Military Surgeons pointed toward the gathered armies in Flanders and Poland. "I have thought much during the past year of the Association, its ends and aims, and . . . what I believe to be the most vital question which the Organized Militia, and especially its Medical Department, has to encounter—that of *Preparedness*," proclaimed Brigadier General Charles Adams, Surgeon General of the Illinois National Guard, at the 1914 meeting of the Association of Military Surgeons.[75] Adams listed five concerns: the state surgeons general scant influence on political matters relating to their own organizations; the absence of uniform entrance and physical examinations for potential candidates in state Medical Corps; the poor state of supply for different state medical departments; the general low recruitment rate of hospital orderlies and sanitary troops; and the lack of instruction programs for state medical officers and enlisted personnel.[76]

Others echoed Adams' assessment. A November 1914 editorial in *The Military Surgeon* announced, "Preparedness is the keystone of the arch of military efficiency," as he attacked the National Guard as an ill-trained rabble. "Patriotism untrained makes a mob, not an army. Medical and surgical knowledge alone make a doctor, not a military surgeon. . . . The National Guard is the chief offender in lack of efficiency. In many states there is practically no consideration of the physical, mental, social, or professional qualifications for medical officers."[77] Division of Militia Affairs chief Mills agreed, pointing out that individual states' inaction in sanitary training and instruction reflected a persistent belief that militia surgeons needed no special training beyond their medical expertise. "The entire matter may be summed up by saying that there is still a generally prevalent idea that a medical officer is merely a doctor practicing his profession under possibly different conditions in the field from those obtaining in civilian life, but that there is no substantial difference in the character of his work."[78]

The War Department ultimately adopted two tracks to promote National Guard readiness. The first extended participation in the Regular Army's service schools to militia, reserve, and National Guard officers. This included the newly established Field Service and Correspondence School for Medical Officers at Fort Leavenworth. Opened in 1912, the school offered courses in military science and tactics following a 1910 Inspector General report noted the Army's medical officers required instruction in "tactical knowledge."[79] The curriculum at the new service school was a correspondence course in military tactics and administration, followed by a six-week course at Fort Leavenworth studying practical problems in medical administration in wartime conditions.[80]

The second track was a regular schedule of cooperative field exercises with equal Regular Army and National Guard participation. In 1906, the War Department scheduled six summertime joint maneuver camps primarily for the line, with only regimental medical establishments attending the exercise. Despite the introduction of sanitation squads made up of enlisted Hospital Corps personnel and contracted civilians, all six camps reported typhoid fever outbreaks. The results were mixed. On one hand, Surgeon General O'Reilly praised the efforts of the sanitation squads; he also claimed the maneuvers brought in too few medical officers to manage the routine needs of a large encampment, let alone assist in the resolution of field problems.[81] Reports from Regular medical officers observing the maneuvers supported his criticism. In the Texas state maneuvers, observers noted, regimental physicians "could accompany the troops or stay at home, as suited their convenience." Of the twenty-one physicians listed on the state's militia roster, only a third appeared for the exercise. Compounding the problem, although the divisional hospital required one hundred and fifty enlisted personnel, regimental commanders only released fifty men for the light duty; even they were reluctant to remain at their posts.[82]

In 1909, three special camps of instruction were set up for National Guard and militia medical officers. Two separate fourteen-day long camps were held at Antietam, Maryland, and Sparta, Wisconsin. Another twenty-one-day long camp was held near San Francisco, California, for Western Guard troops. Altogether, 161 medical officers from thirty-four states attended the camps, receiving instruction in medical field work, administration, military hygiene, and hospital corps drill and first aid. Each camp culminated in a division-size paper exercise, officers given a range of test problems, including how to establish field hospitals, lines of evacuation, and aid stations in combat conditions.[83]

The first camps were considered a huge success by the militia officers who attended them. Not only did the exercises demonstrate the most recent changes and innovations in Regular Army field medical procedure, they also brought participants up to a baseline of expertise in the mundane paperwork and administrative tasks expected of them in wartime. The camps also revealed several problems inherent to the existing militia/reserve system. The most pressing of these was the chaotic state of supply and organization in the National Guard. When supplies and equipment arrived, frequently it was in the last few days of the exercise.[84] The following year's encampments, held in Gettysburg, Pennsylvania, Peoria, Illinois, Fort Benjamin Harrison, Indiana, and a second time in Sparta, revealed greater misgivings by Regular medical officers toward the National Guard. At the 1910 Gettysburg encampment, state guard officers and Regular observers described a poorly managed and ill-equipped encampment. Virginia National Guard Surgeon General Lieutenant Colonel J.T. Lynch, incensed over a typhoid outbreak among Virginia and Maryland Guard troops—twenty-eight cases alone in Troop A of the First Maryland Cavalry

Regiment—argued the $40,000 spent by his state and the Federal government in maintaining the Virginia troops in the encampment "had resulted in practically no benefit."[85] Lt. Colonel Louis Mervin Maus felt few state medical departments were prepared nor equipped for a real mobilization. "None or few of them have field hospitals, ambulance companies, or well organized hospital corps," he stated at the 1910 meeting of the Association of Military Surgeons. "I would not recommend the separate maneuver camps for the National Guard and Regular Army until the National Guard becomes thoroughly equipped for the field."[86]

The fundamental problem for the Guard was a perceived distrust among Regular medical officers toward their militia counterparts. Major H. I. Jones of the Indiana National Guard acknowledged the Guard had much to learn. The Regular establishment, however, only tolerated state militia medical officers, having no expectation they could practice military affairs. And when the Guard attempted to bring itself up to a standard acceptable to the Regulars by asking the Army to detach non-commissioned officers to assist with the training and drill of Guard companies, the War Department objected on the grounds that "the morals and discipline of their men would be seriously impaired by association with the Militia."[87] The cancellation of the 1911 joint medical maneuvers intensified the feelings of mistrust and abandonment by National Guard medical officers toward the Regulars.[88] Some Guard medical officers bristled over the tenor of training they received from the Regular establishment. Too much effort, these critics claimed, was put into basic problems of sanitation at the expense of other military issues. Pennsylvanian Major C. Schultz called for more hands-on exposure to these issues. "If our friends of the Medical Department of the Army would work out some scheme whereby there would be practically available a course of study, theoretical and practical, to meet such requirements, I feel it would be hailed with delight by the medical men of the Militia," he observed.[89] Major Henry H. Doan, a member of the Pennsylvania National Guard, agreed. "Until quite recently, camp sanitation has occupied nearly all of our time, and much has been talked about and written upon this subject. I should not care to have any one think that camp sanitation was not deserving the thought expended upon it, but I am disposed to think it is about time we were issuing the 'Second Reader.'"[90] Doan also complained that the time devoted to maneuvers, generally a single week during the summer, was as much a "game"—an extended camping trip that cost his state and the Federal Government $170,000—as a training exercise. Better to extend the maneuvers to ten days, Doan recommended, so that the attendees could have more time to practice the techniques and methods recently acquired.[91]

While National Guard readiness was debated across the country, the Regular establishment initiated its first full maneuver division exercises along the Texas-Mexico border in the summer of 1911. Ostensibly a training exercise to test the Army's ability to field and administer a division-sized organization, the maneuver was also a signal to Mexico's warring factions that the Army was prepared to enforce security along the border. The Medical Department looked forward to the scheduled exercise, seeing a chance to prove it could support a large body of troops in the field. After arriving at Camp San Houston, outside of San Antonio, Texas, the Medical Department established four field hospitals and four ambulance companies, all of which would participate in the exercises, which included a bivouac march to and from Leon Springs.[92]

Early reports portrayed the exercise as a huge success for the Medical Department, thanks to a new prophylactic tool unveiled at the maneuver: a viable typhoid fever vaccine. "Never in the history of the world has such a large body of troops been so free from typhoid," reported one medical officer, crediting a combination of the new vaccine, careful attention to camp hygiene and sanitary policing, and the natural disinfecting qualities of the bright Texas sun.[93] Closer observation revealed the maneuver was not quite so perfect. While it was true only one case of typhoid appeared during the entire encampment, the victim believed to have already been sick upon his arrival, other camp diseases appeared. There were over eight cases of bacillary dysentery treated in Field Hospital No.4 alone. Venereal disease was also quite present, thanks to the camp's proximity to San Antonio. Despite the ready presence of latrines and urine cans for late-night use, soldiers still relieved themselves in the open in camp and along the line of march. The latrines were flimsily constructed, and hardly fly-proof. Camp water barrels were consistently left unlocked, and the majority of trash incinerators were unsuitable for destroying the camp's daily trash.[94] Then there was the matter of staffing. Even though the exercise fielded only a single division, the War Department was required to mobilize National Guard physicians to bring its field hospitals and ambulance companies to strength. What would happen, observers asked, in the event of a full-scale mobilization? A December 1911 editorial in *The Military Surgeon* raised a solution that had been proposed since the Japanese Army Medical Department craze a few years before: tap the American National Red Cross as a ready reserve. Major Charles Lynch noted how the ANRC remained active in peacetime, providing support as needed throughout the country in emergencies and offering chronic care for victims of tuberculosis. "Suppose war should come, this is the class of men we should most desire for our hospital corps," Lynch wrote. "They are not cast offs, but the selected from the moral, mental and physical standpoints."[95]

CONQUERING TYPHOID FEVER: MAJOR FREDERICK F. RUSSELL AND THE TYPHOID VACCINE

After yellow fever, hookworm, and malaria, it was only natural the Medical Department's attention would turn to typhoid fever. Since the Spanish-American War, medical officers obsessed over the sanitary prevention of the disease in camps, forts, and cantonments. A British Army epidemic in the Transvaal during the Boer War, in which some 31,000 cases were reported, including 5,877 deaths and which cost some four million pounds to control, was cause for renewed concern in the Medical Department.[96]

Major Frederick F. Russell was the first to suggest inoculation with killed typhoid bacteria cultures as an alternative to sanitary prevention. Russell first considered vaccination during a 1908 European visit to study the British and German colonial experiences with typhoid inoculation. The very nature of typhoid in American society, Russell argued, ensured outbreaks inevitably accompanied mobilizations. Not only was it prevalent throughout the United States, but the disease was capable of rapidly spreading through a population despite all the preventive sanitary measures taken. The only method to keep typhoid from infecting a community was to combine strict sanitation with a mandatory vaccination program.[97] Russell cited the comparative admission rates of the Hospital Corps and the Engineer Corps with the rest of the Army (per 1,000 men) over a ten year period, from 1898 through 1907, noting that it appeared among Engineers at a rate double, and at times even quadruple, the rate in the Hospital Corps and the general infection rate in the Army as a whole.[98] Russell maintained this demonstrated typhoid was always present in the Army. So long as the Army remained within its small, peacetime structure, the disease was manageable save for the occasional, regionalized outbreak. Larger gatherings of volunteers or militia, precisely like the joint maneuvers coming into vogue at the same time, or a large-scale mobilization would again quickly swamp the resources of the Medical Department.[99]

Russell proposed Army Medical School faculty and students take the lead in developing an anti-typhoid vaccine. Two German microbiologists, Richard Pfeiffer and Wilhelm Kolle, had already tested the viability of artificial immunity through inoculation in 1896. At the same time in England, Sir Almroth E. Wright tested a serum created from killed typhoid bacteria. Expanding his tests, Wright inoculated 4,000 British soldiers serving in India in 1898. On the basis of this first trial, 400,000 typhoid vaccine points were created. In the end, however, only 19,069 British soldiers were inoculated before going to South Africa. Nevertheless, the comparative incident rates between inoculated and non-inoculated soldiers: 266 cases, or 11.84 cases per 1,000 men inoculated with the vaccine, versus 3,739 cases, or 24.88 cases per 1,000 men not inoculated (from a pool of 150,231 non-treated soldiers) indicated, to Russell the benefits of vaccination.[100]

Russell pled for permission to begin a test program to prove the typhoid vaccination's viability. Early attempts produced dangerous results; symptoms of typhoid, including headaches, nausea, fever, and an adversely affected appetite, were common side effects. Russell sought to restrict inoculation to the two corps most frequently exposed to the disease: the Hospital and the Engineer Corps.[101] The War Department approved Russell's proposal to inaugurate an anti-typhoid inoculation program within the Hospital Corps.

Avirulent cultures of typhoid were grown in the Army Medical Laboratory. Killed by exposure to heat for an hour, the dead bacilli were next suspended and stored as vaccine points for administration and ease of storage. The vaccine was administered in three stages, separated by ten-day intervals to gradually introduce the still dangerous vaccine into the body over time. The third injection separated the American program from the British, who only administered two doses within ten-day intervals, and was acclaimed as responsible for the greater effectiveness of Russell's vaccine. Side effects were limited; primarily stiffness in the arm where the injection was given and in some cases a light rash across the chest and abdomen. Serious side effects, such as fever, nausea, and shortness of breath were rarer.[102]

The Army extended voluntary typhoid vaccination to all personnel in March 1909. Over the next eighteen months the Army Medical Department vaccinated 12,644 men, or roughly one seventh of the Army's strength. A comparison of typhoid incidence between the two populations revealed the program's success. Only five cases appeared in the vaccinated group, compared to 418 cases with thirty-two deaths in the rest of the Army. This was enough for the War Department to mandate typhoid vaccination for all personnel under forty-five years old, beginning on July 1, 1911. The results were felt almost immediately. In 1911, even though the mandatory vaccinations began at mid-year, typhoid incidence among troops in the United States fell to forty-four cases, with six deaths. In 1912, the rate had fallen to fifteen in the entire Army, with another three cases of paratyphoid fever. Only six of these cases appeared among vaccinated men; while another five were recruits who had been infected before their enlistment.[103] By 1913, typhoid fever in the Army had virtually disappeared. Only two cases appeared among troops at domestic stations, while only one case appeared among the 31,038 stationed outside the United States.[104]

Mandatory vaccination came just in time for the Army's 1911 Texas Maneuver Division exercises at San Antonio and Galveston. As recruits arrived at the camps from across the country, they were given the typhoid prophylaxis. The near complete absence of typhoid in the camps, with only one case appearing in a sanitary private during the interval between his second and third inoculation, was offered as definitive proof of Russell's vaccine.[105]

Enlisting the American National Red Cross as a Wartime Ready Reserve Despite the rationalization of the militia into the National Guard, the maneuver camps, and the creation of the Medical Reserve Corps, the Medical Department was still unprepared for a large scale mobilization. The Regular establishment was too small and far-flung to serve as anything more than a cadre to train and flesh out new organizations. Likewise, the National Guard's medical services was woefully understaffed and underequipped for a major mobilization. And though awarded its ready reserve, the Medical Reserve Corps remained a force on paper only. Even with the Medical Reserve Corps, there was no existing contingency to field its members as part of a ready-made sanitary force when they were called up.

In response to this problem, in 1916 the Medical Department overcame its objections to partnering with the American National Red Cross, and established a cooperative reserve organization that could be fielded within weeks of mobilization. The justification for a joint Medical Department/ANRC endeavor dated back to 1904, when Captain Percy Moreau Ashburn and Lieutenant Charles F. Craig recommended the Medical Department reach an accommodation with the Red Cross along the same lines as that in Japan. Both Ashburn and Craig were skeptical of any purported superiority of Japanese military medicine. Nevertheless, they recognized the Japanese scheme did give its military medical service a positive wartime advantage. Not only could it respond quickly to mobilization, but also it was able to share the burden of equipment and supply costs with a civilian organization. This allowed the Japanese services to commission more medical officers in peacetime.

As of 1904, the Red Cross in the United States remained a confused and disorganized civilian aid association, under the direction of the septuagenarian Clara Barton. In 1900, Barton finally achieved the goal of winning a federal charter for the fledgling American National Red Cross (ANRC), but the new organization remained plagued by infighting and the substantial ego of its leader. This changed in January 1905, after Barton's forced retirement and the reincorporation of the American National Red Cross by Congress. At the forefront of the new ANRC's mission was providing volunteer assistance to the Army and Navy in wartime, but no formal contingency was made for how this assistance would be implemented.[106] The Medical Department, albeit skeptical of the Red Cross' capability, recognized its potential. It "must not be forgotten that the very essential of Red Cross service, and the vital thing which caused it to come into being, is the alleviation of the horrors of the battlefield," a February 1916 editorial in *The Military Surgeon* reminded. "Any function of civilian relief is wholly incidental and secondary. Its accomplishments in respect to civilian aid have been most praiseworthy; but this is not enough—its necessary field of usefulness is broader."[107]

Colonel John Van Rennselaer Hoff agreed, comparing the activities of foreign Red Cross organizations with the United States to highlight how the ANRC could be mobilized in wartime. In France, Hoff explained, the Red Cross central committee worked directly with the Army through three distinct organizations. The *Societe de secours aux blesses des armies de terre et de mer* was given charge of establishing reserve sanitary trains and hospitals, while both *l'Association des dames francaises* and *l'Union des Femmes de France* were female auxiliaries to the first society. In peacetime, all three groups stored supplies and trained nurses and orderlies at schools of instruction in Paris, Marseilles, Lille, and Nancy. In Germany, independent aid societies came under the control of a central committee directed by a military officer. The United Kingdom called upon its recent experiences during the Boer War to rationalize the contributions of British aid societies. A Red

Cross Central Committee was established from delegates of the National Society for Aid to Sick and Wounded in War, the St. John Ambulance Association, the Army Nursing Reserve, and the Secretary of State for War. The British Red Cross Central Committee was charged with preparing a peacetime establishment that would support the Army in time of war.[108]

Hoff recommended reconfiguring the ANRC so as to enable it to fulfill a wartime mandate. Proposed state ANRC chapters would form a peacetime bureaucracy to manage any anticipated wartime need. Each would consist of four departments: administration, male personnel, female personnel, and material. The ANRC would also be responsible for sponsoring volunteer ambulance companies that could be quickly mobilized for service. Hoff also suggested the ANRC promote hygienic instruction among the civilian population: "If the object of the Red Cross is to ameliorate the horrors of war, how better can it do this than be teaching the people—prospective soldiers—to take care of themselves in the field? Ill-health from disease, not wounds, has been the largest factor of Red Cross work."[109]

Major Charles Lynch also advocated ANRC integration, pressing for Regular medical officers to be given training and administrative positions in the ANRC. He outlined a three-part program to ensure a smooth transition for the ANRC in wartime, focusing on education, morale, and medical assistance. The ANRC's immediate role, Lynch proposed, would be sanitary hygienic instruction. By instructing Americans in the role of hygiene and sanitation in disease prevention during peacetime, the potential soldier would be indoctrinated in habits conducive to camp sanitation. And as for morale boosting, Lynch considered this to be a vital function of civilian relief agencies, having witnessed first hand Japanese Red Cross workers providing comfort to soldiers and sailors. Lynch proposed the ANRC organize similar stations, to give American soldiers a clear idea of how much civilians back home cared for their welfare.[110]

Though it was assumed the Red Cross would immediately seek to provide humanitarian assistance in the event of war, in accordance with the terms of the 1906 Geneva Convention, the Medical Department also wanted to restrict the ANRC's activities so it did not duplicate or hamper their own efforts. To this end, the Medical Department wished to retain control of its field hospitals, leaving the Red Cross the task of supplying hospital ships and trains, motorized ambulance companies, and base hospitals.[111] Judging from the Japanese model, granting the ANRC responsibility for portable base hospitals was an excellent opportunity for partnership, provided "the magnitude of a war is such that assistance in this direction is required from our Red Cross it is suggested that the organization and supplies be prescribed in the manual for the Medical Department of the Army be followed exactly."[112] Regardless of these appeals, attempts to reconcile the American National Red Cross' wartime relief mission had little public support. In 1907, the ANRC created a War Relief Board, chaired by Surgeon General O'Reilly, but little came of this first effort. Indeed, after the Army presented the

ANRC with its list of demands—the organization was to purchase and supply at least one hospital ship, three hospital trains, and a number of field hospitals and rest stations—the Red Cross balked for lack of funds.[113]

The war in Europe changed the attitude of the ANRC. On December 8, 1915, the American National Red Cross by-laws were amended to incorporate two separate military and civil relief arms. Shortly after the Medical Department signaled its approval, Colonel Jefferson R. Kean was appointed head of the new Department of Military Relief. Kean devoted his energies to a new scheme to provide a reserve of base hospitals staffed by reserve medical officers and organized and maintained by the nation's large urban hospitals. According to Kean's scheme, the 500-bed capacity base hospitals would receive basic material (tents, cots, trucks, ambulances, surgical apparatus, sterilizers, x-ray equipment) from the Federal Government. The individual sponsor hospitals maintained all perishable supplies and pharmaceuticals in their own facilities, and provide the cadre of medical officers, orderlies, and nurses that would form the staff of the base hospital upon mobilization.[114]

The ANRC directors signed on to Kean's proposal, their eagerness heightened by the June 3 passage of the National Defense Act of 1916. In addition to expanding the peacetime Army and National Guard, the act set a new wartime mission for the Medical Department, established appropriate ratios of medical personnel to the line strength of the Army, and most important to the ANRC directors, incorporated volunteer organizations into the wartime Medical Department.[115] On October 26, 1916, Kean hosted a practical field exercise of the new Red Cross base hospital at Fairmount Park, Philadelphia, where personnel from Base Hospital No. 4, affiliated with the Western Reserve Hospital of Cleveland, Ohio, drilled with equipment provided by a New York hospital. In addition to forming ambulance companies, training detachments, and refreshment units, the ANRC organized thirty-three other base hospitals, most in the Northeast and Midwest, just in time for war with Germany.[116] Within a month, six hospitals were sent to support the British Army in Flanders, the first American forces deployed to France. In July, the ANRC authorized another fourteen base hospitals. By the war's end, the ANRC spent over $2,000,000, all private donations, to field fifty base hospitals, nineteen smaller hospital units, and forty-six ambulance companies for service in France and Italy.[117]

With the creation of the Red Cross Base Hospital, the Medical Department successfully fulfilled the last of its readiness schemes less than a year before the war with Germany, signaling a culmination of its efforts since the Dodge Commission report to revamp its organization and structure. The hospitals represented a near-perfect coordination of resources by the Army and the civilian world. Administrative officers, including the hospital adjutant, quartermaster, and registrar, came from the Regular Army, as did the commanding medical officer. All other staff came from the unit's private hospital sponsor. Each hospital's one hundred and fifty enlisted personnel, administrators, and orderlies were either local reservists or hospital employees who "may agree to enlist in the sanitary service when called into active service."[118] All equipment was purchased by the Medical Department with funds provided by the hospital sponsor, to ensure uniformity and standardization.

MEXICO AND THE ARMY MEDICAL DEPARTMENT, 1914–1917

While the specter of war loomed in Europe, American eyes were focused on a crisis much closer. Mexico's collapse into revolution and anarchy in 1911, as Porfirio Diaz's government crumbled under pressure from a host of factions, threatened to spill over into American territory. The civil war in Mexico grew harsher as General Victoriano Huerta seized power following the assassination of Diaz's successor, Francisco Madero. In February 1914, appalled over the violence in Mexico and discomfited with the Huerta government, President Woodrow Wilson ordered the War Department to schedule a second Maneuver Division to signal American concerns.[119] In 1914, Medical Corps Major Weston P. Chamberlain lectured the line officers of the 5th Infantry Regiment on the subject of a possible invasion of Mexico. Retracing Major General Winfield Scott's 1849 march from Veracruz into Mexico City, Chamberlain described four dangers facing an American expedition: the intemperate torrid climate of the Mexican lowlands; the prevalence of infectious diseases, including cholera, malaria, and yellow fever, along the line of march; the risks in "intimate contact with a native population of a low moral tone and living in an unsanitary manner"; and the prospect of homesick soldiers succumbing to the degenerative influences of the region, manifested in alcohol abuse, venereal disease, mental collapse, and suicide.[120] Chamberlain assured his audience the Medical Department was well prepared to meet these challenges. After all, the Army Medical Department had already met and defeated the hidden foe— Reed's and Gorgas's work in Cuba, and the discovery of a viable typhoid vaccine offered as case in point. The sanitary precautions undertaken by both medical staff and line officers would ensure the good health and efficiency of American troops operating in Mexico. Careful attention to diet, hydration, personal hygiene, and sun protection, along with rigorous sanitary policing, would suffice against most disease threats. An important supplement to these hygienic measures for line officers was the need to keep soldiers in Mexico occupied in their free time. Offering plentiful leisure opportunities—sport, reading material, and other entertainments—would keep soldiers out of Mexican brothels and saloons. More than a scheme to stave off boredom, Chamberlain prescribed such official leisure activity as a remedy to stave off homesickness, the inevitable fall into dissipation that would ensue, and hence, a formula to preserve the strategic efficiency of any American force deployed there.[121]

The Medical Department soon had its chance to practice its public health techniques in Mexico. On April 22, 1914, American sailors and marines took control of the Mexican city of Veracruz. On April 23, the 5th Infantry Brigade of the Maneuver Division was ordered to embark at Galveston, Texas, and occupy Veracruz for an indeterminate period. After securing the town, sanitary officers set out to make the area malaria-free. By July 3, 1914, forty cases of malaria were reported among the soldiers and marines occupying the city. Veracruz was similar to cities in Cuba and Panama: open sewers conveyed waste to the ocean; vacant lots provided plentiful breeding grounds for mosquitoes, as did the many open cisterns, cesspools, water barrels, and fountains dotting the town's residential and commercial districts. Major Thomas E. Noble took charge of a local work force to dig a system of drainage ditches while oiling or filling in the free-standing pools of water. He concurrently directed a squad of sanitary inspectors to secure water storage. Within weeks, the town was declared free of malaria, but the threat of infection from the surrounding area held by the Mexican federal troops—off limits to American sanitarians—remained. To remedy this danger, a daily dose of three quinine grains was issued to each man standing guard at the extreme pickets and outposts, while all windows and doors were screened in the city itself.[122]

On November 23, 1914, the Fifth Brigade left Veracruz and returned to Galveston, bearing all moneys and customs receipts collected during their stay in the city. During the occupation of Veracruz, tensions mounted between the two countries, despite the collapse of Huerta's government in mid-July. Hostilities between Mexicans and Americans were manifested in periodic raids across the border by both rebel forces under the direction of Francisco "Pancho" Villa and supporters of the new Mexican president, Venustiano Carranza. The raids culminated in the March 9, 1916, Villista raid on Columbus, New Mexico, an attack that signaled the second American intervention in the Mexican Revolution.[123]

Even before the Columbus Raid, the Medical Department was active in towns and communities all along the border. Historian Alexandra Minna Stern has focused attention on the Medical Departments activities in Texas during the Mexican Intervention as part of a broader discursive construct of "medicalization." Accordingly, official actors from the Army Medical Department, the U.S. Public Health Service, and local and state public health officials used their power and expertise to impose a medical quarantine of the local Mexican-American population. This quarantine, which comprised several levels of coercive discourse, ranging from an ongoing exposition of the threat of degenerative tropicalism to the physical destruction of suspect neighborhoods, is at the core of Stern's placement of medicalization within a broader early-twentieth-century American imperial discourse.[124] While commanding American troops at El Paso, Texas, in 1915, Brigadier General John J. Pershing placed his entire medical staff at the disposal of the city to assist in cleaning up the city's Mexican-dominated Second Ward, called "Chihuahuita" by the locals. Pershing felt justified on the basis of the Medical Department's experience in cleaning up filthy, non-white areas through their earlier imperial service.[125]

After the Columbus raid, Pershing received orders to cross into Mexico to track down Villa. On March 11, 1916, Wilson authorized sending two cavalry brigades into Mexico, one leaving from Culberson's Ranch, New Mexico, the second from Columbus. A third brigade of infantry would follow behind the Columbus column. This provisional division, labeled the "Punitive Expedition, U.S. Army," was supported by two companies from the Second Battalion of Engineers, Signal Corps detachments, two Quartermaster Corps wagon companies, and the First Aero Squadron. Medical support consisted of two field hospitals and two ambulance companies under the command of Lieutenant Colonel Euclid B. Frick. Augmenting the expedition's field medical support was a cantonment hospital at Columbus, which served as an ad hoc evacuation hospital and supply depot, treating serious injuries and illnesses. The base hospital at Fort Bliss served as a third tier of medical support for the worst cases.[126]

The experience was a real-life exercise in the department's capacity to provide division level support in the field. Each regiment traveled into Mexico with a small regimental infirmary, consisting of the regimental surgeon, his assistant, their orderlies, a pack mule with a field medical kit and anywhere between one to three horse-drawn ambulances. These infirmaries provided immediate care for sick and wounded; serious cases were transferred to rest stations along the line of communication to await transportation by Ambulance Company No. 7 to one of the two field hospitals. When the company was refitted with motor ambulances in May, its horse-drawn ambulances were turned over to those regiments whose own equipment was worn out by the constant advance into Mexico. Ambulance Company No. 3 remained in Columbus, where it supported necessary evacuation operations between the cantonment hospital and Fort Bliss and provided reserve capacity for its counterpart in Mexico. Field Hospital No. 3 was set up at the Provisional Division headquarters in Colonia Dublan, Mexico, where it served as a supply depot and the expedition's primary evacuation hospital. Its partner, Field Hospital No. 7, accompanied the second cavalry brigade deeper into Chihuahua, setting up operations at Namiquipa, where it remained until June 18, 1916, when it returned to El Valle.[127]

Problems anticipated during the last six years of field exercises, especially maintaining the flow of supplies to field hospitals constantly on the move, were still a problem. Fortunately, the level of engagement was sufficiently low that it did not overtask the field hospitals' supplies at any time. A second problem was the chronic understaffing of hospital personnel. Overall, the expedition was well cared for. Both Pershing and the division's medical staff were pleased with the overall health and performance of the Medical Department during the expedition.[128]

Thanks to these precautions and the Army's mandatory anti-typhoid vaccination policy, the expedition's disease morbidity and mortality rates were held at approximately 3 percent. The majority of reported sick cases before the onset of the rainy season in October were intestinal-related, primarily diarrhea and dysentery. Bratton linked the diarrhea cases to the Army field ration of "hard tack, bacon and underdone beans [which] is sure, sooner or later to bring on intestinal trouble. Such a diet many of the troops had to live on for days at a time; in fact, some of them lived on much less if reports are correct."[129] The failure of individual soldiers to follow orders and directives to refrain from drinking free-standing and unchlorinated water was likewise blamed for the expedition's dysentery cases: "Unfortunately the chlorinated water is very objectional to many persons and, after a few weeks use it was hard to keep the men on this water. Many of the men drank water from the streams and irrigating ditches and this infected water was undoubtedly the case and starting point of later cases of diarrheoa and dysentery." This was dealt with when new wells were driven in the expedition's winter camps under the supervision of medical officers. Moreover, the majority of troops in the division observed the sanitary guidelines imposed by the Medical Department.[130]

While Pershing led the Provisional Division on its fruitless chase after Pancho Villa's band in the barren Chihuahua Mountains, the Medical Department endured a second test when President Wilson ordered the mobilization of 112,000 National Guard troops along the South Texas border. The experience of the Guard troops differed greatly from that of the Regulars in Mexico. Prior to their arrival, base hospitals were established at Brownsville, San Antonio, El Paso, and Douglas, Texas, while a ten-car hospital train was sent to the region to cope with any unanticipated overflow of sick or wounded Guardsmen. Upon their arrival at train stations in South Texas, each man received a thorough medical examination, the mandatory typhoid vaccination, and a thorough course on sanitary tactics.[131]

Overall, the experience on the Mexican border was a successful, if limited, test of the Medical Department's ability to manage a large scale mobilization and field deployment. General Pershing noted that "Although the detachments of the Medical Department serving with regiments have been short of the personnel prescribed for war service, there has been no lack of medical attention and the efficiency of the officers and men of this Department serving with Command has been marked."[132] More instructive were the findings among in the National Guard's Texas encampments. Despite the best efforts of medical officers, the camps experienced several outbreaks of measles and mumps. An American National Red Cross review board, sent to El Paso to investigate newspaper charges of callousness toward Guardsmen by the Army, cited a higher than expected rate of pneumonia, caused by exposure to temperature extremes in the desert, and noted the lack of trained female nurses. Despite these failings, however, the 1916 National Guard mobilization was cited in the Medical Department's official history of World War I: "This mobilization of the armed forces of the Nation was most fortunate and opportune, therefore, as a training maneuver alike in military and sanitary matters."[133] The department had proven capable of handling a large-scale mobilization. The experience of immunizing large numbers of troops, ensuring standards of sanitation were observed and of evacuating wounded and sick troops under hostile fire (admittedly, however, what American troops experienced in Mexico was a far cry from what waited in Europe) would soon prove invaluable.

On the eve of America's entry into the First World War, the Army Medical Department achieved its long sought goal of exercising the final legitimate authority over matters of health and wellness within its corporate community. Using the intellectual and emotional capital built by sanitarians active in the tropical periphery, medical officers in the United States redefined their professional role within the Army as a whole. After 1905, sanitary-minded physicians asserted dominance within the Medical Department by codifying the public health mindset into a structured set of operational and strategic prerequisites: *sanitary tactics*. They were in turn supported by the Medical Department's researchers—physicians like Colonel Frederick F. Russell, following the tradition established by Surgeon General George Miller Sternberg and Colonel Walter Read—who developed new solutions to old-standing disease threats. In its new guise, the Medical Department promoted itself as an agent of military science as much as a support branch dedicated to preserving life after armed conflict. In creating sanitary tactics, the Army's sanitarians took a gamble: they guaranteed their line counterparts they could deliver on a promise of bringing the most rifles to the firing line in time of war. Whether this promise could be met remained to be seen.

6 Vice and the Soldier
The Army Medical Department and Public Health as Morality, 1890–1917

A critical aspect of sanitary tactics was the Army medical officer's ability to safeguard the health of the American soldier. Nowhere was this taken more seriously than in the Medical Department's campaign against vice. Failure to confront the illicit institutions that promoted sexual promiscuity in civil society, particularly the saloon and brothel culture surrounding military posts, threatened the entire country; as Colonel John Van Rensselaer Hoff cautioned in 1909, "We of the United States have a serious peril confronting us, which threatens national venereal infection."[1] Promoting total abstinence from alcohol and sex was not easily accomplished. Indeed, all save the most naïve officers believed soldiers would always find their way to the barroom and the brothel.

Generally overlooked is how the medical officer' stance on alcohol evolved and how it was directly related to fears of venereal disease after the Spanish-American War. Over the course of twenty-five years, the Medical Department's attitude toward alcohol use—even light beer and wine—shifted from general tolerance and acceptance to outright rejection. More remarkable is how this shift was made against the overall tide of opinion among the line and other staff departments, including the Chaplain Corps.

By 1903, the Medical Department publicly adopted a total prohibition stance on medical and eugenicist grounds. In doing so, the Army Medical Department bolstered its reputation as a leader in the temperance and social hygiene movements. It did so in the face of opposition from other groups within its community—groups which could and would ignore the professional advice of its medical experts when it suited their needs. Ultimately, the Medical Department realized its greatest influence, not in shaping the nation's mobilization against vice before the First World War, but by setting an example for promoting a total ban on alcohol on the eve of national prohibition, rendering morality a component of American public health.

THE CANTEEN CONTROVERSY, 1881–1897

Drunkenness was a familiar problem for the Army. In the 1790s, whiskey was part of the soldier's daily ration. During the antebellum years, enlisted men and officers alike turned to strong drink not only out of boredom, but necessity; considering the poor quality of drinking water in many posts, alcohol was the safer alternative. Many soldiers served through the Civil War in an alcoholic haze, and the culture of drink remained a feature for years after 1865.[2] Medical officers were largely unsympathetic toward alcoholics. Physicians were trained to consider alcohol as both an exciting factor for disease and as a morally corrosive substance. Left to his own devices, the intemperate soldier became a regular figure in the hospital, his health steadily declining, though not as rapidly as his reputation and honor.[3]

Attitudes within the Army toward alcohol were mixed throughout the nineteenth century. Drunkenness was recognized as a serious breach of discipline, frequently compounded by post-binge behavior. Desertions, unapproved absences, fights, petty theft, assaults, insubordination, sexual misconduct, and murders were all linked to alcohol in official reports and anecdotal accounts alike. What was the average soldier to do, others countered. For many soldiers strung across the frontier in small posts, alcohol was the necessary evil, the glue that bound men together while also pulling them apart. Much of this was linked to prevailing ethnic biases held against the lower ranks. Alcoholism was the soldier's disease, thanks to the heavy enrollment of ethnic groups for whom drinking was a matter of casual fact. Adjutant General Henry Clark Corbin noted this in his description of German-American soldiers in 1897. "There are a great many men of German descent, for instance, that are accustomed, and have been all their lives, to drink beer instead of drinking tea and coffee, and other things as some of us do. They want their beer, and that enters into their lives."[4] Irish soldiers were also acclaimed as heavy drinkers, the Surgeon General's Office reporting in 1891 that soldiers of Irish descent had the highest rate of admission—89.54 per thousand—for drunkenness of any enlisted ethnic group in the Army.[5] Yet, while German and Irish soldiers were singled out, the general perception was that all white Americans "the so-called Christian races" of European descent were predisposed to drink, "and among the Caucasian, the Anglo-Saxon stands pre-eminent" as a chronic tippler.[6]

Action was finally taken in 1881. As one of his last acts in office, President Rutherford B. Hayes, a noted teetotaler who substituted lemonade for wine at state dinners, banned the sale of alcoholic beverages on military installations.[7] Praised by temperance societies and civilian social advocates, Hayes' order brought the question of alcohol and the Army to the forefront of the public debate on the connections between morality and the basic rights of the citizen. On one side, social reformists singled out the Army as the focus of their efforts to impose total prohibition of alcohol. Facing them were not only "wet" advocates—men and women who believed alcohol consumption was a private matter of individual consent—but more increasingly, a substantial cadre of line and staff officers who promoted the sale of beer, wine, and cider as an alternative to the climate of unregulated wholesale drunkenness on many posts. Soon, every issue of discipline and public health was linked to the public sale and consumption of alcohol on the Army post.

Even as the ban was circulated, a movement to restore light alcohol was begun by civilian sutlers managing small stores and post exchanges across the country. Individual garrisons joined in, establishing areas for enlisted men on posts offering food, reading material, and where permitted, cheap lager beer. Installations where the new common rooms operated issued favorable disciplinary reports, with monthly guardhouse confinements dropping by two thirds in some cases. As news spread, officers pressed to replace civilian-operated stores—a source of discontent among soldiers tired of high prices and officers worried about the regular sale of toiletries, perfumes, and colognes with a high alcohol content—with a soldier-controlled recreational area. On February 1, 1889, new regulations governing the operation of post canteens were introduced. The old sutlery system was over; in its place was the new recreation room, modeled on European canteens as a place where enlisted men could relax with cheap beer, wine, or soda, while reading newspapers, books, or enjoying games of billiards or cards. After a September 27, 1889 regulation stripped sutlers of their exclusive trade rights on military property, the new canteen began offering dry goods at a fair price to its customers. Unlike the civilian-run shops, however, the canteens reinvested the profits from its operations back into the clubs, by purchasing furniture, books, gymnasium equipment, and other goods.[8]

The canteen was welcomed throughout the Army. At Fort Abraham Lincoln, near Bismarck, North Dakota, "the canteen tends not only to the comfort and pleasure of the men, but prevents dissipation. The morale of this command has improved, the men appear more contented with their surroundings and but few apply to leave the post on passes."[9] Colonel Richard I. Dodge, commanding officer, 11th Infantry Regiment and post commander at Madison Barracks, New York, was amazed at how quickly the canteen replaced local saloons and fleshpots. "Though within the limits of a village abounding in bar rooms and other temptations," Dodge reported, "this post is more free from drunks, disorders, unauthorized absence and neglect of duty than any I have ever commanded. In my opinion no step has been taken for the improvement of the moral, social and intellectual condition of the enlisted man more efficacious than the establishment of the canteen system."[10] An unnamed peer agreed in a letter to the Army and Navy Register:

> To look in upon the canteen in the evening, and there see the men so thoroughly enjoying themselves, seated around the tables, discussing all kinds of subjects, playing games, withal as quiet and orderly a lot of men as could be found in any club room in civil life, is convincing proof to any one that the canteen is a fixture and has come to stay.[11]

Such reports were supported by the official record. Since 1889, desertion rates decreased from just over 8 percent to just over 4 percent in 1900 and

1901.[12] "Alcoholism also has been decreasing in our Army," Surgeon General George Miller Sternberg reported in 1892, but at a slower rate than other conditions and diseases. For this, he blamed recruiting officers rather than the canteen itself, as the worst rates appeared among white soldiers of European descent.[13]

In light of such accounts, it seemed remarkable any resistance to the canteen existed. Yet, almost immediately, temperance crusaders targeted the post canteen system. Leading the charge in Congress against the sale of alcohol on military posts was New Hampshire Republican Senator Henry W. Blair. A staunch moralist and radical on the subject of temperance, Blair believed "Prohibition is the only remedy" for social problems.[14] The very prospect of the federal government supporting the sale of alcohol on its military reservations was anathema to Blair. During Senate hearings on the Army Appropriations Bill on May 9, 1890, Blair lent his name to a supplemental bill prohibiting the canteen, arguing "that the canteen is simply a liquor saloon kept by the United States Government through its agents, the officers, who are usually more in need of prohibitory restraint than the soldiers themselves."[15] Under such administration, Blair continued, the canteen could only spread alcoholism throughout the Army. For the good of the nation, Congress should intervene.

Support from the canteen's defenders was guarded. No one in the Senate wished to be portrayed as promoting drinking, even as they applauded the canteen's effect on reducing drunkenness on duty and desertion. Maryland Senator Arthur P. Gorman, for example, balanced his support with his own personal views on temperance, noting that "I practice it absolutely. ... But at the same time, I recognize it is not possible in this world to enforce that idea upon everybody else, and it would not be wise to do it if we had the power."[16] New York Senator John T. McCall cast his support as recognition that the common soldier was somehow incapable of maintaining control of his basest instincts, and needed a steering hand to guide him when off duty. "Certainly in a community where public opinion justifies the use of intoxicating liquor it would be unwise and hurtful [to legislate temperance]. It may be, in a community of that kind, where there is a military post or encampment, it is far better for the soldier and the interests of temperance that he should satisfy whatever appetite he may indulge within the control and observation of his officers."[17]

This last point spoke to the heart of the canteen controversy. Since the early 1800s, saloons and dive bars existed side by side with military outposts, forts, and barracks. These institutions profited greatly from military garrisons. These saloons generally operated on the same pattern. On payday, soldiers visited for a single drink. Seeking an opening, bartenders offered to treat the next few rounds. After this, it was easy enough to keep the soldier in the saloon for hours, during which time his purse was drained by his own "turn" to treat the house and his companions. Saloons often sported games of chance and card tables to further entice soldiers; a

smaller number maintained back room brothels. And these were the legitimate houses—there was no shortage of gin mills and dives serving watered-
down beer, knock-out specials, or running sliding door-drops, all devoted
to separating the soldier from his money with as little effort and expense
as possible.

Fear of returning to this earlier climate of abuse motivated the canteen's
supporters to resist Senator Blair's efforts to abolish alcohol in the canteen. If the temperance crowd prevailed, Senator McCall argued, it would
only punish the average soldier. Denying access to cheap beer would force
the common soldier "to go a half a mile or a quarter of a mile into the
worst associations and where he will get the vilest and most injurious of
stimulants."[18] McCall's argument helped defeat the bill in the Senate for
now, but temperance supporters would continue to introduce the ban at
every future Army Appropriations hearing until it succeeded.[19]

After Blair's first attempt to ban the canteen was defeated, line officers
rallied around the institution, heralding it as a great boon to morale and
discipline. This was especially true in frontier and border posts, where officers faced extraordinary problems in keeping their men out of the saloon.
"There is no doubt that the canteen, its sales, etc., has improved the discipline of the post, and more contentment exists among the enlisted men,"
wrote Colonel Alexander McCook, commanding the 6th Infantry Regiment, from Fort Leavenworth.[20] Lager beer and wine sales at the canteen
kept his men from the "wiskey dens" that proliferated around the post.
Colonel McCook was seconded by Sergeant A. B. Hamilton at Fort Ringgold, near Rio Grande, Texas. Hamilton recalled:

> In the town of Riogrande City there was almost everything that was
> low and vile. It was the only place the soldiers had to go for amusement
> outside the garrison, and it was almost universal on the part of the
> people in Riogrande to get the soldiers drunk. They would endeavor
> to get them drunk, and after the soldiers had become intoxicated they
> would get in trouble and be robbed, and they would often wind up in
> the police court. I have had my men made drunk and stripped stark
> naked and thrown out into the street. Two months after the canteen
> was established all this was stopped.[21]

Similar testimony was offered by others in defense of the canteen, as even
the most diehard skeptics supported it as preferable to the saloon.

Regardless of such accounts, Senator Blair and the temperance lobby
pressed on for a total alcohol ban on military reservations. Blair insisted,
for example, the Army's policy on drink constituted no less than a rejection of the Articles of War. Instead, he argued, the Army's acceptance of
drunkenness spread throughout the government like a plague, as "the canteen has come to be an institution, and the chaplains, and the officers, and
the secretary of war, and the House Military Committee, and the conference

committee of the two Houses of Congress think on the whole that it is an estimable or excellent institution, and it ought to be sustained 'in the interest of religion and morality.'"[22] Rejection was a bitter pill for Blair, who believed temperance, like abolition, was a matter of the gravest national interest, and alcohol should be treated like an epidemic disease, or invading foe. "All possible local effort should be put forth against the liquor death everywhere," he wrote in 1888, "The yellow-fever should be fought in the by-ways and hospitals by the physician and the nurse as well as by the quarantine of our ports, and the suspension of infected traffic by law; but the enemy will forever come in like a flood, unless a nation, which is assailed as a nation, defends itself as a nation."[23] Like disease or foreign invasion, temperance necessitated a total national mobilization. "Nothing but a general law can be efficient. That has been demonstrated by experience," Blair concluded, arguing for a constitutional amendment for total prohibition.[24] No matter the evidence presented Blair in support of the post canteen, he absolutely could not accept its merits. Not only was the prescribed sanction of the sale and consumption of alcohol anathema, the canteen itself was an obstruction to the moralists' goal of total national prohibition. All that remained for the temperance crowd was to learn how to tip public support their way.

THE DEMISE OF THE CANTEEN, 1898–1901

Official records vary regarding alcohol use during the War with Spain. A post-war study determined the two years associated with the war saw the lowest rate of alcoholism over a twenty-year period from 1887 to 1906. The rates, 15.95 per thousand in 1898, and 18.35 per thousand in 1899, were half of the pre-war average (34.52 per thousand).[25] Before the war, Major General Nelson A. Miles issued a general order requiring all medical officers to "carefully note the effect" of beer and light wine sold in regimental canteen on the rank and file, out of a general fear the tropic clime would quickly overwhelm even the most casual drinker's immune system, making them more susceptible to tropical infection.[26] Results were mixed. Many volunteer regiments downplayed their alcohol consumption, claiming their complement was made up of young men from "good" families who exercised restraint. Abuses in the training camps were always in a neighboring regiment—invariably from another state—where self-control and discipline was always lax. Worse still were charges that "wet" regiments forced young abstinence recruits to work as bartenders in their unit canteen, or face confinement. "I've seen one canteen bar 200 feet long, with 10 bartenders behind it and men in front of it two and three deep," a National Temperance Society observer reported, claiming that in three months $450,000 was spent on alcohol at Chickamauga.[27]

Regular medical officers were less willing to conceal alcohol abuse. Instead they used the mobilization of volunteer and militia regiments as an opportunity to highlight the advantages of the canteen system. National Guard officers joined both sides of the debate. Temperance advocates spared no graphic detail of the debauches and subsequent illness plaguing "wet" regiments. "It is also a matter of public record that during the war with Spain, when the brewery interests established bars at all home camps, the sickness and mortality from 'disease' among the soldiers was the greatest to be found in the annals of the modern armies," wrote temperance proponent Ellwood Bergey. "Also it is notorious that during this war tens of thousands of young men imbibed their first liquor which layed the foundation for a life of subsequent ruin."[28] Likewise, Bergey proclaimed, the majority of officers were besotten ogres, with no regard for their young recruits' welfare. Even worse, many allegedly misused government funds in the Philippines for the purpose of collecting prostitutes under a single roof, where they could be licensed and put to work rather than rehabilitated.[29]

Canteen supporters proudly compared the sick call and desertion rates of their regiments with the "drys." Regular beer and wine issues in the controlled setting of the regimental exchange prevented a wide range of disciplinary breaches. Likewise, the "wet" canteen was acclaimed for keeping illness rates low. This was particularly noted in the fever camps. Not only did the canteen keep men out of the tent brothels and saloons surrounding the camps, it also prevented mingling with typhoid infected rowdies from nearby "dry" regiments.

Canteen advocates found the case of the 3rd Nebraska Volunteer Infantry Regiment—commanded by Colonel William Jennings Bryan, populist Democratic presidential candidate and devoted temperance advocate—especially telling. The Third Nebraska was reputedly created solely for political purposes, specifically to fulfill Bryan's desire to show his own patriotism. As regimental commander, Bryan was reputedly lackluster, more interested in winning over his men—all future voters—than in preparing for military action.[30] His easygoing attitude only won him criticism as typhoid fever and venereal disease spread throughout his command at Camp Cuba Libre, near Jacksonville, Florida. Bryan's unwillingness to take responsibility for the collective health of his regiment was more than an inability to adopt military discipline and order, however. Rather, it reflected his beliefs on health, and how each individual person's morality determined their state of wellness. It is not that Bryan didn't care about his men. He cared a great deal for their social and moral welfare, providing everything for the men's amusement, including games, books, sporting equipment, and regular church services. Everything his men could want was offered, save for the issue of cheap beer and wine at the local canteen. Here, Bryan acted on a moral obligation to protect his men from a practice he considered corrupt.[31]

Bryan's dry regimen was short lived. He left the regiment on December 12, 1898, following a long illness. In leaving, Bryan turned command over to Lieutenant Colonel Victor Vifquain, a Belgian immigrant who rose from the rank of private to Brevet Brigadier General during the Civil War.

Vifquain authorized beer sales at the regimental exchange in part as a disciplinary measure. After opening the canteen, "No doctors, no provost guards, were needed about the 3d Nebraska," Vifquain later commented, as opposed to the situation under Bryan's command, when the regiment "had many drunks every day," and suffered the expected disciplinary infractions. Shortly after the change in command, the regiment departed for Cuba, undertaking garrison duty in Havana, where it reported only minimal illness related to alcohol and venereal disease.[32]

The new colonial tropical possessions, inhabited by various non-white peoples of suspect morality, created a new cause for distress among temperance advocates. The deployment of thousands of soldiers, many citizen soldiers of the National Guard, in the Philippines, Puerto Rico, and Cuba, put many young men at risk from a whole litany of sins of the flesh and soul. Never mind the initial reports of medical officers of little change in incidence of drunkenness between soldiers abroad and soldiers at home. Accounts of Manila streets, lined with small huts each offering local potations of questionable quality, mortified American readers at home. All across the country, newspaper readers became familiar with accounts of "vino," the Filipino choice homebrew. Accounts of its content and manufacture varied. Essential ingredients included some form of tropical fruit, ranging from fermented coconut to bananas to mangoes. Sugar was another critical ingredient. Invariably, other, unsavory ingredients were added to the mix, including tree leaves, food scraps, and the inevitable insects that, once attracted to the brew, died and fell to the bottom of the barrels. Regardless of the ingredients, the effects were always the same. A "fiery and villainous" drink according to one observer,[33] vino was "the most abominable and destructive liquid that I believe the earth can produce," another man noted. "The rottenest American whiskey ever brewed is 'angel food' compared with that vile stuff."[34] Sold in roadside bars and shacks for ten cents a canteenful, vino drinkers invariably ended up blind, roaring drunk, staggering around until they collapsed in a stupor. The lucky ones were robbed of their clothes and sentenced to a month's confinement in the guardhouse. It was not uncommon for drunk Americans to be "boloed" in the street—hacked up by rebel Filipinos. Others went "bino crazy," deserting their units to go native, shacking up with local women, surviving on the run until their next bottle or canteenful.[35]

Then there were the cases of vino poisoning. Even good soldiers were susceptible to lapsing occasionally, but homebrewed vino could kill. Army chaplain Charles S. Pierce described one case he experienced during his deployment in the Philippines in 1899. The man was an eighteen year veteran, with several commendations attesting to his sobriety and good comportment as a soldier. One night, however, the soldier went on a vino spree from which he never recovered. "He had never been a drunkard," Pierce wrote, "but this native poison was so virulent in its effect that he became maddened, and lingered in his delirium a whole week, never having recovered his reason at the time of his death."[36] A general crackdown on vino sales in Manila ensued, but with little effect.

The prevalence of lethal home-brewed potations, combined with the tremendous isolation from home, induced ever more strenuous appeals for the canteen in the imperial periphery. Captain Edward S. Munson, Assistant Surgeon, viewed the canteen as a preventive "in the disuse of stronger spirituous liquors and in a lessening of the evils which followed the free use of spirits in the tropics."[37] Cold American lager beer was a lifeline for young soldiers, not only morally but also physically, since its lower alcohol content was considered far less likely to cause the nervous collapse incident to tropical service. Combined with its ready employment as a morale booster for lonely American men serving abroad—a release valve that could be maintained and controlled by commanding officers as an incentive to guarantee military order—the canteen, Munson argued, "offers inducements to the men to remain at home and spend their idle time within the limits of the post," rather than becoming habitual slaves to the brothels and saloonkeepers willing to extend credit for booze.[38]

Nevertheless, dire accounts from the nation's new imperial periphery reinvigorated the prohibition crowd. On March 2, 1899, Congress closed the canteen; the next day, however, Attorney General John W. Griggs advised Secretary of War Alger of a loophole in the new legislation. While military personnel were barred from selling alcohol, nothing prevented civilian contractors from doing such. Word spread across the Army advising commanders to hire local civilians to manage post canteens. Five months later, Griggs' loophole was reaffirmed by the incoming Secretary of War, Elihu Root, who saw the question not as an issue of soldier morality, but rather of "whether they should be permitted to drink beer in camp, surrounded by the restraining influences of discipline and good association, or whether they should be driven to drink bad whiskey in the vile resorts which cluster around the limits of every military post and camp, and especially around those in which prohibition is maintained."[39]

Fueled by further accounts of depravity and degeneration in the imperial periphery, the temperance forces continued their push for a total ban. The American Anti-Saloon League decried the high percentage—"between 10 and 35 per cent"—of soldiers stationed in the Philippines who "drink to excess habitually."[40] The canteen was decried as "nothing more of less than a polite term for 'saloon,'" preying on the "'morally week.'" [41] The temperance crowd was joined by Army officers and enlisted soldiers who objected to the canteen on moral grounds. This group, which included retired Brigadier General A. S. Daggett, increasingly objected to the system after a long silence on the subject. Whether beer, wine, or cheap rotgut whiskey, alcohol was alcohol, and its sale on government property was an affront to the majority of abstinent Americans. Moreover, the canteen introduced young recruits to a new life constructed of bad habits and gave hard drinkers a substitute when they couldn't get to the local whiskey saloon. Even more outrageous was the premise that the Canteen had improved the over-all quality of life in the Army since its introduction in 1889. The real agent of change were civilian philanthropies, benevolent societies, and a more progressive-minded Army establishment in the late 1870s and 1880s taking a general interest in the welfare of the enlisted soldier. This was realized not merely in the material improvement of life in the barracks, but also in the rate of desertions and hospital admissions for drunkenness in the decade *before* the Canteen was established in 1889. In the case of deser-tions, the argument was harder to make, as there was a higher average rate of desertions—12 percent—between 1881 and 1889, compared with a sharp decrease to an average of 5 percent between 1890 and 1897. Hospital admissions were indeed trending lower, however, with a decrease of 27.3 per thousand in 1881 and 1889 compared to a 12.2 per thousand decrease in 1891–1897. The point, temperance proponents argued, was that the qual-ity of life for the soldier was already improving before the canteen; lauding the system for any changes was a manipulation of the actual facts.[42]

The temporary reprieve for the canteen ended in 1901, when Congress reaffirmed the Canteen ban, extending it this time to sales "by any person in any post exchange or canteen or Army transport or upon any premises used for military purposes by the United States."[43] Across the country and overseas, light alcohol sales were terminated, while plans were drawn up and circulated for a new post exchange, designed with an eye toward the "strenuous Christianity" movement's obsession with sport and fitness. New stone and brick buildings would replace the wood frame canteen shack, providing a clean and imposing venue for physical exercise and mental improvement: gym floors encircled by running tracks, suited for activities and occasions from group calisthenics to formal dances; exercise equip-ment and weight racks; separate rooms for reading, billiards, and classes; kitchens and dining areas; small stores and post office service—everything one could desire, save for the old canteen room, with cheap nickel beer and light wine.[44] As Congress appropriated $500,000 for new buildings at posts at home and abroad, it was clear the canteen would not return until the new buildings were tested.[45]

THE FIGHT FOR THE CANTEEN CONTINUES

Despite the new marble post exchange and its amenities, line officers and their staff peers remained bitter, as social reformer and temperance advo-cate Reverend Charles Parkhurst learned shortly after the ban took effect. While visiting Chicago's Fort Sheridan, Parkhurst was quizzed about his position on the canteen, and if he felt the ban was fair and just to the pri-vate soldiers. Responding diplomatically that he felt many were unaware of all the facts pertaining to the issue, the post commander pounced. "I see that you are perfectly blind, Dr. Parkhurst, to anything we can say to you,"

Colonel James J. Van Horne, commanding 8th Infantry Regiment, lashed. "You are cocked and primed and blind. You came here with your mind made up," he continued, crediting Parkhurst's visit as an occasion to gloat, a charge Parkhurst denied.[46] The exchange reveals how both sides reached a complete impasse, with little hope of compromise on the issue.

Not that there would be any change from the temperance movement. The canteen ban was the first step in a broader effort to bring about a nation-wide prohibition of alcohol sale and consumption. The Army ban was a critical precedent, evidence of the selfless objectives of the movement, itself a collective of the country's most influential moral and health reformers. This attitude was certainly reflected by other churchmen active in the movement, especially Methodist church leaders. Bishop Stephen Aason Merrill, for example, argued that "Any attempt to regulate the sale of intoxicants in the Army or elsewhere is wrong, and can only lead to wrong." Bishop Edward Gayer Andrews, agreed, stating that alcohol "endangers the health, the morals and the efficiency of the soldier, and ought to disappear from our military camps and posts." Bishop William Xavier Ninde expressed his sympathy for the endangered morality of the American soldier. "It seems a cruel thing to place temptation in the way of our noble soldier boys, who are away from the kindly and restraining influences of the home and the home church." For Bishop Charles Cardwell McCabe, there was but one solution. "The establishment of the army canteen, or 'military beer saloon' is a backward step in Christian civilization. It will be a source of great trouble to us if not abolished."[47]

Not all clergymen supported the ban. The leaders of the Catholic temperance movement supported the canteen as a refuge from the saloon. John Archbishop Ireland, Catholic Archbishop of St. Paul, Minnesota, and a temperance advocate, testified before the Senate Committee on Military Affairs on December 13, 1900, offering his assessment on the canteen at Fort Snelling, outside of St. Paul, Minnesota. Since it was "useless to try to prohibit absolutely the use of liquor," he argued, the canteen actually saved young soldiers "from outside temptations of all kinds."[48] When questioned if the canteen was an enticement to sin for young recruits, Archbishop Ireland scoffed, "That sort of man in the army is rather a rare article, but if the rare article does turn up, as it may, and if a man is found in the army who has been able to resist the temptations of the saloons in ordinary life, I think he will be able to resist the evils of the canteen."[49] Ireland's testimony was immediately seized upon by the pro-canteen crowd, as seen in a char-coal drawing titled "And Uncle Sam Permits It!" printed in *Uncle Sam's Magazine* in July 1909. The sketch portrays a valley beneath a mountain pass, with soldiers marching in formation toward the saloons and dives purveying poison and cheap swill. Resting atop a pile of bones—of the dead who have been lured into its hands—is an octopus, its arms waving ominously over the tableau. The caption quotes form the archbishop's testimony: "Along the military reservation it was the custom of three or four miserable saloons to establish themselves, expressly and exclusively for the purpose of furnishing liquor to the soldiers—liquor of the worst kind—and not only furnishing liquor, but furnishing everything that makes for iniquity."[50]

Army chaplains also supported the canteen, frequently in opposition to their individual denomination's public stance on temperance. Chaplains, like medical officers, existed in the Army at the institution's behest and sufferance in the nineteenth century. Considered civilian members of a martial fraternity, like medical officers, the chaplain struggled for authority over moral issues while also striving for legitimacy. Yet the chaplain also occupied two professional spheres simultaneously. As a witness to God and one of the earthly messengers of His will, the chaplain was obligated to speak toward a higher calling, at times against the will of his own secular chain of command and authority. Yet the chaplain's chief constituency was a community of men who existed outside the pale of civilian society, and who were the chief agents of the state's authority. The obligation presented to the chaplain was very great, and one which frequently called for careful interpretations of scripture to meet the circumstances of military life, without undermining their own tenuous status and legitimacy. Thus, many chaplains gave their unstinting support to the canteen as "the best possible solution" to the issue of balancing good health and temperance in the Army.[51] The canteen wasn't perfect; any place that made its trade in beer and wine hardly qualified as a safe environment from temptation. But it was preferable to the alternative, as Chaplain D. R. Lowell argued in 1898: "My advice to the temperance people would be for the present let us try to improve the 'canteen' system until we can see our way clear to something better. . . . I have no doubt that if the 'canteen' were abolished entirely, a worse state of affairs would exist than now obtains."[52]

Chaplains serving abroad were even more convinced of the need for the canteen. Not only a safe refuge from rotgut vino and lax indigenous morals, the canteen was a lifeline to the comforts of home. Henry Swift described his experiences as chaplain to the 24th Infantry Regiment in Santiago, Cuba after the canteen was closed. Within a few weeks, morale plummeted, bringing the reputation of the regiment down as well. "The men herded in the low haunts and dives of the city," Swift wrote. "It was an evil period; and we all felt that it would be far better to keep the canteen open."[53] Charles Pierce agreed; in Manila in 1899, he was shocked by the prevalence of nipa hut brothels and vino sellers all over the city. Pierce abandoned his objections to the canteen, becoming a qualified temperance man in the process. "I should welcome the day when all men, out of the Army as well as in it, might find it agreeable by their abstinence to crush out the market for all malt or spirituous products," he wrote to the Adjutant General. "That millennial age, however, has not dawned, and my opinion is that it is better to accept such forms of restriction as are feasible than to insist upon a theory which, however ideal, is impossible of enforcement."[54]

The support offered by the majority of chaplains for the canteen indicated how it was viewed as essential for the enlisted man's spiritual and physical health. Edmund Banks Smith, chaplain at Governor's Island, New York, recognized that without the canteen, the men in his garrison would routinely visit the fleshpots of New York City, to the embarrassment of the service as a whole. Having considered what the American public already believed regarding alcohol in the Army, Smith considered the loss of the canteen only fed the public's appetite for misleading spectacle. "The average citizen, seeing a soldier under the influence of liquor, in uniform, concludes most illogically that the majority of soldiers are drunkards. This is a cruel injustice to the American soldier and to the Army at large."[55] By the time Chaplain Smith wrote his defense of the canteen, however, it was already too late. The canteen had long since been banned, and in theory, if not yet full practice, the Army was dry. Yet Smith and other chaplains continued to press for the canteen on moral grounds, considering it the lesser of two evils. The enlisted man rarely turned out to be a "lifer," Smith cautioned, so it was best to remember "that the American soldier is an American citizen before and after his enlistment, and that if he contracts evil habits of intemperance in the Army, society will suffer after his discharge. Therefore, everything that can be done for the moral welfare of the soldier is something done for the good of the entire community."[56]

The Chaplaincy's support for the canteen, even in the face of the legislative successes of the temperance faction, reveals the extent to which the Army spoke of a single mind on the subject of temperance and morality. As a whole, the Army is shown to be more concerned with the pragmatic reality of the temperance debate—specifically, soldiers were the primary audience of saloon-keepers, brothel madams, and a criminal element. The canteen's provision of cheap lager beer and wine was an effort to extend a paternal hand of guidance and protection over the susceptible enlisted man—guidance through a dangerous maze of temptation and protection from the worst manifestation of the civilian population's disdain for the uniformed agent of security. Through the 1890s, military officers from all branches considered the canteen an essential tool to prevent the influence and spread of vice in the ranks. At the very moment, however, when the canteen's influence was most needed to safeguard American servicemen in new and exotic foreign posts from the degenerative aspects of their tropical service, the institution was taken away, leaving medical and line officers both to discover new methods to engage and combat the growing tide of venereal infection in the ranks.

VENEREAL DISEASE AND THE MEDICAL OFFICER, 1890–1910

In 1909, Colonel John Van Rensselaer Hoff asked, "Is there a venereal peril for us?"[57] He was speaking from the clinician's perspective. Since the

Civil War, average syphilis and gonorrhea rates in the general population declined. In 1865, the rate of venereal infection was 82 per thousand men. While during the decade after the war, the rate of infection did increase to 87.86 per thousand, from 1876 until 1897 the rate decreased to 73.70 per thousand men, with syphilis specifically falling from 105 per thousand in 1868 to 12 per thousand in 1897.[58] During the Spanish-American War, however, venereal disease rates increased, to 133 per thousand men in 1899. This rate grew over the next nine years, reaching 196.02 per thousand in 1907.[59] Why this increase, Hoff asked, despite the general decline of syphilis and gonorrhea in the general population? And what could the medical officer do to stop it?

The Army was no stranger to venereal disease. Between 1819 and 1839, for example, 2,712 cases of gonorrhea and 1,046 cases of syphilis were reported.[60] Despite this, venereal disease did not warrant any mention in the Medical Department's statistical abstracts, except as an exciting factor in the spread of cholera, influenza, or other epidemics.[61] Only after the Mexican War was more attention paid to venereal disease. Coastal garrisons, notably those in or near cities with an industrious commercial sex trade, were where soldiers were most likely to be infected, while the interior of the Great Plains was considered less threatening. Surgeons like Thomas Madison, stationed at Fort Randall, on the Missouri River in the Dakota Territory, commented favorably in 1857 on the virtue of interior Indian tribes, whose women generally avoided carnal contact with soldiers: "The squaws are very virtuous or very inaccessible, and are not pretty."[62] The same could not be reported for Mexican women in the Southwest and California or the women of the Northwest tribes, both groups accused by surgeons and soldiers of wanton lewdness, and blamed for spreading venereal disease.[63] Stereotypes associating Mexican women with the complaint disease were promulgated by many surgeons, including Assistant Surgeon Israel Moses. Assigned to Ringgold Barracks in South Texas as Post Surgeon in 1854, even while reporting on the low rate venereal diseases there, Moses wrote: "Not a case exists in town, nor among the troops—a fact without precedence! That a Mexican town, in which there are about two hundred women, and mostly of Mexican morals, should exist without syphilis among them, is a wonder."[64]

Venereal diseases were also linked to moral conduct and behavior. Unlike other conditions, the source of infection was readily understood and linked to an alleged or real lapse in morality. The best way to treat syphilis and gonorrhea was to avoid the risk in the first place. Hence the link to alcohol and other stimulants; in the Manichean world of nineteenth-century morality, venereal disease was not only an unfortunate infection related to misbehaving, it was also seen as a just reward for the individual who transgressed the social code and strayed from the moral strictures of polite society.

Venereal disease was seen as the soldier's disease. Enlisted men drawn from the ranks of the nation's poor were traditionally seen as carriers of social taint and suspect morality. Civilians overwhelming viewed soldiers as the lowest of the low, professional debauchees, taking on a job beyond the pale of good civil company. The soldier fulfilled the role of the community's domesticated violent other, defender of civilian property and liberty, but also a hazard to those civilians who came into contact with him, due to his existence on society's moral periphery. One part Judas Goat, one part diseased leper, the soldier simultaneously placed himself in harm's way and threatened the rest of the community with infection.

TREATING VENEREAL DISEASE BEFORE 1900

Another factor affecting the perception of venereal disease was its illusory response to treatment. Since the seventeenth century, physicians reported mixed results treating venereal disease. Cases resulting in horrible disfigurement, painful discharge, social isolation, and death were not unknown. Yet such distressing progressions of syphilis were tallied to repeated moral lapse and habitual abuse by the immoral victim, not necessarily as evidence of a latent infection which could ravage the host's body years after initial infection. Success was often claimed when urethral flushes and injections—painful mixes of zinc, mercury, silver nitrate, and other substances—were frequently employed against both syphilis and gonorrhea. Indeed, mercury became accepted by regular physicians as the best treatment for venereal disease, largely on the basis of the physical reaction it created. By promoting sweating and extensive salivation, it was considered a powerful exciting agent, which, properly administered, restored the humoric imbalance caused by the disease. The regimen was hazardous, however, as more physicians recognized mercury overdose would overwhelm the patient's constitution.[65] Hence the shift from oral administration to the more topical application of mercury flushes and ointments. In more painful and potentially life-threatening cases, local remedies and healers were called upon, no matter how repugnant. Surgeon Madison described one incident of a local *metis* trader hired to administer his own patent remedy on a soldier whose infection blocked his urinary tract. The obstruction was removed, "I am credibly informed, by suction, with the lips applied to the penis. After a few mouthfuls of bloody urine, the bladder was relieved of its enormous detention without further difficulty, for the time being. I found it almost impossible, at first, to introduce the smallest sized bougie or catheter, but he is now perfectly well, and can himself introduce a large catheter without difficulty."[66] Despite such claims of success by army surgeons, the majority of patients were less fortunate. Many doctors reported success in treating gonorrhea or primary syphilis with urethral flushes of mercury or potassium iodide, but they did not take into account the dormancy of the illness. When secondary syphilis inevitably appeared, physicians had no recourse save discharging the afflicted soldiers from the service.

Not until the Civil War did medical officers reconsider the disease's etiology and the appropriate therapeutic response. The sheer number of infected individuals—over 182,750 reported cases of syphilis and gonorrhea in the Union Army alone—determined the re-evaluation of contemporary wisdom regarding venereal disease.[67] Compounding the situation was the wide range of treatments and remedies proffered by volunteer surgeons. These non-regulated physicians used the entire *material medica* on patients, with the same general result as Regular medical officers—which is to say little effect at all.[68]

In the Western Theater, medical and line officers adopted a new course of remediation. After occupying Nashville in the summer of 1862, Union Army military governors and medical officers discovered the city was home to a thriving community of prostitutes. The number of sex workers swelled with the arrival of other like-minded women eager to ply their trade among the thousands of Union soldiers now stationed in each city. Facing the prospect of rampant venereal disease decimating their forces, the city's military governor instituted mandatory medical inspections and licenses of all working prostitutes in July of 1863. Armed with the power to incarcerate, medical officers inspected public women for syphilis and gonorrhea. Women found free of disease were given a certificate allowing them to ply their trade until their next inspection ten days later. Those afflicted with venereal disease were confined until they were "perfectly cured" of their ailment, or forced to leave the city. By April 30, 1864, 352 women were inspected and given licenses, and another 92 were confined in the venereal hospital. By January 31, 1865, 207 women were treated, until the primary symptoms of their condition abated and they were deemed free to return to their occupation or ordered to leave.[69]

The regulation and inspection scheme developed in Nashville was soon copied in Memphis, another town whose indigenous community of prostitutes swelled with new arrivals into a thriving culture of sex for hire. By the summer of 1864, the increase in gonorrhea and syphilis was so great that Major General Cadwaller C. Washburn, commander of the Department of West Tennessee, gave up trying to suppress the sex trade. Washburn placed the city under martial law, and issued a public circular on September 30, 1864. The notice ordered "All women of the town of the City of Memphis and vicinity" ("women of the town" being the polite euphemism to distinguish prostitutes from women of good character) to submit to a weekly medical inspection administered by a medical officer. Those passed with a clean bill of health reported to the Mayor's office, where they were required to purchase a ticket of registry for $10.00, the fee used to pay the upkeep and maintenance of a separate female ward at the City Hospital. Like the Nashville order, the full coercive weight of military authority was extended to policing compliance. "Good conduct will insure relief from detective or police visits, exposure or loss, and a violation of the order will inevitably incur punishment," the order stated. "Any woman of the town, public or private, found in the city or vicinity after the tenth day of October, 1864, without her certificate or registry and her medical exemption certificate, will be arrested by the police and punished." Between October 1, 1864 and the suspension of the program in February 1865, 134 women registered with the department, while the woman's ward at the Memphis City Hospital treated thirty-four women for venereal diseases.[70]

The impetus behind Union Army's brief experiment with regulated prostitution in Nashville and later in Memphis was not the eradication of venereal disease but the acknowledgment that illicit sex for hire was an onerous evil that would not go away. Like the British Contagious Diseases Act of 1864, both infection and intent was gendered. Afflicted male soldiers were confined in their own venereal hospitals, but aside from shame avoided any official punishment. Indeed, according to *The Medical and Surgical History of the War of the Rebellion*, the soldiers bore little responsibility for their infection, but rather were the victims of "the evil" congress with "diseased women." Such language buttressed the impression that women, rather than men, were the primary vectors of venereal disease, and that women should submit to regulated examination, quarantine, fines, imprisonment, and if deemed appropriate, forced exile. The language of the official history also singled out Southern women as the primary culprits in transmitting disease, since "many of the better class of prostitutes had been drawn to Nashville from northern cities by the comparative protection from venereal disease which its license system afforded." Little comment was made of the gender inequities within the regulation policy, other than to quietly laud its success and to note that "after the attempt to reduce disease by the forcible expulsion of the prostitutes had, as it always has, utterly failed, the more philosophic plan of recognizing and controlling an ineradicable evil has met with undoubted success."[71]

VENEREAL DISEASE BECOMES A PUBLIC HEALTH ISSUE, 1890–1910

After the Civil War, venereal disease vexed medical and line officers across the country. As before the war, the disease was not considered a serious threat to the overall public health of a command. But the experiences of the Civil War still haunted medical officers, who now viewed the illness as a detriment to good order and service and as proof of fraternization with unsavory elements of American society. Frontier posts and urban forts were assailed by saloons, brothels, and casinos where alcohol was often used as an enticement to sample the establishment's other unsavory offerings. Colonel Thomas F. Anderson, commanding the 14th Infantry Regiment at Vancouver Barracks, Washington, described the environment around his post in 1890. Directly across the Columbia River from Vancouver Barracks was Portland, Oregon, a town flush with dozens of saloons and bars that lured soldiers in with whiskey and beer on credit. "Connected with many of those are gambling establishments and bawdy houses of the worst description, where the most dangerous diseases are contracted, and where, I am informed, crimes against nature and practices too vile for description are indulged in," Anderson reported. "In the city of Portland at some of the low dance halls it is reported that women clad only in their chemises wait on the men."[72] Meanwhile, at Fort Wingate, New Mexico, on the edge of Apache country, saloon and brothel owners maintained concealed stables in hidden ravines in and around the post for soldiers to sneak off for their illicit entertainment. Of course, following their rendezvous, soldiers were just as likely to be robbed of everything they had, including the uniforms off their back, and sent back to the post, "drunken, demoralized and with venereal diseases," to face court-martial and confinement in the hospital.[73] Given the choice between the rum house and the post canteen, little wonder most Army officers preferred the latter.

Adding to domestic outrage were the dramatic and exotic spectacles in the nation's new imperial periphery. In the Philippines, American soldiers were astounded by the native women's apparent lack of modesty and morality. Some developed closer relationships, occasionally living together in the hut villages surrounding military encampments. Such arrangements were almost always temporary, of course, as American perceptions of racial identity remained attuned to what was acceptable back home. It was one thing to keep a Filipino mistress while stationed abroad; indeed, such relationships were tolerated as a means to keep soldiers out of trouble. But there was no mistaking their consorts for legitimate partners, as Private Richard Johnson recalled: "A few [soldiers] had ventured into regular marriage, but most Americans of that day felt socially above marrying these women of the lower social order, which were the only ones available to them, though not many had scruples about sleeping with them. These women were generally referred to as 'Squaws', a term acquired from association with Indian women on the Western Plains of the United States, and the men who kept them were generally termed 'Squaw men'."[74] Hawaii was equally dangerous and alluring. Long before annexation, prostitution was considered a staple business in Honolulu. Since becoming an American territory in 1898, efforts to clean up the city only scattered prostitutes across the island, with many finding their way to Pearl City, the port town adjacent to the naval base at Pearl Harbor.[75] When a rail spur connecting Schofield Barracks to the Oahu Railway was completed in 1909, soldiers now had direct access to red light districts in Honolulu, Kamakela, and other neighborhoods. Soon the Army's two chief posts in Oahu, Schofield Barracks and Fort Shafter, reported infection rates rivaling the Philippines, 203 and 139 per thousand men respectively in the last quarter of 1911.[76]

While the Philippines and Hawaii were considered hazardous to the overall morality and health of American soldiers, they paled in comparison with China. Following the Boxer Rebellion of 1900, American troops took up permanent stations in Beijing and Tientsin, ostensibly to safeguard American persons and property there. China quickly obtained a reputation as the Army's most exotic—and dangerous—posting for young soldiers. Alcohol, women, and opium were all cheaply obtained, and despite their officers' best efforts, enlisted men flocked to the brothels and bars.[77] The result was infection on an epidemic scale. Major Louis Livingston Seaman, medical officer attached with the First U.S. Volunteer Engineer Regiment, reported that by February 1901 only eight total abstinence men remained in the entire 12th Infantry Regiment. Thanks to their thirst for alcohol, Seaman concluded, American soldiers were led directly into the arms of diseased women. Accordingly, 50 percent of all patients in Camp Reilly's hospital ward in Beijing received treatment for gonorrhea and syphilis, all acquired from local prostitutes. "My own observations in other military hospitals tend to a similar conclusion," Seaman wrote. "The men get their liquor away from the post and leave the rum-hole for the brothel."[78] And matters only got worse. In 1910, the American garrison in Beijing suffered an infection rate of 30 percent, as compared with a rate of under 1 percent in the German Legation garrison.[79] And by 1913, the 15th Infantry Regiment's admission rates for venereal disease reached the incredible level of 226.15 per thousand men.[80]

Little surprise the American public saw the soldier as a lost cause when it came to morality and overall health. The general perception of the enlisted man was captured in a 1909 cartoon published in *Uncle Sam's Magazine*. The cartoon, titled "Just Outside the Gate," shows a soldier in the "Good-Fellows' Grotto," deep into his cups. Surrounding him is a gaggle of harpies and demons—desertion, sin, murder, robbery, disease, want, insanity, and suicide, among them—toasting his health below a list of the house specialties: wood alcohol, knock-out drops, beer swill, good dope, and deadly drugs.[81] The message was clear: the culture of sin surrounding the Army post was slowly killing the average soldier; if not by drink, then through the diseased charms of the prostitute. For the country's honor and the health of its soldiery, something had to change. The public health of the Army was inextricably linked to morality.

Yet medical officers were uncertain what to do, even after identifying the microbial source of infection and making the direct moral association between behavior and disease. The problem was public opinion. In essence, the American public would not tolerate the simplest and most obvious sanitary solution—the registration and regular inspection of prostitutes. Major Edward L. Munson addressed this challenge in a larger paper on the diseases of the soldier in July, 1909. The problem resided within a small yet dangerous core population of diseased individuals. Given the chance to inspect and regulate the female carriers of venereal disease, Munson argued, "we [physicians] could stamp out gonorrhea and chancroids in one generation and syphilis in three. But our hands are tied by ethics and sentiment."[82] Social reformers, united in their zeal to stamp out prostitution, would hardly tolerate the examination and isolation of suspected prostitutes on military posts. Even if the medical officer could act, the unregulated nature of prostitution in the United States meant that, without martial law, there was no way to stamp the practice out completely. "How are we to combat this condition . . . ," Munson asked, "I confess that I do not know. The best that we can do is to cure existing infections and try to prevent the acquirement of new ones."[83] Denied the opportunity to control infected women, Army medical officers sought to address the issue of infected men under their direct control. In Beijing, Major Lyster oversaw an experiment in which a prophylactic station, complete with calomel ointment and disinfectant soaps, was set up in the barracks for use after visiting a prostitute. The effect was negligible, as men simply ignored or forgot to use the station. Even after creating a disposable urethral flush—the "K packet," consisting of a tapered two inch glass tube, filled with three 1–10 gram potassium permangantate tablets and a gelatine capsule filled with 30 percent calomel ointment, all wrapped in wax paper for convenience—little change in infection was reported. When questioned, men simply reported losing or forgetting their packets, prompting Lyster to call for the direct intercession by company-level commanders: "The recruit must learn [about venereal infection] and he usually does so by an experience expensive to the government, to himself and to society. Once instructed as any young man should be, the soldier should be required to comply with orders causing him to care for himself or be cared for after 'exposure.'"[84]

Other medical officers adopted their own version of Lyster's prophylaxis regimen. Beginning in June 1909, venereal inspection was mandated at Schofield Barracks, Hawaii, for any soldier on liberty. Any venereal case found to have evaded inspection was subjected to court-martial on charges of failure to comply with post orders. Over the remaining months of 1909, 504 men reported for prophylaxis inspection, with only fourteen becoming infected after the fact, an overall decrease of over 70 percent from the infection rate between January and May.[85] The garrison's medical officer, Captain C. F. Morse, saw this as an essential first step toward reducing infection: "If the amount of venereal disease can be reduced 50% or even 25%, if 50 or 25 our of every hundred men formerly infected can be saved from that infection by any means adopted we should feel that we have accomplished a good work well worth the trouble incurred."[86]

The quest for a solution to the Army's venereal disease problem was boosted with the introduction of a new pharmaceutical in 1910. The year before, German bacteriologist Paul Ehrlich reported success against syphilis from his laboratory's latest organic chemical compound, 606. Marketed as Salvarsan in Europe, 606 arrived in the United States as arsphenamine. Samples were immediately dispatched to the Army Medical Laboratory, where two researchers, Captains Henry J. Nichols and Charles F. Craig, evaluated its merits. After a year's testing on patients in the Government Hospital for the Insane in Washington, D.C., instructions were released to the Medical Department outlining the proper administration of Salvarsan. The base treatment, indicated for primary stage syphilis, was based on two introductions of the drug a week apart, either intravenously or intramuscularly. Secondary and tertiary stage syphilis warranted additional treatment with a combination of Salvarsan and mercury. In all cases, blood samples marked "606" were to be sent to one of the Army's three General Hospitals for evaluation and control purposes.[87]

The immediate problem with Salvarsan was the drug's side effects. Severe local pain at the site of injection often lasted for days, at times requiring morphine for relief. Low fevers, nausea, vomiting, diarrhea, headache, and at times, cellulitis and soft tissue destruction around the injection area were also reported. Muscle pain and tissue degeneration was reportedly lessened through intravenous administration.[88] Undeterred, Army physicians administered Salvarsan in high doses with supplemental topical administrations of mercury ointment directly to syphilitic lesions, with good results. As the first treatment cases returned negative Wassermann test results a year after final treatment, Surgeon General George H. Torney gave the treatment his final approval in 1912.[89]

Between prophylaxis and Salvarsan, Army physicians were confident they could now deal with syphilis on a case-by-case basis. Yet the prospect of eliminating venereal disease in an Army strung out over 7,000 miles, and whose members were likely to acquire repeat infections, flew in the face of common sense. New cases appeared with stunning regularity. The Army's rate of admission for venereal diseases mounted, from 160.94 per thousand men in 1902, to 188.34 per thousand in 1904, to 196.99 per thousand in 1909.[90] Doctors grasped for alternative solutions: the higher rates were related to chronic gonorrhea cases being reported at sick call; the impact of new diagnostic tools like the Wassermann test; more frequent physical examinations for venereal disease; and the new practice of holding venereal patients in the sick ward until they were cured, were all cited as factors contributing to an illusory rise of cases.[91] Others clung to more fanciful causes—ranging from *trepenoma* carrying bedbugs, to saliva exchange at "kissing parties" involving at least one infected person—for the increase.[92]

In response to repeat infections and the general inability to control individual soldiers outside post, a group of medical officers took aim at the notion of abstinence altogether. After attending an International Conference for the prophylaxis of venereal diseases in 1899, Assistant Surgeon General Valery Havard returned home less sure of the efficacy of relying on the private soldier or citizen to exercise sexual restraint. After attending a second conference in 1902, Havard was convinced regulation and examination were the best means to arrest the venereal disease epidemic in American society and halt its advance in the Army. Unfortunately, Havard noted, the moral climate in the United States made such an approach untenable, leaving no alternative save prophylaxis and education.[93] Not that others were likewise convinced. Medical Corps Major P. C. Fauntleroy, writing in 1909, took aim at the "well known American prudery, false modesty, fanatical puritan narrowness and official weakness" as facilitating an environment of ignorance, in which illicit sexual contact bred venereal infection. In the absence of curing the diseases, the only course was to regulate the practice that spread it. "The *sine qua non* in the control of these diseases has been shown by the military in the Civil War, the Spanish-American and Philippine wars, when they have had the opportunity to do so, to be the effective segregation, inspection and control of prostitution in all its forms."[94]

Proponents of regulated prostitution expanded their venereal disease prevention schema to include a revision of the Army's ban on light alcohol sales in the post exchange. The winning essay in the Association of Military Surgeons' prize contest for 1911 was a serious treatment of the entire issue of venereal disease remediation by Captain Edward B. Vedder. In his essay, Vedder offered a balanced solution to the problem based first on providing a safe environment for soldiers to enjoy a drink while off duty without recourse to local dives or brothels. Considering the steady rise in venereal disease since the abolition of the canteen, it only made sense to re-establish the canteen:

> For the sake of argument only, let us suppose the worst possible apprehensions of the prohibitionists are fulfilled, and that everyone who patronizes the canteen becomes as drunk as you please. The result will be that they will drop into a bed to sleep it off, or will be consigned to the oblivion of the guardhouse. In either case they will acquire no venereal diseases, since no women of bad character ever have or ever will be permitted on the reservation. Thus, whatever may be said of the temperance side of the argument, it is certain that so long as a man stays at the canteen he is safe, while the moment he goes to the average saloon outside the reservation, he is on the road to a possible case of venereal disease.[95]

Combined with the canteen would be the vigorous application of authorized prophylaxis measures under line officer supervision, with the threat of total pay stoppage for soldiers on sick report for venereal disease. These measures, combined with constant moral and civil education classes, were intended to limit visits to prostitutes. In areas where prostitution was widespread and rampant, Vedder proposed regulating select houses. These houses would be mandated as dry establishments, and all women working there would be subject to regular inspection, and if infected, treated in isolation.[96]

Vedder's recommendations brought the issue of Army morality full circle. From 1901, when the Canteen was banned on the grounds it fomented immorality and sent soldiers into the arms of diseased women, the Army reported a steady rise in venereal disease rates. Education, prophylaxis, and treatment were intended to ameliorate syphilis and gonorrhea. But no amount of prevention could overcome the simple reality that young men in uniform who wished to have sex would find no shortage of partners in the environment surrounding military posts and encampments. Little surprise that in 1910, a new call to revive the post canteen as a "wet" environment was made—on the very same moral grounds that closed it a decade earlier.

Indeed, all through the Medical Department's obsession with venereal disease, the canteen had never really gone away. Throughout the Army, line and staff proponents pressed for its return as part of an overall campaign to preserve the morality, good health, and safety of the private soldier. At Fort Sam Houston, in San Antonio, Texas, soldiers of the 9th Infantry Regiment took matters into their own hands in July 1907. After the post canteen was closed in 1901, ten saloons—all gin mills of the lowest sort, with back room beds available for "guests" by the hour—soon opened around the post. The saloons all plied a steady trade until July 6, 1907, when a Private Wolf was shot dead by the owner of Smith's Saloon during an argument over the price of a nickel beer. After a grand jury refused to indict the saloon owner, despite the eyewitness testimony of three witnesses, the regiment's enlisted men opened their own club off of fort premises.[97] The new club made an immediate mark on the community around Fort Sam Houston. After building the two room structure, comprised of a common area bar and a separate back room for non-commissioned officers, the men obtained credit from local merchants, and set out to provide a safe regulated environment where enlisted men could mingle off-duty without recourse to the local saloons. Beer, soda, and cigars were sold under the watchful eye of sergeants and corporals. Soon the club enjoyed a positive reputation with the town police, remaining, unlike nearby saloons, free of any disturbance or disorder during its operation.[98] Individual state militias also pushed back against the ban. In 1906, at the Texas National Guard maneuvers, a canteen was opened offering beer after duty hours. The state attorney general insisted Texas statutes gave him the power to abate prohibition laws in gatherings of state forces as he saw fit, provided the trade was restricted to beer and the proceeds used to improve the quality of the grounds. When pressed for a ruling, the Army's acting Judge Advocate General, Brigadier General Enoch H. Crowder, recommended compliance with the state statute, acknowledging the primacy of the National Guard establishment (and hence, individual states) in managing their own cadre.[99]

And yet the canteen remained closed. One reason lies with the inability of canteen proponents in Congress to persuade their opponents to give the institution a second chance. But no less critical was the strenuous campaign against the canteen as a vehicle to moral and racial degeneration through its promotion of a relaxed climate of moral ambiguity amidst the gravest challenges to American youth. From the 1890s through his retirement in

1915 and afterwards, one officer in particular devoted tremendous energy and much of his own personal reputation to promoting a climate of total abstinence and temperance in the Army. In Colonel Louis Mervin Maus' view, the Army had matured from its frontier days into becoming the chief agent to promote Christian masculinity in a culture under constant pressure from internal and external challenges. While he never gained the highest rank he desired most in the Army Medical Department, Maus exercised great influence on the policies undertaken after 1911 to further cement the War Department's ban on alcohol and vice.

ENTER COLONEL LOUIS MERVIN MAUS, MORALIST CHAMPION

Louis Mervin Maus entered the Army on November 10, 1874, after graduating from the University of Maryland's medical school. By the Spanish-American War, Maus had charted the same course as many of his peers, combining frontier service in the Dakotas and the Arizona Territories with postings in Eastern coastal and urban forts. Maus acquired a reputation as a solid clinician, but after a year's leave in Paris, where he studied at the Pasteur Institute under the founder's personal direction, he pursued specialized training in sanitation, tropical diseases, and bacteriology. At the onset of war with Spain, Maus was appointed chief surgeon of the Seventh Army Corps in Jacksonville, Florida. Under his administration, Seventh Corps reported fewer sick than any other corps in the Spanish-American War.[100]

After arriving in Cuba, Maus put the Second Division's medical infrastructure in order, replenishing the division's medical supplies and establishing a new divisional hospital from the many disparate regimental hospitals. Next, he turned his attention to cleaning up Havana, launching a program of street cleaning and building scrubbing that he claimed, at least temporarily, reduced yellow fever in the city. Maus was transferred from Cuba before the disease returned in full force in 1900, being reassigned to the Philippines as Chief Surgeon for the Department of Northern Luzon.[101] His arrival coincided with a series of disease outbreaks that threatened the entire island. Bubonic plague, cholera, and smallpox were rampant in Manila's slums and the surrounding countryside. The city itself was awash in its own filth, the old quarter's moats and canals used for centuries as cesspools, the foundation stones of the city's oldest buildings oozing fetid slime from accumulated underground wastes. Maus immediately launched a cleaning program similar to that which he undertook in Cuba. The bubonic plague epicenter was identified in Manila's Chinese district, where it was in turn linked to an outbreak in Hong Kong. All houses stricken by the plague were disinfected, while a military-style rat-catching campaign was launched in December 1899. Over 20,000 plates of poisoned bait and 10,000 traps were employed, killing over 600,000 rats over a fifteen-month period. Meanwhile, the new Shiga plague vaccine was distributed to hundreds of thousands of Chinese and Filipinos. Maus declared Manila plague free by March 6, 1902, and opened a similar sanitary campaign against a new cholera outbreak later that month.[102]

Appointed the islands' first Commissioner of Public Health on July 1, 1901, Maus imposed a program of urban cleanliness employing thousands of Filipinos with total power to enter and inspect any private residence and evict inhabitants for up to five days while their home was fully cleaned and disinfected. During the height of the 1902 cholera epidemic, he issued more orders, all aimed at arresting the disease with no regard for how they affected the people under his charge. All city wells were closed, cutting off the water supply to the poor. Produce markets were closed. American troops were sent to guard the Mariquina River, to ensure no water was taken from the river and that no one tried to leave the city through it. A disinformation campaign was unveiled, aimed at denying the disease was cholera, calling it instead a colic resulting from ingesting green rice. These efforts and the introduction of a treatment regimen of mandatory benzozene enemas for the afflicted held in the cholera hospital and detention center established at San Lazero Hospital, inflamed public opinion against the Americans, who were increasingly cast as taking out their frustrations over the recent insurrection on the moribund population.[103]

Yet Maus' real interest lay in the intersection of public health and morality. From his earliest days in uniform, Maus decried the Army's culture of tolerance for alcohol. In fact, Maus declared, alcohol had no beneficial application at all, concluding in 1912 that "After a careful study of alcohol as behavior and medicine, I have been unable to discover one single beneficial or useful purpose it serves in the human economy."[104] In every aspect, he continued, alcohol created misery and ruin. Like an octopus, Maus cautioned, the liquor industry ensnared elected and appointed officials at all levels of government, compelling them to act contrary to the public will of the nation. On the individual level, alcohol was a slow-acting poison, acting first on the nervous system, then targeting the body's ability to void waste, weakening the immune system, and ultimately consuming the body's own organs. Bad enough if this pernicious corrosion was limited to the imbiber, but alcohol's toxicity passed to infants, creating a generation of young cretins, their physical, mental, and moral development stunted before birth.[105]

Physical degeneration, and its linkage to alcoholism, was a signal obsession for Maus. While the last generation of Americans were generally healthy, thanks to the temperance of their parents, these same young people risked their children's future health through their own alcohol-fueled lusts. The penchant for alcohol was passed on to the next generation, affecting their own future character and health. Just as the mark of Cain, "It might be said that the fate of every child is written on its forehead when it enters the world, because its fortune for good or bad is settled in advance by the character and habits of its parents."[106] Alcoholism thus concealed many physical deformities and character defects. Afflicted children grew into flawed adults; indeed, alcohol was ultimately responsible for virtually all of society's miscreants, who in turn found their way into the service. Maus wrote, "It is my opinion that the majority of degenerates, who enter our services, as expressed by flagrant violators of rules, regulations and orders, deserters, the inept, moral perverts, and venereal debauches, result from the use of alcohol beverages or their hereditary effects."[107] In linking venereal disease and alcohol use in such a manner, and by linking it to the Medical Department's other sanitary activities, he firmly associated the two conditions with the public health of the Army, and ultimately, American society at large.

Defending the homeland against the scourge of tropical disease was not enough; by taking on alcohol abuse and venereal disease, Maus sought to prevent the ultimate degeneration of American society itself. Indeed, for Maus, venereal disease was the next great scourge lurking in the bodies of the afflicted, the once and future plague that, if unchecked, would consume American society. He was convinced venereal disease was rampant—with over 10 percent of the population afflicted with syphilis, and as many as 80 percent of all men over twenty-five suffering from gonorrhea.[108] Despite the best efforts of administrators and physicians, this rate of infection remained unaffected, creating more than a public health crisis; the high rate of infection threatened the ultimate degeneration of the American people themselves.[109] "I know of no period in the history of our country when a general moral reform was more greatly needed," Maus cautioned his peers in a December 2, 1912 address before the Providence Medical Society. "The increase of tippling and cigarette smoking is marked among the women of the wealthy classes while their less favored sisters haunt with pernicious frequency places of amusement, which pander to the basest human passions, and chase with utter abandon the voluptuous step of the grizzly bear, bunny hug, and turkey trot."[110] The results of such frivolous distractions were apparent only to physicians, Maus concluded, citing gonorrheal infection rates of 75 to 80 percent among women, with accompanying sterility rates of 20 percent.[111] What Maus saw as a dangerous relaxing of social constraint and morality on the dance floor was the first step in the imminent erosion of the physical and mental health of the American people.

Maus' response to the problem straddled the scientific and the political progressive world views. He counseled the ready application of the newest methods of chemical prophylaxis as they became available. In addresses before public crowds across the country, Maus expressed his full support for the K Packet and its successors, citing their efficacy—when soldiers could be induced to use them properly—in eliminating gonorrheal infection.[112] Treatment was also combined with the tried and true progressive practice of proper statistical collation of all verified cases. Maus believed this collection of vital statistics was one of the most important duties of the medical officer and civil physician, as it provided the foundation not only for the accurate reporting of the disease in the general population, but the ability to track its ebb and flow in specific populations over time. Accurate reporting eluded American physicians, Maus believed, largely because of an ingrained reluctance to discuss the subject born of an outdated morality. He thus proposed increased venereal disease instruction in the nation's medical colleges, to establish a uniform best practice for diagnosing, treating, and reporting the condition nationwide.[113]

While counseling the application of modern medical practice and methods to the diagnosis and treatment of venereal disease, Maus believed the greatest tool to prevent its spread was the strict control of the alcohol and sex trade by the civil authorities. "The role that alcohol plays in the contraction of venereal disease and its association with prostitution, makes its control or prohibition necessary for the successful municipal treatment of the three well known social evils," he argued.[114] The best means to arrest the spread of venereal disease was a combination of counter-intuitive measures. On one hand, communities were best served by banning alcohol sales outright or restricting their public use to specific times and taking steps to make their use as uncomfortable an experience as possible. To facilitate this, Maus proposed removing all furniture and accoutrements of existing saloons, making them "limited to the bar and standing room alone."[115] Even better, Maus argued, for the nation to follow the Army's example in banning alcohol outright. Here he revealed his own lack of trust in the character of the Army's enlisted man. "It must be remembered that the majority of our soldiers are young men, and that their opportunities in life have been limited, especially in regard to education," he wrote. "Many of them have not been reared under the best moral influences and restraints, and they have had little chance to establish a high moral standard."[116] Without the Army's guiding hand, these young men would fall victim to the disease-ridden saloon and brothel culture surrounding military posts.

Yet preaching abstinence was not enough. Line officers, medical officers, and chaplains were all now charged with creating a safer and more moral barracks environment for the private soldier. The line officer was expected to take a more paternal interest in the moral character of his men, establishing an atmosphere of mutual trust and respect in which officers and enlisted men strove to avoid shaming each other. Chaplains would likewise take a more active role in facilitating off-duty activities to engage the men's attention and uplift their morality. By introducing "games of football, competitions in manly sports, musicales, minstrel shows, readings, stereopticon lectures, addresses on historical and other interesting topics, and on appropriate occasions, moral subjects, . . . they are not only keeping the men out of mischief, but are building up character, a priceless heritage to every man."[117]

Medical officers served a dual role—as educators and as first and last lines of defense against venereal infection. As the chief agent of sanitary tactics in the military environment, medical officers were expected to share their expertise with the garrison on hygienic threats and offer their best advice through lecture, practice, and formal exercise in how to prevent the spread of diseases that could have a damaging effect on military effectiveness. Maus argued this obligation should be expanded to include lectures on the effects of alcohol abuse and venereal disease. Such preventive lectures would make up the Army's first defense against the debilitating and degenerative effects of vice. The second line would be taken up by the regular inspection and application of prophylaxis by the medical officer as needed, in an effort to halt the spread of venereal disease beyond the initial exposure.[118]

MAUS AND THE MORALISTS MAKE THEIR CASE

Maus was not a solitary crusader. As early as 1893, there were signs that medical officers were losing faith in the canteen system. In his annual report, Surgeon General Sternberg noted that subordinates questioned the canteen advocates' claims. For example, some observed any benefit from reducing binges was offset by the number of fresh recruits exposed to the habit for the first time in the sanctioned environment of the canteen. Others noted that regardless of intentions, the canteen remained an environment dedicated to promoting drunkenness. Major Charles K. Winne reported, "[T]he canteen as originally proposed, and which had much to commend it, has gradually been modified so that it is for all intents and purposes simply an authorized beer saloon kept open under the auspices and with the approval of the Government. . . . To substitute the quiet narcotism of beer for he active delirium of alcohol is merely to change the action of one poison for another."[119]

As Maus became more vocal with his public opposition to the canteen, others joined to argue in favor of the Army's formal temperance policy. Colonel Joseph K. Weaver, of the Pennsylvania National Guard, noted the overall subject of whether soldiers should have access to beer or whiskey was moot. "The habit of drinking intoxicants is bad. It makes the guard more susceptible to discipline and disobedience; they are therefore not as good soldiers when they get beer. It renders the standing of regiments a good deal lower."[120] Another argument rejecting the canteen was posed by Captain R. H. Pierson, who noted that intemperance was both a "civil . . . and military vice." Alcohol consumption, he wrote, degraded the individual's moral and physical health and brought ruination upon the home of the imbiber. Accordingly, there was no place in the Army for such men: "Persons of dissipated habits must control their appetites or sooner or later be dismissed from the service."[121]

Another temperance proponent was Anita Newcomb McGee, former Acting Assistant Surgeon and founder of the Army Nurse Corps. After entering the Medical Department in 1898, McGee favored the canteen as a means to control enlisted personnel behavior and restrict access to hard liquor. In 1907, however, McGee launched her own investigation. To her own surprise, McGee was convinced that banning the canteen was sound policy.

After analyzing Medical Department statistics on hospital admissions for alcoholism, she determined that following the closure of the canteen, the level of admission had risen only slightly, while remaining radically lower than the period before the canteen opened.[122] She went on to dismiss line and staff officer claims that the canteen's closure created a boom in civilian saloons and grog shops, concluding that Secretary of War Elihu Root's claim of an increase of 341 saloons within a mile of U.S. posts between February 2, 1901 and January 8, 1903, was overstated by seventy saloons. Indeed, closer analysis of individual reports showed no change at all in many areas.[123] In closing her report, McGee dismissed the direst warnings of the canteen advocates, pointing again to the Army's own statistical record of the previous ten years. McGee not only rejected claims of increased desertions and courts-martial related to the closing of the canteen, she also considered the argument that most Army officers and enlisted personnel approved the canteen was wrong. She pointed to the absence of any serious poll on the subject until 1899, when only 15 percent of 3,772 volunteer officers and less than 500 non-commissioned officers even bothered to reply to the survey, rendering it useless. More recent discussion with military personnel indicated either a general indifference to the subject or outright opposition on moral principles. In the end, McGee concluded the question was not whether the canteen should or should not be restored, but what should and could the Army do to resolve the problems of alcoholism and venereal disease: "I have become convinced that the prohibition sentiment of the country makes the restoration of the canteen impossible. The sooner we forget it and adopt other methods for diminishing alcoholism, the better it will be for the army."[124]

Nevertheless, the debate did not end quietly. Medical and line officers, and other civilian advocates, pressed on for the canteen's return. Some, like Colonel Havard, based their objections on the premise that the individual rights and personal liberties of the common soldier were at stake, arguing that "In regard to his eating and drinking he ought to enjoy the same privileges of any citizen, so long as he is not guilty of any excess which, in the opinion of his superiors, might be detrimental to his health and morals."[125] Others, like Major Charles Woodruff, continued to push for the moral high ground, believing that, while nationwide temperance was improving, the abolition of the canteen—especially in the imperial periphery—made soldiers more susceptible to bad habits than if it remained open.[126]

In the end, the canteen's proponents failed to realize the larger issue at stake was not the ability of the soldier to enjoy his alcohol in off-duty hours. Rather, by entering into a new imperial mission, the Army's enlisted men had become unwitting vectors of degeneration and venereal infection. Colonel Louis Mervin Maus and his supporters recognized this connection immediately after the Spanish-American War, and they were well-equipped as military sanitarians and as public speakers to convey their meaning of empire to a broad audience, eager for exotic news of the Republic's new tropical possessions.

By 1917, a new generation of medical officers arrived on the scene, identifying morality as a sanitary problem requiring close management and observation. These young officers readily joined progressives in and out of the government on their crusade to preserve the purity of America's sons in wartime uniform. As Nancy Bristow notes in her book *Making Men Moral: Social Engineering during the Great War*, "Enlisted to bear arms for the United States in the international crusade, American troops became the target of an important domestic reform program. Unlike any army ever before assembled, the American troops were to be kept physically healthy *and* morally pure, free of the traditional degradation of training camp culture."[127] The Army Medical Department was a ready partner in this endeavor. All thoughts of returning to the old canteen were ignored; indeed, to all observers, it appeared the department forgot it even had an earlier position on the canteens. Conventional wisdom had come around to the moralist's point of view, as Colonel John Van Rensselaer Hoff expressed in his April 1918 editorial in *The Military Surgeon*. "Alcoholism is not an instinct. It is an addiction and the result of habit. . . . The liquor men themselves are responsible for the undermining of society by which the drug addicts they have produced act in opposition to law and honor."[128] By promoting total prohibition, the Army proved it could act decisively in the greater cause of public health in wartime. In fact, only the Army, Hoff claimed, could decisively act to close the saloons and gin mills surrounding its camps and cantonments, as local authorities had long since been corrupted by the trade themselves.[129] The War Department itself—not only the Army Medical Department—became an agent of moral, social, and medical change in American society. In acting to cut off the liquor trade, reformers believed the entire cycle of alcoholism and venereal disease would be broken at the moment of inception. As championed by the War Department in cooperation with the nation's leading moral reform groups, prohibition was a public health measure, the only way to eliminate a self-sustaining process of moral and physical degeneration. A long way from the days of debating the merits of nickel beer against the hazards of the saloon, as the onus shifted from the soldier to the community at large surrounding him. In the end, the medical officer's willingness to compromise his communal identity as a member of the military officer fraternity to safeguard the institution at large against an institutionalized culture of tacit acceptance on the subject of alcohol and venereal disease proved, if not the right choice, then the proper one given the circumstances. As self-identified members of the progressive status quo, Army medical officers were drawn into the ranks of the more extreme progressive social moralists despite their wishes to remain close to their brother officers of the line and staff. They would survive this challenge with their status relatively unscathed, thanks to their continued press for relevance in the overall health of the institution and in turn, the overall military effectiveness and readiness of the Army on the cusp of war.

Notes

NOTES TO THE INTRODUCTION

1. Leonard Wood, "The Military Government of Cuba," *Annals of the American Academy of Political and Social Science* (March, 1903), 153–182, 153.
2. *Special Report on Insular Affairs, as Per Instructions of Circular No. 10*, War Department, March 25, 1899, 11–12, quote on 12.
3. *Ibid.*, 11.
4. Wood, "The Military Government of Cuba," 154–155.
5. Jefferson Randolph Kean, "Hospitals and Charities in Cuba," *JAMSUS* 12:3 (March, 1903), 140–149, 141.
6. Kean, "Hospitals and Charities," 142, 143; Wood, "Military Government of Cuba," 173.
7. L. S. Rowe, "The Reorganization of Local Government in Cuba," *Annals of the American Academy of Political and Social Science* (March, 1905), 311–321, 315.
8. William C. Gorgas, *Sanitation in Panama* (D. Appleton and Company, 1915), 6.
9. February 8, 1901 report, Major Valery Havard to Adjutant General, Department of Cuba, February 8, 1901, in *Yellow Fever: A Compilation of Various Publications* (Government Printing Office, 1911), 221–226, 221.
10. William C. Gorgas, *The Practical Mosquito Work Done at Havana, Cuba, Which Resulted in the Disappearance of Yellow Fever From That Locality*, reprint, *Washington Medical Annals* II:3 (July, 1903), 2–3; Hermann Hagedorn, *Leonard Wood: A Biography*, Volume One (Harper & Brothers, Publishers, 1931), 300, 323.
11. Gorgas, "The Practical Mosquito Work," 3; Jefferson R. Kean, "Walter Reed, Dedication of His Birthplace," *Military Surgeon* 62:3 (March, 1928), 293–304, 301.
12. Suzanne Jurmain, *The Secret of the Yellow Death: A True Story of Medical Sleuthing* (Houghton Mifflin Books for Children, 2009); John R. Pierce and Jim Writer, *Yellow Jack: How Yellow Fever Ravaged America and Walter Reed Discovered Its Deadly Secrets* (John Wiley & Sons, Inc., 2005).
13. Frank R. Freemon, *Gangrene and Glory: Medical Care During the American Civil War* (University of Illinois Press, 2001); Alfred J. Bollet, *Civil War Medicine: Challenges and Triumphs* (Galen Press, 2002); Ira Rutkow, *Bleeding Blue and Gray: Civil War Surgery and the Evolution of American Medicine* (Random House, 2007); Albert Cowdrey, *Fighting for Life: American Military Medicine in World War II* (The Free Press, 1994).

14. Paul Steiner, *Disease in the Civil War: Natural Biological Warfare, 1861–1865* (Charles C. Thomas Publishers, Ltd., 1968); Carol R. Byerly, *Fever of War: The Influenza Epidemic in the U.S. Army during World War I* (New York University Press, 2005); Stephen B. Oates, *Women of Valor: Clara Barton and the Civil War* (The Free Press, 1995); Bonnie Ellen Blustein, *Preserve Your Love of Science: Life of William A. Hammond, American Neurologist*, Cambridge Studies in the History of Medicine (Cambridge University Press, 2002); Barbara Tomblin, *G.I. Nightingales: The Army Nurse Corps in World War II* (The University of Kentucky Press, 2003).

15. Important works treating the Army in transition during the Progressive Era include: James L. Abrahamson, *America Arms for a New Century: The Making of a Great Military Power* (The Free Press, 1981); Ronald J. Barr, *The Progressive Army: US Army Command and Administration, 1870–1914* (St. Martin's Press, 1998); Jack C. Lane, *Armed Progressive: General Leonard Wood* (Presidio Press, 1978); John P. Finnegan, *Against the Specter of a Dragon: The Campaign for American Military Preparedness, 1914–1917* (Greenwood Press, 1974); Carol Reardon, *Soldiers and Scholars: The U.S. Army and the Uses of Military History, 1865–1920* (University of Kansas Press, 1990); Russell F. Weigley, *Towards an American Army: Military Thought from Washington to Marshall* (Columbia University Press, 1962).

16. Paul Starr, *The Social Transformation of American Medicine: The Rise of a Sovereign Profession and the Making of a Vast Industry* (Basic Books, 1982), 4–5.

17. Ken Arnold, Klaus Vogel, and James Peto, eds., *War and Medicine* (London: Black Dog Publishing, 2008).

18. Roger Cooter, Mark Harrison, and Steve Sturdy, eds., *War, Medicine and Modernity* (Phoenix Mill: Sutton, 1998).

19. Joanna Bourke, *Dismembering the Male: Men's Bodies, Britain, and the Great War* (Chicago: The University Press of Chicago, 1996), 11.

20. Joanna Bourke, "Suffering and the Healing Profession," in *War and Medicine*, 108–125, 125.

21. The U.S. Army as an imperial army is discussed in: Graham A. Cosmas, *An Army for Empire: The United States Army in the Spanish-American War* (White Mane Publishing, 1971, 1994); John M. Gates, *Schoolbooks and Krags: The United States Army in the Philippines, 1898–1902* (Greenwood Press, 1973); David F. Healy, *The United States in Cuba, 1898–1902: Generals, Politicians, and the Search for Policy* (University of Wisconsin Press, 1963); Brian McAllister Linn, *Guardians of Empire: The U.S. Army and the Pacific, 1902–1940* (University of North Carolina Press, 1997); Brian McAllister Linn, *The U.S. Army and Counter-insurgency in the Philippine War, 1899–1902* (University of North Carolina Press, 1989); Glenn A. May, *Battle for Batangas: A Philippine Province at War* (Yale University Press, 1991); Stuart C. Miller, *"Benevolent Assimilation": The American Conquest of the Philippines, 1899–1903* (Yale University Press, 1982); Allan R. Millett, *The Politics of Intervention: The Military Occupation of Cuba, 1906–1909* (Ohio State University Press, 1968); David Silbey, *A War of Frontier and Empire: The Philippine-American War, 1899–1902* (Hill and Wang, 2008); and David F. Trask, *The War with Spain in 1898* (Macmillan, 1981).

22. For examples of the application of health and wellness as tools of imperial discourse from the European—especially British—perspectives, see: David Arnold, *Colonizing the Body: State Medicine and Epidemic Disease in Nineteenth-Century India* (University of California Press, 1993); David Arnold, ed., *Imperial medicine and indigenous societies* (Manchester

University Press, 1988); Philip D. Curtin, *Disease and Empire: The Health of European Troops in the Conquest of Africa* (Cambridge University Press, 1998); Mark Harrison: *Public Health in British India: Anglo-Indian Preventive Medicine, 1859–1914* (Cambridge University Press, 1994); Anil Kumar, *Medicine and the Raj: British Medical Policy in India, 1835–1911* (AltiMira Press, 1998); Roy Macleod and Milton Lewis, eds., *Disease, Medicine, and Empire: Perspectives on Western Medicine and the Experience of European Expansion* (Routledge, 1988); and Megan Vaughan, *Curing their Ills: Colonial Power and African Illness* (Stanford: Stanford University Press, 1991). For the American experience in the Philippines and elsewhere see: Warwick Anderson, *Colonial Pathologies: American Tropical Medicine, Race, and Hygiene in the Philippines* (Duke University Press, 2006; Anthony De Bevoise, *Agents of Apocalypse: Epidemic Disease in the Colonial Philippines* (Princeton University Press, 1995); and Soma Hewa, *Colonialism, Tropical Disease, and Imperial Medicine: Rockefeller Philanthropy in Sri Lanka* (University Press of America, 1995). Also consider Glenn A. May's *Social Engineering in the Philippines: The Aims, Execution, and Impact of American Colonial Policy, 1900–1913* (Greenwood Press, 1980).

23. The notion of tropicality as a trope of identity and differentiation has been raised in David Arnold's *The Problem of Nature: Environment, Culture, and European Expansion* (Blackwell Publishers, 1996). Arnold presents the case for the construction of "tropicalism" in the eighteenth and nineteenth centuries as a binary signifier, conveying both alluring sensuality and decay and degeneration for Europeans. For a historiography of knowledge schemas as tools of Western expansion, see Michael Adas, *Machines as the Measure of Men: Science, Technology, and Ideologies of Western Dominance* (Cornell University Press, 1989).

24. Nancy Tomes, *The Gospel of Germs: Men, Women, and the Microbe in American Life* (Harvard University Press, 1999).

25. While the professional triad schema (sanitarians, microbiologists, general practitioners) bears some resemblance to Brian McAllister Linn's conceptualization of the Army as driven by three martial philosophies (guardians, heroes, and managers), it is an independent creation that dates back to my original dissertation. See Brian McAllister Linn, *The Echo of Battle: The Army's Way of War* (Harvard University Press, 2007), 5–7; Bobby A. Wintermute, "Waging Health: The United States Army Medical Department and Public Health in the Progressive Era, 1890–1920." Dissertation: Temple University, Department of History 2006, UM# 3247320.

26. Anderson, *Colonial Pathologies*.

NOTES TO CHAPTER 1

1. Percy Moreau Ashburn, *A History of the Medical Department of the United States Army* (Houghton Mifflin Company, 1929), 156.
2. Ibid., 156.
3. James Robb Church, "[Obituary] John Van R. Hoff," *Military Surgeon.* XLVI: 2 (February, 1920), 204–207, 204–205.
4. "A Memorial to Colonel John Van Rensselaer Hoff, Medical Corps, U.S. Army," *Military Surgeon.* 67: 3 (September, 1930), 277–284, 279–280.
5. John Van Rensselaer Hoff, "Resumé of the History of the Medical Department of the United States Army, From 1775 to the Beginning of the Spanish-American War," *JAMSUS* 10: 2 (February, 1902), 347–393, 368

6. See Jefferson R. Kean, "The Army Medical Service," *JAMA*. XLII: 22 (May 28, 1904), 1418–1419.
7. [John Van Rensselaer Hoff], "The Passing of the General Staff," *Military Surgeon*. XLIII: 1 (July, 1918), 74–76, 76.
8. "Increased Rank and More Authority for Medical Officers," *JAMA* LXIX: 19 (November 10, 1917), 1612–1613, 1612; "Restoration of the Record of Colonel John Van R. Hoff, Medical Corps, U.S. Army, Retired,"*Military Surgeon* XLVI: 1 (January, 1920), 108–109, 108.
9. Harvey E. Brown, *The Medical Department of the United States Army from 1775 to 1873* (Surgeon General's Office, 1873), 107.
10. *Regulations of the Medical Department, September,1818*, in Brown, *Medical Department of the Army*, 109–118.
11. Russell F. Weigley, *History of the United States Army* (The Macmillan Company, 1967), 135–137; Leonard D. White, *The Jeffersonians: A Study in Administrative History, 1801–1829* (The Macmillan Company, 1959), 236–237; quote in Letter from Jackson to Brigadier-General Winfield Scott, December 3, 1817, in John Spencer Bassett, ed., *Correspondence of Andrew Jackson*, Volume 2 (Carnegie Institution of Washington, 1927), 339.
12. Brown, *Medical Department of the Army*, 109.
13. *Secretary of War Reports, 1818*; reprinted in Brown, *Medical Department of the Army*, 122.
14. Quote in Letter, John C. Calhoun to Andrew Jackson, August 10, 1819. *The Papers of John C. Calhoun, 1819–1820*. Edited by W. Edwin Hemphill, Volume 4 of 25 Volumes (Columbia: The University of South Carolina Press for the South Caroliniana Society, 1969), 224–226; White, *The Jeffersonians*, 240, 244.
15. *Report of the Secretary of War* [1832], 64–65; *American State Papers*, 5, 6: 820–822; *American State Papers*, 5, 7: 591–593; *Report of the Secretary of War* [1838], 121–123; *Report of the Secretary of War* [1842], 202–203.
16. *Report of the Secretary of War* [1848], 81; *Report of the Secretary of War* [1849], 188; *Report of the Secretary of War* [1857], 62–63.
17. *Regulations for the Army of the United States*, [1863], 505.
18. United States War Department, *Revised United States Army Regulations of 1861. With an Appendix Containing the Changes and Laws Affecting Army Regulations and Articles of War to June 25, 1863*, 526; Quote in Brown, *Medical Department of the Army*, 221.
19. Bonnie E. Blustein, "'To Increase the Efficiency of the Medical Department': A New Approach to U.S. Civil War Medicine," *Civil War History* 33: 1 (March, 1987), 22–41, 25; Brown, *Medical Department of the Army*, 221–222, quote in *Regulations of 1863*, 532.
20. *Regulations* [1863], 534; Mary C. Gillett, *The Army Medical Department, 1818–1865*. Army Historical Series (Center of Military History, United States Army, 1987), 181.
21. Jonathan Letterman, *Medical Recollections of the Army of the Potomac* (D. Appleton and Company, 1866), 48. Quote in Bell Irvin Wiley, *The Life of Billy Yank: The Common Soldier of the Union* (Louisiana State University Press, 1952, 1971), 131.
22. Ashburn, *History of the Medical Department*, 89; Brown, *Army Medical Department*, 219, 245, 248–250.
23. *Report of the Secretary of War* [1869], 425; U.S. Statutes at Large 16 (1869): 318.
24. Brown, *Medical Department of the Army*, 256; Mary C. Gillett, *The Army Medical Department, 1865–1917*. Army Historical Series (Center of

Military History, United States Army, 1994), 13–16; U.S. Statutes at Large 18–3 (1874): 245.

25. U.S. Statutes at Large 19 (1876): 61; U.S. Statutes at Large 22 (1883): 456–457; U.S. Statutes at Large 24 (1886): 95; U.S. Statutes at Large 28 (1894): 235, 403.

26. *Report of the Surgeon General*, in *Report of the Secretary of War* [1828], 63.

27. NARA, RG112 E.2. Letters and Endorsements Sent, April 1818–October 1889, Volume 6, Surgeon General Joseph Lovell to Secretary of War Lewis Cass, November 15, 1835, 53.

28. *Regulations of the Medical Department, September, 1818*, in Brown, *Medical Department of the Army*, 120; Gillett, *Army Medical Department, 1818–1865*, 128.

29. *Report of the Surgeon General*, in *Report of the Secretary of War* [1850], 241.

30. *Regulations* [1863], 313–314; Azel Ames, "The Acting Assistant Surgeon of the Army of the United States," *JAMSUS* 13: 3 (September, 1903), 121–133, 122–123; quote in Gillett, *Army Medical Department, 1818–1865*, 181.

31. H. Rep. 33 (40–3), 1388, 49.

32. *General Regulations for the Army; or Military Institutes*, 1825, 14–15; *General Regulations for the Army of the United States; also, the Rules and Articles of War, and Extracts from Laws Relating to Them*, 1835, 2–3.

33. U.S. Statutes at Large 5 (1847): 124–125.

34. Brown, *Medical Department of the Army*, 182; Gillett, *Medical Department, 1818–1865*, 129.

35. Brown, *Medical Department of the Army*, 202; Adjutant General's Office, General Orders No. 28, September 21, 1850.

36. Gillett, *Medical Department, 1818–1865*, 129; quote in Brown, *Medical Department of the Army*, 202–203

37. James Chester, "'The Place of the Medical Department in the Army'," *JMSI* 11: 46 (September, 1890), 823–827, 824.

38. Hoff, "Resumé of the Medical Department," 369.

39. C. L. Linley, "Pride and Prejudice—Tenting on the Old Camp Ground," *The Transactions of the Second Annual Meeting of the Association of Military Surgeons of the National Guard of the United States* (Becktold & Co., 1892), 151–159, 152.

40. Brown, *Medical Department of the Army*, 141.

41. *American State Papers* 5 Military Affairs 4: 802. The surgeon's emoluments included three daily ration allowances, at $18.00 a month, a monthly forage allowance of $16.00 for two horses, and $13.00 monthly pay for a personal servant. Assistant surgeons received $12.00 monthly for two rations, $16.00 forage for two horses, and a personal servant allowance of $13.00

42. *American State Papers* 5 Military Affairs 4, 801–802. In 1828, Congress authorized a graded pay scale for Naval medical officers, with surgeon's mates receiving $69.00 for pay and rations (compared with $52.00 monthly for Army assistant surgeons) and surgeons receiving up to $100.00 monthly (opposed to $57.00 for Army surgeons.

43. *Ibid.*, 66

44. *American State Papers* 5 Military Affairs 4, 849; U. S. Statutes at Large 4 (1834): 714; Brown, *Medical Department of the Army*, 135; Gillett, *Medical Department, 1818–1865*, 30–31.

45. Letter, Surgeon General Thomas Lawson to Major S. Cooper, Assistant Adjutant General, July 5, 1839, in Brown, *Medical Department of the Army*, 165.

46. *General Regulations for the Army of the United States, 1841*, 371.
47. Letter, Adjutant General Jones to Surgeon General Thomas Lawson, August 3, 1843, in Brown, *Medical Department of the Army*, 173.
48. Alfred A. Woodhull, "The Place of the Medical Department in the Army," *JMSI*. XI: 45 (July, 1890), 544–565, 555.
49. Gillett, *Army Medical Department, 1818–1865*, 53–54; Brown, *Medical Department of the Army*, 159; James Evelyn Pilcher, "The Surgeon Generals of the United States Army, IX, Brevet Brigadier General Thomas Lawson, Surgeon General of the United Army, 1836–1861," *JAMSUS* 14: 6 (June, 1904), 406–410, 407–409.
50. Brown, *Medical Department of the Army*, 253.
51. Quote in *American State Papers*, 5, 5: 654; Gillett, *The Army Medical Department, 1818–1865*, 31–32.
52. *American State Papers*, 5, 6: 839; 7: 621; *Report of the Surgeon General*, in *Report of the Secretary of War*, 1838 145; 1839 147; 1840 197; 1842 359; 1843 79; 1844 152; 1846 199; 1847 722; 1848 366; 1849 207; 1850 340; 1852 138; 1854 82; 1856 262; 1857 167; 1858 805; 1859 626; 1860 243; 1861, 61; Quote in *Report of the Surgeon General*, 1839, 147.
53. *Report of the Surgeon General*, 1839, 148.
54. John S. Haller, Jr., *American Medicine in Transition, 1840–1910* (University of Illinois Press, 1981), 200–209; Richard Harrison Shryock, *Medical Licensing in America, 1650–1965* (The Johns Hopkins Press, 1967), 14, 28, 30–31; Paul Starr, *The Social Transformation of American Medicine: The Rise of a Sovereign Profession and the Making of a Vast Industry* (Basic Books, 1982), 44–45; John Harley Warner, *The Therapeutic Perspective: Medical Practice, Knowledge, and Identity in America, 1820–1885* (Princeton University Press, 1997), 16.
55. Robert W. Haxall, "Report of the Committee appointed under the fourth resolution of the National Medical Convention, which assembled in New York, in May, 1846," Note A, in *Report of the Committee on the Organization of the National Medical Association* (National Medical Convention, 1846), 11.
56. N. S. Davis. *History of the American Medical Association, From its Organization Up to January, 1855. To Which is Appended Biographical Notices, with Portraits of the Presidents of the Association, and of the Author*, Edited by S. W. Butler, M.D. (Lippincott, Grambo and Co., 1855), 67.
57. Gillett, *Army Medical Department, 1818–1865*, 129–130; *Report of the Secretary of War*, 1853, 147.
58. *Report of the Secretary of War*, 1853, 147, 148.
59. *Report of the Secretary of War*, 1856, 262.
60. Brown, *Medical Department of the Army*, 219.
61. House Ex.Doc. 23, 1879 (45–3), 12; Gillett, *Army Medical Department, 1818–1865*, 156.
62. *Report of the Secretary of War*, 1833, 58–59.
63. *General Regulations,1841*, 291–295.
64. Depletive therapies relied upon mineral and vegetative substances like calomel, antimony, or ipecac, in combination with bleeding, diet, and blistering or sweating to reduce the levels of fluids and toxins in the body causing illness. Antiphlogistic therapies used many of the same tools as the depletives to target inflammation and fever. Beginning in the 1840s, stimulative therapies were implemented to achieve the opposite effect from the depletive and antiphlogistic regimens. Instead of decreasing the body's humoric imbalance, it sought to restore that which was reduced by the disease. Quinine, alcohol, iron supplements, and vigorous massage were employed to stimulate

the body into shaking off the illness. Warner, *The Therapeutic Perspective*, 58–60, 91–100; John S. Haller, Jr., *Medical Protestants; The Eclectics in American Medicine, 1825–1939* (Southern Illinois University Press, 1994), 37–55.

65. George M. Frederickson, *The Inner Civil War: Northern Intellectuals and the Crisis of the Union* (The University of Illinois Press, 1965, 1993), 211–215.
66. Blustein, "'To Increase the Efficiency,'" 25.
67. Joseph Janvier Woodward and George A. Otis, eds., *The Medical and Surgical History of the War of the Rebellion. Appendix to Part I, Containing Reports of Medical Directors, and Other Documents*. Reprinted as *The Medical and Surgical History of the Civil War*. Volume 12 (Broadfoot Publishing Company, 1990), 877.
68. *Medical and Surgical History of the Rebellion*. Volume 3, 2; Volume 5, 1; Paul E. Steiner, *Disease in the Civil War, Natural Biological Warfare in 1861–1865* (Charles C. Thomas, Publisher, 1968), 8–10
69. William Alexander Hammond, *A Treatise on Hygiene with Special Reference to the Military Service*, Reprinted with a Biographical Introduction by Ira M. Rutkow (Norman Publishing, 1991), viii.
70. Included among the morbid factors Hammond cited as modifiers influencing one's personal state of well-being were nostalgia, epistaxis, flatulence, constitutional disorders, and masturbation. *Ibid.*, 127–145.
71. *Ibid.*, 305–306.
72. *Ibid.*, 306–309; quote on 425–426
73. *Ibid.*, 427–431
74. *Medical and Surgical History of the Civil War*, Volume 6, 896–901, 932–941; Circular No. 6, November 1, 1865, 164.
75. Charles E. Rosenberg, *The Care of Strangers: The Rise of America's Hospital System* (The Johns Hopkins University Press, 1995), 18–29.
76. Benjamin F. Butler, *Autobiography and Personal Reminiscences of Major-General Benjamin F. Butler, Butler's Book* (A. M. Thayer & Co., 1892), 401.
77. *Ibid.*, 403–407.
78. Objections to Butler's sanitary policy pale in comparison with the outrage over his General Order No. 28, the so-called "Woman Order," which threatened to treat any woman who insulted or harmed a Union soldier as a "woman of the town plying her avocation." (*Ibid.*, 418.) *Medical and Surgical History*, Vol. 6, 675.
79. *Ibid.*, 676.
80. *Medical and Surgical History*, Vol. 1, 636–637, 684–685. In her book, *Yellow Fever and the South*, Margaret Humphreys observes Butler's quarantine and sanitary policing of New Orleans, though attacked by southern physicians as "tyrannical," were recognized by others as highly efficacious, and were perceived as being "evidence for the power of modern sanitary science to protect a population" (Margaret Humphreys, *Yellow Fever and the South* [The Johns Hopkins University Press, 1999] 27).
81. Roger Cooter and Steve Sturdy, "On War, Medicine and Modernity: Introduction," in Roger Cooter, Mark Harrison, and Steve Sturdy, eds., *War, Medicine and Modernity* (Sutton Publishing, 1998), 1–21. Examples of the militarized aspect of the USPHS uniform may be found in Alan M. Kraut, *Silent Travelers: Germs, Genes and the "Immigrant Menace"* (The Johns Hopkins University Press, 1994), 54, and "John Walter Kerr," in *Military Surgeon*. 49: 2 (August, 1921), 120–124, 120.
82. *Regulations of 1863*, 10.
83. *Ibid.*, 84, 519.

84. Emory Upton, *The Military Policy of the United States* (Government Printing Office, 1904), 410, 411.
85. *Ibid.*, quote on 411, 412.
86. Cited in Brown, *Medical Department*, 240–241.
87. *Ibid.*, 242.
88. General Orders No. 306, War Department. AGO. December 27, 1864, in *Compendium of General Orders, Adjutant General's Office, 1864* (Government Printing Office, 1864), 182–183; Brown, *Medical Department*, 242.
89. *Army Regulations, Prepared and Submitted to a Board of Officers* (1868)
90. *Ibid.*, 3.
91. *Ibid.*, quote on 3, 4.
92. General Orders No. 65, Adjutant General's Office, Headquarters of the Army, July 9, 1884, 8.
93. Woodhull, "The Place of the Medical Department," 546, 555.
94. Tasker Bliss, quoted in Ashburn, *History of the Medical Department*, 112.
95. House Report 74, 1873 (42: 3), 140–141.
96. House Misc. Doc. 56, 1878 (45: 2), 9.
97. Wesley Merritt, "Comment and Criticism: 'Place of the Medical Department in the Army,'" *JMSI* 11: 45 (July, 1890), 657–658.
98. Carol Reardon, *Soldiers and Scholars: The U.S. Army and the Uses of Military History, 1865–1920* (The University Press of Kansas, 1990), quote on 23, 24.
99. Chester, "Place of the Medical Department," 823–824.
100. *Ibid.*, 823.
101. *Ibid.*, 824.
102. *Ibid.*, 824.
103. *Ibid.*, 825.
104. Thomas M. Anderson, "The Place of the Medical Department in the Army," *JMSI* 14: 62 (March 1893), 340–341, 341.
105. "The Status of Medical Officers," *JMSI* 18: 80 (March 1896), 429–431, 430.
106. "The Status of Medical Officers," *JMSI* 20: 85 (January 1897), 216–218, 217.
107. James A. Tobey, *The Medical Department of the Army: Its History, Activities and Organization* Institution for Government Research, Service Monographs of the United States Government, No. 45 (The Johns Hopkins Press, 1927), 20.

NOTES TO CHAPTER 2

1. John S. Haller, Jr., *Medical Protestants: The Eclectics in American Medicine, 1825–1939* (Southern Illinois University Press, 1994), 37–55; John Harley Warner, *The Therapeutic Perspective: Medical Practice, Knowledge, and Identity in America, 1820–1885* (Princeton University Press, 1997), 41.
2. *Medical and Surgical History of the War of the Rebellion*, Volume 1, iii–iv; Harvey E. Brown, *The Medical Department of the United States Army from 1775 to 1873* (Surgeon General's Office, 1873), 225.
3. Surgeon General's Office, Circular No. 5, June 9, 1862, in D. S. Lamb, "A History of the United States Army Medical Museum, 1862–1917" manuscript, 1917, The College of Physicians of Philadelphia, 3.
4. Lamb, "History of the Army Medical Museum," 28–29.
5. *Ibid.*, 16–17.

6. Surgeon General's Office, Circular No. 2, May 21, 1862, in Brown, *Medical Department of the Army*, 226.
7. Carleton B. Chapman, *Order Out of Chaos: John Shaw Billings and America's Coming of Age*. (The Boston Medical Library in the Francis A. Countway Library of Medicine, 1994), 79–80; Circular No. 6. War Department. Washington, November 1, 1865. *Reports on the Extent and Nature of the Materials Available for the Preparation of a Medical and Surgical History of the Rebellion*. (J.P. Lippincott & Co., 1865), 3–7, 96, 152; *Report of the Secretary of War 1885*, 732; Charles Richard, "The U. S. Army Medical School," *The Interstate Medical Journal* [St. Louis, Missouri]. 22: 9 (September, 1915), 912–922, 914; Brown, *Medical Department of the Army*, 257.
8. *Report of the Surgeon General, 1890*, 6–7.
9. Lamb, "History of the Army Medical Museum," 18; Staff Surgeon Dr. Ehrlich, "Contemporary Comment: A German View of the American Army Medical School, and Museum," *JAMSUS* 15: 4 (October, 1904), 317–323, 317–319; John Eric Erichsen, "Impressions of American Surgery," *Lancet* (1874), II, 720.
10. Circular No. 6, November 1, 1865, 90.
11. Quoted in Lamb, "History of the Army Medical Museum," 61–62.
12. *Medical and Surgical History of the War of the Rebellion*, Volume 1, xvi–xviii; quotes *Ibid.*, Vol. 3, 374.
13. Review, "The Medical and Surgical History of the War. Vol. II" in *The Medical Record: A Weekly Journal of Medicine and Surgery* [New York]. 11 (August 12, 1876), 519–520, 519; Review, "The Medical and Surgical History of the War of the Rebellion. Part II. Volume I" in *American Journal of the Medical Sciences* [Philadelphia] LXXIX: 1 (January 1880), 163–180, 180.
14. Rudolf Virchow quoted in Frank R. Freemon, "Lincoln Finds a Surgeon General: William A. Hammond and the Transformation of the United States Army Medical Bureau," *Civil War History*. 33: 1 (March, 1987), 5–21, 14.
15. Review in *Lancet* (London), N.S. (August 30, 1873), 302–303, 302.
16. John Shaw Billings, "The Military Medical Officer at the Opening of the Twentieth Century," *JAMSUS* 12: 6 (June, 1903), 349–357, 349–350.
17. Fielding H. Garrison, *John Shaw Billings: A Memoir* (The Knickerbocker Press, 1915), 153–154, 161, 172, 176–177.
18. U.S. War Department, Surgeon General's Office *A Report on the Hygiene of the United States Army, with Descriptions of Military Posts*, Circular No. 8, 1875, xvii. Billings concluded that between 1870 and 1874, of a mean strength of 25,989 white troops, the total losses, discharged and deceased, for consumption and respiratory diseases per 1,000 men were 5.29 and 2.867 respectively, compared with 2.486 and .788 in the civilian population over the same period.
19. *Ibid.*, x.
20. *Ibid.*, x.
21. Cited in Garrison, *John Shaw Billings*, 217–218.
22. *Report of the Surgeon General, 1895*, 8.
23. *Index Catalogue of the Library of the Surgeon General's Office, United States Army*, Sixteen Volumes (General Printing Office, 1880–1895); Chapman, *Order Out of Chaos*, 183–186, 197–198.
24. Circular No. 6, 148–149; Joseph Janvier Woodward, "On Photo-micrography with the highest powers, as practised in the Army Medical Museum," *American Journal of Science and Arts*, XLII: 125 (September, 1866), 189–195; Joseph Janvier Woodward, *Report to the Surgeon General, of the*

United States Army, on the Magnesium and Electric Lights, as Applied to Photo-Micrography. (War Department, Surgeon General's Office, 1870), 1–2; Joseph Janvier Woodward, International Exhibition of 1876. The Medical Staff of the United States Army, and Its Scientific Work. An Address Delivered to the International Medical Congress at Philadelphia. Wednesday Evening, September 6, 1876 (N.P., 1876), 22–23; Mary C. Gillett, The Army Medical Department, 1865–1917. Army Historical Series. (Center of Military History, United States Army, 1994), 28.

25. Louis A. Lagarde, "Can a Septic Bullet Infect a Gunshot Wound? A Special Report to the Surgeon-General, U.S. Army," New York Medical Journal (October 22, 1872), 458–464, 458, 460–464, quote on 464.

26. Louis A. Lagarde, "Poisoned Wounds by the Implements of Warfare," JAMA XL: 16 (April 18, 1903), 1062–1069, 1069.

27. James Evelyn Pilcher, "The Surgeon Generals of the United States Army, XVII, Brigadier General Charles Sutherland, Surgeon General of the United States Army, 1890–1893" JAMSUS 16: 2 (February, 1905), 129–132, 132.

28. The New York Times, May 31, 1893, 12; Ibid., June 1, 1893, 4.

29. The Medical News. LXII: 23 (June 10, 1893), 627.

30. Texas Medical Journal, IX: 2 (August, 1893), 89.

31. "Sketch of George M. Sternberg," Appleton's Popular Science Monthly (New York), LVI: 1 (November, 1899), 116–121, 116.

32. See Paul Starr, The Social Transformation of American Medicine: The Rise of a Sovereign Profession and the Making of a Vast Industry (Basic Books, 1982), 102–110.

33. George M. Sternberg, "The Address of the President. Delivered at the Forty-ninth Annual Meeting of the American Medical Association, held at Denver, Colorado, June 7–10, 1898," JAMA XXX: 24 (June 11, 1898), 1373–1380, 1373.

34. Carol Reardon, Soldiers and Scholars: The U.S. Army and the Uses of Military History, 1865–1920. (University Press of Kansas, 1990), 1.

35. Samuel P. Huntington, The Soldier and the State: The Theory and Politics of Civil-Military Relations (The Belknap Press of Harvard University Press, 1957, 1985), 7–18; Reardon, Soldiers and Scholars, 2–3.

36. Morris Fishbein, A History of the American Medical Association 1847 to 1947 (W.B. Saunders Company, 1947), 74–75, 135.

37. Michael D. Doubler, Civilian in Peace, Soldier in War: The Army National Guard, 1636–2000 (University Press of Kansas, 2003), 111–114.

38. Ibid., 118; The National Guard Association of the State of New York. Sixth Annual Convention, Held in Albany, N.Y., January 23, 1884 (Matthews, Northrup & Co., 1884), 12.

39. Proceedings of the Second Annual Convention of the National Guard Association of Ohio, held at Columbus, Ohio, January 15–16, 1885 (Gazette Press, 1885), 4–5, quote on 4.

40. A. C. Sharpe, "Organization and Training of a National Reserve for Military Service," JMSI X: XXXVII (March, 1889), 1–31, 16, 18, 20;

41. Jerry Cooper, The Rise of the National Guard: The Evolution of the American Militia, 1865–1920 (University of Nebraska Press, 1997), 66–69, 92–93.

42. Reardon, Soldiers and Scholars, 21–23.

43. "Editorial Expression: Vale, Nicholas Senn," Military Surgeon 22: 2 (February, 1908), 144–151, 146–148; Fishbein, History of the American Medical Association, 1847–1947, 671–673.

44. William K. Beatty, "Nicholas Senn," in American National Biography, Volume Nineteen. Twenty-four Volumes (Oxford University Press, 1999), 639–640, 639. "Vale, Nicholas Senn," 144–151.

45. Nicholas Senn, "The Mission of the Association of the Military Surgeons of the National Guard of the United States," *Transactions of the Second Annual Meeting of the Association of Military Surgeons of the National Guard of the United States* (Becktold & Co., 1892), 18–31, 21.
46. Senn, "Mission of the Association," 21.
47. *Ibid.*, 22.
48. *The Transactions of the Association of Military Surgeons of the National Guard of the United States for the Year 1891* (Burdick, Armitage & Allen, Printers, 1891), 34–35.
49. *Ibid.*, 4–10, 13, 26, 32.
50. George Miller Sternberg, "Address of President Sternberg," *Proceedings of the Fifth Annual Meeting of the Association of Military Surgeons of the United States* (Earhart & Richardson, Superior Printers, 1896), 8–22, 9.
51. "Register of Members," *Proceedings of the Seventh Annual Meeting of the Association of Military Surgeons of the United States* (Berlin Printing Co., 1897), 656–674.
52. *The Transactions of the Third Annual Meeting of the Association of Military Surgeons, of the National Guard of the United States* (Buxton & Skinner Stationery Co., 1894), 84; *Proceedings of the Fifth Annual Meeting of the Association of Military Surgeons of the United States* (Earhart & Richardson, Superior Printers, 1896), 70.
53. NLM MS.C142, Box 3, Association of Military Surgeons of the U.S. Personnel Records; Edgar Erskine Hume, "The Golden Jubilee of the Association of Military Surgeons of the United States, A Brief History of Its First Half-Century, 1891–17 September 1941," *Military Surgeon.* 89: 3 (September, 1941), 247–594, 467.
54. Russell F. Weigley, "The Long Death of the Indian-Fighting Army," in Garry D. Ryan and Timothy K. Nenninger, editors, *Soldiers and Civilians: The U.S. Army and the American People.* (National Archives and Records Association, 1987), 27–39, 29–30.
55. See: James M. Ingalls, "The Resistance of the Air to the Motion of Oblong Projectiles as Influenced by the Shape of the Head," *Journal of the United States Artillery.* IV: 2 (April, 1895), 191–213; Albert Cushing Crehore and George O. Squier, "Experiments with a new Polarizing Photo-Chronograph Applied to the Measurement of the Velocity of Projectiles," *Journal of the United States Artillery.* IV: 3 (July, 1895), 409–452; J. G. Galbraith, "The Principles of Military Administration: Their Application to Methods of Supplying Horses for the Cavalry Service; With Suggestions for the Remount of the First Cavalry," *Journal of the United States Cavalry Association* VIII: 29 (June, 1895), 105–117; Allan K. Capron, "Notes on Feeding Cavalry Horses," *Journal of the United States Cavalry Association* X: 36 (March, 1897), 32–38.
56. See: Wesley J. Merritt, "Life and Services of General Philip St. George Cooke, U.S. Army," *Journal of the United States Cavalry Association* VIII: 29 (June, 1895), 79–92; John F. McBlain, "With Gibbon on the Sioux Campaign of 1876," *Journal of the United States Cavalry Association* IX: 33 (June, 1896), 139–148; Charles D. Rhodes, "The History of the Cavalry of the Army of the Potomac, Including that of the Army of Virginia, (Pope's) and also the History of the Operations of the Federal Cavalry in West Virginia During the War," *Journal of the United States Cavalry Association* XI: 40 (March, 1898), 1–101.
57. Charles D. Rhodes, "The Cavalry of the German Empire," *Journal of the United States Cavalry Association* IX: 33 (June, 1896), 126–138.
58. See: E. G. Nicholls, "The Training Together in Peace Time the Garrison Artillery Forces of the Empire, Including Regular Militia, Volunteer and

Colonial Artillery," *Journal of the United States Artillery* IV: IV (October, 1895), 677–712; C. G. Treat, "Moving Targets in Use in the Light Artillery of England, Germany, France and Italy, and Some Forms Recently Tried by the Light Artillery Battalion at Fort Riley, Kansas," *Journal of the United States Artillery*. IX: III (May–June, 1898), 265–282.

59. William Wallace, "Our Military Decline," *Infantry Journal* IX: 5 (March–April, 1913), 625–644, 637. Original emphasis.

60. *Ibid.*, 637.

61. A. L. Mills, "The Military Geography of Mexico," *Journal of the United States Cavalry Association* X: 39 (December, 1897), 397–416.

62. See William G. Haan and W. W. Witherspoon, "What Has Been Done Since 1892 for the Defense of Our Coast Line Outside the Coast Forts," *Journal of the United States Artillery* 39: 2 (March–April, 1913), 129–136.

63. James Parker, "The Value of Cavalry as a Part of Our Army," *Journal of the United States Cavalry Association* XXV: 103 (July, 1914), 5–13, 7.

64. *Ibid.*, 13.

65. Herbert L. Burrell, "Gunshot Wounds of Joints," *Transactions of the Third Annual Meeting of the Association of Military Surgeons of the National Guard of the United States*. (Buxton & Skinner Stationery Co., 1894), 90–99; J. D. Griffith, "Gunshot Wounds of the Abdomen," *Ibid.*, 135–144; Louis A. Lagarde, "Septic Bullets and Septic Powders," *Proceedings of the Fifth Annual Meeting of the Association of Military Surgeons of the United States* (Earhart and Richardson, Superior Printers, 1896), 169–174; Frank R. Keefer, "Observations on the Physical Examination of the Recruit," *Transactions, Third Annual Meeting*, 166–192; Paul R. Brown, "Determination of the Personal Identity of the United States Soldier," *Proceedings of the Sixth Annual Meeting of the Association of Military Surgeons of the United States* (Cleveland: Medical Gazette Publishing Co., 1896), 263–272; John Van Rensselaer Hoff, "The Travois—A New Sanitary Appliance in the First Line of Battlefield Assistance," *Proceeding of the Fourth Annual Meeting of the Association of Military Surgeons of the United States* (Burton & Skinner, Stationery, Co., 1894), 73–84; Charles R. Greenleaf, "Ambulance Construction," *Proceedings, Fifth Annual Meeting*, 264–274.

66. B. J. D. Irwin, "Notes on the Introduction of Tent Hospitals in War," *Proceedings, Fourth Annual Meeting*, 107–136, 107–108; Henry R. Stiles, "The Medical and Surgical Equipment of a Fifteenth Century French Military Expedition," *Proceedings, Sixth Annual Meeting*, 185–191.

67. Charles R. Greenleaf, "The Practical Duties of the Army Surgeon in the Field, During Time of War," *The Transactions of the Second Annual Meeting of the Association of Military Surgeons of the National Guard of the United States* (Becktold & Co., 1892), 9–14, 11.

68. *Report of the Surgeon General* in *Report of the Secretary of War, 1862*, 56.

69. Charles H. Alden, "The Special Training of the Medical Officer with Brief Notes on Army Medical Schools Abroad and At Home," [May 3, 1894], 8; Lamb, "History of the Army Medical Museum," 24; Mary C. Gillett, *The Army Medical Department, 1818–1865*, Army Historical Series (Center of Military History, United States Army, 1987), 202.

70. Alfred A. Woodhull, "The Place of the Medical Department in the Army," *JMSI* 11: 45 (July, 1890), 544–565, 561, 562.

71. *Ibid.*, 562–563.

72. Senn, " Mission of the Association of Military Surgeons," *Transactions, Second Annual Meeting*, 19–31, quote on 29.

73. Alden, "Special Training," 3–7; Charles H. Alden, "The U.S. Army Medical School, Washington, D.C." *National Medical Review* [Washington, D.C.]

7:8 (January, 1898), 211–215, 211; John Van Rensselaer Hoff, "Military Medical Education," *JAMSUS* 17:3 (September, 1905), 195–203, 195–196.

74. *Report of the Surgeon General, 1893*, 15.
75. Edgar Erskine Hume, *Victories of Army Medicine*. (J. B. Lippincott Company, 1943), 55. The Army established four other service schools before the Army Medical School. At the end of the Civil War, the Engineer School of Application was established at Washington Barracks, District of Columbia, along with a School of Submarine Defense at Fort Totten, New York. In 1867, the long moribund Artillery School—originally founded in 1824, but soon disregarded—was re-opened at Fort Monroe, Virginia. The School of Application for infantry and cavalry, the precursor of the General Staff College, was opened in 1881 to introduce young officers to the latest developments in military theory. Another service school was convened in 1893 with the Army Medical School, the School of Application for Cavalry and Field Artillery was also convened in 1893 at Fort Riley Kansas. William C. Borden, *The Education of the Medical Officer of the Army* (The Association of Military Surgeons, 1903), 5.
76. *Circular of Information: In relation to appointment in the medical corps of the United States Army, the requisite qualifications, examination of applicants, etc.* Form 132. War Department, Surgeon General's Office, Revised August 17, 1916, 10, 12.
77. Richard, "U. S. Army Medical School," 912, 917; "Editorial: The Education of the Medical Officer—The Army Medical School," *JAMSUS* 13: 4 (October, 1903), 249–251, 250–251; Diary, Perry L. Boyer papers, Box Two, USAHEC; Hoff, "Military Medical Education, " 198–199.
78. Richard, "U.S. Army Medical School," 919.
79. *Surgeon General's Report, 1894*, 28–29.
80. *Ibid.*, 29–30; Perry Boyer Papers, Box One, USAHEC, Carlisle Barracks.
81. *Surgeon General's Report, 1894*, 27–28; Alden, "Special Training of the Medical Officer," 9–11, 15.
82. *Ibid.*, 23, 26–27, 32.
83. Edward L. Munson, commentary on John Nelson Goltra, "The Executive Element in the Training and Skill of the Army Surgeon," *JAMSUS* 12: 4 (April, 1903), 206–219, 216.
84. *Report of the Surgeon General, 1897*, 6, 21; *Report of the Surgeon General, 1898*, 14.
85. Gillett, *Army Medical Department, 1865–1917*, 97–99, 382; William C. Borden, "The Walter Reed General Hospital of the United States Army," *Military Surgeon* 20: 1 (January, 1907), 20–35, 24–25; Richard, "The U. S. Army Medical School," 914.
86. *Army and Navy Register (Army and Navy Illustrated)* 31: 1163, April 5, 1902, 27; Hoff, "Military Medical Education" 198–199; "The Army Medical School," *JAMSUS* 17: 3 (September, 1905), 241–244, 244; Gillett, *Army Medical Department, 1865–1917*, 320.
87. Edward B. Vedder, "A Plea for Specialism," *Military Surgeon* 24: 4 (April, 1909), 317–324, 321.
88. *Ibid.*, 322.

NOTES TO CHAPTER 3

1. SAW Survey Collection, Box 254, 1898-W-809, USAHEC.
2. Letter, May 29, 1898, SAW Survey Collection, Box 254, 1898-W-809,USAHEC.

3. Letter, June 9, 1898, SAW Survey Collection, Box 254, 1898-W-809, USAHEC.
4. *Ibid.*
5. Letter, June 30, 1898, SAW Survey Collection, Box 254, 1898, W-809, USA-HEC. Goddard is referring to the Krag-Jorgensen Rifle, the Regular Army's standard magazine-fed bolt-action rifle.
6. Letter, July 26, 1898, SAW Survey Collection, Box 254, 1898-W-809, USAHEC.
7. Letter, August 14, 1898, SAW Survey Collection, Box 254, 1898-W-809, USAHEC.
8. Walter Reed, Victor C. Vaughan, and Edward O. Shakespeare, *Report on the Origin and Spread of Typhoid Fever in U.S. Military Camps During the Spanish War of 1898.* Volume 1 (Government Printing Office, 1904), 675; SAW Survey Collection, Box 258, 1898, W-603, USAHEC.
9. Charles Adams, "Minutes of the Meeting," in *Proceedings of the Association of Military Surgeons of the United States* (The Association of Military Surgeons, 1901), 47–73, 67–68.
10. *Ibid.*, 67–68.
11. Francis A. Winter, "Preparedness of the Medical Department of the Army, in the Matter of Field Supplies," (Paper read before the 1912 Army War College Class), 2.
12. *Ibid.*,1.
13. Vincent J. Cirillo, "The Spanish-American War and Military Medicine," UMI Number 9936178, Rutgers, 1999, 158, 167.
14. *Report of the Commission Appointed by the President to Investigate the Conduct of the War Department in the War With Spain, Volume I.* 1899, 265.
15. *Ibid.*, 265.
16. *Annual Reports of the War Department, 1898. Report of the Secretary of War. Miscellaneous Reports,* 1–2, 18, 253, 257–259.
17. *Army and Navy Journal.* 35: 37 (May 14, 1898), 715.
18. *The New York Times,* May 13, 1898, 2.
19. *Army and Navy Journal.* 35: 38 (May 21, 1898), 737; *Surgeon General Report, 1899,* 389.
20. *Surgeon General Report, 1899,* 390, 417; General Orders 100, War Department, Adjutant General's Office, July 16, 1898.
21. *Army and Navy Journal.* 35: 51 (August 20, 1898), 1059.
22. *The New York Times,* May 13, 1898, 2; *Surgeon General Report, 1899,* 389.
23. *Surgeon General Report, 1899,* 389.
24. *Annual Report, 1898,* 688; General Orders No. 52, Headquarters of the Army, Adjutant General's Office, May 24, 1898.
25. *Annual Report, 1898,* 178; *Surgeon General's Report, 1899,* 422.
26. *Surgeon General's Report, 1899,* 424.
27. *Ibid.*, 560.
28. *Ibid.*, 405. .
29. *Ibid.*, 425.
30. *Ibid.*, 422.
31. General Orders No. 58, Headquarters of the Army, Adjutant General's Office, May 31, 1898; General Orders No. 82, Headquarters of the Army, Adjutant General's Office June 27, 1898.
32. Correspondence from the Adjutant General, U.S.A., Relating to the Campaign in Cuba, in *Report of Conduct of War Department,* 872–873; Todd Richard Brereton, "An Impractical Sort of Officer: The Army Career of

Arthur L. Wagner, 1875–1905," Dissertation: Texas A&M University, Department of History, 1994. UM# 9432648, 129–133.
33. *Surgeon General's Report, 1899*, 490–493.
34. The Isle of Pines, located off the southern coast of Cuba, was one of the few places in Cuba that was free from yellow fever. Miles felt that it would provide an ideal staging camp for an invasion of the main island, not to mention a sanitary refuge for the sick and wounded. Miles also considered Nipe, on the northeastern coast of Cuba, an essential safe harbor and coaling station for the Navy. *Annual Reports 1898*, 19, 27, quote on 20; Graham A. Cosmas, *An Army for Empire: The United States Army in the Spanish-American War* (White Mane Publishing, 1971, 1994), 96–98.
35. *Surgeon General's Report, 1898*, 4–7, Cosmas, *Army for Empire*, 96–98.
36. *Surgeon General's Report, 1899*, 390.
37. *Surgeon General's Report, 1899*, 388, 406, 709–719, 751; Cosmas, *Army for Empire*, 129.
38. *Surgeon General's Report, 1899*, 388; Cosmas, *Army for Empire*, 91.
39. *The New York Times*, May 16, 1898, 3; S. D. Bodeham and J. P. Fitzgerald, *Ashland Boys at the Front in the Spanish-American War, A Record of the Experiences of Co. L, 2nd Wis. Vol. Inf., Leahy on the "Oregon," Scott and Oakey at Manilla, Warner in Cuba* (Daily Press, N.D.), 29; James E. Payne, *History of the Fifth Missouri Volunteer Infantry*, (Press of James E. Payne, 1899), 11; Letter, June 16, 1898, SAW Survey Collection, Box 254, 1898-W-809, USAHEC; Reed, Shakespeare, and Vaughan, *Typhoid Board Report*, Vol. 1, 273.
40. Circular No. 1, Surgeon-General's Office, April 25, 1898 in *Surgeon General's Report, 1898*, 727–728.
41. Circular No. 3, Surgeon-General's Office, May 18, 1898, in *Surgeon General's Report, 1898*, 728–730; Circular No. 5, Surgeon-General's Office, August 8, 1898, in *Surgeon General's Report, 1898*, 731.
42. Harry E. Webber, *Twelve Months with the Eighth Massachusetts Infantry in the Service of the United States* (Newcomb & Gauss, Printers, 1908), 88; Surgeon General's Report, 1899, 390.
43. Reed, Shakespeare, Vaughan, *Typhoid Board Report*, Vol. 1, 17, 20.
44. *Surgeon General's Report, 1899*, 558.
45. Reed, Vaughan, and Shakespeare, *Typhoid Board Report*, Vol. 1, 75.
46. Bodeham and Fitzgerald, *Ashland Boys at the Front*, 42; Edward Champe Carter, "Typhoid and Malarial Fevers at Chickamauga in 1898," *JAMSUS* 14: 2 (February 1904), 104–110, 104.
47. Robert W. Leonard, "Sanitation of Troops," *JMSI* 51: 180 (Nov/Dec, 1912), 367–370, 368; Cirillo, "The Spanish American War," 69.
48. Charles Craig Papers, Box 1, Book 1, 36, USAHEC; *The Washington Post*, (ND—September 29, 1898?).
49. Bodeham and Fitzgerald, *Ashland Boys at the Front*, 51.
50. *Ibid.*, 57.
51. Carter, "Typhoid and Malarial Fevers," 105; Payne, *History of the Fifth Missouri*, 12.
52. Carter, "Typhoid and Malarial Fevers," 105; Letter, June 16, 1898, SAW Survey Collection, Box 254, 1898-W-809, USAHEC; Webber, *Eighth Massachusetts Infantry*, 89; *Surgeon General's Report, 1899*, 624–625; Payne, *History of the Fifth Missouri*, 13.
53. Carter, "Typhoid and Malarial Fevers," 106
54. *Ibid.*, 106; quote in Webber, *Twelve Months with the Eighth Massachusetts Infantry*, 87.
55. Carter, "Typhoid and Malarial Fevers, 106, Webber, *Twelve Months with the Eighth Massachusetts Infantry*, 89–90.

56. Bodeham and Fitzgerald, *Ashland Boys at the Front*, 45.
57. *Surgeon General's Report, 1899*, 392–393, 407. The First Division hospital contained 120 beds, Second Division contained 150 beds, Third Division held 206 beds, and the Reserve Hospital had a 250 bed capacity.
58. *Surgeon General's Report, 1899*, 392.
59. *Surgeon General's Report, 1899*, 392; General Order 140, War Department, Adjutant General's Office, September 3, 1898; General Order 142, War Department, Adjutant General's Office, September 14, 1898; *The Evening Bulletin* [Philadelphia], August 16, 1898, 2; *Chattanooga Daily Times*, October 19, 1898, in Charles Craig Papers, Box 1, Book 1, 101.
60. *Surgeon General's Report, 1899*, 393; *The Philadelphia Inquirer*, August 13, 1898, 5.
61. General Order 117, War Department, Adjutant General's Office, August 10, 1898.
62. Walter Miller Warren, "Malaria in Mobilization Camps During the Late War," *Military Surgeon* 2: 7 (September 1899), 219–221, 219; Reed, Shakespeare, and Vaughan, *Typhoid Fever Board*, Vol. 1, 1898, 298.
63. General Order 114, War Department, Adjutant General's Office, August 9, 1898.
64. *The Phildelphia Inquirer*, August 22, 1898, 1, 10.
65. *The Philadelphia Inquirer*, August 25, 1898, 1; W. A. Holbrook, "Some Lessons of the War with Spain," *Army and Navy Register*. 38: 1350 (October 25, 1905), 3–5, 4; Charles D. Smith, *Cases of Chickamauga Typhoid Treated at the Maine General Hospital* (Stephen Berry, 1899), 5, 16.
66. Leonard, "Sanitation of Troops," 369.
67. Webber, *Twelve Months with the Eighth Massachusetts Infantry*, 82–84.
68. Cirillo, "The Spanish-American War and Military Medicine," 71; Charles Craig Papers, Box 1, Book 1, 1; Reed, Shakespeare, and Vaughan, *Typhoid Review Board*, Volume 1, 301; *Chattanooga Daily Times*, October 29, 1898; *Chattanooga Daily Times*, October 31, 1898; *The Washington Post*, September 29, 1898.
69. *Chattanooga Daily Times*, September 16, 1898.
70. *Surgeon General's Report, 1899*, 390.
71. *Ibid.*, 391, 624; Cosmas, *Army for Empire*, 129.
72. Noel Garraux Harrison, *City of Canvas: Camp Russell A. Alger and the Spanish-American War* (Falls Church Historical Commission, Fairfax County Historical Commission, 1988), 1, 5, 38; *Surgeon General's Report, 1899*, 393; Anthony Fiala, *Troop "C" in Service, An Account of the Part Played by Troop "C" of the New York Volunteer Cavalry in the Spanish-American War of 1898* (Eagle Press, 1899), 35; Reed, Shakespeare, and Vaughan, *Typhoid Board Report*, Vol. 1, 311, 370.
73. Fiala, *Troop "C" in Service*, 31; quote in *Surgeon General's Report, 1899*, 393, 394; Harrison, *City of Canvas*, 2, 59; Reed, Shakespeare, and Vaughan, *Typhoid Board Report*, Vol. 1, 311.
74. Alfred C. Girard, *The Management of Camp Alger and Camp Meade*, reprint, *New York Medical Journal*, September 24, 1898 (D. Appleton Company, 1898), 4; Harrison, *Camp Alger*, 53–54.
75. Girard, "Camp Alger and Camp Meade," 1.
76. *Ibid.*, 5.
77. *Surgeon General's Report, 1899*, 393.
78. Harrison, *Camp Alger*, 78.
79. *Surgeon General's Report, 1899*, 393; Fiala, *Troop "C" in Service*, 48; Harrison, *City of Canvas*, 39; Quote in Curtis V. Hard, *Banners in the Air: The Eighth Ohio Volunteers and the Spanish-American War*, Edited by Robert H. Ferrell (The Kent State University Press, 1988), 13.

80. Reed, Shakespeare, and Vaughan, *Typhoid Board Report*, Vol. 1, 312.
81. Girard, "Camp Alger and Camp Meade," 7.
82. Reed, Shakespeare, and Vaughan, *Typhoid Board Report*, Vol. 1, 339, 366, 370.
83. *Ibid.*, 367; Harrison, *City of Canvas*, 59; *Surgeon General's Report, 1899*, 394; Medwin Leale, "Some Experiences with the New York Volunteer Cavalry During the Spanish-American War," *Military Surgeon*, 20: 6 (June, 1907), 468–483, 470; Hard, *Banners in the Air*, 9, 11, 26; James Cooper, *Campaign of the First Troop Philadelphia City Cavalry, April 25—November 11, 1898* (Hallowell Co. Ltd., N.D.), 40–41.
84. Reed, Shakespeare, and Vaughan, *Typhoid Board Report*, Vol. 1, 372–373, 378, quote on 378.
85. Harrison, *City of Canvas*, 67; quote in Fiala, *Troop "C" in Service*, 31.
86. Fiala, *Troop "C" in Service*, 42; Reed, Shakespeare, and Vaughan, *Typhoid Board Report*, Vol. 1, 315, 316, 318, 342.
87. Map of Camp Meade, The Samuel B. Young Papers, Box 14, USAHEC. The area encompassing Camp Meade has since been developed as part of the Pennsylvania State University's Capitol Campus and the Harrisburg International Airport. *The Philadelphia Inquirer*, August 11, 1898, 12; *Surgeon General's Report, 1899*, 394–395, 401–402; Reed, Shakespeare, and Vaughan, *Typhoid Board Report*, Vol. 1, 315, 318, 320, 321, 323, 324, 326, 331, 334, 336, 338, 381–382.
88. Reed, Shakespeare, and Vaughan, *Typhoid Board Report*, Vol. 1, 392–393, 408, 412.
89. T. A. Turner, *Story of the Fifteenth Minnesota Volunteer Infantry* (Lessard Printing Co., N.D.), 33–37; Alger, *Spanish-American War*, 448; Reed, Shakespeare, and Vaughan, *Typhoid Board Report*, Vol. 1, 416
90. *Surgeon General's Report*, 395–396; *The Philadelphia Inquirer*, August 13, 1898, 5.
91. *The Philadelphia Inquirer*, August 26, 1898, 1; *Surgeon General's Report, 1899*, 402.
92. *Surgeon General's Report, 1899*, 396, 401–402.
93. *Ibid.*, 420; Reed, Vaughan, and Shakespeare, *Typhoid Fever Report*, Vol. 1, 502, 507; Cosmas, *Army for Empire*, 129.
94. *Surgeon General's Report, 1898*, 771; *Surgeon General's Report, 1899*, 417–418; Reed, Vaughan, and Shakespeare, *Typhoid Board Report*, Vol. 1, 504.
95. Reed, Vaughan, and Shakespeare, *Typhoid Board Report*, Vol. 1, 592, 593, 595, quote on 596.
96. *Ibid.*, 542, 548, 550.
97. *Ibid.*, 505, 540, 543; *Surgeon General's Report, 1899*, 445.
98. Cited in Reed, Vaughan, and Shakespeare, *Typhoid Board Report*, Vol. 1, 577.
99. *Ibid.*, 577; *Surgeon General's Report, 1899*, 445.
100. Reed, Vaughan, and Shakespeare, *Typhoid Board Report*, Vol. 1, 504–505.
101. *Surgeon General's Report, 1899*, 418.
102. *Ibid.*, 447.
103. *Ibid.*, 448.
104. *Ibid.*, 417, 446–447; Reed, Vaughan, and Shakespeare, *Typhoid Board Report*, Vol. 1, 518–519.
105. *Surgeon General's Report, 1899*, 418, 446; Reed, Vaughan, and Shakespeare, *Typhoid Board Report*, Vol. 1, 504.
106. *Surgeon General's Report, 1899*, 447.
107. *Ibid.*, 447.

108. *Ibid.*, 448.
109. Reed, Vaughan, and Shakespeare, *Typhoid Board Report*, Vol. 1, 675.
110. *The Atlanta Constitution*, August 30, 1898, 1.
111. *The New York Herald*, September 10, 1898, 4.
112. *The New York Herald*, September 2, 1898, 8.
113. *The Chicago Daily Tribune*, September 2, 1898, 1.
114. *The Chicago Daily Tribune*, September 3, 1898, 6.
115. *The New York Daily Tribune*, September 2, 1898, 3.
116. *The New York Daily Tribune*, September 9, 1898, 6.
117. *The Philadelphia Inquirer*, August 25, 1898, 6.
118. *The Atlanta Constitution*, August 31, 1898, 4.
119. *The New York Herald*, September 2, 1898, 5.
120. *The Chicago Daily Tribune*, September 1, 1898, 1.
121. *The New York Herald*, September 10, 1898, 5.
122. *The Minneapolis Journal*, September 5, 1898, 1.
123. *The New York Herald*, September 22, 1898, 5
124. *The Chicago Daily Tribune*, August 22, 1898, 1.
125. *The New York Herald*, September 23, 1898, 5.
126. *Report of Conduct of War Department*, 3–4, 11–12.
127. *Ibid.*, 773–774.
128. *Ibid.*, quote on 43, 7, 8, 44.
129. *Ibid.*, quote on 66, 8.
130. *Ibid.*, 71, 74, 76, 85.
131. Reed, Vaughan, and Shakespeare, *Report on Typhoid*, Vol. 1, xv–xvi, 675; Cirillo, "Spanish-American War and Military Medicine," 77–79; Reed to Adjutant General, August 8, 1898, NLM, MS C 48, Orders 1898 Folder; *Surgeon General's Report, 1899*, 626; Victor C. Vaughan, "Typhoid Fever Among the American Soldiers in the Recent War with Spain," *JAMSUS* 25: 100 (July, 1899), 85–88, 85; George Miller Sternberg, *Sanitary Lessons of the War and Other Papers* (American Medical Association, 1899), 20.
132. Victor C. Vaughan, *A Doctor's Memories* (The Bobbs-Merrill Company, 1926), 392–395.
133. Reed, Vaughan, Shakespeare, *Typhoid Fever Report*, Vol. 1, 656, 659, 660.
134. Vaughan, "Typhoid Fever," 85; Reed, Vaughan, Shakespeare, *Typhoid Fever Report*, Vol. 1, 662.
135. Reed, Shakespeare, and Vaughan, *Typhoid Fever Report*, Vol. 1, 663, 666; Vaughan, "Typhoid Fever," 85–86.
136. Reed, Vaughan, and Shakespeare, *Typhoid Board Report*, Vol. 1, 663.
137. *Ibid.*, 664.
138. *Ibid.*, 664–666, 672, quote on 664
139. Vaughan, "Typhoid Fever," 86–87; Sternberg, *Sanitary Lessons*, 16, 19–20; *Surgeon General's Report, 1899*, 622–623.
140. Turner, *Story of the Fifteenth Minnesota*, 40–41.
141. Memorandum, January 25, 1899, 1. NLM MS C 48, Box 1 of 2, Folder "Preliminary Report on Typhoid Fever in Military Camps."
142. *Ibid.*, 3.
143. *Ibid.*, 7.
144. *Ibid.*, 8–9.
145. *Ibid.*, 10.
146. *Ibid.*, 13.
147. *Ibid.*, 18.
148. *Ibid.*, 22.
149. Turner, *Story of the Fifteenth Minnesota*, 40.

NOTES TO CHAPTER 4

1. Charles J. Proben, "The Climate of Puerto Rico," *Atlanta Journal-Record of Medicine* II:2 (May, 1900), 73–87), 84.
2. Azel Ames, "The Vaccination of Porto Rico—A Lesson to the World," *JAMSUS* 12:5 (May, 1903), 293–313, 299–300.
3. Ronald Ross, "Medical Science and the Tropics," *Bulletin of the American Geographical Society* 45:6 (1913), 435–438, 435–436, 438.
4. The concepts of colonial and tropical medicine have become so intertwined they are virtually interchangeable. See Roy Macleod, "Introduction," in Roy Macleod and Milton Lewis, eds., *Disease, Medicine, and Empire: Perspectives on Western Medicine and the Experience of European Expansion* (Routledge, 1988), 1–18, and David Arnold, *Colonizing the Body: State Medicine and Epidemic Disease in Nineteenth-Century India* (University of California Press, 1993).
5. Michael Adas, *Machines as the Measure of Men: Science, Technology, and Ideologies of Western Dominance* (Cornell University Press, 1989), 292–293.
6. Edward Said, *Orientalism* (Vintage Books, 1974, 1998), 7, 12.
7. David Arnold, *The Problem of Nature: Environment, Culture and European Expansion* (Blackwell, 1996), 141–142
8. *Ibid.*, 142–151.
9. Arnold, *Colonizing the Body*, 28–29, 43; Warwick Anderson, "Colonial Pathologies: American Medicine in the Philippines, 1898–1921," Dissertation: University of Pennsylvania, Department of History and Sociology of Science, 1992, UM# AAT9235108; Warwick Anderson, "The Trespass Speaks: White Masculinity and Colonial Breakdown," *AHR* 102:5 (December, 1997), 1343–1370, 1345–1347; Adas, *Machines as the Measure*, 206.
10. Cited in Ernest R. May, *Imperial Democracy: The Emergence of America as a Great Power* (Harper & Row, 1961), 253.
11. See Louis A. Pérez, Jr., *The War of 1898: The United States and Cuba in History and Historiography* (The University of North Carolina Press, 1998), 29–35.
12. Mattew Frye Jacobson, *Barbarian Virtues: The United States Encounters Foreign Peoples at Home and Abroad, 1876–1917* (Hill and Wang, 2000), 144–147, 153–157.
13. Jacob R. Wolf, Troop K, 3ʳᵈ US Cavalry, United Spanish War Veterans Collection, Box Misc. "A," USAHEC.
14. *Ibid.*
15. *The People of the Philippines. Letter from the Secretary of War, Transmitting an Article on the People of the Philippines, Compiled in the Division of Insular Affairs of the War Department.* Senate Document No. 218, 56ᵗʰ Congress, 2d Session, February 15, 1901, 18–19
16. Letter, May 31, 1899, A. Milliard to Major William Kobbe, William August Kobbe Papers, Box Three, Folder One, USAHEC.
17. Willard B. Gatewood, Jr., *"Smoked Yankees" and the Struggle for Empire: Letters from Negro Soldiers, 1898–1902* (University of Illinois Press, 1971), 294–295.
18. L. Mervin Maus, "Sanitary and Economical Improvement in the Philippines Since American Intervention," [November 23ʳᵈ, 1912], in SPI Pamphlets, Vol. 29, Number One, New York Public Library, 4.
19. Private Kenneth Fleming, Hospital Corps, Box 242, Accession Number 1898-W-1149, USAHEC.
20. *Ibid.*

21. J. Hamilton Stone, "Our Troops in the Tropics—From the Surgeon's Stand-point," *JMSI* 26:105 (May, 1900), 358–369, 365.
22. Proben, "The Climate of Puerto Rico," 74.
23. *Ibid.*, 83–84
24. Charles E. Woodruff, *Medical Ethnology* (New York: Rebman Company, 1915), 133–138.
25. Charles Francis Mason, "Notes from the Experience of a Medical Officer in the Tropics," *JAMSUS* 13:5 (November, 1903), 306–314, 306; W. W. King, "Tropical Neurasthenia," *JAMA* 46:20 (May 19, 1906), 1518–1519, 1518.
26. Silas Weir Mitchell, *Wear and Tear, or Hints for the Overworked* (J. B. Lippincott & Co., 1871), 20–21.
27. *Ibid.*, 53–59.
28. King, "Tropical Neurasthenia," 1518.
29. Henry P. Birmingham, "Some Practical Suggestions on Tropical Hygiene," *JAMSUS* 12:1 (January, 1903), 45–54, 46.
30. F. Smith, "The Soldier's Heart, and the Civilian's," *Journal of the Royal Army Medical Corps* VIII:1 (January, 1907), 1–7, 2; Henry A. Fairbairn, "Cardiac Degeneration as Exemplified in the Soldier of the Late War," *Albany Medical Annals* 20:4 (April, 1899) 191–199, 192–193.
31. Stuart, "Tropical Hygiene," 77.
32. Mason, "Notes from a Medical Officer," 306.
33. Birmingham, "Practical Suggestions," 47.
34. King, "Tropical Neurasthenia," 1519; Mason, "Notes from a Medical Officer," 306.
35. King, "Tropical Neurasthenia," 1519.
36. "Obituary: Colonel Charles E. Woodruff," *Medical Record* [New York]. 87:25 (June 19, 1915), 1034; *The Lancet-Clinic* [Cincinnati] 64:26 (June 26, 1915), 703; Anderson, "The Trespass Speaks," 1358.
37. Charles E. Woodruff, *The Effects of Tropical Light on White Men* (Rebman Company, 1905), 2.
38. Obituary, *JAMA*, 64:26 (June 26, 1915), 2154; Woodruff, *Tropical Light*, 4–12.
39. Woodruff, *Tropical Light*, 4.
40. Woodruff, *Medical Ethnology*, 244
41. *Ibid.*, 290.
42. *Ibid.*, 290–304, quote on 306.
43. Charles Richard, "The U. S. Army Medical School," *Interstate Medical Journal* [St. Louis, Missouri]. 22:9 (September, 1915), 919.
44. Report of Maj. V. Havard, Medical Corps, United States Army, Headquarters Department of Cuba, Office of Chief Surgeon, Havana, February 8, 1901, in *Yellow Fever, A compilation of Various Publications*, (Government Printing Office, 1911), 221–226, 222.
45. H. Harold Scott, *A History of Tropical Medicine*, Volume One (The Williams & Wilkins Company, 1939), 367.
46. William Crawford Gorgas, *A Few General Directions With Regard to Destroying Mosquitoes, Particularly the Yellow Fever Mosquito* (Government Printing Office, 1904), 8; Leonard Wood, "The Military Government of Cuba," *Annals of the American Academy of Political and Social Science* (March 1903), 153–182, 169.
47. Report of Maj. W.C. Gorgas, Medical Corps, United States Army, Headquarters Department of Cuba, Office of Chief Sanitary Officer of Habana, July 12, 1902, in *Yellow Fever, A Compilation of Various Publications*, 234–250.
48. (Charles Finlay), Report of the Habana Yellow Fever Commission, January 3, 1902, in *Yellow Fever: A Compilation of Various Publications*, 227–233,

230; William Crawford Gorgas, "A Short Account of the Results of Mosquito Work in Havana, Cuba," *JAMSUS* 12:3 (March, 1903), 133–139, 133.
49. Finlay January 3, 1902 report, 229; Gorgas July 12, 1902 Report, 236–237.
50. Gorgas, *A Few General Directions*, 245; Gorgas, "Short Account in Havana," 134.
51. Gorgas, "Short Account in Havana," 135.
52. William Crawford Gorgas, *Mosquito Work in Havana* (William Wood and Company, 1902) , 2; Gorgas, "Short Account in Havana," 134–135; Gorgas, *A Few General Directions*, 246.
53. *Ibid.*, 4; Gorgas, "Short Account in Havana," 135–136.
54. William Crawford Gorgas, *Sanitation in Panama* (D. Appleton and Company, 1915), 52–55; *Report of W. C. Gorgas, Major, Surgeon U.S. Army, Chief Sanitary Officer, for the Current Year 1901*, March 29, 1902, 6; Gorgas, "Short Account in Havana," 136–137.
55. William Crawford Gorgas, *The Practical Mosquito Work Done at Havana, Cuba, Which Resulted in the Disappearance of Yellow Fever from that Locality*, reprint, *Washington Medical Annals* II:3 (July, 1903), 10–11.
56. *Ibid.*, 9–10
57. Gorgas, *Sanitary Work on the Isthmus*, 14–15.
58. William Crawford Gorgas, *Sanitation in the Canal Zone* (Press of The American Medical Association, 1907), 7–8.
59. Gorgas, "Short Account in Havana," 138–139.
60. Gorgas, *Mosquito Work in Havana*, 3; Gorgas, *Sanitation in Panama*, 63–64; Gorgas, "A Few General Directions," 246.
61. *Ibid.*, 141–143.
62. Joseph McFarland, "The Isthmian Canal Zone," *Medicine* [Detroit], XI:5 (May, 1905), 336–343, 336.
63. *Ibid.*, 337, quote on 339, 341.
64. Roland G. Curtin, "Medical Conditions of the Isthmus of Panama, With Other Notes," *Medicine* [Detroit], XI:5 (May, 1905), 343–349, 344.
65. William P. Buel, "Notes on the Medical Topography, Climate, and Diseases of Panama, N.G.," *The American Journal of the Medical Sciences* 37 (January, 1859), 131–135, 134.
66. G. Halsted Boyland, "The DeLesseps Canal in its Relation to Hygiene," *The Independent Practitioner* [Baltimore]. 1:7 (July, 1880), 317–333, 320–321; quote in Buel, "Notes on the Medical Topography," 132.
67. Seneca Egbert, "The History of Panama and the Panama Canal," *Medicine* [Detroit], XI:5 (May, 1905), 329–335, 333.
68. Gorgas, *Sanitation in Panama*, 138–139; Wolfred Nelson, *Yellow Fever, Absolute Protection Secured by Scientific Quarantine* (W. Nelson, 1889), 38; William Crawford Gorgas, *Sanitary Work on the Isthmus of Panama During the Last Three Years* (William Wood & Company, 1907), 4; William Crawford Gorgas, *Population and Deaths from Various Diseases in the City of Panama, by Months and Years, from November 1883, to August 1906; Number of Employees and Deaths from Various Diseases Among Employees of the French Canal Companies, by Months and Years, from January, 1881, to April, 1904* (Government Printing Office, 1906), 19–25; Merritt W. Ireland, "Obituary: General William Crawford Gorgas," *Military Surgeon* XLVII:2 (August, 1920), 252–254, 253; December 15, 1910, Letter, James Thorington to William Crawford Gorgas, in James Thorington Papers, 1889–1941, Box Two, Envelope Three, "Correspondence, Letter to W.C. Gorgas, Canal Zone, XII-15–1910", Z10164, College of Physicians, Philadelphia.

69. William Crawford Gorgas, *Sanitary Conditions as Encountered in Cuba and Panama, and What is Being Done to Render the Canal Zone Healthy* (William Wood and Company, 1905), 6.
70. *Army and Navy Register* XXXVII:1327 (May 20, 1905), 9; William Crawford Gorgas, "The Sanitary Organization of the Isthmian Canal as it Bears Upon Anti-Malarial Work," *Military Surgeon* XXIV:4 (April, 1909), 261–267, 262.
71. Gorgas, *Sanitation in Panama*, 151–152.
72. William Crawford Gorgas, *Sanitation of the Canal Zone* (William Wood and Company, 1908), 9–10.
73. Gorgas, *Sanitation in Panama*, 152.
74. Gorgas, "Isthmian Canal Sanitary Organization," 264.
75. Gorgas, *Sanitation in Panama*, 183; Gorgas, "Isthmian Canal Sanitary Organization," 265.
76. *Army and Navy Register* XXXVII:1318 (March 18, 1905), 9; Gorgas, *Sanitation in Panama*, 151.
77. Gorgas, "Isthmian Canal Sanitary Organization," 265.
78. Gorgas, *Sanitary Work on the Isthmus*, 8–9.
79. *Ibid.*, 10.
80. Gorgas, "Isthmian Canal Sanitary Organization," 266.
81. William Crawford Gorgas, "The Conquest of the Tropics for the White Race," *JAMA* LII (June 19, 1909), 1967–1969, 1968.
82. "When the Army took possession of Cuba in 1898, one of its great objects was to control yellow fever in that island so that the importation of the disease into the neighboring States of the United States would not be a constant menace" (Gorgas, *The Practical Mosquito Work*, 1); Ireland, "Obituary," 253–254; Scott, *History of Tropical Medicine*, 369–371;
83. Charles H. Alden, "Puerto Rico: Its Climate and Its Diseases," *New York Medical Journal* 74:1 (July 6, 1901), 17–22, 21.
84. Ames, "The Vaccination of Porto Rico," 299–300; Alden, "Puerto Rico," 18.
85. Ames, "The Vaccination of Porto Rico," 300.
86. *Ibid.*, 301.
87. Official Gazette, No. 2, January 3, 1899, in U.S. Army Adjutant General's Office, *Military Orders Having the Force of Law Promulgated by the Commanding General Department of Porto Rico from October 18th, 1898, to April 30th, 1900. Volume Two*. (N.P., 1900), 6.
88. Ames, "The Vaccination of Porto Rico," 305.
89. *Ibid.*, 313.
90. Proben, "The Climate of Puerto Rico," 77.
91. Allan Stuart, "Tropical Hygiene in Reference to Clothing, Houses, Routine, and Diet," *Military Surgeon* 20:2 (February, 1907), 75–93, 77; Bailey K. Ashford, "Where Treatment of All Infected is the Surest Prophylactic Measure—The Problem of Epidemic Uncinariasis in Porto Rico," *Military Surgeon* 20:1 (January, 1907), 40–55, 42; Stone, "Our Troops in the Tropics," 366.
92. *Army and Navy Register* XXVI:14 (September 30, 1899), 211.
93. Bailey K. Ashford and Pedro Gutierrez Igaravidez, *Uncinariasis (Hookworm Disease) in Porto Rico, A Medical and Economic Problem* (Government Printing Office, 1911), 6.
94. José Lugo-Viña, "Public Hygiene in Porto Rico," *JAMSUS* 13:3 (September, 1903), 150–153, 152–153.
95. Alden, "Puerto Rico ", 20. "For the ten years beginning 1890 there was a yearly average of 4,513 deaths from this cause [tropical chlorosis] out of a yearly average of 27,915 total deaths."

96. Ashford, "Problem of Epidemic Uncinariasis," 41
97. "Obituary: Colonel Bailey K. Ashford," *Military Surgeon*, 75:6 (December 1934), 405; "Obituary: Bailey Kelly Ashford," *Science* 80:2084 (December 7, 1934), 516–518, 516; Bailey K. Ashford, "Observations on the Campaign in Western Porto Rico During the Spanish-American War," *JAMSUS* 15:3 (September 1903), 157–168, 157, 159, 162.
98. Bailey K. Ashford, *A Soldier in Science* (William Morrow & Company, 1934), 38–40.
99. Henry J. Nichols, "Hook-worm Disease and Pellagra," *Military Surgeon* 26:6 (June, 1910), 646–657, 647–648; Bailey K. Ashford and Walter W. King, "A Study of Uncinariasis in Porto Rico," *American Medicine* 6:10 (September 5, 1903), 391–396, 394–396.
100. Ashford, *Soldier in Science*, 4–5.
101. Ashford and Igarividez, *Uncinariasis in Porto Rico*, 25.
102. *Ibid.*, 26–27.
103. Bailey K. Ashford and Walter W. King, "A Study of Uncinariasis in Porto Rico," *American Medicine* 6:11 (September 12, 1903), 431–438, 431–432.
104. *Ibid.*, 432.
105. *Ibid.*, 432; Ashford, "Problem of Epidemic Uncinariasis," 45–46; Bailey K. Ashford and Pedro Gutierrez Igaravidez, "Summary of a Ten Years' Campaign Against Hookworm Disease in Porto Rico," *JAMA* 54:22 (May 28, 1910), 1757–1761, 1751.
106. Ashford, "Problem of Epidemic Uncinariasis," 42.
107. Ashford and Igaravidez, "Summary of a Ten Years' Campaign," 1759; *Army and Navy Register*, XXXVI:1283 (July 16, 1904), 1.
108. Ashford and Igaravidez, "Summary of a Ten Years' Campaign," 1761; *Army and Navy Register*, XXXVIII:1352 (November 11, 1905), 11.
109. Ashford, "Problem of Epidemic Uncinariasis," 47–49, quote on 49.
110. *Ibid.*, 52.
111. Ashford, *Soldier in Science*, 381.
112. Ashford and Igarividez, "Summar of a Ten Years' Campaign," 1761.
113. Ashford and Igarividez, *Uncinariasis in Porto Rico*, 235–238.
114. *Ibid.*, 30–31.
115. *Ibid. Rico*, 31.
116. Charles Wardell Stiles, "A New Species of Hookworm (*Uncinaria americana*) Parasitic in Man, *American Medicine* III:19 (May 10, 1902), 777–778, 777.
117. John Ettling, *The Germ of Laziness: Rockefeller Philanthropy and Public Health in the New South* (Harvard University Press, 1981) 34–42.
118. Ashford, *Soldier in Science*, 94–95.
119. *Ibid.*, 95.
120. *Ibid.*, 94.
121. *Ibid.*, 96.
122. Lewis Hackett's Notes for IHD History, RAC, RG 3.1, Ser. 908, Box 3, Fldr. 191, 546.
123. Transcript of Charles Wardell Stiles, "'Early History, in Part Esoteric, of the Hookworm Campaign in Our Southern United States,' *Journal of Parasitology*, Vol. 25, p. 283, August 1939," RAC RG3.1, Ser. 908, Box 3, Fldr. 191.
124. Lewis Hackett's Notes for IHD History, RAC RG3.1, Ser. 908, Box 3, Fldr. 191, 546.
125. Adas, *Machines as the Measure*, 201–203; Richard S. Fogarty, *Race & War in France: Colonial Subjects in the French Army, 1914–1918* (The Johns Hopkins University Press, 2008), 9–12; Mark Harrison, *Public Health in British India: Anglo-Indian Preventive Medicine, 1859–1914* (Cambridge

University Press, 1994), 200–201, 229; David P. Barrows, "The Governor-General of the Philippines Under Spain and the United States," *AHR* 21:2 (January, 1916), 288–311, 302.

126. Elihu Root, *The Military and Colonial Policy of the United States* (AMS Press, Inc., 1970), 11–12.

127. Richard Johnson, "My Life in the Army, 1899–1922" (Unpublished manuscript), 39, 46, Richard Johnson Papers, USAHEC; Nancy Tomes, *The Gospel of Germs: Men, Women, and the Microbe in American Life* (Harvard University Press, 1998), 1–20, 91–112. The title of Tomes' book indicates the quasi-religiosity with which American society embraced germ theory in the late nineteenth century.

NOTES TO CHAPTER 5

1. Percy Moreau Ashburn, *The Elements of Military Hygiene, Especially Arranged for Officers and Men of the Line* (Houghton Mifflin, 1909), 146.

2. U.S. Statutes at Large, 31 (1901), 752–753, 755; James A. Tobey, *The Medical Department of the Army: Its History, Activities and Organization*, Institution for Government Research, Service Monographs of the United States Government, No. 45 (The Johns Hopkins Press, 1927), 31.

3. James Evelyn Pilcher, *The Surgeon Generals of the Army of the United States of America* (The Association of Military Surgeons, 1905), 86–88; U.S. Statutes at Large, 32 (1902), 339.

4. Pilcher, *Surgeon Generals of the Army*, 89–90; Mary C. Gillett, *The Army Medical Department, 1865–1917*, Army Historical Series (Center of Military History, United States Army, 1995), 315.

5. Pilcher, *Surgeon Generals of the Army*, 91; Gillett, *Army Medical Department, 1865–1917*, 315.

6. "Obituary: Major General Robert Maitland O'Reilly," *Military Surgeon*. 31:6 (December, 1912), 741–743, 742.

7. Gillett, *Army Medical Department,1865–1917*, 319.

8. *Ibid.*, 320–321; *Efficiency of the Medical Department*, 60th Cong., 1st Session, 1908, S.R.41, 4–5.

9. "Army Medical Reorganization: The Proposed Army Medical Corps and Medical Reserve Corps," *JAMSUS* 14:3 (March, 1904), 201–206; Senate, *Efficiency of Medical Department*, 10.

10. Charles Lynch, Frank W. Weed, and Loy McAfee, *The Medical Department of the United States Army in the World War, Volume I: The Surgeon General's Office* (Government Printing Office, 1923), 59.

11. *Report of the Surgeon General, 1904*, 119.

12. U.S. Statutes at Large, 35 (1909), 66–67; Tobey, *The Medical Department of the Army*, 31–32.

13. U.S. Statutes at Large, 35 (1909), 68–69; *War Department Annual Reports, 1909*, Volume Two, 172–173; Gillett, *Army Medical Department, 1865–1917*, 322–323.

14. "Editorial Expression: The Army Medical Reorganization Bill," *Military Surgeon* 38:3 (March, 1916), 324–325, 324; quote in *Annual Reports, 1909*, 173.

15. Henry C. Cox, "The 'Inactive' Medical Reserve Corps," *Military Surgeon* 28:4 (April, 1911), 377–382, 377.

16. *Ibid.*, 381.

17. "Editorial: Brigadier General George H. Torney, Surgeon General of the United States Army," *Military Surgeon*. 24:2 (February, 1909), 144–147, 145.

18. Gillett, *Army Medical Department, 1865–1917*, 316–318.
19. Marie D. Gorgas and Burton J. Hendrick, *William Crawford Gorgas, His Life and Work* (Doubleday, Page and Company, 1924), 268–270.
20. Gustavus M. Blech, "National Guard and National Defense, With Special Reference to the Sanitary Service," *Military Surgeon* 33:2 (August, 1913), 144–148, 144.
21. "The Surgeons in Manchuria," *Army and Navy Register* 36:1300 (November 22, 1904), 7.
22. John Van Rensselaer Hoff, "Russian Sanitary Organization in the Far East: Medical Statistics and the Medical Department," [January 4, 1906], USA-HEC, Carlisle, Pennsylvania, 11–13.
23. Surgeon Raymond Spear, "Report on the Russian Medical and Sanitary Features of the Russo-Japanese War to the Surgeon General, U.S. Navy, 1906," USAHEC, Carlisle, Pennsylvania, 10–11; Hoff, "Russian Sanitary Organization," 12, 24.
24. Hoff, "Russian Sanitary Organization," 13–14.
25. *Ibid.*, 2–4, 18–19; Spear, "Report on Russian Medical Features," 60–64.
26. Charles Lynch, *Medical Department of the Japanese Army* (The Old Corner Bookstore, 1906), 8–10, 12–15.
27. Percy M. Ashburn and Charles F. Craig, "Observations Made During a Visit to Japan by the United States Army Board for the Study of Tropical Diseases as They Exist in the Philippine Islands," *Military Surgeon* 22:2 (February, 1908), 116–136, 127–128, 130; John F. Hutchinson, *Champions of Charity: War and the Rise of the Red Cross* (Westview Press, 1996), 211.
28. Lynch, *Medical Department of Japanese Army*, 19–20, 22–23.
29. Louis L. Seaman, "Address of Major Louis L. Seaman Before the International Congress of Military and Naval Surgeons," (N.P., 1904), 20–21. See also Louis L. Seaman, *From Tokio through Manchuria with the Japanese* (D. Appleton and Company, 1905), 228.
30. Louis Livingston Seaman, *The Real Triumph of Japan: The Conquest of the Silent Foe* (D. Appleton & Co., 1908), 1.
31. Seaman, "Address," 27–28.
32. *Ibid.*, 31.
33. *Ibid.*, 31, 29.
34. Ashburn and Craig, "Observations Made by the Army Board," 116–124, quote on 126.
35. "Dr. Seaman and the Japanese," *Army and Navy Register* 37:1310 (January 14, 1905), 6
36. Ashburn and Craig, "Observations Made by the Army Board," 122–125 .
37. *Ibid.*, 134.
38. Ashburn and Craig, "Observations Made by the Army Board," 134
39. Edgar Erskine Hume, *The Golden Jubilee of the Association of Military Surgeons of the United States* (The Association of Military Surgeons, 1941), 247.
40. Peter E. Traub, "Military Hygiene: How Best to Enforce its Study in our Military and Naval Schools and Promote its Intelligent Practice in Our Army," *JAMSUS* 36:133 (January–February, 1905), 1–38, 4.
41. *Ibid.*, 6.
42. Alfred A. Woodhull, "Comment and Criticism: Military Hygiene," *JMSI* 36:134 (March–April, 1905), 349–353, 351.
43. D. H. Broughton, "Command and Criticism: Military Hygiene," *JMSI* 36:134 (March–April, 1905), 353–357, 356.
44. *Army and Navy Register* 35:1275 (May 21, 1904), 2.
45. Percy Moreau Ashburn, *A History of the Medical Department of the United States Army* (Houghton Mifflin Company, 1929), 246.

46. Charles Lynch, "The Scope of Teaching that Should be Followed in the Newly-Established Chair of Hygiene and Sanitation in our Military and Naval Schools, and the Practical Results to be Expected Therefrom," *JMSI* 44:157 (January–February, 1909), 194–213, 194.

47. *Ibid.*, 194, 195.

48. Alfred A. Woodhull, "The Scope of Teaching That Should be Followed in the Newly Established Chair of Hygiene and Sanitation in our Military and Naval Schools, and the Practical Results to be Expected Therefrom," *JMSI* 42:152 (March–April, 1908), 157–192, 157.

49. *Ibid.*, 158.

50. *Ibid.*, 158–159.

51. Lynch, "The Scope of Teaching," 213.

52. Woodhull, "The Scope of Training," 160.

53. *Ibid.*, 190.

54. *War Department Annual Reports, 1908.* Volume Four, 107–108; Gillett, *Army Medical Department, 1865–1917*, 325; Frank R. Keefer, "The Functions of the Medical Department of the Army, Especially in the Field," *JMSI* 99:174 (November–December, 1911), 347–359, 347.

55. Keefer, "Functions of the Medical Department," 349.

56. Alfred A. Woodhull, *Notes on Military Hygiene for Officers of the Line* (John Wiley & Sons, 1890, 1898, 1904).

57. Alfred A. Woodhull, *Military Hygiene for Officers of the Line* (John Wiley & Sons, 1909), 4.

58. Vincent J. Cirillo, *Bullets and Bacilli: The Spanish-American War and Military Medicine* (Rutgers University Press, 2004), 132–133.

59. *War Department Annual Reports, 1908*, 45–46.

60. Ashburn, *Elements of Military Hygiene*, 145.

61. *Ibid.*, 145.

62. Edward Lyman Munson, *The Principles of Sanitary Tactics* (Edward L. Munson, 1911), 63, 87, 132, 240.

63. *Ibid.*, 36.

64. *Ibid.*, 59–60.

65. H.L. Gilchrist, "The Necessity for a Uniform Organization for the Medical Corps of the National Guard," *Military Surgeon* 34:1 (January, 1914), 22–26, 23–24.

66. *Ibid.*, 24.

67. Blech, "National Guard and National Defense," 147.

68. Gillett, *Army Medical Department, 1865–1917*, 322; *War Department Annual Reports, 1912.* Volume 1, 694; *Field Service Regulations, United States Army, 1910*, 33. According to the Regulations, "The Medical Department consists of a surgeon-general, and of the commissioned and enlisted personnel, nurses, and dental surgeons authorized by law for that department. The personnel of the department and all other persons assigned to duty with that department are collectively called *sanitary troops*" (Ibid., 33.)

69. Henry D. Thomason, "Sanitary Troops in the Organized Militia of the United States," *Military Surgeon* 29:5 (November, 1911), 511–526, 511.

70. "The Organization of the Medical Department of State Forces," *Military Surgeon* 21:6 (December, 1907), 550–551, 550.

71. *Ibid.*, 551; H.C. Fisher, "Preparedness of the Medical Department for War," *Military Surgeon* 38:2 (February, 1916), 123–130, 124; Thomason, "Sanitary Troops," 512–513.

72. Thomason, "Sanitary Troops," 515, 518; "Annual Report of Brigadier General A.L. Mills, G.S., U.S.A., Chief of the Division of Militia Affairs," *Military Surgeon* 34:3 (March, 1914), 249–256, 249.

73. "Annual Report of Brigadier General Mills," 253–254.
74. Fisher, "Preparedness," 124–125, 126, 128, 129.
75. Charles Adams, "Preparedness, Presidential Address," *Military Surgeon* 35:5 (November, 1914), 411–414, 411.
76. *Ibid.*, 412–413.
77. "Editorial: Preparedness," *Military Surgeon* 35:5 (November, 1914), 430–432, 431.
78. "Annual Report of Brigadier General Mills," quote on 249, 252.
79. Gillett, *Army Medical Department, 1865–1917,* 324.
80. *War Department Annual Reports, 1912,* 790–791.
81. Day Allen Willey, "Summer Encampments," *Army and Navy Life and the United Services* 9:1 (July, 1906), 17–24, 18; Robert M. O'Reilly, *War Department Annual Reports, 1907,* Volume II, 97.
82. *Report of the Surgeon General, 1904,* 25.
83. George S. Crampton, "Camps of Instruction for Militia Medical Officers in 1909," *Military Surgeon.* 27:4 (October, 1910), 355–363, 356–358, 360–361.
84. *Ibid.*, 359.
85. A. S. Stayer, "Report on the 1910 Camp of the Division of the Pennsylvania National Guard at Gettysburg, PA.," *Military Surgeon* 29:1 (January, 1911), 1–28, 17, quote on 26; Daniel W. Rogers, "Report of the Chief Sanitary Officer of the Division, Camp of Illinois National Guard, at Peoria, Illinois, 1910," *Military Surgeon.* 28:1 (January, 1911), 35–44, 42–43.
86. Stayer, "Report on the 1910 Camp," 27.
87. H. J. Jones, "The Army and the National Guard from the View-point of a National Guard Officer," *Military Surgeon* 28:1 (January, 1911), 45–47, 45.
88. "Editorial," *Military Surgeon.* 28:2 (February, 1911), 227–228, 227; Stayer, "Report on the 1910 Camp," 17, C. Schultz, "Benefits Derived from Camps of Instruction, to the Medical Officers, in Conjunction with the Field and Line Officers," *Military Surgeon* 34:2 (February, 1914), 131–133, 131.
89. Schultz, "Benefits Derived from Camps of Instruction," 132.
90. Henry H. Doan, "A Plea for More Camps of Instruction, Under Government Supervision, for Officers of the Organized Militia," *Military Surgeon* 32:1 (January, 1913), 75–77, 76.
91. *Ibid.*, 76–77.
92. Editorial, *Military Surgeon* 28:4 (April, 1911), 475–477; *War Department Annual Reports, 1911,* Volume One, 12–13; Herbert A. Arnold, "Report on Maneuver Camps at San Antonio and Leon Springs and on Juarez, Mexico," *Military Surgeon.* 29:1 (July, 1911), 21–28, 21.
93. Frank W. Foxworthy, "Report of Sanitary Conditions at Maneuver Camp, San Antonio, Texas," *Military Surgeon* 29:2 (August, 1911), 196–197, 196; "Editorial," *Military Surgeon* 29:2 (August, 1911), 233–234.
94. Arnold, "Report on Maneuver Camps," 22–24.
95. "Editorial," *Military Surgeon* 29:6 (December, 1911), 698.
96. Frederick F. Russell, "The Prevention of Typhoid Fever by Vaccination and by Early Diagnosis and Isolation," *Military Surgeon* 24:6 (June, 1909), 479–518, 480.
97. Frederick F. Russell, *Results of Antityphoid Vaccination in the Army in 1911, and its Suitability for Use in Civil Communities* (American Medical Association, 1912), 2–3.
98. Russell, "The Prevention of Typhoid Fever," 512.
99. *Ibid.*, 512–514.

100. *Ibid.*, 481–482; Russell, *Results of Antityphoid Vaccination*, 4–5. In 1904 the Germans returned to typhoid inoculation in their Herero Campaign in German South West Africa (current day Namibia) where half of the German troops deployed were inoculated. The mixed results of the inoculation—with a decline in the infection rate between those who refused inoculation and those who received it of only 50 percent—indicate the German inoculation was flawed. Russell, *Results of Antityphoid Vaccination*, 5.

101. Russell, *Results of Antityphoid Vaccination*, 513–514

102. *Ibid.*, 6–7; Albert G. Love, "Typhoid Prophylaxis in the British Army in India and in the American Army in the United States," *Military Surgeon* 32:3 (March, 1913), 250–258, 257–258.

103. Love, "Typhoid Prophylaxis," 257; Russell, "Antityphoid Vaccination During 1913," 1.

104. Russell, "Antityphoid Vaccination During 1913," 1, 2.

105. Russell, *Results of Antityphoid Vaccination*, 9–10.

106. Hutchinson, *Champions of Charity*, 229–231; John Van Rensselaer Hoff, "Military Hygiene: And How Can the People of the United States be Educated to Appreciate its Necessity?" *JMSI* 40:147 (May–June, 1907), 353–376, 368–369.

107. "Editorial: At Last a Red Cross for War," *Military Surgeon* 38:2 (February, 1916), 205–207, 206.

108. Hoff, "Military Hygiene: Appreciate its Necessity," 367–368.

109. *Ibid.*, 369, 373, quote on 370.

110. Charles Lynch, *What is the Most Efficient Organization of the American National Red Cross for War and What Should be Its Relations with the Medical Departments of the Army and Navy?* (The Association of Military Surgeons, 1907), 8, 10, 17, 24.

111. *Ibid.*, 14.

112. *Ibid.*, 27.

113. Hutchison, *Champions of Charity*, 235.

114. "Editorial: Red Cross for War," 205; Tobey, *The Medical Department of the Army*, 37; *History of the Pennsylvania Hospital Unit (Base Hospital No. 10, U.S.A.) in the Great War* (Paul B. Hoeber, 1921), 15, 18–19.

115. *Manual for the Medical Department, United States Army*, 1916, 179; Tobey, *The Medical Department of the Army* 34; Edgar Erskine Hume, *Victories of Army Medicine; Scientific Accomplishments of the Medical Department of the United States Army* (J.B. Lippincott Company, 1943), 34; *Regulations Governing the Employment of the American Red Cross in Time of War* (December 18, 1916, War Department, 2475835, A.G.O., 3.

116. *History of Base Hospital No. 10*, 20

117. Henry P. Davison, *The American Red Cross in the Great War* (Macmillan, 1920), 143; Tobey, *The Medical Department of the Army*, 37.

118. *Regulations Governing American Red Cross*, 7.

119. Clarence C. Clendenen, *Blood on the Border: The United States Army and the Mexican Irregulars* (Macmillan, 1969), 132, 152–153.

120. Weston P. Chamberlain, "Hints for Line Officers Regarding the Diseases Liable to be Met With in Mexico and the General Methods of Combating Them," *JMSI* 54:189 (May–June, 1914), 341–359, 341.

121. Chamberlain, "Hints for Line Officers," 355–359.

122. Clendenen, *Blood on the Border*, 158–162; "Disease Among Our Troops at the Front," *Military Surgeon* 35:2 (August, 1914), 163–166, 164–166.

123. Clendenan, *Blood on the Border*, 200–209.

124. Alexandra Minna Stern, "Buildings, Boundaries, and Blood: Medicalization and Nation-Building on the U.S.-Mexico Border, 1910–1930," *Hispanic*

American Historical Review 79:1 (February, 1999), 41–81, 42–43. Stern describes, "I treat medicalization as a far-reaching cultural and scientific formation pivotal to United States imperialism and nation-building in the early twentieth century" (*Ibid.*, 50.)

125. *Ibid.*, 55–56.
126. John J. Pershing, Punitive Division Report, October 10, 1916, 1–5. USAHEC.
127. Punitive Division Report, Appendix "D," (Report, George E. Bratton, Acting Division Surgeon, October 7, 1916), 67–68.
128. William J.L. Lyster, "Sterilization of Drinking Water by Calcium Hypochlorite in the Field," *Military Surgeon.* 36:3 (March, 1915), 222–228, 223; *Ibid.*, 68.
129. Punitive Division Report, Appendix "D," 68.
130. Punitive Expedition Report, 38; *Ibid.*, 68.
131. Irving Goff McCann, *With the National Guard on the Border: Our National Military Problem* (C.V. Mosby Company, 1917), 136, quote on 138.
132. Punitive Expedition Report, 39.
133. *History of Base Hospital No. 10*, 20–21; quote in Lynch, Weed, and McAfee, *Medical Department of the Army*, Vol. 1, 71.

NOTES TO CHAPTER 6

1. John Van Rensselaer Hoff, "Is There a Venereal Peril for Us?" *The Military Surgeon* XXV:6 (December, 1909), 732–748, 747.
2. Edward M. Coffman, *The Old Army: A Portrait of the American Army in Peacetime, 1784–1898* (Oxford University Press, 1986), 21,63, 99, 263.
3. James Mann, *Medical Sketches of the Campaigns of 1812, 13, 14* (H. Mann and Co. 1816), 36.
4. J.A. Dapray, "The Army Canteen Question," *Uncle Sam's Magazine* XV:3 (July, 1909), 66–73, 71.
5. *Report of the Surgeon General, 1891*, 31.
6. George Augustus Lung, "Alcohol a Depreciating Factor of Efficiency," *JAMSUS* 18:1 (January, 1906), 69–88, 74.
7. Jack D. Foner, *The United States Soldier Between Two Wars* (Humanities Press, 1970), 79; John Thomas Murphy, "Pistol's Legacy: Sutlers, Post Traders, and the American Army, 1820–1895." Dissertation: University of Illinois at Urbana-Champaign, 1993. UMI Number: 9314919, 285.
8. *Ibid.*, 289–293; *Army and Navy Register*, XXII:21 (November 20, 1897), Supplement, 3.
9. *Army and Navy Register*, XI:3 (January 18, 1890), 31.
10. *Ibid.*, 31.
11. *Ibid.*, 31.
12. "A Study of Desertion," U.S. War Department Report, 1920, USAHEC, 7.
13. *Report of the Surgeon General, 1892*, 47, 87.
14. *The New York Times*, December 26, 1883, 4.
15. *Congressional Record.* 51:1 Congress, Volume XXI, 1889, 4378.
16. *Ibid.*, 4375.
17. *Army and Navy Register*, XI:20 (May 17, 1890), 319.
18. *Ibid.*, 319.
19. *Army and Navy Register*, XI:22 (May 31, 1890), 395.
20. *Ibid.*, 349.
21. "Fact, Not Fiction," *Uncle Sam's Magazine* XV:3 (July, 1909), 99.

22. *Cong. Rec.*, 51:1, 5477.
23. Henry W. Blair, *The Temperance Movement, or the Conflict Between Man and Alcohol* (William E. Smythe Company, 1888), 381.
24. *Ibid.*, 385.
25. Anita Newcomb McGee, "Facts About the Army Canteen," *Military Surgeon* XXIII:4 (October, 1908), 260–271, 261.
26. General Orders No. 87, Headquarters of the Army, Adjutant General's Office, July 2, 1898.
27. *Army and Navy Register.* XXVI:26 (December 23, 1899), 408.
28. Ellwood Bergey, *Why Soldiers Desert from the United States Army* (Wm. F. Fell & Company, 1903), 87.
29. *Ibid.*, 32, 108–109.
30. John Reuben Johnson, "Nebraska in the Spanish-American War and the Philippine Insurrection, A Study in Imperialism." Dissertation: University of Nebraska, January 2, 1937. No UM#, 34–35.
31. *Ibid.*, 206, 220–221.
32. *Army and Navy Register*, XXIX:1101 (January 26, 1901), quote on 68; Johnson, "Nebraska in the Spanish-American War," 226, 235
33. *Report of the Surgeon General, 1901*, 172–173; *Army and Navy Register* XXVII:1065 (May 12, 1900), 319.
34. *Army and Navy Register* XXIX:1113 (April 20, 1901), 303.
35. *Ibid.*, 303.
36. *Army and Navy Register* XXVII:1065 (May 12, 1900), 319.
37. House Document 2, 56ᵗʰ Congress, First Session, V. 2, *Report of the Adjutant General of the Army to the Secretary of War on the Canteen Section of the Post Exchange.* November 24, 1899, 266.
38. *Ibid.*, 276.
39. "The Army Canteen Question," 66–73, 66–67, quote on 69.
40. Senate Document 51: 27ᵗʰ Congress, 2ⁿᵈ Session, *Address to American Public on the Subject of the Canteen, Etc.*, 1.
41. *Army and Navy Register*, XXXIX:1384 (June 23, 1906), 6.
42. *Ibid.*, 4–5.
43. *Army and Navy Register*, XXXIX:1384 (June 23, 1906), 6; Two years later, additional laws were passed banning the sale of alcohol in immigrant processing stations and the Capitol. *Army and Navy Register*, XXXIX:1369 (March 10, 1906), 27.
44. *Army and Navy Register*, XXXIV:1254 (December 26, 1903), 5–7, 5.
45. Senate Doc. 51, 15.
46. *Army and Navy Register*, XXIX:1116 (May 11, 1901), 370.
47. All quoted in *Army and Navy Register*, XXIV:5 (July 30, 1898), 72.
48. *The New York Times*, December 14, 1900, 5.
49. *Ibid.*, 5.
50. "And Uncle Sam Permits It!" *Uncle Sam's Magazine* XV:3 (July, 1909), 73.
51. Edmund Banks Smith, "The Army Canteen," *Army and Navy Life* XIV:4 (April, 1909), 310–313, 313.
52. *Army and Navy Register* XXIV:8 (August 20, 1898), 121.
53. House Report 1701, (56:1), 11.
54. *Ibid.*, 10.
55. Smith, "The Army Canteen," 311.
56. *Ibid.*, 313.
57. Hoff, "Is There a Venereal Peril," 732.
58. *Ibid.*, 733–734.
59. *Ibid.*,736.

60. Samuel Forry and Thomas Lawson, *Statistical Report on the Sickness and Mortality of the Army of the United States* (J. Gideon, Jr., 1840), 330.
61. *Ibid.*, 92.
62. Report of T. C. Madison, 1857, in Richard H. Coolidge, *Statistical Report on the Sickness and Mortality of the Army of the United States, 1855–1860* (George W. Bowman, Printer, 1860), 40.
63. E. P. Langworthy, "Medical Topography and Diseases of Fort Conrad," in Richard H. Coolidge, *Statistical Report on the Sickness and Mortality of the Army of the United States, 1839–1855,*(A.O.P. Nicholson, Printer, 1856), 415–416; J. M. Haden, "Medical Topography and Diseases of Fort Steilacoom," in *Statistical Report, 1839–1855*, 480; Coffman, *The Old Army*, 107–108, 181; McCaffrey, *Army of Manifest Destiny*, 104.
64. Israel Moses, "Medical Topography and Diseases of Ringgold Barracks," *Statistical Report, 1839–1855*, 360.
65. Abraham Colles, *Practical Observations on the Venereal Disease, and on the Use of Mercury* (A. Waldie, 1837), 3–4
66. Report of T. C. Madison in *Statistical Report, 1855–1860*, 37–41, 40–41.
67. Charles Smart, *The Medical and Surgical History of the War of the Rebellion*. Volume 6 (Government Printing Office, 1888), 891.
68. Thomas P. Lowry, *The Story the Soldier's Wouldn't Tell: Sex in the Civil War* (Mechanicsburg, Pennsylvania: Stackpole Books, 1994), 104–105.
69. *Ibid.*, 76–83; *Medical and Surgical History*, Vol. 6, 893–895.
70. *Ibid.*, 894–896; quotes on 895.
71. *Ibid.*, 891; quotes on 894. The British Contagious Diseases Act of 1864 permitted the police in cities and towns where army and navy posts were located to accost women to determine if they had a medical inspection certificate. The police were also given the power to confine women without a certificate in prison until they underwent an examination for venereal disease; if the test revealed the presence of a disease, the afflicted woman could remain in prison until "cured." Aside from the national scope of the British act, the greatest distinction between the CDA and the Union Army's policies in Nashville and Memphis was the extension of absolute power to the male police in Britain, who had the ability to stop any woman on the street to demand proof of health. For more on the Contagious Diseases Act, and the reaction of British women to its coercive power, see Judith R. Walkowitz, *Prostitution and Victorian Society: Women, Class, and the State* (Cambridge University Press, 1980), 67–147.
72. *Army and Navy Register*, XI:23 (June 7, 1890), 373.
73. *Ibid.*, 373.
74. Richard Johnson Papers, Folder One, "My Life in the Army, 1899–1922" (Unpublished Manuscript), 60, USAHEC, Carlisle, Pennsylvania.
75. C. F. Morse, "The Prevalence and Prophylaxis of Venereal Diseases at One Military Post," *Military Surgeon*. 27:3 (September, 1910), 268–273, 268.
76. Henry I. Raymond, "Prophylaxis under G.O. #31, War Department, 1912, for the Hawaiian Department," *Military Surgeon*. 34:2 (February, 1914), 134–139, 135–136.
77. "Report of Operations in China from November 30, 1900 to May 19, 1901, by Maj. Gen. Adna R. Chaffee, U.S.A.," in *Reports of the War Department, 1901*. Part Four (of Five), *Division of Insular Affairs*, 498–505, 505; Edward M. Coffman's essay "The American 15th Infantry Regiment in China, 1912–1938," *Journal of Military History*. 58:1 (January, 1994), 57–74, captures the appeal—and very real hazards—of China service for this generation of soldiers. While beyond the scope of this project, the 15th Infantry's rate of drunkenness led or tied all other regiments in the Army for ten out of eleven

years (1928–1938), with drunkenness rates reaching 43.8 per thousand in 1928. *Op.Cit.*, 71.

78. Louis Livingston Seaman, "Observations in China and the Tropics on the Army Ration and the Post Exchange or Canteen," *JMSI.* XXIX:CXIII (September, 1901), 289–293, 292, quote on 293.

79. William Lyster, "Venereal Prophylaxis in the Army—The Necessity of Cooperation with Line Officers," *Military Surgeon* 29:1 (July, 1911), 67–72, 67.

80. Coffman, "The American 15th Infantry," 72.

81. "Just Outside the Gate," *Uncle Sam's Magazine.* XV:3 (July, 1909), 65

82. Edward L. Munson, "Diseases of the Soldier and Their Prophylaxis," *Military Surgeon* 25:1 (July, 1909), 24–37, 34.

83. *Ibid.*, 34.

84. Lyster, "Venereal Prophylaxis in the Army," 69, quote on 70–71.

85. Morse, "The Prevalence of Venereal Diseases," 269–270.

86. *Ibid.*, 268.

87. Mary C. Gillett, *The Army Medical Department, 1865–1917* (Center of Military History, United States Army, 1995), 350; Circular No. 2, Office of the Surgeon General, War Department, June 3, 1911.

88. James S. Fox, "Prophylaxis of Syphilis and Practical Points on its Treatment by Salvarsan," *Military Surgeon* 32:1 (January, 1913), 91–97, 95–96

89. Gillett, *The Army Medical Department*, 351.

90. Edward B. Vedder, "What are the Best Available Measures to Diminish Venereal Diseases Among Soldiers and Sailors, and Along What Lines Should We Seek the Cooperation of Federal, State and Municipal Authorities?" *Military Surgeon* 29:5 (November, 1911), 484–510, 489.

91. Deane C. Howard, "Venereal Prophylaxis," *Military Surgeon* 29:6 (December, 1911), 669–673, 669.

92. W. P. McIntosh, "Syphilis: Especially in Regard to its Communication by Drinking Cups, Kissing, Etc.," *Military Surgeon* 32:2 (February, 1913), 184–191, 187, 189.

93. Valery Havard, "The Prophylaxis of Venereal Disease," *JAMSUS* 15:1 (July, 1904), 1–17, 1, 10–11.

94. P.C. Fauntleroy, "Venereal Disease in the Army and the Necessity of Proper Action by State and Municipal Authorities for its Effectual Control," *Military Surgeon* 25:6 (December, 1909), 772–774, 773, 774.

95. Vedder, "Best Available Measures to Diminish Venereal Diseases," 489.

96. *Ibid.*, 487, 495, 498,500, 505–508.

97. Bremner Mere, "What They Did in Texas," *Army and Navy Life* XIV:4 (April, 1909), 319–323, 319–320.

98. *Ibid.*, 322–323.

99. Enoch H. Crowder, "The Canteen at the Camps," *Army and Navy Register* XL:1387 (July 14, 1906), 29.

100. Robert D. Gorodetzer, "A Concise Biography of Colonel Louis M. Maus, MC," April 1971, USAMEDD Historical Unit, 4, 6, 8.

101. *Ibid.*, 4, 9.

102. James Carson, "The Army's Fight with Plague and Cholera in Manila," *The San Francisco Chronicle*, October 19, 1902, 10; William Atherton Du Puy, "Each of These Men Saved One Million Lives," *The Sunday Oregonian* [Portland]. June 14, 1914, 5.

103. Carson, "Plague and Cholera in Manila," 10.

104. L, Mervin Maus, "Does the Moderate Use of Alcohol Lower Health and Efficiency and Should it be Prohibited Among Officers and Officials of the Military, Naval and Civil Services?" *JMSI* 51:180 (November–December,1912), 301–320, 301.

105. *Ibid.*, 302–305.
106. L. Mervin Maus, "Injurious Effects Resulting from the Moderate Use of Alcohol," *JMSI* 54:187 (January–February, 1914), 1–8, 1–2.
107. *Ibid.*, 318.
108. L. Mervin Maus, "Further Observations on the Prophylaxis of Venereal Diseases in the United States Army," *Military Surgeon* 27:6 (December, 1910), 636–644, 636.
109. L. Mervin Maus, "Venereal Diseases in the United States Army—Their Prevention and Treatment," *Military Surgeon* 27:2 (August, 1910), 130–148, 130–131.
110. L. Mervin Maus, "The Suppression of Vice Diseases Through Personal Prophylaxis and Municipal Control of the Saloon and Courtesan," *Chicago Medical Recorder* 35:1 (January, 1913), 11–22, 15.
111. Maus, "Further Observations," 637.
112. Maus, "The Suppression of Vice Diseases," 18.
113. L. Mervin Maus, "Venereal Diseases in the United States Army—Their Prevention and Treatment [Continued]," *Military Surgeon* 27:3 (September, 1910), 248–267, 262.
114. Maus, "The Suppression of Vice Diseases," 11.
115. *Ibid.*, 12.
116. Maus, "Venereal Diseases in the Army," 135.
117. *Ibid.*, 130
118. *Ibid.*, 134–135.
119. *Report of the Surgeon-General, 1893*, 138, quote on 139.
120. McGee, "Facts About the Canteen," 270.
121. R.H. Pierson, "The Relation of Military Officers to Military Discipline," *Military Surgeon* XXXII:6 (June, 1913), 527–542, 537–538.
122. McGee, "Facts About the Canteen," 261.
123. *Ibid.*, 264–265.
124. *Ibid.*, 267–268, quote on 269.
125. *Ibid.*, 269.
126. *Ibid.*, 270.
127. Nancy K. Bristow, *Making Men Moral: Social Engineering during the Great War* (New York University Press, 1996), 7.
128. "Military Prohibition Prohibits," *Military Surgeon* XLII:4 (April, 1918), 455–456, 456.
129. *Ibid.*, 456.

Bibliography

PRIMARY SOURCES

Archival Records

College of Physicians of Philadelphia, Philadelphia, Pennsylvania
    James Thorington Papers, 1889–1941.
    Sturgis Image Collection.
National Archives and Records Administration, Washington, D.C.
    RG 112.
    RG 165.
National Library of Medicine, Bethesda, Maryland.
    MS C 48.
    MS C 142.
Rockefeller Archive Center, Pocantico Hills, New York.
    RG 3.1, Series 908.
United States Army Heritage and Education Center, Carlisle, Pennsylvania.
    "A Study of Desertion," U.S. War Department Report, 1920.
    Perry L. Boyer Papers.
    Charles Craig Papers.
    Richard Johnson Papers.
    William August Kobbe Papers.
    John J. Pershing, Punitive Division Report, October 10, 1916.
    RG 92S—Halstead-Maus Photographic Collection.
    RG 112S—Military Order of the Loyal Legion of the United States (MOLLUS)
        Photographic Collection.
    United Spanish War Veterans Collection.
    Samuel B. Young Papers.

Newspapers

Chattanooga Daily Times
The Atlanta Constitution
The Chicago Daily Tribune
The Evening Bulletin (Philadelphia)
The Minneapolis Journal
The New York Herald
The New York Times
The Oregonian (Portland)

The Philadelphia Inquirer
The San Francisco Chronicle
The Washington Post

Journals and Magazines (without citation)

Army and Navy Journal
Army and Navy Register
Army and Navy Register (Army and Navy Illustrated)
The Lancet-Clinic (Cincinnati)
The Medical News
Texas Medical Journal

Journal Title Abbreviations (individual citations follow)

AHR (American Historical Review)
JAMA (Journal of the American Medical Association)
JAMSUS (Journal of the Association of Military Surgeons of the United States)
JMSI (The Journal of the Military Service Institution of the United States)
Proceedings (Proceedings of the Association of Military Surgeons of the United States)

Government Publications

American State Papers.
Circular No. 2, Office of the Surgeon General, War Department, June 3, 1911.
Circular No. 6, War Department. Washington, November 1, 1865.
Circular of Information: In relation to appointment in the medical corps of the United States Army, the requisite qualifications, examination of applicants, etc. Form 132. War Department, Surgeon General's Office, Revised August 17, 1916.
Compendium of General Orders, Adjutant General's Office, 1864.
Congressional Record. 51:1 Congress, Volume XXI, 1889,
Efficiency of the Medical Department, 60th Cong., 1st Session, 1908, S.R.41.
Field Service Regulations, United States Army, 1910.
General Orders 28, Adjutant General's Office, September 21, 1850.
General Orders 65, Adjutant General's Office, Headquarters of the Army, July 9, 1884.
General Orders 58, Headquarters of the Army, Adjutant General's Office, May 31, 1898.
General Orders 82, Headquarters of the Army, Adjutant General's Office June 27, 1898.
General Orders 87, Headquarters of the Army, Adjutant General's Office, July 2, 1898.
General Orders 100, War Department, Adjutant General's Office, July 16, 1898.
General Orders 114, War Department, Adjutant General's Office, August 9, 1898.
General Orders 117, War Department, Adjutant General's Office, August 10, 1898.
General Orders 140, War Department, Adjutant General's Office, September 3, 1898.
General Orders 142, War Department, Adjutant General's Office, September 14, 1898.

General Regulations for the Army of the United States, 1841.

General Regulations for the Army; or Military Institutes, 1825.

General Regulations for the Army of the United States; also, the Rules and Articles of War, and Extracts from Laws Relating to Them. 1835.

House Document 2, 56ᵗʰ Congress, First Session, V. 2, *Report of the Adjutant General of the Army to the Secretary of War on the Canteen Section of the Post Exchange.* November 24, 1899.

House Misc. Doc. 56, (45:2).

House Ex.Doc. 23, (45:3).

House Report 33, (40:3).

House Report 74, 1873, (42:3).

House Report 1701, (56:1).

Manual for the Medical Department, United States Army, 1916.

The People of the Philippines. Letter from the Secretary of War, Transmitting an Article on the People of the Philippines, Compiled in the Division of Insular Affairs of the War Department. Senate Document No. 218, 56ᵗʰ Congress, 2d Session, February 15, 1901.

Regulations for the Army of the United States, 1863.

Regulations Governing the Employment of the American Red Cross in Time of War. December 18, 1916, War Department, 2475835, A.G.O.

Report of the Commission Appointed by the President to Investigate the Conduct of the War Department in the War With Spain, 1899.

Reports of the Secretary of War.

Reports of the Surgeon General.

Report of W. C. Gorgas, Major, Surgeon U.S. Army, Chief Sanitary Officer, for the Current Year 1901, March 29, 1902.

Revised United States Army Regulations of 1861. With an Appendix Containing the Changes and Laws Affecting Army Regulations and Articles of War to June 25, 1863.

Senate Document 51: 27ᵗʰ Congress, 2ⁿᵈ Session, *Address to American Public on the Subject of the Canteen, Etc.*

Special Report on Insular Affairs, as Per Instructions of Circular No. 10, War Department, March 25, 1899.

U.S. Army Adjutant General's Office, *Military Orders Having the Force of Law Promulgated by the Commanding General Department of Porto Rico from October 18ᵗʰ, 1898, to April 30ᵗʰ, 1900.* Two Volumes. N.P., 1900.

U.S. Statutes at Large.

U.S. War Department, Surgeon General's Office, *A Report on the Hygiene of the United States Army, with Descriptions of Military Posts,* Circular No. 8. 1875.

War Department, U.S.A. Annual Reports, 1907–1912.

Yellow Fever: A Compilation of Various Publications. Government Printing Office, 1911.

Speeches

Alden, Charles H., "The Special Training of the Medical Officer with Brief Notes on Army Medical Schools Abroad and at Home." [May 3, 1894].

Hoff, John Van Rensselaer, "Russian Sanitary Organization in the Far East: Medical Statistics and the Medical Department." [January 4, 1906] U.S. Army Heritage and Education Center, Carlisle, Pennsylvania.

Maus, L. Mervin, "Sanitary and Economical Improvement in the Philippines Since American Intervention." [November 23, 1912] In SPI Pamphlets, 29:1, New York Public Library.

Seaman, Louis L., "Address of Major Louis L. Seaman Before the International Congress of Military and Naval Surgeons," (St. Louis, Missouri: N.P., 1904).

Spear, Raymond, "Report on the Russian Medical and Sanitary Features of the Russo-Japanese War to the Surgeon General, U.S. Navy, 1906," U.S. Army Heritage and Education Center, Carlisle, Pennsylvania.

Winter, Francis A., "Preparedness of the Medical Department of the Army, in the Matter of Field Supplies," [1912] U.S. Army Heritage and Education Center, Carlisle, Pennsylvania.

Articles

Adams, Charles, "Minutes of the Meeting," in *Proceedings*. Association of Military Surgeons, 1901, 47–73.

———, "Preparedness, Presidential Address," *Military Surgeon* 35:5 (November, 1914), 411–414.

Alden, Charles H., "Puerto Rico: Its Climate and Its Diseases," *New York Medical Journal* 74:1 (July 6, 1901), 17–22.

———, "The U.S. Army Medical School, Washington, D.C.," *National Medical Review* [Washington, D.C.] 7:8 (January, 1898), 211–215.

Ames, Azel, "The Acting Assistant Surgeon of the Army of the United States," *JAMSUS* 13:3 (September, 1903), 121–133.

———, "The Vaccination of Porto Rico—A Lesson to the World," *JAMSUS* 12:5 (May, 1903), 293–313.

"And Uncle Sam Permits It!" *Uncle Sam's Magazine* XV:3 (July, 1909), 73.

Anderson, Thomas M., "The Place of the Medical Department in the Army,"*JMSI* 14:62 (March, 1893), 340–341.

"Annual Report of Brigadier General A.L. Mills, G.S., U.S.A., Chief of the Division of Militia Affairs," *Military Surgeon* 34:3 (March, 1914), 249–256.

"Army Medical Reorganization: The Proposed Army Medical Corps and Medical Reserve Corps," *JAMSUS* 14:3 (March, 1904), 201–206.

"The Army Medical School," *JAMSUS* 17:3 (September, 1905), 241–244.

Arnold, Herbert A., "Report on Maneuver Camps at San Antonio and Leon Springs and on Juarez, Mexico," *Military Surgeon* 29:1 (July, 1911), 21–28.

Ashburn, Percy M., and Charles F. Craig, "Observations Made During a Visit to Japan by the United States Army Board for the Study of Tropical Diseases as They Exist in the Philippine Islands," *Military Surgeon* 22:2 (February, 1908), 116–136.

Ashford, Bailey K., "Observations on the Campaign in Western Porto Rico During the Spanish-American War," *JAMSUS* 15:3 (September, 1903), 157–168.

———, "Where Treatment of All Infected is the Surest Prophylactic Measure—The Problem of Epidemic Uncinariasis in Porto Rico," *Military Surgeon* 20:1 (January, 1907), 40–55.

Ashford, Bailey K., and Pedro Gutierrez Igaravidez, "Summary of a Ten Years' Campaign Against Hookworm Disease in Porto Rico," *JAMA* 54:22 (May 28, 1910), 1757–1761.

Ashford, Bailey K., and Walter W. King, "A Study of Uncinariasis in Porto Rico," *American Medicine* 6:10 (September 5, 1903), 391–396.

———, "A Study of Uncinariasis in Porto Rico," *American Medicine* 6:11 (September 12, 1903), 431–438.

Barrows, David P., "The Governor-General of the Philippines Under Spain and the United States," *AHR* 21:2 (January, 1916), 288–311.

Billings, John Shaw, "The Military Medical Officer at the Opening of the Twentieth Century," *JAMSUS* 12:6 (June, 1903), 349–357.

Birmingham, Henry P., "Some Practical Suggestions on Tropical Hygiene," *JAMSUS* 12:1 (January, 1903), 45–54.

Blech, Gustavus, "National Guard and National Defense, With Special Reference to the Sanitary Service," *Military Surgeon* 33:2 (August, 1913), 144–148.

Borden, William C., "The Walter Reed General Hospital of the United States Army," *Military Surgeon* 20:1 (January, 1907), 20–35.

Boyland, G. Halsted, "The DeLesseps Canal in its Relation to Hygiene," *Independent Practitioner* [Baltimore] 1:7 (July, 1880), 317–333.

Broughton, D. H., "Command and Criticism: Military Hygiene," *JMSI* 36:134 (March–April, 1905), 353–357.

Brown, Paul R., "Determination of the Personal Identity of the United States Soldier," *Proceedings of the Sixth Annual Meeting of the Association of Military Surgeons of the United States* (Medical Gazette Publishing Co., 1896), 263–272.

Buel, William P., "Notes on the Medical Topography, Climate, and Diseases of Panama, N.G.," *American Journal of the Medical Sciences* 37 (January, 1859), 131–135.

Burrell, Herbert L., "Gunshot Wounds of Joints," *Transactions of the Third Annual Meeting of the Association of Military Surgeons of the National Guard of the United States* (Buxton & Skinner Stationery Co., 1894), 90–99.

Capron, Allan K., "Notes on Feeding Cavalry Horses," *Journal of the United States Cavalry Association* 10:36 (March, 1897), 32–38.

Carter, Edward Champe, "Typhoid and Malarial Fevers at Chickamauga in 1898," *JAMSUS* 14:2 (February, 1904), 104–110.

Chamberlain, Weston P., "Hints for Line Officers Regarding the Diseases Liable to be Met With in Mexico and the General Methods of Combating Them," *JMSI* 54:189 (May–June, 1914), 341–359.

Chester, James, "The Place of the Medical Department in the Army," *JMSI*, 11:46 (September, 1890), 823–827.

Church, James Robb, "[Obituary] John Van R. Hoff," *Military Surgeon*, XLVI:2 (February, 1920), 204–207.

Cox, Henry C., "The 'Inactive' Medical Reserve Corps," *Military Surgeon* 28:4 (April, 1911), 377–382.

Crampton, George S., "Camps of Instruction for Militia Medical Officers in 1909," *Military Surgeon* 27:4 (October, 1910), 355–363.

Crehore, Albert Cushing, and George O. Squier, "Experiments with a new Polarizing Photo-Chronograph Applied to the Measurement of the Velocity of Projectiles," *Journal of the United States Artillery* 4:3 (July, 1895), 409–452.

Crowder, Enoch H., "The Canteen at the Camps," *Army and Navy Register.* XL:1387 (July 14, 1906), 29.

Curtin, Roland G., "Medical Conditions of the Isthmus of Panama, With Other Notes," *Medicine* [Detroit] 11:5 (May, 1905), 343–349.

Dapray, J. A., "The Army Canteen Question," *Uncle Sam's Magazine* XV:3 (July, 1909), 66–73.

"Disease Among Our Troops at the Front," *Military Surgeon* 35:2 (August, 1914), 163–166.

Doan, Henry H., "A Plea for More Camps of Instruction, Under Government Supervision, for Officers of the Organized Militia," *Military Surgeon* 32:1 (January, 1913), 75–77.

"Dr. Seaman and the Japanese," *Army and Navy Register* 37:1310 (January 14, 1905).

"Editorial," *Military Surgeon* 28:2 (February, 1911), 227–228.

———, *Military Surgeon* 28:4 (April, 1911), 475–477.

———, *Military Surgeon* 29:2 (August, 1911), 233–234.

258 Bibliography

————, *Military Surgeon* 29:6 (December, 1911), 698.

"Editorial: At Last a Red Cross for War," *Military Surgeon* 38:2 (February, 1916), 205–207.

"Editorial: Brigadier General George H. Torney, Surgeon General of the United States Army," *Military Surgeon* 24:2 (February, 1909), 144–147.

"Editorial Expression: The Army Medical Reorganization Bill," *Military Surgeon* 38:3 (March, 1916), 324–325.

"Editorial Expression: Vale, Nicholas Senn," *Military Surgeon* 22:2 (February, 1908), 144–151.

"Editorial: Preparedness," *Military Surgeon* 35:5 (November, 1914), 430–432.

"Editorial: The Education of the Medical Officer—The Army Medical School," *JAMSUS* 13:4 (October, 1903), 249–251.

Egbert, Seneca, "The History of Panama and the Panama Canal," *Medicine* [Detroit] XI:5 (May, 1905), 329–335.

Ehrlich, Staff Surgeon Dr., "Contemporary Comment: A German View of the American Army Medical School, and Museum," *JAMSUS* 15:4 (October, 1904), 317–323.

Erichsen, John Eric, "Impressions of American Surgery," *Lancet* (1874), 2, 720.

"Fact, Not Fiction," *Uncle Sam's Magazine* XV:3 (July, 1909).

Fairbairn, Henry A., "Cardiac Degeneration as Exemplified in the Soldier of the Late War," *Albany Medical Annals* 20:4 (April, 1899), 191–199.

Fauntleroy, P. C., "Venereal Disease in the Army and the Necessity of Proper Action by State and Municipal Authorities for its Effectual Control," *Military Surgeon* 25:6 (December, 1909), 772–774.

Fisher, H. C., "Preparedness of the Medical Department for War," *Military Surgeon* 38:2 (February, 1916), 123–130.

Fox, James S., "Prophylaxis of Syphilis and Practical Points on its Treatment by Salvarsan," *Military Surgeon* 32:1 (January, 1913), 91–97.

Foxworthy, Frank W., "Report of Sanitary Conditions at Maneuver Camp, San Antonio, Texas," *Military Surgeon* 29:2 (August, 1911), 196–197.

Galbraith, J. G., "The Principles of Military Administration: Their Application to Methods of Supplying Horses for the Cavalry Service; With Suggestions for the Remount of the First Cavalry," *Journal of the United States Cavalry Association* 8:29 (June, 1895), 105–117.

Gilchrist, H. L., "The Necessity for a Uniform Organization for the Medical Corps of the National Guard," *Military Surgeon* 34:1 (January, 1914), 22–26.

Goltra, John Nelson, "The Executive Element in the Training and Skill of the Army Surgeon," *JAMSUS* 12:4 (April, 1903), 206–219.

Gorgas, William Crawford, "A Short Account of the Results of Mosquito Work in Havana, Cuba," *JAMSUS* 12:3 (March, 1903), 133–139.

————, "The Conquest of the Tropics for the White Race," *JAMA* LII (June 19, 1909), 1967–1969.

————, "The Sanitary Organization of the Isthmian Canal as it Bears Upon Anti-Malarial Work," *Military Surgeon* XXIV:4 (April, 1909), 261–267.

Gorodetzer, Robert D., "A Concise Biography of Colonel Louis M. Maus, MC," April 1971, USAMEDD Historical Unit.

Greenleaf, Charles R., "Ambulance Construction," *Proceedings of the Fifth Annual Meeting of the Association of Military Surgeons of the United States* (Earhart & Richardson, Superior Printers, 1896), 264–274.

————, "The Practical Duties of the Army Surgeon in the Field, During Time of War," presented at the Second Annual Meeting of the Association of Military Surgeons of the National Guard of the United States, St. Louis, Missouri, April 19, 1892; in *Transactions of the Second Annual Meeting of the Association of Military Surgeons of the National Guard of the United States* (Becktold & Co., 1892), 9–14.

Griffith, J. D., "Gunshot Wounds of the Abdomen," *Transactions of the Third Annual Meeting of the Association of Military Surgeons of the National Guard of the United States* (Buxton & Skinner Stationery Co., 1894), 135–144.

Haan, William G., and W. W. Witherspoon, "What Has Been Done Since 1892 for the Defense of Our Coast Line Outside the Coast Forts," *Journal of the United States Artillery* 39:2 (March–April, 1913), 129–136.

Havard, Valery, "The Prophylaxis of Venereal Disease," *JAMSUS* 15:1 (July, 1904), 1–17.

Hoff, John Van Rensselaer, "Is There a Venereal Peril for Us?" *Military Surgeon* XXV:6 (December, 1909), 732–748.

———, "Military Hygiene: And How Can the People of the United States be Educated to Appreciate its Necessity?" *JMSI* 40:147 (May–June, 1907), 353–376.

———, "Military Medical Education," *JAMSUS* 17:3 (September, 1905), 195–203.

———, "The Passing of the General Staff," *Military Surgeon* XLIII:1 (July, 1918), 74–76,

———, "Resumé of the History of the Medical Department of the United States Army, From 1775 to the Beginning of the Spanish-American War," *JAMSUS* 10:3 (January, 1902), 347–398.

———, "The Travois—A New Sanitary Appliance in the First Line of Battlefield Assistance," *Proceedings of the Fourth Annual Meeting of the Association of Military Surgeons of the United States* (Buxton & Skinner Stationery Co., 1894), 73–84.

Holbrook, W. A., "Some Lessons of the War with Spain," *Army and Navy Register* 38:1350 (October 25, 1905), 3–5.

Howard, Deane C., "Venereal Prophylaxis," *Military Surgeon* 29:6 (December, 1911), 669–673.

"Increased Rank and More Authority for Medical Officers," *JAMA* LXIX:19 (November 10, 1917), 1612–1613.

Ingalls, James M., "The Resistance of the Air to the Motion of Oblong Projectiles as Influenced by the Shape of the Head," *Journal of the United States Artillery* IV:2 (April, 1895), 191–213.

Ireland, Merritte W., "Obituary: General William Crawford Gorgas," *Military Surgeon*. XLVII:2 (August, 1920), 252–254.

Irwin, B. J. D., "Notes on the Introduction of Tent Hospitals in War," *Proceedings of the Fourth Annual Meeting of the Association of Military Surgeons of the United States* (Buxton & Skinner Stationery Co., 1894), 107–136.

"John Walter Kerr," *Military Surgeon* 49:2 (August, 1921), 120–124.

Jones, H. J., "The Army and the National Guard from the View-point of a National Guard Officer," *Military Surgeon* 28:1 (January, 1911), 45–47.

"Just Outside the Gate," *Uncle Sam's Magazine* XV:3 (July, 1909), 65.

Kean, Jefferson Randolph, "Hospitals and Charities in Cuba," *JAMSUS* 12:3 (March, 1903), 140–149.

———, "The Army Medical Service," *JAMA* XLII:22 (May 28, 1904), 1418–1419.

Keefer, Frank R., "Observations on the Physical Examination of the Recruit," *Transactions of the Third Annual Meeting of the Association of Military Surgeons of the National Guard of the United States*. (Buxton & Skinner Stationery Co., 1894), 166–192.

Keefer, Frank R., "The Functions of the Medical Department of the Army, Especially in the Field," *JMSI* 99:174 (November–December, 1911), 347–359.

King, W. W., "Tropical Neurasthenia," *JAMA* 46:20 (May 19, 1906), 1518–1519.

Lagarde, Louis A., "Can a Septic Bullet Infect a Gunshot Wound? A Special Report to the Surgeon-General , U.S. Army," *New York Medical Journal* (October 22, 1872), 458–464.

——, "Poisoned Wounds by the Implements of Warfare," *JAMA* 40:16 (April 18, 1903), 1062–1069.

——, "Septic Bullets and Septic Powders," *Proceedings of the Fifth Annual Meeting of the Association of Military Surgeons of the United States* (Earhart and Richardson, Superior Printers, 1896), 169–174.

Leale, Medwin, "Some Experiences with the New York Volunteer Cavalry During the Spanish-American War," *Military Surgeon* 20:6 (June, 1907), 468–483.

Leonard, Robert W., "Sanitation of Troops," *JMSI* 51:180 (November/December, 1912), 367–370.

Linley, C. L., "Pride and Prejudice—Tenting on the Old Camp Ground," *Transactions of the Second Annual Meeting of the Association of Military Surgeons of the National Guard of the United States* (Becktold & Co., 1892), 151–159.

Love, Albert G., "Typhoid Prophylaxis in the British Army in India and in the American Army in the United States," *Military Surgeon* 32:3 (March, 1913), 250–258.

Lugo-Viña, José, "Public Hygiene in Porto Rico," *JAMSUS* 13:3 (September, 1903), 150–153.

Lung, George Augustus, "Alcohol a Depreciating Factor of Efficiency," *JAMSUS* 18:1 (January, 1906), 69–88,

Lynch, Charles, "The Scope of Teaching that Should be Followed in the Newly-Established Chair of Hygiene and Sanitation in our Military and Naval Schools, and the Practical Results to be Expected Therefrom," *JMSI* 44:157 (January–February, 1909), 194–213.

Lyster, William J. L., "Sterilization of Drinking Water by Calcium Hypochlorite in the Field," *Military Surgeon* 36:3 (March, 1915), 222–228.

——, "Venereal Prophylaxis in the Army—The Necessity of Cooperation with Line Officers," *Military Surgeon* 2.9:1 (July, 1911), 67–72.

Mason, Charles Francis, "Notes from the Experience of a Medical Officer in the Tropics," *JAMSUS* 13:5 (November, 1903), 306–314.

Maus, L. Mervin, "Does the Moderate Use of Alcohol Lower Health and Efficiency and Should it be Prohibited Among Officers and Officials of the Military, Naval and Civil Services?" *JMSI* 51:180 (November–December,1912), 301–320.

——, "Further Observations on the Prophylaxis of Venereal Diseases in the United States Army," *Military Surgeon* 27:6 (December, 1910), 636–644.

——, "Injurious Effects Resulting from the Moderate Use of Alcohol," *JMSI* 54:187 (January–February, 1914), 1–8.

——, "The Suppression of Vice Diseases Through Personal Prophylaxis and Municipal Control of the Saloon and Courtesan," *Chicago Medical Recorder* 35:1 (January, 1913), 11–22.

——, "Venereal Diseases in the United States Army—Their Prevention and Treatment," *Military Surgeon* 27:2 (August, 1910), 130–148.

——, "Venereal Diseases in the United States Army—Their Prevention and Treatment [Continued]," *Military Surgeon* 27:3 (September, 1910), 248–267.

McBlain, John F., "With Gibbon on the Sioux Campaign of 1876," *Journal of the United States Cavalry Association* 9:33 (June, 1896), 139–148.

McFarland, Joseph, "The Isthmian Canal Zone," *Medicine* [Detroit] 11:5 (May, 1905), 336–343.

McGee, Anita Newcomb, "Facts About the Army Canteen," *Military Surgeon* XXIII:4 (October, 1908), 260–271.

McIntosh, W. P., "Syphilis: Especially in Regard to its Communication by Drinking Cups, Kissing, Etc.," *Military Surgeon* 32:2 (February, 1913), 184–191.

"A Memorial to Colonel John Van Rensselaer Hoff, Medical Corps, U.S. Army," *Military Surgeon* 67:3 (September, 1930), 277–284.

Mere, Bremner, "What They Did in Texas," *Army and Navy Life* XIV:4 (April, 1909), 319–323.

Merritt, Wesley J., "Life and Services of General Philip St. George Cooke, U.S. Army," *Journal of the United States Cavalry Association* 8:29 (June, 1895), 79–92.

———, "Comment and Criticism: 'Place of the Medical Department in the Army,'" *JMSI* 11:45 (July, 1890), 657–658.

"Military Prohibition Prohibits," *Military Surgeon* XLII:4 (April, 1918), 455–456.

Mills, A. L., "The Military Geography of Mexico," *Journal of the United States Cavalry Association* 10:39 (December, 1897), 397–416.

Morse, C. F., "The Prevalence and Prophylaxis of Venereal Diseases at One Military Post," *Military Surgeon* 27:3 (September, 1910), 268–273.

Munson, Edward L., "Diseases of the Soldier and Their Prophylaxis," *Military Surgeon* 25:1 (July, 1909), 24–37.

Nicholls, E. G., "The Training Together in Peace Time the Garrison Artillery Forces of the Empire, Including Regular Militia, Volunteer and Colonial Artillery," *Journal of the United States Artillery* 4:4 (October, 1895), 677–712.

Nichols, Henry J., "Hook-worm Disease and Pellagra," *Military Surgeon* 26:6 (June, 1910), 646–657.

"Obituary," *JAMA* 64:26 (June 26, 1915), 2154.

"Obituary: Colonel Charles E. Woodruff," *Medical Record* [New York] 87:25 (June 19, 1915), 1034.

"Obituary: Bailey Kelly Ashford," *Science* 80:2084 (December 7, 1934), 516–518.

"Obituary: Colonel Bailey K. Ashford," *Military Surgeon* 75:6 (December, 1934), 405.

"Obituary: Major General Robert Maitland O'Reilly," *Military Surgeon* 31:6 (December, 1912), 741–743.

"The Organization of the Medical Department of State Forces," *Military Surgeon* 21:6 (December, 1907), 550–551.

Parker, James, "The Value of Cavalry as a Part of Our Army," *Journal of the United States Cavalry Association* 25:103 (July, 1914), 5–13.

Pierson, R. H., "The Relation of Military Officers to Military Discipline," *Military Surgeon* XXXII:6 (June, 1913), 527–542.

Proben, Charles J., "The Climate of Puerto Rico," *Atlanta Journal-Record of Medicine* 2:2 (May, 1900), 73–87).

Raymond, Henry I., "Prophylaxis under G.O. #31, War Department, 1912, for the Hawaiian Department," *Military Surgeon* 34:2 (February, 1914), 134–139.

"Restoration of the Record of Colonel John Van R. Hoff, Medical Corps, U.S. Army, Retired," *Military Surgeon* XLVI:1 (January, 1920), 108–109.

Review, "The Medical and Surgical History of the War of the Rebellion. Part II. Volume I" in *American Journal of the Medical Sciences* [Philadelphia] 79:1 (January, 1880), 163–180.

Review, "The Medical and Surgical History of the War. Vol. II" in *The Medical Record: A Weekly Journal of Medicine and Surgery* [New York] 11 (August 12, 1876), 519–520.

Rhodes, Charles D., "The Cavalry of the German Empire," *Journal of the United States Cavalry Association* IX:33 (June, 1896), 126–138.

———, "The History of the Cavalry of the Army of the Potomac, Including that of the Army of Virginia, (Pope's) and also the History of the Operations of the Federal Cavalry in West Virginia During the War," *Journal of the United States Cavalry Association* XI:40 (March, 1898), 1–101.

Richard, Charles, "The U. S. Army Medical School," *Interstate Medical Journal* [St. Louis, Missouri] 22:9 (September, 1915), 912–922.

Rogers, Daniel W., "Report of the Chief Sanitary Officer of the Division, Camp of Illinois National Guard, at Peoria, Illinois, 1910," *Military Surgeon* 28:1 (January, 1911), 35–44.

Ross, Ronald, "Medical Science and the Tropics," *Bulletin of the American Geographical Society* 45:6 (1913), 435–438.

Rowe, L. S., "The Reorganization of Local Government in Cuba," *Annals of the American Academy of Political and Social Science* (March, 1905), 311–321.

Russell, Frederick F., "The Prevention of Typhoid Fever by Vaccination and by Early Diagnosis and Isolation," *Military Surgeon* 24:6 (June, 1909), 479–518.

Schultz, C., "Benefits Derived from Camps of Instruction, to the Medical Officers, in Conjunction with the Field and Line Officers," *Military Surgeon* 34:2 (February, 1914), 131–133.

Seaman, Louis Livingston, "Observations in China and the Tropics on the Army Ration and the Post Exchange or Canteen," *JMSI* XXIX:CXIII (September, 1901), 289–293.

Senn, Nicholas, "The Mission of the Association of the Military Surgeons of the National Guard of the United States," *Transactions of the Second Annual Meeting of the Association of Military Surgeons of the National Guard of the United States* (Becktold & Co., 1892), 18–31.

Sharpe, A.C., "Organization and Training of a National Reserve for Military Service," *JMSI* 10:37 (March, 1889), 1–31.

"Sketch of George M. Sternberg," *Appleton's Popular Science Monthly* [New York] 56:1 (November, 1899), 116–121.

Smart, Charles, "The Medical Department of the Army," *JMSI* 15:70 (July, 1894), 740–751.

Smith, Edmund Banks, "The Army Canteen," *Army and Navy Life* XIV:4 (April, 1909), 310–313.

Smith, F., "The Soldier's Heart, and the Civilian's," *Journal of the Royal Army Medical Corps* VIII:1 (January, 1907), 1–7.

Smyth, John, "Lessons of the War Which May be Applicable to Civil Practice," *Military Surgeon* 47:1 (July, 1920), 100–108.

"The Status of Medical Officers," *JMSI* 18:80 (March, 1896), 429–431.

"The Status of Medical Officers," *JMSI* 20:85 (January, 1897), 216–218.

Stayer, A. S., "Report on the 1910 Camp of the Division of the Pennsylvania National Guard at Gettysburg, PA.," *Military Surgeon* 29:1 (January, 1911), 1–28.

Sternberg, George M., "Address of President Sternberg," *Proceedings of the Fifth Annual Meeting of the Association of Military Surgeons of the United States* (Earhart & Richardson, Superior Printers, 1896), 8–22.

———, "The Address of the President. Delivered at the Forty-ninth Annual Meeting of the American Medical Association, held at Denver, Colorado, June 7–10, 1898," *JAMA* 30:24 (June 11, 1898), 1373–1380.

Stiles, Charles Wardell, "A New Species of Hookworm (*Uncinaria americana*) Parasitic in Man, *American Medicine* 3:19 (May 10, 1902), 777–778.

Stiles, Henry R., "The Medical and Surgical Equipment of a Fifteenth Century French Military Expedition," *Proceedings of the Sixth Annual Meeting of the Association of Military Surgeons of the United States* (Medical Gazette Publishing Co., 1896), 185–191.

Stone, J. Hamilton, "Our Troops in the Tropics—From the Surgeon's Standpoint," *JMSI* 26:105 (May, 1900), 358–369.

Stuart, Allan, "Tropical Hygiene in Reference to Clothing, Houses, Routine, and Diet," *Military Surgeon* 20:2 (February, 1907), 75–93.

"The Surgeons in Manchuria," Army and Navy Register 36:1300 (November 22, 1904), 7.

Thomason, Henry D., "Sanitary Troops in the Organized Militia of the United States," *Military Surgeon* 29:5 (November, 1911), 511–526.

Traub, Peter E., "Military Hygiene: How Best to Enforce its Study in our Military and Naval Schools and Promote its Intelligent Practice in Our Army," *JMSI* 36:133 (January–February, 1905), 1–38.

Treat, C. G., "Moving Targets in Use in the Light Artillery of England, Germany, France and Italy, and Some Forms Recently Tried by the Light Artillery Battalion at Fort   Riley, Kansas," *Journal of the United States Artillery* 9:3 (May–June, 1898), 265–282.

Vaughan, Victor C., "Typhoid Fever Among the American Soldiers in the Recent War with Spain," *JMSI* 25:100 (July, 1899), 85–88.

Vedder, Edward B., "A Plea for Specialism," *Military Surgeon* 24:4 (April, 1909), 317–324.

———, "What are the Best Available Measures to Diminish Venereal Diseases Among Soldiers and Sailors, and Along What Lines Should We Seek the Cooperation of Federal, State and Municipal Authorities?" *Military Surgeon* 29:5 (November, 1911), 484–510.

Wallace, William, "Our Military Decline," *Infantry Journal* 9:5 (March–April, 1913), 625–644.

Warren, Walter Miller, "Malaria in Mobilization Camps During the Late War," *Military Surgeon* 2:7 (September 1899), 219–221.

Willey, Day Allen, "Summer Encampments," *Army and Navy Life and the United Services* 9:1 (July, 1906), 17–24.

Wood, Leonard, "The Military Government of Cuba," *Annals of the American Academy of Political and Social Science* (March, 1903), 153–182.

Woodhull, Alfred A., "Comment and Criticism: Military Hygiene," *JMSI* 36:134 (March–April, 1905), 349–353.

———, "The Place of the Medical Department in the Army," *JMSI* 11:45 (July, 1890), 544–565.

———, "The Scope of Teaching That Should be Followed in the Newly Established Chair of Hygiene and Sanitation in our Military and Naval Schools, and the Practical Results to be Expected Therefrom," *JMSI* 42:152 (March–April, 1908), 157–192.

Woodward, Joseph Janvier, "On Photo-micrography with the highest powers, as practised in the Army Medical Museum," *American Journal of Science and Arts* 42:125 (September, 1866), 189–195;

Books

Ashburn, Percy Moreau, *The Elements of Military Hygiene, Especially Arranged for Officers and Men of the Line* (Houghton Mifflin, 1909).

Ashford, Bailey K., *A Soldier in Science* (William Morrow & Company, 1934).

Ashford, Bailey K., and Pedro Gutierrez Igaravidez, *Uncinariasis (Hookworm Disease) in Porto Rico, A Medical and Economic Problem* (Government Printing Office, 1911).

Bassett, John Spencer, ed., *Correspondence of Andrew Jackson*. Six Volumes. (Carnegie Institution of Washington, 1927).

Bergey, Ellwood, *Why Soldiers Desert from the United States Army* (Wm. F. Fell & Company, 1903).

Blair, Henry W., *The Temperance Movement, or the Conflict Between Man and Alcohol* (William E. Smythe Company, 1888).

Bodeham, S. D., and J. P. Fitzgerald, *Ashland Boys at the Front in the Spanish-American War, A Record of the Experiences of Co. L, 2nd Wis. Vol. Inf., Leahy on the "Oregon," Scott and Oakey at Manilla, Warner in Cuba.* (Daily Press, N.D).

Borden, William C., *The Education of the Medical Officer of the Army* (The Association of Military Surgeons, 1903).

Butler, Benjamin F., *Autobiography and Personal Reminiscences of Major-General Benjamin F. Butler, Butler's Book* (A. M. Thayer & Co., 1892).

Colles, Abraham, *Practical Observations on the Venereal Disease, and on the Use of Mercury* (A. Waldie, 1837).

Coolidge, Richard H., *Statistical Report on the Sickness and Mortality in the Army of the United States, 1839–1855* (A.O.P. Nicholson, Printer, 1856).

———, *Statistical Report on the Sickness and Mortality in the Army of the United States, 1855–1860* (George W. Bowman, Printer, 1860).

Cooper, James, *Campaign of the First Troop Philadelphia City Cavalry, April 25–November 11, 1898* (Hallowell Co. Ltd., N.D).

Fiala, Anthony, *Troop "C" in Service, An Account of the Part Played by Troop "C" of the New York Volunteer Cavalry in the Spanish-American War of 1898* (Eagle Press, 1899).

Forry, Samuel, and Thomas Lawson, *Statistical Report on the Sickness and Mortality of the Army of the United States* (J. Gideon, Jr., 1840).

Gatewood, Willard B., Jr., *"Smoked Yankees" and the Struggle for Empire: Letters from Negro Soldiers, 1898–1902* (University of Illinois Press, 1971).

Girard, Alfred C., *The Management of Camp Alger and Camp Meade.* Reprint, *New York Medical Journal*, September 24, 1898 (D. Appleton Company, 1898).

Gorgas, William C., *A Few General Directions With Regard to Destroying Mosquitoes, Particularly the Yellow Fever Mosquito* (Government Printing Office, 1904).

———, *Mosquito Work in Havana* (William Wood and Company, 1902).

———, *Population and Deaths from Various Diseases in the City of Panama, by Months and Years, from November 1883, to August 1906; Number of Employees and Deaths from Various Diseases Among Employees of the French Canal Companies, by Months and Years, from January, 1881, to April, 1904* (Government Printing Office, 1906).

———, *Sanitary Conditions as Encountered in Cuba and Panama, and What is Being Done to Render the Canal Zone Healthy* (William Wood and Company, 1905).

———, *Sanitary Work on the Isthmus of Panama During the Last Three Years* (William Wood & Company, 1907).

———, *Sanitation in Panama* (D. Appleton and Company, 1915).

———, *Sanitation in the Canal Zone* (Press of The American Medical Association, 1907).

———, *Sanitation of the Canal Zone* (William Wood and Company, 1908).

———, *The Practical Mosquito Work Done at Havana, Cuba, Which Resulted in the Disappearance of Yellow Fever from that Locality*, reprint, *Washington Medical Annals* II:3 (July, 1903).

———, *Work of the Sanitary Department of Havana* (Press of the American Medical Association, 1911).

Hammond, William Alexander, *A Treatise on Hygiene with Special Reference to the Military Service*, Reprinted with a Biographical Introduction by Ira M. Rutkow (Norman Publishing, 1991).

Hemphill, W. Edwin, ed. *The Papers of John C. Calhoun*, Twenty-five Volumes (The University of South Carolina Press for the South Caroliniana Society, 1969).

Letterman, Jonathan, *Medical Recollections of the Army of the Potomac* (D. Appleton and Company, 1866).

Lynch, Charles, *Medical Department of the Japanese Army* (The Old Corner Bookstore, 1906).

———, Frank W. Weed, and Loy McAfee, *The Medical Department of the United States Army in the World War*, Fifteen Volumes (Government Printing Office, 1923).

———, *What is the Most Efficient Organization of the American National Red Cross for War and What Should be Its Relations with the Medical Departments of the Army and Navy?* (The Association of Military Surgeons, 1907).

Mann, James, *Medical Sketches of the Campaigns of 1812, 13, 14* (H. Mann and Co., 1816).

McCann, Irving Goff, *With the National Guard on the Border: Our National Military Problem* (C.V. Mosby Company, 1917).

Mitchell, Silas Weir, *Wear and Tear, or Hints for the Overworked* (J. B. Lippincott & Co., 1871).

Munson, Edward Lyman, *The Principles of Sanitary Tactics* (Edward L. Munson, 1911).

The National Guard Association of the State of New York, Sixth Annual Convention, Held in Albany, New York, January 23, 1884 (Matthews, Northrup & Co., 1884).

Nelson, Wolfred, *Yellow Fever, Absolute Protection Secured by Scientific Quarantine* (W. Nelson, 1889).

Payne, James E., *History of the Fifth Missouri Volunteer Infantry* (Press of James E. Payne, 1899).

Proceedings of the Fifth Annual Meeting of the Association of Military Surgeons of the United States (Earhart & Richardson, Superior Printers, 1896).

Proceedings of the Second Annual Convention of the National Guard Association of Ohio, held at Columbus, Ohio, January 15–16, 1885 (Gazette Press, 1885).

Reed, Walter, Victor C. Vaughan, and Edward O. Shakespeare, *Report on the Origin and Spread of Typhoid Fever in U.S. Military Camps During the Spanish War of 1898*, Two Volumes (Government Printing Office, 1904).

Report of the Committee on the Organization of the National Medical Association (National Medical Convention, 1846).

Reports on the Extent and Nature of the Materials Available for the Preparation of a Medical and Surgical History of the Rebellion (J.P. Lippincott & Co., 1865).

Root, Elihu, *The Military and Colonial Policy of the United States* (AMS Press, 1970).

Russell, Frederick F., *Results of Antityphoid Vaccination in the Army in 1911, and its Suitability for Use in Civil Communities* (American Medical Association, 1912).

Seaman, Louis L., *From Tokio through Manchuria with the Japanese* (New York: D. Appleton and Company, 1905).

———, *The Real Triumph of Japan: The Conquest of the Silent Foe* (D. Appleton & Co., 1908).

Smith, Charles D., *Cases of Chickamauga Typhoid Treated at the Maine General Hospital* (Stephen Berry, 1899).

Sternberg, George Miller, *Sanitary Lessons of the War and Other Papers* (American Medical Association, 1899).

The Transactions of the Association of Military Surgeons of the National Guard of the United States for the Year 1891 (Burdick, Armitage & Allen, Printers, 1891).

The Transactions of the Third Annual Meeting of the Association of Military Surgeons, of the National Guard of the United States (Buxton & Skinner Stationery Co., 1894).

Turner, T. A., *Story of the Fifteenth Minnesota Volunteer Infantry* (Lessard Printing Co., N.D).
Upton, Emory, *The Military Policy of the United States* (Government Printing Office, 1904).
Vaughan, Victor C., *A Doctor's Memories* (The Bobbs-Merrill Company, 1926).
Webber, Harry E., *Twelve Months with the Eighth Massachusetts Infantry in the Service of the United States* (Newcomb & Gauss, Printers, 1908).
Woodhull, Alfred A., *Military Hygiene for Officers of the Line* (John Wiley & Sons, 1909).
———, *Notes on Military Hygiene for Officers of the Line*, Third Edition (John Wiley & Sons, 1890, 1898, 1904).
Woodruff, Charles E., *Medical Ethnology* (Rebman Company, 1915).
———, *The Effects of Tropical Light on White Men* (Rebman Company, 1905).
Woodward, Joseph Janvier, *International Exhibition of 1876. The Medical Staff of the United States Army, and Its Scientific Work. An Address Delivered to the International Medical Congress at Philadelphia. Wednesday Evening, September 6, 1876* (N.P., 1876).
———, *Report to the Surgeon General, of the United States Army, on the Magnesium and Electric Lights, as Applied to Photo-Micrography* (War Department, Surgeon General's Office, 1870).
Woodward, Joseph Janvier, and George A. Otis, eds., *The Medical and Surgical History of the War of the Rebellion*. Reprinted as *The Medical and Surgical History of the Civil War*, Twelve Volumes (Broadfoot Publishing Company, 1990).

Secondary Sources Dissertations and Theses

Anderson, Warwick, "Colonial Pathologies: American Medicine in the Philippines, 1898–1921," Dissertation: University of Pennsylvania, Department of History and Sociology of Science, 1992, UM# 9235108.
Brereton, Todd Richard, "An Impractical Sort of Officer: The Army Career of Arthur L. Wagner, 1875–1905," Dissertation: Texas A&M University, Department of History, 1994, UM# 9432648.
Cirillo, Vincent J., "The Spanish-American War and Military Medicine," Dissertation: Rutgers: State University of New Jersey, Department of History 1999, UM# 9936178.
Johnson, John Reuben, "Nebraska in the Spanish-American War and the Philippine Insurrection, A Study in Imperialism." Dissertation: University of Nebraska, January 2, 1937, No UM# .
Murphy, John Thomas, "Pistol's Legacy: Sutlers, Post Traders, and the American Army, 1820–1895." Dissertation: University of Illinois at Urbana-Champaign, Department of History 1993, UM# 9314919.
Wintermute, Bobby A., "Waging Health: The United States Army Medical Department and Public Health in the Progressive Era, 1890–1920." Dissertation: Temple University, Department of History 2006, UM# 3247320.

Articles

Anderson, Warwick, "The Trespass Speaks: White Masculinity and Colonial Breakdown," *AHR* 102:5 (December, 1997), 1343–1370.
Blustein, Bonnie E., "'To Increase the Efficiency of the Medical Department': A New Approach to U.S. Civil War Medicine," *Civil War History* 33:1 (March, 1987), 22–41.

Cassedy, James H., "The 'Germ of Laziness' in the South, 1901–1915: Charles Wardell Stiles and the Progressive Paradox," *Bulletin of the History of Medicine* 45 (1971), 159–169.

Coffman, Edward M., "The American 15th Infantry Regiment in China, 1912–1938," *Journal of Military History* 58:1 (January, 1994), 57–74.

Freemon, Frank R., "Lincoln Finds a Surgeon General: William A. Hammond and the Transformation of the United States Army Medical Bureau," *Civil War History* 33:1 (March, 1987), 5–21.

Hume, Edgar Erskine, "The Golden Jubilee of the Association of Military Surgeons of the United States, A Brief History of Its First Half-Century, 1891–17 September 1941," *Military Surgeon* 89:3 (September, 1941), 247–594.

Kean, Jefferson R., "Walter Reed, Dedication of His Birthplace," *Military Surgeon* 62:3 (March, 1928), 293–304.

Pilcher, James Evelyn, "The Surgeon Generals of the United States Army, IX, Brevet Brigadier General Thomas Lawson, Surgeon General of the United Army, 1836–1861," *JAMSUS* 14:6 (June, 1904), 406–410.

——, "The Surgeon Generals of the United States Army, XVII, Brigadier General Charles Sutherland, Surgeon General of the United States Army, 1890–1893" *JAMSUS* 16:2 (February, 1905), 129–132.

Stern, Alexandra Minna, "Buildings, Boundaries, and Blood: Medicalization and Nation-Building on the U.S.-Mexico Border, 1910–1930," *Hispanic American Historical Review* 79:1 (February, 1999), 41–81.

Books

Abrahamson, James L., *America Arms for a New Century: The Making of a Great Military Power* (The Free Press, 1981).

Adas, Michael, *Machines as the Measure of Men: Science, Technology, and Ideologies of Western Dominance* (Cornell University Press, 1989).

American National Biography, Twenty-four Volumes (Oxford University Press, 1999).

Anderson, Warwick, *Colonial Pathologies: American Tropical Medicine, Race, and Hygiene in the Philippines* (Duke University Press, 2006).

Arnold, David, *Colonizing the Body: State Medicine and Epidemic Disease in Nineteenth-Century India* (University of California Press, 1993).

——, ed., *Imperial medicine and indigenous societies* (Manchester University Press, 1988).

——, *The Problem of Nature: Environment, Culture and European Expansion* (Blackwell, 1996).

Arnold, Ken, Klaus Vogel, and James Peto, eds., *War and Medicine* (London: Black Dog Publishing, 2008).

Ashburn, Percy Moreau, *A History of the Medical Department of the United States Army* (Houghton Mifflin Company, 1929).

Barr, Ronald J., *The Progressive Army: US Army Command and Administration, 1870–1914* (St. Martin's Press, 1998).

Blustein, Bonnie Ellen. *Preserve Your Love of Science: Life of William A. Hammond, American Neurologist*, Cambridge Studies in the History of Medicine (Cambridge University Press, 2002).

Bollet, Alfred J., *Civil War Medicine: Challenges and Triumphs* (Galen Press, 2002).

Bourke, Joanna, *Dismembering the Male: Men's Bodies, Britain, and the Great War* (The University Press of Chicago, 1996).

Bristow, Nancy K., *Making Men Moral: Social Engineering during the Great War* (New York University Press, 1996).

Brown, Harvey, E., *The Medical Department of the United States Army from 1775 to 1873* (Surgeon General's Office, 1873).

Byerly, Carol R., *Fever of War: The Influenza Epidemic in the U.S. Army during World War I* (New York University Press, 2005).

Chapman, Carleton B., *Order Out of Chaos: John Shaw Billings and America's Coming of Age* (The Boston Medical Library in The Francis A. Countway Library of Medicine, 1994).

Cirillo, Vincent J., *Bullets and Bacilli: The Spanish-American War and Military Medicine* (Rutgers University Press, 2004).

Clendenen, Clarence C., *Blood on the Border: The United States Army and the Mexican Irregulars* (Macmillan, 1969).

Coffman, Edward M., *The Old Army: A Portrait of the American Army in Peacetime, 1784–1898* (Oxford University Press, 1986).

Cooper, Jerry, *The Rise of the National Guard: The Evolution of the American Militia, 1865–1920* (University of Nebraska Press, 1997).

Cooter, Roger, Mark Harrison, and Steve Sturdy, eds., *War, Medicine and Modernity* (Sutton Publishing, 1998).

Cosmas, Graham A., *An Army for Empire: The United States Army in the Spanish-American War* (White Mane Publishing, 1971, 1994).

Cowdrey, Albert, *Fighting for Life: American Military Medicine in World War II* (The Free Press, 1994).

Curtin, Philip D., *Disease and Empire: The Health of European Troops in the Conquest of Africa* (Cambridge University Press, 1998).

Davis, N.S., *History of the American Medical Association, From its Organization Up to January, 1855. To Which is Appended Biographical Notices, with Portraits of the Presidents of the Association, and of the Author*, Edited by S. W. Butler, M.D. (Lippincott, Grambo and Co., 1855).

Davison, Henry P., *The American Red Cross in the Great War* (Macmillan, 1920).

De Bevoise, Anthony, *Agents of Apocalypse: Epidemic Disease in the Colonial Philippines* (Princeton University Press, 1995).

Doubler, Michael D., *Civilian in Peace, Soldier in War: The Army National Guard, 1636–2000* (University Press of Kansas, 2003).

Ettling, John, *The Germ of Laziness: Rockefeller Philanthropy and Public Health in the New South* (Harvard University Press, 1981).

Finnegan, John P., *Against the Specter of a Dragon: The Campaign for American Military Preparedness, 1914–1917* (Greenwood Press, 1974).

Fishbein, Morris, *A History of the American Medical Association, 1847–1947* (W.B. Saunders Company, 1947).

———, ed., *Doctors at War* (E.P. Dutton & Company, Inc, 1945).

Fogarty, Richard S., *Race and War in France: Colonial Subjects in the French Army, 1914–1918* (The Johns Hopkins University Press, 2008).

Freemon, Frank R., *Gangrene and Glory: Medical Care During the American Civil War* (University of Illinois Press, 2001).

Foner, Jack D., *The United States Soldier Between Two Wars: Army Life and Reforms, 1865–1898* (Humanities Press, 1970).

Frederickson, George M., *The Inner Civil War: Northern Intellectuals and the Crisis of the Union* (The University of Illinois Press, 1965, 1993).

Garrison, Fielding H., *John Shaw Billings: A Memoir* (The Knickerbocker Press, 1915).

Gates, John M., *Schoolbooks and Krags: The United States Army in the Philippines, 1898–1902* (Greenwood Press, 1973).

Gillett, Mary C., *The Army Medical Department, 1818–1865*, Army Historical Series (Center of Military History, United States Army, 1987).

————, *The Army Medical Department, 1865–1917*, Army Historical Series (Center of Military History, United States Army, 1994).

Gorgas, Marie D., and Burton J. Hendrick, *William Crawford Gorgas, His Life and Work* (Doubleday, Page and Company, 1924).

Hagedorn, Hagedorn, *Leonard Wood: A Biography*, Two Volumes (Harper & Brothers, 1931).

Haller, John S., *Medical Protestants; The Eclectics in American Medicine, 1825–1939* (Southern Illinois University Press, 1994).

Haller, Jr., John S., *American Medicine in Transition, 1840–1910* (University of Illinois Press, 1981).

Hard, Curtis V., *Banners in the Air: The Eighth Ohio Volunteers and the Spanish-American War*, Edited by Robert H. Ferrell (The Kent State University Press, 1988).

Harrison, Mark, *Public Health in British India: Anglo-Indian Preventive Medicine, 1859–1914* (Cambridge University Press, 1994).

Harrison, Noel Garraux, *City of Canvas: Camp Russell A. Alger and the Spanish-American War* (Falls Church Historical Commission, Fairfax County Historical Commission, 1988).

Healy, David F., *The United States in Cuba, 1898–1902: Generals, Politicians, and the Search for Policy* (University of Wisconsin Press, 1963).

Hewa, Soma, *Colonialism, Tropical Disease, and Imperial Medicine: Rockefeller Philanthropy in Sri Lanka* (University Press of America, 1995).

History of the Pennsylvania Hospital Unit (Base Hospital No. 10, U.S.A.) in the Great War (Paul B. Hoeber, 1921).

Hume, Edgar Erskine, *The Golden Jubilee of the Association of Military Surgeons of the United States* (The Association of Military Surgeons, 1941).

————, *Victories of Army Medicine; Scientific Accomplishments of the Medical Department of the United States Army* (J. B. Lippincott Company, 1943).

Humphreys, Margaret, *Yellow Fever and the South* (The Johns Hopkins University Press, 1999).

Huntington, Samuel P., *The Soldier and the State: The Theory and Politics of Civil-Military Relations* (The Belknap Press of Harvard University Press, 1957, 1985).

Hutchinson, John F., *Champions of Charity: War and the Rise of the Red Cross* (Westview Press, 1996).

Index Catalogue of the Library of the Surgeon General's Office, United States Army, Sixteen Volumes (General Printing Office, 1880–1895).

Jacobson, Mattew Frye, *Barbarian Virtues: The United States Encounters Foreign Peoples at Home and Abroad, 1876–1917* (Hill and Wang, 2000).

Jurmain, Suzanne, *The Secret of the Yellow Death: A True Story of Medical Sleuthing* (Houghton Mifflin Books for Children, 2009).

Kraut, Alan M., *Silent Travelers: Germs, Genes and the "Immigrant Menace"* (The Johns Hopkins University Press, 1994).

Kumar, Anil, *Medicine and the Raj: British Medical Policy in India, 1835–1911* (AltiMira Press, 1998.

Lamb, D. S., "A History of the United States Army Medical Museum, 1862–1917" manuscript, 1917, in the Library of the College of Physicians of Philadelphia.

Lane, Jack C., *Armed Progressive: General Leonard Wood* (Presidio Press, 1978).

Linn, Brian McAllister, *The Echo of Battle: The Army's Way of War* (Harvard University Press, 2007).

————, *Guardians of Empire: The U.S. Army and the Pacific, 1902–1940* (University of North Carolina Press, 1997).

————, *The U.S. Army and Counter-insurgency in the Philippine War, 1899–1902* (University of North Carolina Press, 1989).

Lowry, Thomas P., *The Story the Soldier's Wouldn't Tell: Sex in the Civil War* (Stackpole Books, 1994).

Macleod, Roy and Milton Lewis, eds., *Disease, Medicine, and Empire: Perspectives on Western Medicine and the Experience of European Expansion* (Routledge, 1988).

May, Ernest R., *Imperial Democracy: The Emergence of America as a Great Power* (Harper & Row, 1961).

May, Glenn A, *Social Engineering in the Philippines: The Aims, Execution, and Impact of American Colonial Policy, 1900–1913* (Greenwood Press, 1980).

———, *Battle for Batangas: A Philippine Province at War* (Yale University Press, 1991).

Miller, Stuart C., *"Benevolent Assimilation": The American Conquest of the Philippines, 1899–1903* (Yale University Press, 1982).

Millett, Allan R., *The Politics of Intervention: The Military Occupation of Cuba, 1906–1909* (Ohio State University Press, 1968).

Oates, Stephen B. *Women of Valor: Clara Barton and the Civil War* (The Free Press, 1995).

Pérez, Louis A., Jr., *The War of 1898: The United States and Cuba in History and Historiography* (The University of North Carolina Press, 1998).

Pierce, John R. and Jim Writer, *Yellow Jack: How Yellow Fever Ravaged America and Walter Reed Discovered its Deadly Secrets* (John Wiley & Sons, 2005).

Pilcher, James Evelyn, *The Surgeon Generals of the Army of the United States of America* (The Association of Military Surgeons, 1905).

Reardon, Carol, *Soldiers and Scholars: The U.S. Army and the Uses of Military History, 1865–1920* (The University Press of Kansas, 1990).

Rosenberg, Charles E., *The Care of Strangers: The Rise of America's Hospital System* (The Johns Hopkins University Press, 1995).

Rutkow, Ira, *Bleeding Blue and Gray: Civil War Surgery and the Evolution of American Medicine* (Random House, 2007).

Ryan, Garry D., and Timothy K. Nenninger, eds., *Soldiers and Civilians: The U.S. Army and the American People* (National Archives and Records Association, 1987).

Said, Edward, *Orientalism* (Vintage Books, 1974, 1998).

Scott, H. Harold, *A History of Tropical Medicine*, Two Volumes (The Williams & Wilkins Company, 1939).

Shryock, Richard Harrison, *Medical Licensing in America, 1650–1965* (The Johns Hopkins Press, 1967).

Silbey, David, *A War of Frontier and Empire: The Philippine-American War, 1899–1902* (Hill and Wang, 2008).

Starr, Paul, *The Social Transformation of American Medicine: The Rise of a Sovereign Profession and the Making of a Vast Industry* (Basic Books, 1982).

Steiner, Paul E., *Disease in the Civil War: Natural Biological Warfare, 1861–1865* (Charles C. Thomas, 1968).

Tobey, James A., *The Medical Department of the Army: Its History, Activities and Organization*, Institution for Government Research, Service Monographs of the United States Government, No. 45 (The Johns Hopkins Press, 1927).

Tomblin, Barbara Brooks, *G.I. Nightingales: The Army Nurse Corps in World War II* (The University Press of Kentucky, 2003).

Tomes, Nancy, *The Gospel of Germs: Men, Women, and the Microbe in American Life* (Harvard University Press, 1999).

Trask, David F., *The War with Spain in 1898* (Macmillan, 1981).

Vaughan, Megan, *Curing their Ills: Colonial Power and African Illness* (Stanford University Press, 1991).

Walkowitz, Judith R., *Prostitution and Victorian Society: Women, Class, and the State* (Cambridge University Press, 1980).

Warner, John Harley, *The Therapeutic Perspective: Medical Practice, Knowledge, and Identity in America, 1820–1885* (Princeton University Press, 1997).

Weigley, Russell F., *History of the United States Army* (Macmillan, 1967).

———, *Towards an American Army: Military Thought from Washington to Marshall* (New York: Columbia University Press, 1962).

White, Leonard D., *The Jeffersonians: A Study in Administrative History, 1801–1829* (Macmillan, 1959).

Wiley, Bell Irvin, *The Life of Billy Yank: The Common Soldier of the Union* (Louisiana State University Press, 1952, 1971).

Index